LUTYENS, MACONCHY, WILLIAMS AND TWENTIETH-CENTURY BRITISH MUSIC

Lutyens, Maconchy, Williams and Twentieth-Century British Music
A Blest Trio of Sirens

RHIANNON MATHIAS

ASHGATE

© Rhiannon Mathias 2012

All rights reserved. No part of this publication may be reproduced, stored in a retrieval system or transmitted in any form or by any means, electronic, mechanical, photocopying, recording or otherwise without the prior permission of the publisher.

Rhiannon Mathias has asserted her right under the Copyright, Designs and Patents Act, 1988, to be identified as the author of this work.

Published by
Ashgate Publishing Limited
Wey Court East
Union Road
Farnham
Surrey, GU9 7PT
England

Ashgate Publishing Company
Suite 420
101 Cherry Street
Burlington
VT 05401-4405
USA

www.ashgate.com

British Library Cataloguing in Publication Data
Mathias, Rhiannon.
  Lutyens, Maconchy, Williams and twentieth-century British
  music : a blest trio of sirens.
  1. Lutyens, Elisabeth, 1906-1983--Criticism and interpretation. 2. Maconchy, Elizabeth, 1907-1994--Criticism and interpretation. 3. Williams, Grace, 1906-1977--Criticism and interpretation. 4. Women composers--Great Britain. 5. Music--Great Britain--20th century--History and criticism.
  I. Title
  780.9'22'41-dc23

Library of Congress Cataloging-in-Publication Data
Mathias, Rhiannon, 1968-
  Lutyens, Maconchy, Williams, and Twentieth-century British music : a blest trio of sirens / Rhiannon Mathias.
     p. cm.
  Includes bibliographical references and index.
  ISBN 978-0-7546-5019-5 (hardcover) 1. Music--Great Britain--20th century--History and criticism. 2. Lutyens, Elisabeth, 1906-1983--Criticism and interpretation. 3. Maconchy, Elizabeth, 1907-1994--Criticism and interpretation. 4. Williams, Grace, 1906-1977--Criticism and interpretation. I. Title.
  ML285.5.M34 2012
  780.92'52--dc23
  [B]
                                                                    2011038472
ISBN 9780754650195 (hbk)
ISBN 9781409444039 (ebk)

Printed and bound in Great Britain by the
MPG Books Group, UK

Contents

List of Music Examples		*vii*
Acknowledgements		*xi*
	Introduction	1
PART I 1926–1935		
1	The Musical Evangelization of Kensington	9
2	Professional Composers: Study Abroad and the Macnaghten–Lemare Concerts	33
PART II 1935–1955		
3	Lutyens: Music in London	65
4	Maconchy: An Impassioned Argument	93
5	Williams: To the Wild Hills	121
PART III 1955–1994		
6	Lutyens: *And Suddenly It's Evening*	157
7	Maconchy: *My Dark Heart*	203
8	Williams: *My Last Duchess*	249
	Conclusion	291
Appendix		*293*
Selected Bibliography		*299*
Index		*305*

List of Music Examples

	Opening of *Sirens' Song* by Elizabeth Maconchy (1974)	7
1.1	*The Birthday of the Infanta* by Elisabeth Lutyens	26
1.2	Concertino for Piano and Small Orchestra by Elizabeth Maconchy, opening theme	28
1.3	Psalm 137 for Voice and Small Orchestra by Grace Williams, opening	29
2.1	*The Land* by Elizabeth Maconchy. I 'Winter', opening theme	36
2.2	*The Land* by Elizabeth Maconchy. IV 'Autumn'	37
2.3	*Tuscany* for Mezzo-Soprano and Orchestra by Grace Williams	38
2.4	'Stay, O Sweet' for Soprano and String Quartet by Elisabeth Lutyens	43
2.5	String Quartet No. 1 by Elizabeth Maconchy, opening	51
2.6	*Movement* for Trumpet and Chamber Orchestra by Grace Williams, opening	55
2.7	*Movement* for Trumpet and Chamber Orchestra by Grace Williams, trumpet theme	56
2.8	*Elegy* for String Orchestra by Grace Williams, opening	58
3.1	String Quartet No. 1, IV 'tema di Frescobaldi'	67
3.2	Chamber Concerto No. 1, I 'Theme and Variations'	72
3.3	*Jungle Mariners*, introduction theme	78
3.4	*O Saisons, O Châteaux!*, soprano entry	81
3.5	*Requiem for the Living*, 2 'Requiem Aeternam', chorus refrain	85
3.6	String Quartet No. 6, Primo	87
3.7	String Quartet No. 6, Secondo	88
3.8	Motet Prime Row with Interval Sequence	90
3.9	*Excerpta Tractati-Logico-Philosophici*, opening	91
4.1	String Quartet No. 2, opening themes from movements I, II, III and IV	95
4.2	String Quartet No. 2, I	97
4.3	String Quartet No. 3, opening	99
4.4	String Quartet No. 4, opening	102
4.5	String Quartet No. 4, themes from II, III and IV	103
4.6	*Sonnet Sequence* (piano reduction), opening	110

4.7	String Quartet No. 5, excerpts from I and II	112
4.8	Fifth String Quartet by Elizabeth Maconchy, III	113
4.9	*Sea Sketches* for String Orchestra by Grace Williams, I 'High Wind', opening	113
4.10	String Quartet No. 6, I, passacaglia theme	114
4.11	Concertino for Bassoon and String Orchestra, II, opening	116
4.12	Symphony for Double String Orchestra, II	118
4.13	Symphony for Double String Orchestra: I, opening theme and IV, opening	119
5.1	*Four Illustrations for the Legend of Rhiannon*, I 'The Conflict', opening	123
5.2	*Four Illustrations for the Legend of Rhiannon*, II 'The Nuptial Feast', fanfare theme	124
5.3	*Four Illustrations for the Legend of Rhiannon*, III, *Hen Ddarbi* theme	124
5.4	*Four Illustrations for the Legend of Rhiannon*, IV, *Cainc Dafydd Broffwyd* theme	125
5.5	Williams's annotated list of traditional tunes in the *Fantasia on Welsh Nursery Tunes*	127
5.6	*Fantasia on Welsh Nursery Tunes*	129
5.7	Sinfonia Concertante for Piano and Orchestra, III	132
5.8	Symphony No. 1, opening	135
5.9	Symphony No. 1, I, trumpet theme	136
5.10	Symphony No. 1, IV, opening	138
5.11	*Sea Sketches* for String Orchestra, III 'Channel Sirens', opening	141
5.12	*Sea Sketches* for String Orchestra, III	142
5.13	*Sea Sketches* for String Orchestra, V 'Calm Sea in Summer', opening	143
5.14	Violin Concerto, I, solo violin theme	149
5.15	*The Dancers*, III 'Roundelay'	151
5.16	*The Dancers*, V 'To the Wild Hills'	153
6.1	*The Country of the Stars*, opening	163
6.2	Prime note row for *De Amore*	163
6.3	*Quincunx*, Tutti 3	167
6.4	*6 Tempi for 10 Instruments*, Prime note row	169
6.5	*6 Tempi for 10 Instruments*, I: 3/8, $\eighthnote$ = 144 – opening	170
6.6	*6 Tempi for 10 Instruments*, II: 7/4, $\quarternote$ = 44 – opening	171
6.7	*Music for Orchestra II*	176
6.8	*Catena*, 2a 'Hachi No Ki'	179
6.9	*The Valley of Hatsu-Se*, I 'Fuyu-komori'	181
6.10	*Akapotik Rose*, III 'Kakafon Kakkoon'	184
6.11	*And Suddenly It's Evening*, I 'On the Willow Boughs'	190

6.12	*Essence of Our Happinesses*, I 'The Mi'raj of Abu Yasid'	193
6.13	*Driving Out the Death*, opening	196
6.14	*Plenum II*	200
7.1	String Quartet No. 7, themes from II, III and IV	206
7.2	*The Departure*	213
7.3	Serenata Concertante, opening	217
7.4	Serenata Concertante, I	218
7.5	Clarinet Quintet, opening	220
7.6	Three Settings of Poems by Gerard Manley Hopkins, I 'The Starlight Night'	224
7.7	Three Settings of Poems by Gerard Manley Hopkins, III 'A May Magnificat'	226
7.8	*The Leaden Echo and the Golden Echo*, 'The Leaden Echo'	228
7.9	*The Leaden Echo and the Golden Echo*, 'The Golden Echo'	229
7.10	String Quartet No. 9, III	231
7.11	String Quartet No. 10, opening	234
7.12	*Epyllion* for Solo Cello and Strings, opening	236
7.13	*Epyllion* for Solo Cello and Strings, I	238
7.14	String Quartet No. 11, *Lento*	240
7.15	String Quartet No. 12, IV 'challenge' chords	241
7.16	*My Dark Heart*, I 'Life is Flying from Me'	245
7.17	*My Dark Heart*, II 'The South Wind is Coming Back'	246
7.18	*My Dark Heart* and *Music for Strings*	247
8.1	*Penillion* for Orchestra, I	252
8.2	*Penillion* for Orchestra, Finale, 'hwyl' rhythms	253
8.3	Symphony No. 2, opening	258
8.4	Symphony No. 2, II, main theme	259
8.5	Symphony No. 2, IV, opening	260
8.6	*The Parlour*, Grandmamma's theme	265
8.7	Four Mediaeval Welsh Poems, I 'Stafell Gynddylan'	268
8.8	Trumpet Concerto, opening	270
8.9	Trumpet Concerto, II, passacaglia theme	271
8.10	*Ballads* for Orchestra, IV	275
8.11	*Missa Cambrensis*, I 'Kyrie', opening	278
8.12	*Missa Cambrensis*, I 'Kyrie', first chorus entry	279
8.13	*Missa Cambrensis*, IV 'Sanctus'	281
8.14	*Missa Cambrensis*, V 'Agnus Dei', final bars	282
8.15	*Ave Maris Stella*, opening	286
8.16	'To Sea! To Sea!' from Two Choruses	289

Acknowledgements

I wish to thank the composers' families, Rose and Mohammed Abdalla, Teresa Fetherstonhaugh, Nicola LeFanu, Eryl and David Freestone for enduring my many questions with patience. Thanks must also go to Anthony Payne, Jane Manning, Robert Saxton, Brian Elias, Glyn Perrin, Heward Rees, Jenny Doctor, Wyn Thomas and Graeme Cotterill for their support for and interest in this book. I am grateful to Sophie Fuller and Sarah Tenant-Flowers, both of whom have undertaken research into areas relevant to the subject of this book, for letting me include extracts from their dissertations.

Some of the research for this book was carried out during my time as an Edison Fellow at the British Library, and I would like to acknowledge the help I received from Jonathan Summers of the National Sound Archive, Tim Day (formerly of the Sound Archive), Nicolas Bell and the excellent team in Library's Music Department. I would also like to thank Trish Hayes at the BBC Written Archives, and staff at the Royal College of Music Archive, Bangor University Archive, the National Library of Wales and St. Hilda's College, Oxford for their assistance.

George Mowat-Brown and John Hywel read through various drafts of this lengthy project and I am grateful for their invaluable comments. I would also like to raise a glass to Frank Zappa, Stevie Ray Vaughan and Eric Clapton for providing moments of necessary catharsis during the finishing stages of checking and editing. A final toast must go to my family, and I thank John, Seren Grace and my mother Yvonne for their understanding and love.

I am especially grateful to the following people for allowing me to reproduce extracts from the materials listed below:

Glyn Perrin, Executor to the Estate of Elisabeth Lutyens, for Lutyens's unpublished music and words from *Requiem for the Living* (1948) and *Time Off? Not a Ghost of a Chance* (1967–68), and for Lutyens's unpublished papers, radio interviews and *A Goldfish Bowl* (Cassell, London) © Elisabeth Lutyens 1972.

Nicola LeFanu, Executor to the Estate of Elizabeth Maconchy, for Maconchy's unpublished music, correspondence and radio interviews.

Eryl Freestone, Executor to the Estate of Grace Williams, for Williams's unpublished music, correspondence, radio interviews and her annotated list of traditional tunes in the *Fantasia on Welsh Nursery Tunes*.

I am very grateful to the following publishers for allowing me to reproduce extracts from music by Lutyens, Maconchy and Williams, and would particularly like to thank:

James Rushton and Carolyn Fuller at Music Sales Group (Chester Music Limited, Novello & Co. Limited); Simon Wright and Khol Dieu at Oxford University Press; Laurence Scott at Universal Music Group (Alfred Lengnick & Co. Ltd.); Claire Urwin at the University of York Music Press; Chris Painter at Oriana Publications Limited; Sally Groves and Colin Green at Schott Music Limited, London; Troy Schreck at Alfred Music Publishing Company (Mills Music Ltd., Belwin-Mills Publishing Corp.) and Ruth Edwards at Cyhoeddiadau Curiad / Curiad Publications.

The image of the autograph score of Lutyens's *The Birthday of the Infanta* reproduced with the permission of the British Library Board. All rights reserved.

The image of the autograph score of Williams's 'To Sea! To Sea!' from *Two Choruses* supplied by The National Library of Wales / Darparwyd gan Llyfrgell Genedlaethol Cymru.

The extracts from the Patron's Fund reports reproduced with the permission of the Royal College of Music.

Kenneth Wright, Internal BBC Memo (30 July 1951) © BBC reproduced by permission of the BBC Written Archives.

Words from Vita Sackville-West's *The Land* and *Tuscany* reproduced with the permission of Curtis Brown Group Ltd., London on behalf of the Estate of Vita Sackville-West.

Wittgenstein's *Tractatus Logico-Philosophicus*, translated by David Pears and Brian McGuiness, reprinted by permission of Taylor & Francis Books (UK).

Words from Kathleen Raine's *To the Wild Hills* reprinted by kind permission of Brian Keeble, Executor to the Estate of Kathleen Raine.

Eduardo Paolozzi's *Kakafon Kakkoon* reprinted by kind permission of Toby Treves, Trustee of the Paolozzi Foundation.

Every effort has been made to trace all the copyright holders, but if any have been inadvertently overlooked the publishers will be pleased to make the necessary arrangement at the first opportunity.

Introduction

Part of the title of this book is intended to resonate with a piece composed by Hubert Parry, one of the father figures of the so-called British Musical Renaissance.[1] His *Blest Pair of Sirens (At a Solemn Music)*, a setting of Milton's ode for chorus and orchestra, was commissioned and premiered by Charles Villiers Stanford's Bach Choir in 1887. The piece established Parry as the leading choral composer of his day and was written while the composer was Professor of Composition and Music History at the then newly founded Royal College of Music in London. It was a favourite piece of his pupil Ralph Vaughan Williams – another seminal renaissance figure – who, in turn, became the teacher of Elizabeth Maconchy (1907–94) and Grace Williams (1906–77) at the Royal College in the late 1920s. Elisabeth Lutyens (1906–83), an exact College contemporary of this blest pair, has been added to form a trio.

It was in this stimulating college environment that the three young students were able to absorb the ideals and musical values of their British musical heritage. This remarkable trio would go on to make different, but important, contributions to British music, extending the themes of the renaissance initiated by Parry and Stanford further into the twentieth century. At the same time, Lutyens, Maconchy and Williams belonged to a new generation of British composers – including Michael Tippett (1905–98) and Benjamin Britten (1913–76) – who were also strongly influenced by continental musical developments. Lutyens became, not without controversy, one of the first English composers to embrace 12-note music; Maconchy's sophisticated personal idiom was inspired by both continental and local influences; and Williams emerged as one of the first professional composers from Wales to assimilate aspects of her Welsh cultural heritage into a cosmopolitan and individual musical style.

While the compositional styles of these three composers evolved independently and in different ways – very much reflecting the major trends in twentieth-century British music – there were common themes that bound their lives together, not least the challenge of being a woman in a predominantly male profession. In the

---

[1] The 'British Musical Renaissance' is a phrase commonly applied to the emergence of a new school of British composers in the period 1880–1914: the movement is also often referred to as the 'English Musical Renaissance'. Most accounts tend to take the first performance of Parry's cantata *Scenes from Shelley's Prometheus Unbound* at the Gloucester Festival in 1880 as a starting point for the Renaissance. Parry, Stanford and Alexander Mackenzie, principal of the Royal Academy of Music, were generally thought to be the leading figures in the new movement.

nineteenth century, a few women had succeeded in establishing careers in Britain as composers (particularly of popular songs), but opportunities had been limited at a time when women were simply not encouraged to take up composition as a serious pursuit.[2] The formidable Ethel Smyth (1858–1944) proved to be an isolated exception. The daughter of a general in the Royal Artillery, Smyth studied at the Leipzig Conservatoire and composed a Mass in D which was performed at the Royal Albert Hall, London in 1893. *Grove's Dictionary of Music and Musicians* noted that 'this work definitely placed the composer easily at the head of all those of her own sex'.[3] Yet this fact seemed to be the one that provoked the most outrage. By Smyth's own account, 'the Press went for the Mass almost unanimously – some with scorn, some with aversion, in all cases adopting a tone of patronage it was hardest of all to bear'.[4] Although her music was later championed in England by Thomas Beecham and Henry Wood,[5] Smyth also achieved a distinctive profile as an ardent campaigner for women's suffrage. She contributed a *March of the Women* (1911) to the cause which was frequently heard in London as an accompaniment to women's marches: on one occasion, the piece was famously conducted by the composer with a toothbrush from the window of a cell in Holloway Prison. Such a detail seems beside the point but for the fact that Smyth inevitably became better known as a celebrity and campaigner in England rather than as a serious composer.[6]

Smyth's musical accomplishments and involvement in the most acrimonious years of the campaign for women's suffrage did, however, prepare the ground for the young women who reached student age in the first decades of the twentieth century. Lutyens, Maconchy and Williams were among a number of young, highly gifted women – including Dorothy Gow (1893–1982), Imogen Holst (1907–84), Helen Glatz (née Hunter) (1908–96) and Helen Perkin (1909–96) – who studied composition at the Royal College in the late 1920s. It was not unusual for the College to have women music students – both the Royal College and the Royal Academy of Music were co-educational institutions – but it was remarkable to have several women studying composition at the same time. Significantly, although Smyth's music did not have any direct influence on the three composers' creative development, they were acutely aware of the impact the women's suffrage

---

[2] For a detailed discussion, see Sophie Fuller, *The Pandora Guide to Women Composers: Britain and the United States, 1629–Present* (London: HarperCollins, 1994).

[3] *Grove's Dictionary of Music and Musicians* (Fifth Edition), ed. E. Blom (London: Macmillan, 1954), vol. vii, p. 860. Note that this comment originally appeared in Smyth's entry in the Second Edition of *Grove's Dictionary*, ed. J.A. Fuller-Maitland (London: Macmillan, 1900).

[4] Smyth, *As Time Went On ...* (London: Longmans, Green and Co., 1936), p. 172.

[5] Beecham conducted the English premiere of her third opera *The Wreckers* (1903–04) at His Majesty's Theatre, London on 22 June 1909.

[6] 'This is celebrity indeed! ... but it does not alter the fact that after having been on the job, so to speak, for over forty years, I have never yet succeeded in becoming even a tiny wheel in the English music machine'. Smyth, *As Time Went On*, pp. 288–289.

movement had had on attitudes in society. As a teenager, Lutyens received some early encouragement in her aspiration to be a composer from her aunt Lady Constance Lytton, who was both a fine musician and a suffragette. Maconchy believed that the emancipation of women had 'started earlier in England than anywhere else', and that the resulting shift of perspective helped to account for the fact that there were 'more women composers [of about the same age] in Great Britain than anywhere else'.[7] When asked if any woman composer had influenced her, Williams later recalled:

> It's strange but there was no central guru or Svengali figure who'd sparked off all the girl composers who emerged in the 1920s or 30s. The woman composer who might have influenced me as a child was Cécile Chaminade whose pieces everyone played and whose picture adorned the cover of one of them. I seem to remember curls, luminous eyes and lace. Very different from Dame Ethel's rough tweeds! ... I discovered that she and Ethel were born within a year of each other in the 1850s, and this I find intriguing because it seems to link up with what Elizabeth Maconchy said about our generation of women composers – all of us coming at roughly the same time. It's as though the muse has been putting us on trial, waiting to see how we shaped before launching some more of us.[8]

The first part of this book opens at the Royal College of Music in the 1920s. Maconchy and Williams won most of the College's composition prizes and scholarships between them, and formed their own composers' club – other members included Imogen Holst and Dorothy Gow – where they were able to discuss contemporary music and to receive useful comments and criticisms about their own pieces. Lutyens was not part of this particular circle. She had a different teacher at college and her priority at this stage was to acquire a solid compositional technique. All three students, however, found the conservatism of College attitudes striking. Lutyens recalled that 'the great modern hero was Brahms'[9] during her time there and that most contemporary music from the Continent tended to be viewed with suspicion. Interestingly, the forceful originality of Bartók, whose work first became known in Britain in the late 1920s, struck a chord within: all three young composers wrote early pieces that reveal an awareness of his music.

The second chapter considers the composers' transition from music student to professional composer, and details their first experiences of the world of public concerts, broadcasts, music critics and publishers. After graduating, all three were confronted by the daunting question – what next? The young, unknown British composer faced enormous challenges at this time in a country that lacked both

---

[7] Maconchy in 'Women as Composers' (BBC radio broadcast, 2 August 1973) [National Sound Archive (NSA) Catalogue Number: BBC Archive Cprd name: 60417 (1)].

[8] Williams in 'Women as Composers', ibid.

[9] Lutyens in interview with Stephen Plaistow (BBC Radio 3, 5 July 1971) [NSA Cat. No. P654R BD 1].

the institutional infrastructure to support new creative work and audiences for contemporary music. As Maconchy later recalled, 'in London in the 1920s no one had given a thought to helping a composer to establish himself – let alone herself – or even to learn the craft of composition by hearing his work performed'.[10] Lutyens complained about this situation to friends in 1931 and suggested that composers should find a way of putting on performances of their own works. Her idea gave birth to the launch of the ground-breaking Macnaghten–Lemare Concerts, an enterprising series which provided a platform for music by a new generation of British composers. All three composers had new work premiered at some of these concerts in the 1930s – often heard alongside new pieces by other unknown youngsters such as Britten, Tippett, Gerald Finzi and Alan Rawsthorne. The importance of these concerts should not be underestimated. More than 30 British composers had pieces performed during the first six years of the series, and as the musicologist Sophie Fuller has noted, 'the fact that, unlike Smyth, the later generation of women composers has been taken seriously and has achieved a fair degree of success must be largely due to the opportunities and encouragement that they found in the Macnaghten–Lemare concerts'.[11]

Part II of the book discusses the composers' musical development in the years 1935 to 1955 and considers the impact the Second World War had on their careers. By 1935 all three had begun to establish themselves in the musical world, but their particular musical paths and idioms would begin to diverge in the ensuing years. In recognition of this broadening out, each composer is discussed in a separate chapter. Chapter 3 considers the nature of Lutyens's radical breakthrough in the 1930s, and her first use of 12-note technique in pieces such as the Chamber Concerto No. 1 (1939–40). While many of her pieces of the 1940s were marked by an attempt to refine her technical skills, she also revealed that she possessed a rare musical versatility, one which could at once encompass the tonal narratives of the ebullient orchestral suite *En Voyage* (1944) and the uncompromising brand of serialism encountered in the Sixth String Quartet (1952).

Chapter 4 examines the way in which Maconchy chose to develop her distinctive musical voice. She found the string quartet to be an ideal medium for the expression of her ideas. Quartet writing enabled her to deal 'with the bones of music',[12] as she put it, and it is evident from the five big-boned quartets she wrote – Quartets Nos. 2, 3, 4, 5 and 6 (1936–50) – that she was continuously refining her contrapuntal writing in order to meet this challenge. Her work was not, however, confined to chamber music and she composed for other genres throughout this period.

---

[10] Maconchy, 'The Composer Speaks' (BBC Radio 3, 17 October 1971) [NSA Cat. No. M4263W C1].

[11] Fuller, '"Putting the BBC and T. Beecham to shame …": The Macnaghten–Lemare Concerts in the Thirties', BMus diss. (King's College, London, 1988), p. 21.

[12] Maconchy, 'Composer's Portrait' (BBC Third Programme, 15 June 1966) [NSA Cat. No. 1CDR0003352 BD3–BD6 NSA].

Whereas Lutyens and Maconchy initially chose to explore the medium of chamber music, Williams preferred to work with larger canvases. The *Fantasia on Welsh Nursery Tunes* (1939–40), a work of bold and colourful tonal contrasts, revealed her prodigious flair for orchestral writing. This piece was largely responsible for bringing her name to the attention of a wider public, and it was followed a few years later by the equally popular *Sea Sketches* for string orchestra (1944). Wales was a natural source for her creativity (both musically and imaginatively) and many, although not all, of her works were inspired by Welsh sources. Pieces discussed in Chapter 5 include her First Symphony (1942–43) – the first modern symphony to be written by a composer from Wales – and the elegant choral suite *The Dancers* (1951).

The third and final part of this book considers the composers' mature works – again, discussed in three separate chapters. Given the combined quantity of pieces, I have chosen to focus on core works and pieces that I consider to be of particular interest. Chapter 6 considers some of the most significant pieces Lutyens wrote between the years 1955 and 1983, the period in which she experienced her greatest critical success. She had now attained a new level of technical command, and her extraordinary compositional fluency – to some extent enhanced by her experiences of meeting tight deadlines for film companies – enabled her to produce over 140 compositions (in all genres ranging from a meticulously timed four-minute brass fanfare to a two-hour opera). Some of her most salient works were composed for the voice and include *The Valley of Hatsu-Se* (1965), an exquisite setting of Japanese poems, and the remarkably poignant *And Suddenly It's Evening* (1966).

Maconchy composed over 100 pieces between the years 1955 and 1994, and continued to explore new musical territory on her own terms. The string quartet remained at the very centre of her art, and, following a break of several years after her Quartet No. 7 (1955), she returned to the medium, composing the Quartets Nos. 8–13 (1966–83). Vocal works now formed an increasingly significant part of her output and during the late 1950s she turned to opera, composing three one-act chamber operas. Chapter 7 concludes with discussions of the masterly *Epyllion* for cello and string orchestra (1975) and the striking vocal cycle *My Dark Heart* (1984).

Williams always insisted on very high standards in her own work and composed some 40 pieces in the final decades of her life. Although her output appears relatively small, this should not necessarily imply that she lacked fluency. She was a compulsive reviser, one who constantly questioned the value of her art: from time to time, she would even 'make a bonfire of works' she considered 'beyond reprieve'.[13] Chapter 8 explores the music Williams composed between 1955 and 1977, the period in which she underwent her most exciting creative phase. She broke new ground with *Penillion* for orchestra (1955), an original adaptation of some of the metrical and melodic characteristics of a traditional

---

[13] Williams, 'Composer's Portrait' (BBC Radio 3, 19 February 1976), transcribed in 'Grace Williams: A Self Portrait', *Welsh Music* 8/5 (Spring 1987), p. 14.

Welsh vocal practice, and her expanded musical vocabulary now energized other orchestral works such as the compelling Symphony No. 2 (1956). In common with Lutyens and Maconchy, she became more interested in writing vocal music in her later years, and some of her most ambitious vocal/choral works, including the *Missa Cambrensis* (1968–71), date from this period. Her successful one-act opera *The Parlour* (1960–66) revealed that she possessed a great gift for dramatic stage works.

This book forms an essential part of any reading of twentieth-century British music. Throughout, I have attempted to enter into the spirit of the composers' time by including reactions to their music from critics, scholars, performers, friends and colleagues. I have also sought to let the composers speak for themselves as much as possible in the form of quotations from published writings, interviews and broadcast talks. What was it like to be a British composer in the twentieth century? And how did these composers respond to the often daunting professional challenges they faced? Although Lutyens, Maconchy and Williams each made a significant contribution to British music, their music was often misunderstood in their own lifetimes, and continues to suffer from neglect to this day. The playwright, music critic and feminist George Bernard Shaw once wrote that 'English society did not care about music – did not know good music from bad'.[14] This, then, is a book about good music.

---

[14] G.B. Shaw, *London Music in 1888–89 as heard by Corno di Bassetto* (London: Constable, 1937), p. 264.

PART I
1926–1935

Opening of *Sirens' Song* by Elizabeth Maconchy (1974)

Source: Copyright © 1977 Chester Music Limited. All Rights Reserved. International Copyright Secured. Reprinted by Permission.

> One of the good works done by the Royal College of Music has been the evangelization of Kensington.
>
> G.B. Shaw, *Music in London 1890–94* (London: Constable, 1932), vol. 1, p. 153.

Chapter 1
The Musical Evangelization of Kensington

The Royal College of Music lies at the heart of South Kensington. Situated in Prince Consort Road, its ornate red brick and terracotta facade – a cross between a cathedral and a Victorian folly – gazes at the curve of the Royal Albert Hall. Every aspect of this illustrious building is designed to be impressive. Originally conceived in 1853 by Prince Albert and Sir Henry Cole, two of the major forces behind the Great Exhibition of 1851, the foundation stone of the College was laid by Edward, Prince of Wales in 1890, and work was completed four years later. Designed by Arthur Blomfield and funded by the memorably named industrialist Samson Fox, the building owes its existence to the confidence, ambition and vision of the Imperial age. When you walk through the College's entrance you are immediately welcomed by alabaster statues of Edward, Prince of Wales (later Edward VII) and his bride Alexandra – a reminder, if one was needed, of the College's regal patrons and its distinguished history. But it is the vibrant 'hum' of the building that gives it a special distinction. Walk out of the main reception area into the labyrinth of dimly lit corridors, stairs and rooms, and you will be greeted by a cacophony of scales, arpeggios, arias and fragments of pieces from every period in music history. This ethereal fanfare, which appears to emanate from every nook of the building, accompanies you as you negotiate your way through swarms of students possessively clutching their double basses, French horns and mobile phones. And as you pass students busily practising in rooms, or rushing to their lessons, you realize that this concerted activity is merely part of one ordinary day for the College.

Passion, persistence and energy have always been fundamental 'Collegian' characteristics. After a temporary National Training School for Music was established in South Kensington in the late 1870s – transforming into the Royal College of Music in 1882 – residents in the area soon became aware of a dramatic rise in the temperature of the British musical climate.[1] Even the indomitable George Bernard Shaw, an astute music critic but never the greatest supporter of Royal institutions or the 'academic musician', noted with approval the link in the 1890s between the glowing musical talent on display in Kensington and the rapid improvement in standards in most areas of professional musical activity. A portrait by Shaw of one of the College's public concerts in March 1890 vividly captures the pioneering spirit of the young institution. He was enthralled by an invigorating performance of Brahms's Second Piano Concerto and made certain that news of

---

[1] The College was originally located nearby in Kensington before moving to its current building in 1894.

the Amazonian prowess of the young soloist spread fast. Miss Polyxena Fletcher played the piano 'courageously and even aggressively', and at the most intense moments of her performance 'thumped the keyboard as if it were Brahms' head. And she was quite right', concluded a delighted Shaw: 'why should she forbear at that age, with an orchestra thundering emulously in her ears?'[2]

Advancing age did not diminish this celebrated Collegian's penchant for giving notable performances. Polyxena Fletcher continued to thump the nation's pianos throughout her professional career – as a concert pianist and as one of London's most prominent piano teachers. It is impossible to say how many pupils this 'weird, grey, spinsterish figure'[3] mesmerized with her robust piano playing. But to Elisabeth Lutyens, the 15-year-old daughter of the celebrated architect Sir Edwin Lutyens, her playing was astounding:

> Polyxena Fletcher had genius ... and became the greatest single influence in my life [at that time]. Music, life and people were inseparable to her, and our lessons, which lasted hours and seemed timeless, were occupied as much with talk and discussion as piano playing. When the talk was of music it was from the widest and most all-embracing point of view and she became to me the yardstick by which to measure all my new intellectual and musical experiences and values of life.[4]

Lessons with Polyxena Fletcher must also have provided Lutyens with a bird's-eye view of the musical world – its personalities, customs and expectations. Miss Fletcher possessed a hardy sense of humour and regaled her pupil with amusing tales of musical life – of friendships and feuds, new musical discoveries and of the best and worst performances of Brahms, Mendelssohn and Schumann, the holy trinity of music at that time. She had studied privately in Vienna with the renowned piano teacher Theodor Leschetizky, and in all respects seemed to embody her teacher's axiom 'no art without life, no life without art'. Furthermore, like Lutyens's own 'Aunt Con' (Lady Constance Lytton), Miss Fletcher's mother had been a pupil of Clara Schumann, then a hallowed institution in England. These factors conspired to make Lutyens want to improve her piano skills so that she too might study abroad, gain entry to a music college and have a glittering career on the concert stage. Miss Fletcher, no doubt, impressed on her the work that would be required for this path – the hours of daily practice, the attention to tone, the detailed knowledge of pieces, the ability to make music and not noise. Yet Lutyens's youthful dreams of becoming a concert pianist proved to be unrealistic: as she divulged 51 years later, 'no amount of work has enabled me to play the

---

[2] Shaw, *London Music in 1888–89 as heard by Corno di Bassetto*, p. 328.
[3] Lutyens's first impression of Miss Fletcher as recounted in her autobiography *A Goldfish Bowl* (London: Cassell, 1972), p. 18.
[4] Ibid. Lutyens was also at this time having violin lessons with Miss Fletcher's friend Marie Motto, another former Collegian, who was the leader of the English String Quartet.

piano better than a typist using one finger'.[5] Even so, those mind-stretching hours spent with Polyxena Fletcher were not wasted. Eventually, Lutyens plucked up courage to show her teacher some of her 'secret' compositions and was rewarded with effusive encouragement and some badly needed harmony lessons.

Although Lutyens was grateful for the opportunities her piano teacher provided, Polyxena Fletcher must have seemed like a character from the distant past to this sophisticated and well-travelled teenager.[6] Miss Fletcher's performance of Brahms's Concerto had taken place 16 years before Lutyens was born – at a time when the piece was only ten years old and its composer was still alive. Unlike the other teachers and governesses, however, Miss Fletcher had a flair for bringing history alive, and it was through her many enthralling tales that Lutyens probably first became acquainted with old Collegians such as Hubert Parry (1848–1918) and Charles Stanford (1852–1924); indeed, it was Stanford, the College's energetic professor of composition and orchestral playing, who had conducted that remarkable Brahms performance in 1890. Although Stanford achieved renown in his day as a composer and composition teacher – his extensive output includes the *Irish Symphony* (No. 3, 1887), several oratorios and a considerable amount of choral music – he was also a superb orchestral trainer. He continued to conduct the College orchestra until 1921 and his exacting standards and eruptive temperament ensured, as Parry noted, that College forces were led 'to brilliant victories times out of number'.[7] Both Stanford and Parry had been recruited onto the College staff in 1883 by George Grove (1820–1900), a man whose life's work Shaw once described as having been 'of more value than that of all the Prime Ministers of the century'.[8] Founding editor of the famous *Dictionary of Music and Musicians* and the College's first director, the visionary Grove sought to introduce ambitious and far-reaching reforms into British musical life.[9] With Stanford and Parry appointed to key cabinet posts at the College, an agenda for national musical renewal was put into place. Known irreverently as 'the Mandarins, both within and outside the College, these men helped to nurture several fertile generations of English composers including Charles Wood, Gustav Holst, Ralph Vaughan Williams, John Ireland, Frank Bridge and Herbert Howells.

---

[5] Ibid., p. 19.

[6] Sir Edwin Lutyens was the government-appointed architect of New Delhi from 1912 to 1930. Elisabeth and her family visited India on several occasions, and she also accompanied her mother on Theosophy tours in Europe and Australia.

[7] Parry as quoted in H.C. Colles and J. Cruft, *The Royal College of Music: A Centenary Record 1883–1983* (London: Royal College of Music, 1982), p. 19. By 1921 the College had three orchestras, 'to provide a ladder for players' attainment'. Adrian Boult succeeded Stanford as conductor of the first orchestra.

[8] Shaw, *Music in London 1890–94*, vol. ii, p. 214.

[9] Although famous as a musician, Grove trained as a civil engineer. Early on in his career he worked on the construction of Robert Stephenson's Britannia Bridge, a railway bridge linking the Isle of Anglesey with the Welsh mainland.

By the time Lutyens entered the College in 1926, Stanford and Parry belonged firmly to the past, but their influence lingered on in the curriculum, the performance repertoire and in the creed of the College.[10] Through their activities as composers, scholars, administrators and teachers, they had helped to outline British borders on the musical map of Europe, and their achievements amounted to one of the first conscious strikes against Britain's unenviable image (both at home and abroad) as *das Land ohne Musik*. Victorian Britain had long assumed the superiority of continental composers and performers, and this, together with inadequate professional training opportunities for musicians in Britain, had created an acceptance that serious music of a high quality could not be home-grown.[11] The reasons for Victorian negative attitudes towards national music were complex, but evidence suggests that this was a distinctly local problem that was intimately connected with the class structure of British society. The musicologist Nicholas Temperley has argued, for example, that attitudes held by a musically philistine aristocracy were greedily embraced by the various lower echelons of the nineteenth-century British class structure, smothering any real sense of national musical growth. As he has stated:

> Social emulation of the upper classes was the spur that energized the middle classes to the great achievements of the Victorian age. It was highly desirable, no doubt, in the army, and navy, the civil and colonial services, the law, medicine and business. It did no damage in the arts of the word: fiction, poetry, drama, oratory, where the English language naturally reigned. In music, emulation of the upper classes was disastrous, because they had long since downplayed its value and adopted foreignness as the shibboleth.[12]

With the emergence of new musical institutions, and renewed general interest in English folk song and the Elizabethan composers, music began to gain a certain 'respectability' in British society.[13] Edward Elgar (1857–1934), the exceptional English composer of his day, was the first to break the mould when he achieved national prominence with works such as the *'Enigma' Variations* (1898–99), the

---

[10] Parry succeeded Grove as Director of the College in 1894. Both he and Stanford remained at the College until their deaths.

[11] It is significant that some of the most prolific British composers of the second half of the nineteenth century – Sterndale Bennett, Arthur Sullivan, Frederick Cowen and Ethel Smyth, for example – had been trained at Mendelssohn's Leipzig Conservatoire.

[12] N. Temperley, 'Xenophilia in British Music History', in Bennett Zon (ed.), *Nineteenth-Century British Music Studies* (Aldershot: Ashgate, 1999), vol. 1, p. 14.

[13] Cecil Sharp (1859–1924), for example, was a major pioneering force in the collecting, publication and revival of English folk song and dance in the twentieth century. He founded the English Folk Dance Society in 1911, and this society was later amalgamated with the older Folk Song Society (founded in 1898) to form the English Folk Dance and Song Society.

oratorio *The Dream of Gerontius* (1899–1900) and the *Pomp and Circumstance Marches* Nos. 1–5 (1901–30). Yet although efforts were made by Elgar, Stanford, Parry and others to raise the profile of British music, change proceeded at a glacial pace. In 1926 it remained for a younger generation, notably Vaughan Williams, Holst and Ireland, to extend the themes of what had become loosely known as the 'British Musical Renaissance'.[14] The fight against a deeply engrained musical philistinism in Britain, however, would be long and difficult. Shortly before taking up his place at the Royal College in July 1930, for instance, a young Benjamin Britten was asked by a guest at a party what career he wished to pursue. He replied that he wanted to be a composer – to which the response was, 'yes, but what else?'

Lutyens wanted to study composition with Vaughan Williams or Ireland, the College's two most illustrious composition teachers, and was perturbed when Hugh Allen, the College's smooth, autocratic Director, attempted to discourage her from studying composition as a first subject.[15] Not only did he seem unimpressed with the examples of work she showed him in her interview but he also appeared ambivalent about the musical training she had received thus far: she had studied harmony and counterpoint in 1923 at the École Normale de Musique in Paris, and had also had some composition lessons from the English composer John Foulds. Allen eventually relented in the face of a persistent Lutyens (and possibly to avoid offending her well-connected parents). Although he refused to let her study with Vaughan Williams or Ireland, he did allow her take theory and composition with the organist and composer Harold Darke. As there was a dire shortage of viola players at the College, Lutyens was persuaded to take viola as her second study.[16]

Rake-thin, witty and idealistic, but prone to bouts of self-consciousness, Lutyens was grateful for the chance to further her musical aspirations. She felt herself to be different from her peers and initially found it difficult to adjust to College life. In truth, music had not always been her central focus. In keeping with the Theosophical doctrines embraced by her mother Lady Emily Lutyens, she had been brought up to chant quaint creeds, to be a strict vegetarian and to believe that only the life of 'Krishna' (Jiddu Krishnamurti), the chosen World Teacher of the new era, had any real meaning. The Theosophical Society had been founded in the

---

[14] Elgar had an uncomfortable relationship with London-based colleagues such as Parry and Stanford. Although a champion of British music, his success and international profile owed nothing to the Renaissance movement.

[15] Hugh Allen (1869–1946) was a quintessential Renaissance man and was highly regarded as a musician, conductor and administrator. He succeeded Parry as Director of the College in 1918.

[16] Records confirm that Lutyens entered College in the middle of the Christmas term of 1926 and that she was registered to study theory (first study) with Darke and viola (second study) with Ernest Tomlinson [Register of Students 1926, Royal College of Music Archive (RCMA)]. Lutyens later concluded that Allen's decision to send her to Darke had been a wise one. She possessed a raw but undisciplined talent for music but her grasp of technique was, by her own admission, weak at this stage of her development.

1870s by Helena Petrovna Blavastky, among others, and its promotion of a new world view found many followers in the English upper classes and throughout Europe during the first decades of the twentieth century. Lutyens's younger sister Mary described the dogmas that she and her siblings were brought up to believe:

> Theosophy was the philosophy on which I was nurtured – that is, the belief in reincarnation and karma, that inexorable law by which you reap what you have sown of good and evil through a succession of lives (I was brought up to think of good and bad karma rather than of good or bad luck); the equality of all the great religions, and, since 1902, a conviction that the World Teacher was shortly to come back into incarnation. It was the great Lord Maitreya – he who had taken the body of Jesus 2000 years ago and had founded Christianity – who was, in the near future, to take the body of Krishna, my friend and almost-brother, and sow the seed of yet another religion.[17]

Lutyens spent a great deal of her adolescence being a reluctant disciple, following her adored, impressionable mother and Annie Besant to Theosophical Society meetings around the world. Indeed, between the years 1923 and 1925 alone, her musical interests were somewhat curtailed by extensive trips to the Austrian Tyrol, Pergine in the Dolomites, Calcutta, Delhi, Adyar (the spiritual centre of the Theosophy world) and Sydney. In Sydney, while undergoing preparation to ascend the ladder of perfection in 1925, she and Mary were encouraged by Bishop Leadbeater, one of the Society's leaders, to float on the astral plane through meditation. Even her mother, now adrift in the vast, eternal mists of meditation, realized that her daughter might find it difficult 'to return to a normal world and keep English hours and adapt … to English standards'.[18] The strain of being part of this spiritual circus began to take its toll on Lutyens. As she recalled, Theosophy 'was having a devastating effect, in practice, on my physical and mental health', and she became 'quite frozen emotionally and incapable of any spontaneous reaction'.[19] Ill health and a seriously agitated father prompted her to reassess her life.[20] Declining to accompany her mother and sister to a Theosophical retreat in California in 1926, and gaining entry to the Royal College of Music, were both part of the cure.

---

[17] Mary Lutyens, *To Be Young: Some Chapters of Autobiography* (London: R. Hart-Davis, 1959), p. 13. The Theosophy movement had admirers in the music world. Both John Foulds (Elisabeth's one-time teacher) and Cyril Scott were declared theosophists, for example, and Raymond Head has suggested that theosophical ideas may also have had an influence on the music of Gustav Holst. See Head, 'Holst – Astrology and Modernism in "The Planets"', *Tempo* 187 (December 1993), pp. 15–22.

[18] Lady Emily Lutyens, *Candles in the Sun* (London: R. Hart-Davis, 1957), p. 114.

[19] Lutyens, *Goldfish Bowl*, p. 37.

[20] Edwin Lutyens was never a disciple of Theosophy and the family's involvement with the Society caused a serious rift between him and his wife.

Fortunately, Lutyens got on well with her theory tutor. Harold Darke (1888–1976) was generally regarded as being one of the finest English organists of his day. He was the organist of St. Michael's, Cornhill in the City of London and his regular Monday recitals at midday were frequently broadcast by the BBC in the 1920s and 30s. A former composition pupil of Stanford's, Darke also became known for his well-crafted organ and choral pieces, including his popular setting of the carol *In the Bleak Midwinter*. Thorough and scrupulous in his teaching methods, he took an interest in the unrefined exercises and pieces Lutyens brought to her Tuesday morning tutorials and encouraged her in her quest to acquire a solid musical technique. His interest bolstered her brittle confidence. She was also now beginning to make a few friends at College and became particularly close to Dorothy Gow, who had been studying composition at the College since 1924.[21] Gentle and generous in character, Gow became a surrogate older sister to Lutyens and together they spent many hours poring over the details of their latest pieces.

As Lutyens began to settle into her new environment, she became aware that a number of her contemporaries had already achieved varying degrees of success for their compositions. In her first term she collided with a beautiful but 'disdainful' young man who had been hurrying out of the College's Parry Room Library. The man was Constant Lambert (1905–51), a former star Collegian, whose ballet *Romeo and Juliet* (1924–25) had recently been performed by Diaghilev's Ballet Russes in Monaco, Paris (where it caused a riot) and London.[22] And it was in December 1926 that Lutyens probably first encountered the music of Elizabeth Maconchy at one of the coveted Patron's Fund rehearsals.

The Patron's Fund played an important role in College life. The Fund was instituted in 1903 by Ernest Palmer primarily to encourage young British composers by arranging professional performances of their works, but provision was also given for providing scholarships for further study abroad, publishing works and supporting British performers.[23] Although the Fund was administered by the College, and was primarily intended for past and present Collegians, it was open, in theory, to all British subjects. Each year, composers submitted pieces to the Fund's reading panel, and the best works were performed by professionals at either an orchestral concert during the summer term or a chamber concert at the end of the Christmas term. In 1919 these concerts were replaced by public rehearsals which were held in the College concert hall. Maconchy's *Fantasy* for flute, harp and string orchestra and *Elegy* for flute, horn and string orchestra were selected by the Fund's examiners in 1926, and on 10 December Adrian Boult and members of the London Symphony Orchestra rehearsed both works in a hall packed with students and visitors. Although it was the first time this 19-year-old composer had heard professional musicians perform her music, Maconchy was well prepared. The *Fantasy*, one of her earliest attempts at writing for larger

---

[21] Dorothy Gow – Appendix.
[22] Constant Lambert – Appendix.
[23] Ernest Palmer – Appendix.

instrumental forces, had been performed at a College concert earlier in July, and both works had received a run-through at a concert given the week before the big event. Admittedly, her pieces had received an unusual amount of attention and rehearsal time by ordinary College standards, but then Maconchy was not an average student. She had already started to collect a number of prizes and had had five pieces performed at the College in that year alone.[24] To have had *two* works selected by the Patron's Fund, however, placed her in an entirely different league from her peers. People at the College suddenly knew who she was; heads would turn in corridors as she walked past.

Maconchy had been totally unprepared for the life of a music student when she first entered the College in September 1923. She was much younger than most of the other students and was still grieving over the recent loss of her father.[25] Certainly, the accelerated tempo of College life and the emphasis placed on high, professional standards were in marked contrast to the sedate, amateur musical world she had known as a child. Maconchy was born in Broxbourne, Hertfordshire, but grew up in Ireland, her family's ancestral home. Her maternal grandfather Captain Poe was distantly related to the Domville family, owners of the Santry domain, near Dublin, and he acted as the executive and agent-in-residence of the family's magnificent Jacobean mansion Santry Court and its gardens. Although her parents Gerald and Violet Maconchy lived in Howth, overlooking Dublin Bay, she and her two sisters spent most of their childhood summers at Santry Court.

Maconchy's musical talent was noticed from the very start. Indeed, when her parents discovered their six-year-old daughter carefully picking out the sound of the church bells on the piano, they quickly sought advice from a local music teacher. Fascinated by the musical sound worlds she was discovering, Maconchy easily mastered her piano teacher's modest province of scales, arpeggios and small piano pieces. She was educated at home by a succession of governesses and, when not attending general lessons, would write her own piano pieces simply for pleasure. Such was her musical progress that she was sent for more advanced lessons to Mrs Boxhill, one of Dublin's most celebrated piano teachers, and, unusually for a girl at that time, to the Dublin-based composer and scholar John Larchet for harmony and counterpoint lessons.[26] After a time both teachers recommended that Maconchy go to London for further study. Her mother – by this time a young widow – decided that she would move to England with her three daughters so that Maconchy could study at the College.

Interestingly, despite her musical talent and specialist training, Maconchy's actual experience of music at this time was limited. Apart from her own activities

---

[24] Maconchy was awarded the following during her time at the College: Foli Scholarship (in 1926 and 1927), the Blumenthal Scholarship (1927 for two years), the Arthur Sullivan Prize (1928) and the Cobbett Prize (1929).

[25] Gerald Maconchy contracted tuberculosis during the First World War and died in 1921.

[26] John Larchet – Appendix.

there had been little music to be heard inside the house, and with a Dublin music scene largely devoid of professional opera companies, orchestras and chamber groups, opportunities to hear music had been scarce. Indeed, by the time she entered the College in 1923, she had attended only one orchestral concert.[27]

It took her some time to find her feet. She took piano as her first study, with the pianist Arthur Alexander, and enjoyed her composition lessons with the distinguished Irish composer Charles Wood (1866–1926).[28] She also took theory as an extra study with the didactic harmonist Herbert Kitson – a very 'dry old stick' according to Maconchy;[29] indeed, in later years she and fellow Collegian Michael Tippett would swap amusing stories about Kitson's good but terrifyingly rigid teaching methods. Both Maconchy and Tippett were particularly attracted to the string quartet form in their student days, an interest almost certainly encouraged by their teacher Charles Wood, himself the composer of eight quartets. Maconchy first heard a string quartet played at one of the College concerts put on by students and, enthralled by the intimacy and sonority of the medium, was eager to explore the form for herself. She would, undoubtedly, have written quartets in imitation of existing models as a means of learning her craft, but her *Suite for Strings* in E minor, a short piece of four contrasting movements, was one of the first pieces she wrote at College that she was later prepared to acknowledge. The work was performed at a concert in November 1924 by some of her student friends, a month after Tippett had his own *Suite for Strings* (in C major) performed by the same quartet group. Although exploratory in concept, Maconchy later came to regard this work as being 'the first thing I wrote with a decidedly personal flavour'.[30]

A breakthrough came in the Christmas term of 1925 when she was sent to Vaughan Williams for composition lessons. Every student would have been acutely aware of Vaughan Williams's and Holst's positions at the forefront of British musical life in the 1920s, and of their towering successes with works such as the *Fantasia on a Theme by Thomas Tallis* (1910, final rev. 1919) and *The Planets* (1914–16). Indeed, Maconchy must have first approached the front door of 13 Cheyne Walk, Chelsea – Vaughan Williams often taught his students from his London home – with a mixture of trepidation and excitement. Yet Vaughan Williams neither encouraged nor needed musical disciples and was always on the

---

[27] A performance of Beethoven's Seventh Symphony by the Hallé Orchestra in Dublin. See Maconchy, 'Serenata Concertante – an analytical note', in *Twenty British Composers* (London: Chester Music for the Feeney Trust, 1975), p. 50.

[28] Charles Wood – Appendix.

[29] Maconchy interviewed in the Channel 4 television documentary, 'Elizabeth Maconchy: A Video Portrait', directed and produced by Margaret Williams (Arbor International Productions and Arts Council of Great Britain, 1984).

[30] Maconchy, 'Talk on String Quartets' (Radio 3, 9 October 1976) [NSA Cat. No. NP2788AW C1]. Tippett's *Suite for Strings* was performed at an informal College concert on 23 October 1924, and Maconchy's *Suite for Strings* in E minor was premiered on 25 November 1924 [RCMA Concert Programmes].

side of the young. He believed that young composers should discover their true musical voices through trial, error and sheer hard work – just as he had done. Large and heavy with a shambling gait, the 53-year-old composer was totally devoid of conceit, possessed a vital individuality and had an unusually wide-ranging musical vision. The impact of his formidable personality on Maconchy was revelatory. 'Everything suddenly opened out to me', she recalled, 'it was a whole new World when I became a pupil of his'.[31] She later wrote about her experience of his unorthodox teaching methods:

> [He] had little respect for the rules and conventional methods of teaching composition, and never followed a formal scheme.
>
> The reason for this apparent lack of method was his complete rejection of ready-made solutions. ... His teaching, though he never said it in so many words – was always directed towards making his pupils think for themselves in their own musical language. He fully recognised the importance of an adequate technique, but for him the purpose of technique was how to give the clearest expression to the musical ideas of each individual composer in his own way. It is something for which there is no formula, and which cannot be learnt at second hand. He taught one to learn direct from the great music of the past – Bach, in particular, but many others too, and never from books.[32]

From the 1920s onwards, Vaughan Williams's music was often thought to epitomize a particular type of English national identity – one which was pastoral and, in the view of some, parochial. Although he held strong views about the regenerative value of national music (both past and present), the clumsy image of a parochial composer failed to do justice to his rich and multifaceted musical personality. Continental influences were crucial to Vaughan Williams's development – he had studied at Leipzig and then briefly with Ravel in Paris – and his range of musical expression was such that it could encompass works as different as the *Pastoral Symphony* (No. 3, 1921) and the turbulent Symphony No. 4 (1931–34). During Maconchy's time at the College, he would often refer to the works he was writing, including his Piano Concerto (1926–31) and the operas *Sir John in Love* (1924–28), *Riders to the Sea* (1925–32) and *The Poisoned Kiss* (1927–29). She recalled seeing sections of the Blake-inspired masque *Job* (1927–30) as it began to emerge, and she acted as a repetiteur for some of the preliminary choral rehearsals of *Flos Campi* (1925). She also attended the College's premiere of his ballad opera *Hugh the Drover* on 4 July 1924.[33] Muriel Nixon, who sang the lead role of Mary in the opera, was a friend, and Nixon went on to perform some of her songs at

---

[31] Maconchy in conversation with John Skiba, *Composer* 63 (Spring 1978), p. 7.

[32] Maconchy, 'Vaughan Williams as a Teacher', *Composer* 2 (1959), pp. 18–19.

[33] The first public performance of the opera took place on 14 July 1924 at His Majesty's Theatre, Haymarket, London.

a College concert in March 1926.[34] These songs, together with other works she wrote at this time, naturally reflected the influence of her teacher, yet it would be wrong to assume that Vaughan Williams expected his pupil to seek a personal style which used English folk song and the Tudor composers as primary stimulants. Far from imposing his own style and philosophy, he actively encouraged Maconchy to respond and react to the different styles of contemporary music.

After Maconchy had been studying with Vaughan Williams for about a year, she discovered the music of Bartók which was then just beginning to be known in England. The radical and uncompromising nature of Bartók's early scores had an enormously liberating effect on her musical thinking. Significantly, his Piano Suite, Op. 14 (1916) was to be the only work she performed at College when she gave a piano recital in March 1927.[35] Her performance was flawless, but several elderly professors were seen to flinch violently in their seats at some of the dissonant, more acerbic gestures in the piece; indeed, some confusion arose at the time as to whether the pianist was playing the right notes.[36] Such responses simply served to highlight both the insularity of some sections of British musical life at this time, and the genuine bewilderment that often greeted contemporary musical developments from the Continent. Lutyens vividly captured the slightly stultifying atmosphere at College when she recalled that during her time there Brahms was still thought to be 'the god of *new* music'.[37] Bartók's reception in Britain was an interesting case. The composer visited London several times during the 1920s to perform his works, and his performances were, on the whole, greeted with a certain amount of hostility. Such was the furore created by Bartók's broadcast performances in 1927, for example, that it prompted the critic and broadcaster Percy Scholes to pen a deliciously verbose article in the *Radio Times* (9 December 1927) entitled 'Is Bartók Mad – Or Are We?':

> A great many listeners have written to me about a recent programme of music by the Hungarian composer, Bela Bartók. The gist of many of the matters is a question – *Is Bartok Mad – or are we?* ...
>
> There is nothing to be astonished at in it because there is nothing new. What he is doing, in the introduction of a new idiom, has been done several times before, and what people are now saying has always on such occasions been said ...

---

[34] Three of Maconchy's songs for soprano and piano – 'The Call', 'There is a Lady Sweet and Kind' and 'My Sweet Sweeting' – was performed by Nixon on 11 March 1926. [RCMA Concert Programmes].

[35] Maconchy played Bartók's Suite on 1 March 1927 [RCMA Concert Programmes].

[36] A detail provided by Nicola Lefanu, Maconchy's daughter, in interview with the author.

[37] Lutyens, *Goldfish Bowl*, p. 38.

I am not very sure, but I *believe* that Bartók is a great composer. I am very sure that he is a clever one. I have a suspicion that what has been wrong with listeners who have written to protest against Bartók's music has been, in the main, not Bartók's composing but their hearing. *The human ear is a very conservative member.*

Scholes received hundreds of letters from listeners in response to his article, some of which were published in subsequent issues of the *Radio Times*. One Eric Lewis of Chelsea thought that Bartók's 'originality must, I suppose, be offensive to the average British listener whose favourite musical diet is Faust and Schubert's *Unfinished*'. Arguing that the modern music 'treatment' had been rather 'too drastic' in recent months, he suggested that if 'Bartók, Stravinsky and Co.' (*sic*) were to be 'administered in somewhat smaller doses' by the BBC, 'it might be possible to persuade the patients "to keep them down"'.[38]

Shaw captured the prevailing late-nineteenth-century English attitude to music when he wrote that 'art in England is regarded as a huge confectionery department, where sweets are made for the eye and ear just as they are made for the palate in the ordinary "tuck-shop"'.[39] This view, however, together with the opinions of the radio listeners in 1927, would certainly not have been endorsed by members of the College's new composers' club. Founded in the Christmas term of 1926 by Maconchy and Grace Williams, the club was comprised of a predominantly female group of composition students, including Dorothy Gow and Imogen Holst. These resourceful friends met once a week to debate the latest contemporary music and to discuss and criticize their own work – much to the pleasure of Vaughan Williams (or 'Uncle Ralph' as they called him) who thought he was witnessing a new 'golden age' of composers. Bartók's music particularly fired their imaginations. Imogen Holst recalled that they were all 'overjoyed when Bartók himself came to London to play his recent *Sonata for Pianoforte* and *Three Open Air Pieces* as well as the *Rumanian Folkdances from Hungary*'.[40] Indeed, club members eagerly rushed to acquire ringside seats in the Arts Theatre Club in London's West End for the live BBC radio broadcast given by Bartók on 4 March 1929. The earlier part of the concert – which included his two new Violin Rhapsodies – was broadcast, but the composer deliberately placed his Piano Sonata at the end of the programme (not broadcast by the BBC), fearing that it would simply be too difficult for radio listeners.

The impact of Bartók's music on Maconchy's musical development was significant. In the Christmas term of 1927, she submitted a work entitled *Bluebeard and Fatima* to the Patron's Fund for consideration. Although the

---

[38] Letters to the Editor, 'The Madness of Bartók and Other Matters', *Radio Times* (6 January 1928), p. 713.

[39] Shaw, *Music in London*, vol. ii, p. 147.

[40] Imogen Holst in 'Grace Williams: A Symposium (Part 1)', *Welsh Music* 5/6 (Summer 1977), p. 19.

manuscript has been lost, it seems reasonable to infer from the title that the work may have been based on the seventeenth-century version of the tale of Bluebeard by Charles Perrault, and not Balázs's libretto for Bartók's opera *Bluebeard's Castle* (1911, rev. 1918, 1921).[41] The work was not accepted for performance but the Fund examiners' succinct reports survive. Both examiners thought that the work was 'discordant' and 'ugly', verdicts which suggest that the piece may have been one of Maconchy's earliest attempts to assimilate Bartókian harmonies and techniques into her own music.[42] For his part, Vaughan Williams appears to have encouraged Maconchy's enthusiasm for Bartók, a composer whose musical outlook in some respects resonated with his own. Interestingly, Maconchy's fascination with the music of Bartók was shared by Grace Williams, and the two quickly became close friends and musical *confrères*. Indeed, for Maconchy, this time would mark 'the beginning of the life-long habit between Grace and me of mutual consultation and criticism'.[43]

Williams had entered the College in September 1926 to study composition with Vaughan Williams. Striking and slender in appearance with a distinctive slanting smile, she had already completed a music degree at Cardiff University and quickly settled into the routines of College life. Dorothy Gow recalled that while the other club members admired Williams, many were also slightly envious of the fact that music 'seemed to be the very essence of her being, and seemed to flow from her so easily'.[44] Williams's interest in music had, like Maconchy and Lutyens, started at an early age, but unlike her peers she had the good fortune of having been born into a house filled with music. Her father, a school teacher with a great love of music, encouraged her to learn music and gave his daughter her first piano lesson. After several years of racing through volumes of keyboard exercises and piano tutors, Williams hungered for further challenges. Curious about the mysterious piles of music which were stacked in the front room of the family house in Barry, South Wales, she would start with the piece at the top and gradually work her way down through a pile. During the course of these expeditions, she encountered Beethoven sonatas, Chopin waltzes, songs, oratorios, Wagner operas, chamber music and – the latest craze then – ragtime pieces. As a teenager, she spent hours improvising at

---

[41] In the Perrault tale, it is Fatima, the seventh and last wife of Bluebeard, who opens the forbidden doors in the castle revealing her predecessors' horrific fate. Bartok's opera retains much of the plot and many of the themes of the original, but Judith, Bluebeard's fourth wife, is featured as a main character and the ending is different.

[42] The Fund reports by Sidney Waddington and Eric Coates are dated 16 and 29 of January 1928 respectively, and make interesting reading. Waddington thought the piece was 'very discordant'. Coates bluntly described the piece as being 'extremely ugly … very unoriginal and totally unnecessary' [RCMA Register of Patron's Fund Concerts, 1928 (shelfmark 016.06)].

[43] Maconchy in 'Grace Williams: A Symposium (Part 1)', *Welsh Music* 5/6, p. 18.

[44] Gow in 'Grace Williams: A Symposium (Part 2)', *Welsh Music* 5/7 (Winter 1977), p. 46.

the piano, playing the violin in chamber groups *en famille*, and she also frequently accompanied her father's choir in public concerts and competitions.[45] In 1920, when she was 14 years old,

> the "National" [Eisteddfod] came to my home town, Barry ... it was there I first saw paintings of Monet – and I heard music by Stravinsky ... and Vaughan Williams. Vaughan Williams was there in person; he was one of the adjudicators. Little did I think then that eight years later I'd become a pupil of his.[46]

The 1920 National Eisteddfod introduced several innovative features which may have made an early impression on Williams. For the first time in its history, new composition competitions were held for an orchestral tone poem and a piece for chorus and orchestra, and the winning pieces were then premiered by the London Symphony Orchestra at the event. The adjudicators for these competitions were Vaughan Williams and Walford Davies, and both concluded that although the winning works showed few signs of originality, they were successful in avoiding 'mere slavish imitation of mid-Victorian [i.e. Mendelssohn] models'. The London Symphony Orchestra also accompanied the various competing choirs in performances of Stanford's cantata *The Revenge* during Eisteddfod week. Vaughan Williams advocated that the performers needed to pay greater attention to detail, memorably counselling that choral performance was 'not an affair of stunts and monkey tricks'. Walford Davies lamented the choirs' clumsy phrasing and lack of appreciation of overall musical structure, but felt that this problem could be overcome if 'a natural appreciation of the subtleties of orchestral music' could be developed.[47]

Something of this advice may have struck a chord within Williams. She had always been thrilled by the *sound* of an orchestra and was particularly drawn to instrumental forms from the very start of her musical development. When she began studying harmony and counterpoint at Barry County School for Girls at the age of 15, she soon realized that she 'could go one better than a text-book exercise' and started composing short instrumental pieces as well as songs.[48] Her unusual musical ability was noticed in school, and a fully-qualified music teacher was

---

[45] Williams's father William Matthew Williams was renowned for founding one of the most outstanding boys' choirs in Europe. Under his directorship, the Romilly Boys' Choir won the Gold Crown at the Paris International Musical Festival in 1912, and in 1914 the choir performed for President Wilson at the White House while on a tour of North America.

[46] Williams, 'A Self Portrait', *Welsh Music* 8/5 (Spring 1987), p. 8. The London Symphony Orchestra gave a performance of Stravinsky's *Firebird Suite* at the 1920 National Eisteddfod. See the National Eisteddfod of Wales – Appendix.

[47] Alfred Kalisch's review in *The Musical Times* of the 1920 National Eisteddfod, quoted in D.I. Allsorbrook, *Music for Wales: Walford Davies and the National Council of Music 1918–1941* (Cardiff: University of Wales Press, 1992), p. 80.

[48] Williams, *Welsh Music* 8/5, p. 8.

appointed. Rhyda Jones, a student of Walford Davies and recent graduate from Aberystwyth University, immediately recognized her pupil's musical abilities and creative drive. She encouraged Williams in her work, gave her freedom to develop and was rewarded with regular gifts of small pieces. By the time Williams came to take her 'Higher' (A-level) music examination, she was devoting a great deal of time to music. Her parents encouraged her to further her studies and she began her BMus course at Cardiff University in September 1923.

Life in Cardiff was a bit like wearing shoes two sizes too small. Although Williams enjoyed the social life – the student dances, the friendships and romances – the somewhat rigid degree course did not measure up to her expectations, and she quickly grew tired of writing strict counterpoint and fugues week after week. The music department did, however, have a fairly lively concert schedule, and Williams became a member of the choral society, played violin in the orchestra and had some of her compositions performed at concerts. The music professor David Evans considered her to be very gifted as a composer, but Williams felt that individuality and freedom of thought were neither encouraged nor valued. As she later recalled, 'if one wrote anything off the beaten track the reaction was "what would the external examiner say?", so I really was imprisoned in that place as far as composing was concerned'.[49] Convinced that it was necessary to get as far away as possible from Wales to acquire essential professional training, she was relieved when her professor suggested that she apply to one of the London music colleges. After graduating in 1926, she entered the Royal College to study composition (first study) and to take the teacher's training course (second study). 'The atmosphere of the place really bowled me over', she remembered. 'Here at last was what I had been aching for – real live musical activity'.[50]

College life had a liberating impact on Williams. She was now able to test new ideas in her compositions, to write for new combinations of instruments, and to enjoy and be stimulated by the company of like-minded fellow students. Vaughan Williams had a profound and lasting influence on her, both as a composer and as a mentor, and she continued to seek his advice right up until his death in 1958. As a teacher, he never failed to inspire. As Williams noted:

> The finest thing about being Vaughan Williams's pupil was that, just because he was a man of such great integrity, it was impossible to show him anything but the very best one could do. As a teacher he was very critical, but not in too detailed a way ... we learnt from the first to be self-critical ...

---

[49] Williams, 'Views and Revisions', *Welsh Music* 5/4 (Winter 1976–77), reprinted in *Welsh Music* 10/9–10 (Summer 2006), p. 11.

[50] Williams, letter to Daniel Jones, 5 April 1940 [Daniel Jones Archive, National Library of Wales (NLW), Aberystwyth].

V.W. [*sic*] liked to remind us that he, too, had been through the mill in his young days. One of the first pieces of advice he gave me was, "If you're going to be a composer you'll need the hide of a rhinoceros."[51]

It was typical of Vaughan Williams that he should support Williams and Maconchy's efforts to form a composers' club. He was particularly keen that they learn from each other's criticisms – advice which was entirely in keeping with his own view that 'the benefit that one obtains from an academy or college is not so much from one's official teachers as from one's fellow students'.[52] Cheered on by supportive friends, Williams submitted an orchestral work entitled *Sea Dirge* to the Patron's Fund in her first term at College. Although the work was not accepted for performance – the examiners thought the piece clever but 'bizarre'[53] – Williams soon made her mark. In the following year, she completed her *Two Psalms* for contralto, harp and strings, and the piece was performed at a College concert, conducted by a young Malcolm Sargent, on 9 December 1927.[54] Further exposure came when, in 1928, she won second prize in the Cobbett Competition with her *Fantasy Quintet* for piano and string quartet. The first prize was awarded to Imogen Holst for her *Phantasy String Quartet*, but Holst later graciously confessed that she felt that Williams deserved the first prize: 'For I knew Grace was a real composer; she was utterly single-minded'.[55]

Lutyens knew all the members of the composers' club, but looked on at all this single-minded activity from the sidelines. Although Dorothy Gow remained one of her closest friends, Lutyens was perhaps all too aware that she lacked the necessary training credentials to join what was, in essence, a clique of Vaughan Williams's students. As she wryly liked to say of her student days, 'people with real talent (such as Elizabeth Maconchy) went to Vaughan Williams, whereas people without talent (such as Elisabeth Lutyens) were sent to Harold Darke'.[56] Her compositional development proceeded at a much slower pace than that of

---

[51] Williams, 'Vaughan Williams: A Tribute', in *The RCM Magazine*, 55/1 (1959), pp. 36–37.

[52] Vaughan Williams, 'A Musical Autobiography', *National Music and Other Essays* (Oxford, 1934; reprint 1987), p. 185.

[53] The reports on *Sea Dirge* (dated 12 and 19 May 1927 respectively) reveal that Herbert Howells thought the work 'clever enough in a bizarre sort of way', but Sidney Waddington felt that it was 'laboured', and 'sometimes near to grotesque' in places [RCMA Register of Patron's Fund Concerts, 1927]. The manuscript of *Sea Dirge* does not survive.

[54] College Concert no. 866 [RCMA Concert Programmes]. From 1921 Malcolm Sargent conducted many concerts given by the first and second College orchestras.

[55] Holst in 'Grace Williams: A Symposium (Part 1)', *Welsh Music* 5/6, p. 21. In addition to the Cobbett Prize, Williams was awarded the Foli Scholarship (in 1927 and 1929) and the Ernest Farrar Prize (1930) during her time at College.

[56] Lutyens as recounted by Robert Saxton in 'Fairest Isle: Lutyens and Maconchy' (Radio 3, 11 September 1995) [NSA Cat. No. H5688/1/1].

Maconchy or Williams. Certainly, she was not thought of as being a particularly interesting composer at College. Indeed, she was much better known as a viola player in her first few years, playing in the second orchestra and taking part in performances of chamber music.

Although Lutyens had comparatively few pieces performed at College, she continued to work hard on her own. In 1927, for instance, she wrote an exploratory string quartet in one movement and an ambitious setting of the Book of Job in the style of Brahms for soloists, chorus and orchestra. Neither of these works were entered for competitions or performed at College, nor did she win any composition prizes or scholarships as a student.[57] She did, however, make progress with Darke, who, in addition to supervising her compositions, gave her organ lessons and encouraged her to develop a greater knowledge of the repertoire – in particular, the music of Bach and Brahms. 'How I dislike [Brahms's] pretentious bombastic symphonies with their creaking technique, bulging at the seams with inflated sentiment', she later confessed.[58] She must have had rather mixed feelings when Darke succeeded in sandwiching her setting of Keats's *To Sleep* for contralto and orchestra between Brahms's Third Symphony and Rossini's Overture to the *Barber of Seville* at a College concert in June 1929.[59]

To Sleep is an immature student work, one which Lutyens quickly buried after its first performance, but it is interesting because it reflects the musical preoccupations she had at the time. The piece has a melancholic pastoral air, contains sections of undigested Debussy – her musical god at this time – and is self-conscious in its orchestral and vocal writing. Even in 1929, despite being buoyed up with the prospect of hearing a piece of hers for the first time, she found the performance to be an immense disappointment. 'I think I had expected "a sea change Into something rich and strange"', she recalled. 'But no – it was exactly as I had originally heard it – though without the added faulty intonation and "blobs"'.[60]

Lutyens realized that she faced a tough battle to properly master her craft. In times of frustration she perhaps drew strength from the example of her father, who once told her that he too had been very conscious of his lack of technique when he had been a young, unknown architect. Yet she had inherited her father's gritty determination and capacity for hard work, and these qualities were now put to good use. A breakthrough finally came in 1931 when she discovered that her new ballet *The Birthday of the Infanta* (after Oscar Wilde) had unexpectedly been selected by the Patron's Fund for performance in July of that year. Although the circumstances surrounding the work's selection nearly succeeded in souring what should have been the highlight of her College career, the performance itself

---

[57] The only prize Lutyens won at College was the Alfred Gibson Prize for viola in 1930.

[58] Lutyens, *Goldfish Bowl*, p. 38.

[59] RCMA College Programme. Note that this was a College concert and not a Patron's Fund rehearsal.

[60] Lutyens, *Goldfish Bowl*, p. 39.

Example 1.1 *The Birthday of the Infanta* by Elisabeth Lutyens

Source: Reproduced by kind permission of the Estate of Elisabeth Lutyens.

aroused a great deal of interest.[61] In particular, the ballet fired the imagination of the English dancer and choreographer Penelope Spencer (1901–93) who served as the College's ballet teacher between the years 1923 and 1939. She had a keen interest in contemporary music and had collaborated with a number of

---

[61] As Lutyens recalled, 'Hugh Allen told me he had used his vote to get the work accepted by the reading panel. Naturally, I was delighted and asked his opinion of the work. I was horribly disillusioned and disgusted when he answered that he hadn't looked at it but thought its choice and performance would please Father' (ibid.). According to the College's Patron's Fund records, the promised performance of the *Infanta* (orchestral version only) took place on 9 July 1931.

composers. Lambert's *Elegiac Blues* (1927), for example, a tribute to the late cabaret dancer Florence Mills, was performed several times by Spencer, and in addition to other projects she arranged the dances for the College premiere of Vaughan Williams's *Sir John in Love* in March 1929. She had been using some sections of Lutyens's *Infanta* for students in her College ballet class when she was asked to suggest and choreograph a new production for the Camargo Society. Spencer nominated the *Infanta*.

The Camargo Society had been founded in 1930 to galvanize English ballet, and was the precursor to the Sadler's Wells Ballet and the Royal Ballet companies. Constant Lambert was appointed musical director, and the founding board boasted luminaries such as the music critic Edwin Evans, the economist John Maynard Keynes, and the ballerinas Lydia Lopokova (Keynes's wife), Marie Rambert, Ninette de Valois and Phyllis Bedells. The new production marked Lutyens's second collision with Lambert. She had to endure a lunch with Lambert and Lopokova where the former insisted on making alterations to the *Infanta* score. 'I disliked him ... heartily at this lunch', she remembered. 'He was extremely arrogant and patronizing for someone only a year older than myself, proclaiming, didactically, that the *only* ballet requiring a chorus was [his own] *Rio Grande*'.[62] Her fascinating tangle with the professional ballet world proved to be something of an eye-opener, with rather too much time spent changing the score to placate ruffled egos. Rex Whistler designed the scenery and costumes for the production and after a great deal of frantic activity, the *Infanta*, its dramatic impact enhanced by wet paint dripping from the scenery on the opening night, was performed at London's Adelphi Theatre on 4 December 1932.[63] The performance was well received on the whole, and although one of the London critics concluded that the work was 'banal and derivative',[64] the audience was at least treated to the sight of Dame Ethel Smyth violently shouting her support for the music from the balcony.

A Patron's Fund performance of Maconchy's new Concertino for piano and small orchestra on 30 November 1928 also led to further developments.[65] Adventurous in scope, the Concertino grows from an arresting musical idea which is stated at the opening of the work.

---

[62] Ibid., p. 61. Lutyens went on to point out that 'first impressions can be misleading; Constant became one of the very best friends I ever had'.

[63] Although Lutyens does not refer to other performances in her autobiography, the *Infanta* may also have been performed by Spencer's ballet at a charity event at the Savoy Theatre, London on 11 March 1932. For further details, see Anne Robinson, 'Penelope Spencer (1901–93) Dancer and Choreographer: A Chronicle', *Dance Research* 28/1 (May 2010), p. 74.

[64] *Daily Mail* review, quoted in M. Harries and S. Harries, *A Pilgrim Soul: The Life and Work of Elisabeth Lutyens* (London: Joseph, 1989), p. 65.

[65] Maconchy's Piano Concertino was premiered at the College by Gwendoline Paul (piano) and members of the London Symphony Orchestra, conducted by Adrian Boult.

Example 1.2 Concertino for Piano and Small Orchestra by Elizabeth Maconchy, opening theme

Source: Copyright © Alfred Lengnick & Co. Ltd. Reproduced by permission of the publisher.

Vaughan Williams was particularly fond of this piece and, conscious of the fact that Maconchy was now approaching the end of her time at College, suggested that his brilliant pupil should consider a period of study abroad.[66] Aware of her enthusiasm for new music, he mentioned Prague as a possible place to study. He had attended the Prague premiere of his *Pastoral Symphony* (conducted by Boult) at the International Society for Contemporary Music (ISCM) Festival in 1925, and had been impressed with the quality and range of musical activities in the city. Excited at the prospect of travelling abroad for the first time, Maconchy put in for the coveted Mendelssohn Scholarship, the College's most prestigious award for overseas study. She recalled that the adjudicators at her interview were mostly 'aged about ninety', and that the following day a beaming Hugh Allen had congratulated her on winning the scholarship. When Maconchy told Allen that the scholarship had been awarded to someone else, he replied that the adjudicators must have changed their minds after he had left the room. He then added, 'but anyway, if we'd given it to you, you'd have only got married and never written another note!'[67] The inept ruling of the elderly adjudicators was not, however, allowed to interfere with Maconchy's progress. Justice was partly restored towards the end of 1928 when she discovered that she had been awarded the College's Octavia Travelling Scholarship to pursue further studies in Prague.

Vaughan Williams also encouraged Williams to think of spreading her wings, and, mindful of her love of Wagner and late Romantic Austro-Germanic music (Williams had been a zealous Wagnerite since her schooldays), recommended Vienna as a place of study. He had always had considerable faith in her abilities and had a particularly high regard for her *Two Psalms*, striking settings of Psalms 137 ('By the waters of Babylon') and 126 ('When the Lord turned again the captivity of Zion'), which had first been performed at a College concert in 1927. Williams revised the work after its premiere and the new version (for soprano and small orchestra) was accepted by the Patron's Fund for rehearsal. Predictably, the examiners had certain reservations, but the piece went forward and was performed

---

[66] Overseas study was usually recommended to the most outstanding compositional students.

[67] Maconchy interviewed in the television documentary 'Elizabeth Maconchy: A Video Portrait'.

at the College on 1 July 1932 by Meriel St. C. Green (soprano) and members of the London Symphony Orchestra, conducted by Iris Lemare.[68]

Example 1.3 Psalm 137 for Voice and Small Orchestra by Grace Williams, opening

---

[68] Sidney Waddington thought the 'brash' Psalms had 'an evident purpose in them' but were 'curiously dry and repellent', whereas Eric Coates described the piece as 'purely note-juggling and nothing else' [RCMA Register of Patron's Fund Concerts, 1932].

Example 1.3 continued

Source: Reproduced by kind permission of the Estate of Grace Williams.

According to Williams, the rehearsal went well although the players had to count like 'grim death' to cope with the 7/8 metre of the first Psalm, and consequently did not quite manage to convey the intended impression of the piece.[69] Even so, many in the packed College hall were impressed by the piece – including a young Benjamin Britten, then in his second year at College. The *Two Psalms* would be one of the first works by Williams to be heard by a wider public when it was broadcast by the BBC in December 1934.

College life had been an essential training ground for Lutyens, Maconchy and Williams, one which had been free of prejudice against their gender. They would find it more difficult, however, to gain a secure foothold in the often treacherous and unpredictable professional music world which lay outside the College. One of the most serious challenges facing these young composers

[69] Williams, letter to Reginald Redman, October 1934 [BBC Written Archive Centre (BBC WAC), WAI/61/1: Grace Williams, Welsh Region Composer, 1934–37].

would be the lack of performance opportunities for their works. As Maconchy recalled, 'there was no SPNM [Society for the Promotion of New Music], no BBC concerts of contemporary music or "Music in our Time" series, ... no Arts Council grants or commissions, no platform for new composers at local festivals, and very little interest in new music at the universities'.[70] Then came the equally dispiriting realization that despite the example of Ethel Smyth, a ballet, concerto or symphony composed by a woman was still considered to be a curious aberration in a predominantly male profession. Consequently, 'publishers would not consider seriously publishing anything by a young woman – except possibly some little songs'.[71] In time, and partly through the musical achievements of these composers, attitudes and outlooks would change. Indeed, the British musical establishment of the 1920s and 30s would have done well to heed Shaw's words when he declared in 1893 that 'whenever I hear the dictum, "Women cannot compose", uttered by some male musician ... I always chuckle and say to myself, "Wait a bit, my lad, until they find out how much easier it is than literature"'.[72]

---

[70] Maconchy, 'The Composer Speaks' (Radio 3, 17 October 1971).
[71] Ibid.
[72] Shaw, *Music in London*, vol. ii, p. 234.

Chapter 2
Professional Composers: Study Abroad and the Macnaghten–Lemare Concerts

> There were our English composers reiterating folksongish [*sic*] platitudes (or so it seemed to me), and there was Stravinsky, Bartók, Hindemith and a new world of sound … Stravinsky so Russian, Bartók so Hungarian and Hindemith so German. It all seemed … a glorious future whilst England seemed to be rustically resuscitating songs no one had heard of … [T]his confrontation of different styles [was bewildering] … There was no getting away from the fact that I wasn't Russian, Hungarian or German. I was English.[1]

When Lutyens left the Royal College of Music in 1931, she and her contemporaries could have been forgiven for being bewildered by the fragmented and changeable musical climate. Where did the young, unknown composer stand in relation to 'this confrontation of different styles'? The very nature, identity and future direction of contemporary music was a fiercely contested issue in British musical life during the interwar period. From the beginning of the twentieth century, traditional English music (from folk songs to Purcell) had been published and performed with increasing regularity and, with the advent of BBC radio music broadcasts in the late 1920s, began to reach much wider audiences than before. The concepts of English musical nationalism, evolution and tradition which had been instigated by Grove, Parry, Stanford and others were extended by the succeeding pre-war generation of musicians, most of whom were now established figures in the British musical firmament. Although receptive to certain contemporary European styles, Vaughan Williams, in particular, was convinced that English music could be revitalized by creatively engaging with national musical sources, convictions which he outlined in his 1934 book entitled *National Music*.

At the same time, and largely thanks to the efforts of the BBC's pioneering music department, audiences were gradually being introduced to the advanced musical idioms of continental composers such as Schoenberg, Stravinsky, Bartók and Berg. Schoenberg conducted a BBC broadcast performance of his *Gurrelieder* in January 1928, for example, and listeners were able to tune in to the first British broadcast of Berg's opera *Wozzeck* in March 1934. Within the musical world, the different styles of the European modernists continued to provoke intense debate – opinion ranged from open hostility to unbridled zeal – with disagreement between those who favoured native values and those who embraced an internationalist perspective. William Walton and Constant Lambert, both known to 1930s

---

[1] Lutyens, notes for a lecture on 'Contemporary English Music' (private collection).

audiences and hailed as leaders of the younger generation of composers, contested the nationalism of the pre-war British musical establishment, and looked to more 'contemporary' sources of influence (notably jazz, Debussy and Stravinsky) to revitalize English music.[2] Lambert underlined his objections to nationalist values in his celebrated critique *Music Ho!*, arguing that

> The English folk song, except to a few crusted old farmhands in those rare districts which have escaped mechanization, is nothing more than a very pretty period piece ... The particular type of self-conscious Englishry practised by the folk-song composers is in itself curiously un-English. England has never produced an artist so "*echt*-English" as Mussorgsky is "*echt*-Russian," or Renoir "*echt*-French." The strength of the English tradition in art is that it has always been open to fruitful foreign influences, which have been grafted on to the native plant without causing it to wither away. The Elizabethans, and Purcell after them, drew what they could from their Italian contemporaries without in any way submerging their own personalities. Even in our day Elgar and Delius have, in their widely different ways, written music that is essentially English in feeling without having to dress itself up in rustic clothes or adopt pseudo-archaic modes of speech.[3]

For some, however, the distance between the English coast and Europe's musical mainland remained an unnavigable channel. Indeed, Hubert Foss, Oxford University Press's influential music editor, could complain in 1927 that 'the worst sign of the times to me is the insularity of the British composer ... he does not know the names, much less the works, of his fellow craftsmen in Germany, in Prague, in Holland ... as a result of all this, Musical England fears modern music'.[4] Foss's comments may well have applied to some British composers, but they bear little relation to the comparatively sophisticated outlooks of Lutyens, Maconchy and Williams. In common with contemporaries such as Britten and Tippett, these composers were deeply affected in different ways by the clamour of European musical modernism, and during the 1930s the music they wrote showed an awareness of a wide range of prevailing ideas and styles. Significantly, all three benefitted from a brief period of study on the Continent after leaving the Royal College. Maconchy was the first to graduate in 1929 and left Britain for Prague, visiting Paris on the way. Williams went to study in Vienna in the following year, and Lutyens returned briefly to Paris in 1931.

Tellingly, Maconchy's decision to study in Prague was influenced by the city's well-established appetite for new music. The International Society for

---

[2] William Walton – Appendix.

[3] Lambert, *Music Ho! A Study of Music in Decline* (London: Faber and Faber, 1934; 3rd ed., 1948), p. 124.

[4] Foss, 'A Survey of Modern Day English Composers', *The Musician* (March, 1927), p. 34.

Contemporary Music – an organization founded in 1922 by Rudolph Réti, Egon Wellesz and Edward Dent, among others – had chosen to hold the orchestral sections of its second and third annual festivals in the city, bringing eagerly anticipated performances of Schoenberg's *Erwartung* (world premiere, 1924), Bartók's *Dance Suite* (Prague premiere, 1925), Janáček's *The Cunning Little Vixen* (Prague premiere, 1925) and Vaughan Williams's *Pastoral Symphony* (European premiere, 1925).[5] In 1929 Prague audiences could discuss with relish the latest microtonal compositions of the radical Czech composer Alois Hába, a leading member of the Czechoslovakian section of the ISCM and a tutor in microtonal music at the Prague Conservatoire.[6]

Maconchy soon came to taste Prague's eclectic character and tempo. 'It was a small ... independent sort of place', she recalled, and 'everybody was very much working on their own'.[7] It was here that she first encountered the music and radical spirit of Janáček, a composer then little known outside Czechoslovakia.[8] Excited by her discovery, she was able to explore more of his work while attending composition lessons with Karel Jirák (1891–1972). Jirák was considered to be one of the more dynamic Czech composers, and he also held the positions of Professor of Composition at the Prague Conservatoire and Musical Director of Czech Radio. He was impressed by Maconchy's musical abilities and, realizing that there was little he could teach his young student, introduced her to many of the leading figures in Czechoslovakian musical life, including the influential composer and pianist Ervín Schulhoff (1894–1942). Both Jirák and Schulhoff thought highly of her recently composed Piano Concertino (1928), and decided to include the work in the 1929/30 season of the Czech Philharmonic Orchestra. With Jirák conducting and Schulhoff as soloist, Maconchy's revised Concertino (now retitled Piano Concerto) received its European premiere on 19 March 1930 – her 23rd birthday – at the Smetana Hall in Prague.[9] Grace Williams travelled from Vienna to hear the performance:

> Prague is almost next door to Vienna ... So of course I went to Prague, and arrived in time for the second rehearsal. Betty was quite happy after the first rehearsal, and at the end of the second things were going terribly well ... but as the concert drew near we developed the usual fear that something would go

---

[5] ISCM – Appendix.

[6] Alois Hába – Appendix.

[7] Maconchy, 'Third Ear' (Radio 3, 29 March 1990) [NSA Cat. No. B5698/2].

[8] Janáček's striking musical independence and originality was not fully appreciated until after the Second World War. The British premiere of *Jenůfa* (1894–1903, rev. 1907–08), for instance, did not take place until 1956.

[9] The full programme for the Prague concert was Mozart's Symphony in G minor (K. 550), Maconchy's Piano Concerto, Schulhoff's Suite from the incidental music for Moliere's *Bourgeois gentilhomme*, and *Komorni Sinfonietta* by Osvald Chlubna, a pupil of Janáček's.

wrong in the middle and spoil it … But the concert performance was even better than the rehearsal … I've always thought the whole work astonishingly good, and I know it very well because, in the old days at the R.C.M. Betty and I used to play it on two pianos. The audience at Prague liked it tremendously …[10]

Another victory followed for Maconchy in that same year when her orchestral suite *The Land* was unexpectedly accepted by Sir Henry Wood for inclusion in the 1930 Proms season. The suite was premiered by the BBC Symphony Orchestra, conducted by Wood, on 30 August 1930, a week after Maconchy's marriage to the Irish scholar and librarian William LeFanu. The work's immediate impact may be gauged by the unrestrained enthusiasm of the critics. Under the headline 'Girl Composer Triumphs', the *Daily Telegraph*'s Herbert Hughes described *The Land* as being not only 'one of the best pieces of orchestral music written by any women in recent years, but by far the most important and interesting work to be produced, so far, at the Promenade Concerts during this present season'. The suite was 'a work of art that is in every way distinguished and masterly', Hughes wrote, and was the creation of 'a first rate intelligence, sensitive and subtle, and yet capable of creating things on big lines' (*Daily Telegraph*, 1 September 1930). Hailed as one of the triumphs of the 1930 Proms season, *The Land* earned Maconchy the reputation of being one of the most exciting young British composers to emerge on the London musical scene.

The Land takes its title from the award-winning poem of 1926 by Vita Sackville-West.[11] Each of the work's four movements presents a seasonal, musical portrait of the English countryside using the poem as a point of departure. The piece opens quietly with a stark, slow theme in low strings (Example 2.1) which heralds the onset of Winter, the ensuing broad, contrapuntal lines in strings illustrating the verse: 'Here is no colour, here is but form and structure, The bones of trees, the magpie bark of birches'.[12]

Example 2.1 *The Land* by Elizabeth Maconchy. I 'Winter', opening theme

Source: Copyright © Alfred Lengnick & Co. Ltd. Reproduced by permission of the publisher.

---

[10] Williams, 'A Letter from Vienna', *RCM Magazine* 26/2 (1930), p. 66.
[11] *The Land* won the Hawthornden Prize for Literature. Victoria ('Vita') Sackville-West – Appendix.
[12] V. Sackville-West, *The Land*. Copyright © Vita Sackville-West.

Spring (movement II) comes in the form of an animated fugue with vigorous cross-rhythms played out in the whole orchestra. Summer (III) is a meditative *Lento* of intense colour, and the work concludes with a vigorous, autumnal finale (IV) imbued with rhythmic vitality. The overall form of the work is tightly wrought, and the main themes from the suite's movements reveal Maconchy's tendency for working with highly concentrated motifs comprised of groups of close intervals. The use of alternating major and minor thirds and the tritone is particularly characteristic of her writing, a feature which she no doubt absorbed from the music of both Bartók and Vaughan Williams. Another aspect of the piece is its remarkable economy of texture. Vaughan Williams once observed that over-scoring was usually a sign of lack of confidence in the quality of musical material, but the orchestration of *The Land* is highly sophisticated and denotes a particular clarity and potency of vision. There are few passages where the orchestra is fully mustered, and when it is, the writing remains clear and uncluttered. The influence of Holst can be detected in the deft handling of the orchestra and in the attention to the effects of sound; indeed, there are striking similarities between the opening of the third movement (Summer) and Saturn, the fifth movement of *The Planets*. Yet this is not derivative music in any sense and the result is entirely fresh and original.

Idiomatically, the music is Eastern European rather than English in its allegiance; indeed, *The Land* is no English pastoral idyll. The rhythmic characters of some of the themes have a fierce, Bartókian flavour and the harmonies also possess continental bite.

Example 2.2 *The Land* by Elizabeth Maconchy. IV 'Autumn'

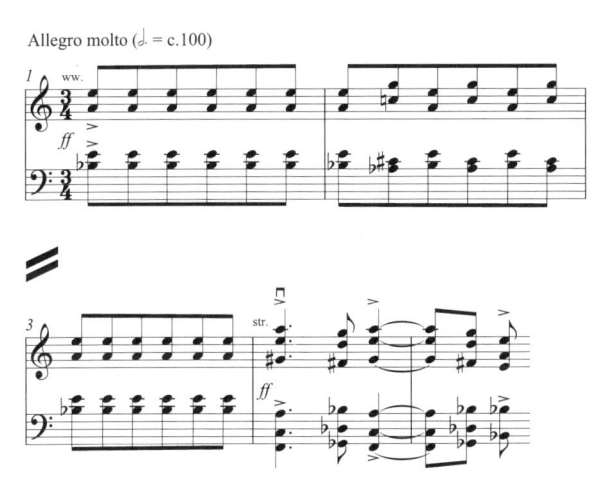

Source: Copyright © Alfred Lengnick & Co. Ltd. Reproduced by permission of the publisher.

The few passages which suggest a familiarity with the music of Shostakovich are probably coincidental, but all these elements have been naturally absorbed into an individual style of remarkable maturity. Assured and powerful in character, *The Land* is a work that both exudes and inspires confidence.

Sackville-West's poetry also proved to be the starting point for a song which Williams wrote during her time in Vienna; indeed, her choice of text may well have been inspired by discussions about poetry with Maconchy at this time. In *Tuscany*, a setting for mezzo-soprano and orchestra, Williams's music and Sackville-West's words combine to evoke a timeless portrait of the rural Tuscan landscape and the 'vine-yard folk' who make their living from the soil. Great care has been taken in this song over the orchestration and the overall effect of sound and mood. The hushed, shimmering opening of the work is enigmatic, with a recitative-like passage for the mezzo heard against quiet strings and a sustained cymbal trill. The poem's soothing, unhurried tempo is emphasized throughout by low, sultry *Andante* phrases for the voice, with gently undulating lines in the orchestra.

Example 2.3 *Tuscany* for Mezzo-Soprano and Orchestra by Grace Williams

Source: Music reproduced by kind permission of the Estate of Grace Williams. Words by Vita Sackville-West reproduced with permission of Curtis Brown Group Ltd., London on behalf of the Estate of Vita Sackville-West. Copyright © Vita Sackville-West.

Vaughan Williams's influence hovers over this song, particularly in its use of modal inflexions, but the work also shows an awareness of the Strauss–Mahler Lied tradition in the use of the orchestra. Williams had a voracious interest in fine examples of orchestral writing and had long held the view that Strauss in particular possessed 'the intellectual grasp and power that are needed in handling the complete modern orchestra'; indeed, in her opinion, Strauss's 'mastery of instrumentation' was 'greater even than Wagner's'.[13]

Similar musical preoccupations recur in Williams's setting of Hilaire Belloc's *Tarantella* (also for mezzo-soprano and orchestra) which she composed around the same time. The manuscript containing *Tuscany* and *Tarantella* is dated 'Vienna, June 1930' and these songs were probably intended to be performed together. In contrast to the tranquil lyricism of the first setting, however, *Tarantella* is an exuberant *Allegro Vivace* showpiece which demonstrates Williams's natural sense of drama and wit. Again, the attention to particular sounds and effects is noticeable in the scoring. An arsenal of percussion instruments is deployed (side drum, cymbals, triangle and castanets), often in antiphonal exchanges with the voice and the rest of the orchestra: in one instance, when the opening lines 'Do you remember an Inn, Miranda?' are restated, they are scored for voice and side drum only.

Both songs were composed while Williams was studying composition with the Viennese composer and scholar Egon Wellesz (1885–1974), and the spirit of adventurousness in the orchestral scoring may be partly the result of her teacher's encouragement. Wellesz was Professor of Music at Vienna University and occupied an exalted position in Viennese musical life. Very much a cultural aristocrat, he possessed an encyclopedic knowledge of Austro-Germanic culture and was a great admirer of Mahler and Strauss.[14] As a composer he had been associated with the Second Viennese School. Early on in his career he studied composition with Schoenberg – he later became his first biographer – and enjoyed lasting friendships with Berg and Webern. Some of his works embraced atonal and 12-note techniques but he remained firmly committed to the tonality of his Viennese heritage throughout his creative career. By the time Williams came to study with him, he had rejected serialism but he did employ Schoenberg's analytical teaching methods in tutorials with his composition students. Whenever she bought her work to him, his criticisms were precise and direct. As she recalled, '[Vaughan Williams] would say "I know there's something wrong, but I can't put my finger on it", but Egon Wellesz could. He had a way of saying "It begins to get weak at this point, so you will scrap from here onwards and re-write"'.[15]

---

[13] Williams, notes on 'The Symphony and the Tone Poem' in an exercise book written while she was a student at University College, Cardiff [Grace Williams Archive, NLW, Aberystwyth].

[14] Hugo von Hofmannsthal, Strauss's librettist, provided the libretto (after Euripides) for Wellesz's opera *Alkestis* (1924).

[15] Williams, 'Views and Revisions', *Welsh Music* 10/9–10, p. 10.

Shortly after she completed her studies with him, Wellesz wrote a testimonial for her which brings aspects of her training into sharper focus:

> It gives me much pleasure to testify that Miss Grace Williams has studied with me in Vienna during the year 1930.
>
> And it is further pleasure to testify to her <u>extraordinary ability</u> in music and <u>very remarkable</u> gifts as a composer, which have developed so quickly and promise a considerable contribution to English music. Furthermore, I should like to insist that she already has a broad outlook and grasp of all musical "Form." Miss Grace Williams has always worked <u>very hard</u> having written a great number of exercises which I have specially set for her, and having also composed prolifically.
>
> I have noted a <u>great</u> improvement in her work in modern orchestral technique. This has been greatly helped by her study of scores, and by her tremendous enthusiasm for the Viennese Opera and the Viennese Orchestral-concerts.[16]

Williams had been intrigued when Vaughan Williams had first suggested that she study with one of Schoenberg's former pupils, but it was the tantalizing prospect of experiencing Vienna's vibrant musical culture and tradition that had initially sparked her imagination. Then there was the anticipation of hearing Wagner and Strauss (two of her musical gods) in Vienna. That these enthusiasms were considered unfashionable by many of her fellow Collegians mattered little to Williams. Conventional wisdom held that Wagner and Strauss belonged to the past rather than the future, and it is interesting to note that when it came to choices for places to study abroad, both Lutyens and Maconchy felt that Vienna had lost its hegemony as the foremost European centre for new music to other European capitals such as Paris and Prague.[17] Vienna did not disappoint, however. Williams attended performances of, among other things, Strauss's *Salome*, 'a profusion of [Wagner's] Ring Cycles'[18] and the Viennese premiere of Berg's *Wozzeck*[19] during her time there. *Wozzeck* made a particularly profound impression on her: she described the opera as being 'ausgezeichnet schön – und wie traurig' (outstandingly beautiful – and yet desolate).[20] Furthermore, it was in Vienna that Williams had her first close encounter with the music of Webern:

---

[16] Wellesz, testimonial dated 5 February 1931 (private collection).

[17] Maconchy recalled that she had been told that 'if you want the classics go to Vienna, but if you want new music go to Prague'. Maconchy, 'Third Ear' (Radio 3, March 1990).

[18] Williams, 'A Letter from Vienna', *RCM Magazine*, 26/2 (1930), p. 65.

[19] *Wozzeck* was premiered by the Berlin State Opera in 1925 but was first performed in Vienna by the Vienna State Opera in 1930.

[20] Williams, letter to the composer Daniel Jones, 5 April 1940 (Daniel Jones Archive, NLW). Daniel Jones – Appendix.

> I went to a concert once where I heard Webern's music for the first time, and I must confess I nearly had hysterics! It was an audience full of terribly serious-faced people in a very small hall, and I was alone. The music consisted of sudden tiny little notes and long silences ... it was all so incredibly strange.[21]

Although Williams found that she was not able to react positively to the music of Webern as a composer or listener, her responses to the music of the Second Viennese School (particularly to that of Berg) were, in a broader sense, rather enlightened for the time. British musical tastes in the 1930s remained deeply conservative and the music establishment was generally hostile to the music of 'mittel-European' composers. Atonal and 12-note methods were considered particularly heinous at a time when some still held that it was unpatriotic, if not immoral, to eschew English musical traditions in favour of what were thought to be crazed European deities. A review of a London recital of Schoenberg's music given in 1932 captured some of the more typical reactions (*The Times*, 16 December 1932):

> There may be ... musicians who understand what Schoenberg is driving at in his music, which to ears unacclimatized to the strange airs of Central Europe simply makes no sense at all. He has, we are told, invented a 12-tone system, substituting an arbitrary for a natural kind of organization ...
>
> In a group of songs, sung by Mme Alice Schuster, the vocal line is determined by the words, so that the difficulty of knowing at least what the composer is aiming at is much reduced, even though the piano accompaniment sounds like the projection on paper of a barbed-wire entanglement. No, it is no use: Schoenberg may be understood in Vienna but he has no future here.

Interestingly, had Lutyens decided to study in Vienna rather than Paris in 1931, it is quite possible that her musical development might have taken a different path. She cited her growing boredom with the insularity of the British musical world and the oppressive predominance of English pastoral music – an abundance of 'folky-wolky modal melodies on the cor anglais',[22] – as one of the reasons for wanting to escape abroad. Her decision to go to Paris, however, was determined by an earlier love affair with the city. Ever since her first visit in 1923 (for studies at the École Normale), she had come to regard England as France's poorer musical relation, the latter being to her a sophisticated, glamorous country which was open to the most exciting cultural and musical developments. She had vivid memories of 'the atmosphere then – remember, after a world war – of new hope, of modern art ... of Picasso, rumours of Joyce's work in progress, of Debussy'. Somehow, she recalled, 'all of it was more exciting, more modern'.[23] Returning to Paris in

---

[21] Williams, 'Views and Revisions', *Welsh Music* 10/9–10, p. 10.
[22] Lutyens, notes to a lecture as quoted in Harries, *A Pilgrim Soul*, p. 53.
[23] Lutyens in interview (Radio 3, 5 July 1971).

1931, she was able to relish again something of that atmosphere while attending private lessons with the composer Georges Caussade, a teacher she shared with Olivier Messiaen. Lutyens was stimulated by Caussade's lessons and never forgot two of his principles: 'even if writing an exercise in first species counterpoint, always write as *music* to be sung or played by human beings, and, above all, learn to become *maître de votre pensée*'.[24] Her visit also gave her the opportunity to rekindle her friendship with the organist and composer Antoine Geoffroy-Dechaume, the son of a family friend. She had fallen under the spell of the young, 'extremely beautiful' Antoine on her previous visit to Paris, and came to share his enthusiasm for early music. Indeed, it was Antoine who first introduced her to the music of the seventeenth-century composers Frescobaldi, Titelouze and Buxtehude, and it was largely as a result of his influence that she acquired a Dolmetsch clavichord in the late 1920s.[25]

While in Paris, Lutyens revised a set of songs which she had originally composed at the College. Her *Five Songs* for soprano and string quartet (and/or piano) form an interesting example of *entente cordiale*, in that two French songs – 'Nuits de Juin' (words, Hugo) and 'Recueillement' (words, Baudelaire) – are grouped with three English songs (words by Bronte, Meredith and Donne), and the group as a whole derives its style largely from the dual influences of early music and French impressionism.[26] Her setting of John Donne's brief and sensual love poem 'Stay, O Sweet' possesses a beguiling simplicity and contains a number of interesting features. Succinct and compact in structure, the music follows the words closely, with little attempt to develop or elaborate the musical material. Much of the bittersweet tension of the opening phrase of the song (Example 2.4) derives from the gentle ambiguity between C♯ major and C♯ minor (through the use of a raised and flattened third of the tonic), and the soprano's second phrase – 'the day breaks not it is my heart, because that you and I must part' – is delivered in a quasi-recitative manner over descending chords in the strings. In the last phrase, the use of chromatic harmonies reflects the more anguished tone of the poem – 'Stay or else my joys will die, and perish in their infancy' – as the lover's departure draws ever closer.

---

[24] Lutyens, *Goldfish Bowl*, p. 56. Caussade (1873–1936) was Professor of Harmony and Counterpoint at the Paris Conservatoire at this time.

[25] The musician and instrument maker Arnold Dolmetsch (1858–1940) was one of the foremost figures in the twentieth-century revival of interest in early English music. In 1917 he established an instrument-making workshop in Haslemere, Surrey, which specialized in making early instruments including lutes, viols, recorders, clavichords and harpsichords. Dolmetsch and his family were also performing musicians and frequently gave concerts of early music on authentic instruments in London and further afield.

[26] Manuscripts of *Five Songs* in Lutyens Collection, British Library (BL Adds 64683, 64686 and 64690).

Example 2.4 'Stay, O Sweet' for Soprano and String Quartet by Elisabeth Lutyens

Source: Reproduced by kind permission of the Estate of Elisabeth Lutyens.

Lutyens's *Five Songs* were premiered on 3 December 1931 by Margaret Rees (soprano), the Anne Macnaghten String Quartet and Rene Cook (piano) at the Ballet Club Theatre, London. The following details appeared in the programme for that concert:

Imogen Holst	Quintet for Oboe and Strings*
Henry Purcell	Three four-part Fantasias for Strings, nos. 2, 9 and 4
	(transcribed by Peter Warlock, edited by André Mangeot)
Betty Lutyens	Five Songs for Soprano*
	(three with string quartet and two with piano)
Arnold Foster	Fantasy for Piano Quartet in one movement*
Carl Stamitz	Quartet for Oboe and Strings op. 8, no. 4 in E flat.[27]

---

[27] Asterisks indicate a world premiere.

The *Times* critic was lavish in his praise of all of the new works performed, and singled out Lutyens's song 'Stay, O Sweet' for showing 'most clearly the composer's feeling for a vocal line and a felicitous touch in the figuration of the accompaniment for string quartet' (5 December 1931). He noted that the concert was the first of three 'organized by a party of energetic young ladies', although he failed to mention names or the rationale which lay behind the series. The idea for these concerts had, in fact, sprung from Lutyens's frustration at the lack of performance opportunities for herself and other young (and, at that stage, unknown) composers in Britain. She had vented her fury at this bleak situation to the young violinist Anne Macnaghten, suggesting that young composers and musicians would be better off if they organized their own concerts.[28] Macnaghten responded enthusiastically and volunteered her recently formed female string quartet as performers. In the ensuing days and weeks, the idea gained weight and more people were recruited to the new enterprise. Lutyens introduced Macnaghten to Iris Lemare, a friend who had studied conducting at the College, and who was now keen to find conducting opportunities in the musical world.[29] Thrown back on their own resources, these three young women planned the first ground-breaking chamber concert series. The Ballet Club Theatre (later, the Mercury Theatre) in Notting Hill, London – home to the Ballet Rambert in the 1930s – was chosen as the venue, and the programmes for the three concerts were drafted. The series reflected Lutyens's policy that concerts should concentrate on showcasing works by young British composers and that they should also include early music repertoire which could not necessarily be heard anywhere else in London.

These concerts were essentially a necessary self-help venture. Apart from the College's Patron's Fund rehearsals and other occasional public outlets, the young British composer faced enormous obstacles in getting works performed in the first few decades of the twentieth century. In recognition of this situation, several attempts had been made to establish organizations which supported home-grown music. In 1907 Elgar and Delius, then the leading composers in Britain, had launched a contemporary music concert series called the League of Music which had to be dissolved after two years because of organizational and financial difficulties. The British Music Society, founded in 1919, was more successful, although its activities were not initially focused on giving concerts. In 1920, however, the Society inaugurated the London Contemporary Music Centre which became one of the few enduring contemporary music concert associations in Britain. Smaller organizations such as The Music Society (1919–35), founded by the violinist André Mangeot, featured a number of works by younger British composers but they were not exclusively concerned with promoting contemporary music. Even Maconchy felt that her early success with *The Land* at the 1930 Proms was an exception to the rule in a country that appeared to be indifferent to new creative work.

---

[28] Anne Macnaghten – Appendix.
[29] Iris Lemare – Appendix.

The new series of concerts initiated by Lutyens, Macnaghten and Lemare was the only series to possess an unwavering commitment to the work of young British composers. Although Lutyens was more than happy to let Macnaghten and Lemare shoulder the general organization and administration of the series, all those involved were expected to help with the promotion of concerts. Infused with a spirit of confidence, common purpose and camaraderie, performers and composers helped one another in frantic eleventh-hour preparation for performances. 'We were a family', Lutyens recalled, 'all helping in comradeship with the necessary part-copying, arranging and playing'.[30] Macnaghten's youthful quartet formed the central core of chamber music players, and featured composers found themselves either playing in Lemare's newly formed chamber orchestra or performing in other capacities. Lutyens's String Quartet in one movement (1927) was premiered at the second concert on 14 December 1931 in a programme that also included the first performance of a String Quintet by Maconchy. The third concert was given on 28 January 1932 and featured Maconchy's *Fantasy for Children* for chamber orchestra (1927) and Lutyens's new arrangements for strings of music by Frescobaldi and Titelouze.

The heady mixture of brand-new pieces with 'classics' by Purcell, Frescobaldi and others proved to be a winning combination. The Ballet Club Theatre had a capacity of 120 people and Lemare remembered that the packed audience for these concerts 'consisted entirely of the composers' friends, the music critics and Betty Lutyens' relations and Anne Macnaghten's relations and my own darling aunt because I hadn't got any other relations'.[31] The presence of the music critics was significant in that they ensured that the concerts, performers and composers received coverage in the national newspapers and the music press. Most responded to these concerts with enthusiasm, although some were clearly startled by the number of young women taking part. One of the more lively reactions was penned by the critic and composer Cecil Gray when he reviewed the second concert for the *Daily Telegraph*. Gray had already revealed that he was perhaps not the greatest admirer of women composers when he had famously responded to a work by the French composer Germaine Tailleferre by saying, 'one could only repeat Dr. Johnson's dictum transposed into terms of music: "Sir, a woman's composing is like a dog walking on its hind legs; it is not done well but you are surprised to see it done at all"'.[32] Gray was, it seems, forced to reconsider his views after encountering the work of Maconchy:

> The second of a series of three concerts chiefly devoted to the music of young English composers ... took place last night. It proved to be a decidedly feminist affair, since out of the seven executants only one, the accompanist, was a

---

[30] Lutyens, *Goldfish Bowl*, p. 67.
[31] Lemare, quoted in Fuller, '"Putting the BBC and T. Beecham to shame ..."', p. 18.
[32] Gray, *A Survey of Contemporary Music* (London: Oxford University Press, 1924), pp. 245–246.

> male, while out of the four modern composers represented in the programme only one – Mr Patrick Hadley – was of the masculine gender. The contrast, incidentally, between his gentle, melancholy and reflective little songs and the almost aggressive virility of the string quintet of Miss Elizabeth Maconchy was striking and piquant.
>
> This latter was an interesting work, probably the best of the four ... Her future will be watched with interest. (*Daily Telegraph*, 15 December 1931)

Although the presence of 'young ladies' proved to be something of a gift for the exclusively male members of the press, these concerts were never intended as a deliberate feminist gesture. 'It just so happened', recalled Macnaghten, 'that the first people to have this idea [were] young women'. Furthermore, the unusually high number of women composers featured in the concerts simply reflected the fact that 'there were a number of very gifted young women writing music [at this time] and because they were women they had a rather greater need to try to get a hearing'.[33] Most of these young women believed that their gender would not hinder their progress in the music profession, but prejudice did exist. Lutyens occasionally appeared as 'A. E.' Lutyens at concerts 'to avoid the sex war',[34] and Maconchy experienced a particularly noxious form of discrimination in the early 1930s when her work was rejected for publication by the London music publishers Boosey and Hawkes. Herbert Hughes, author of that glowing *Telegraph* review of *The Land*, tried to persuade the proprietor Leslie Boosey to offer her a contract, but Boosey recoiled at the idea of publishing anything substantial by a young woman. It was an attitude which proved to be remarkably prevalent in the music world. As Maconchy bitterly recalled, 'concert promoters, conductors too, and publishers more than anything wouldn't look at things by a woman ... [and] that really was a very difficult thing to get over'.[35]

Such experiences serve to underline the importance of the Macnaghten–Lemare concerts (as they became known) in providing composers – of both sexes – with the opportunity to have their works performed in public. Following the success of the first three events it was decided that concerts should continue on a regular basis, and established figures including Vaughan Williams, Holst, Bliss, the tenor Steuart Wilson and the soprano Sophie Wyss rallied round to offer encouragement and advice.[36] During the first six years of the series, composers such as William

---

[33] Macnaghten in 'Elizabeth Maconchy: A Video Portrait' (Channel 4), and quoted in Fuller, '"Putting the BBC and T. Beecham to shame ..."', p. 19.

[34] Lutyens, *Goldfish Bowl*, p. 61.

[35] Maconchy, 'Talking About Music' (Radio 3, 1977) [NSA Cat. No. 1LP0202427 S2 BD3].

[36] Macnaghten was in charge of running the series for the first three years (1931–34) but resigned from her position because she wished to concentrate on her performing career. Lemare took over the management of the concerts from 1934–37 when the series became

Alwyn, Phyllis Tate and Alan Bush had works premiered. Most critics were quick to grasp that, as *The Musical Times* (vol. 76, 1935) noted, these concerts provided 'a direct glimpse into what is going on in British music today'.

Alliances and friendships formed at College between Lutyens, Maconchy and Williams were strengthened through their involvement with the concert series: Williams later recalled that there was a strong sense of banding together by the women composers of similar age (including Dorothy Gow and Imogen Holst).[37] These like-minded women were driven by a serious and passionate attitude to music and music-making and had a common desire to maintain the very highest standards. Many of the pieces that Lutyens, Maconchy and Williams had performed at these concerts were exploratory in the sense that they reveal preoccupations with testing out new ideas. Only a few were ever published, the composers later tending to withdraw what they had come to regard as immature works. Even so, the pieces provide insights into the composers' early development and helped to advance their profiles in the music profession. Interestingly, although some critics were prepared to take their work seriously, for others the issue of women composers continued to overshadow the merits of any pieces that were performed. The following advance notice, for example, appeared in the *Glasgow Herald* about a concert in February 1935 which featured music by all three composers:

London Day by Day: WOMEN COMPOSERS

It has been observed that more and more women composers are finding their way into musical programmes – the more remote and superior kind of programmes, that is, and not the kind that are given at the Queen's Hall – and that, as they do so, they get more and more superior and remote in their music. Two of the most prominent of these cerebrals are Miss Elizabeth Maconchy and Miss Elisabeth Lutyens both of whom are to be represented at tomorrow's Lemare-Macnaghten concert. With a work by Miss Grace Williams as an ending this will be an all-female, all-modern concert. Moreover, the conductor is of the same serious and mentally-burdened sex. Musicians who have been looking on with considerable interest at this branch of the feminist movement are beginning to wonder when a woman composer is going to write some music reminiscent of the sex as it used to be.[38]

---

known as the Lemare Concerts. The concerts resumed after the Second World War with Vaughan Williams as President and Macnaghten as manager of the renamed Macnaghten New Music Group. Although Macnaghten handed the management of the concerts to others in 1957, she continued to be involved and the organization survived until the mid-1990s.

[37] 'We didn't know Elisabeth Lutyens so well because she had a different teacher [at the College] … I got to know [her] afterwards because we were all concerned with the Macnaghten Concerts'. Williams, 'Views and Revisions', p. 10.

[38] *Glasgow Herald*, 4 February 1935. This tiny notice appeared a few pages after the

Such comments reflected the then widely-held platitude that it was natural for a woman to focus on the cultivation of 'the feminine instinct' in her music, most typically expressed by graceful, tuneful music in smaller genres such as delicate songs or piano pieces.[39] 'No lipstick, silk stocking or saucily titled hat adorns the music', wrote the critic William McNaught in the *Evening News* (5 February 1935) after failing to find any suitably ladylike tunes in the pieces performed at that February concert. 'All is grim, intense, and cerebral', he complained before concluding that 'these three ladies were too formidably clever, or tried to be'.

Lutyens may have attracted the rather English pejorative associations of being 'cerebral' and 'too clever', but a significant amount of the press attention she received in the 1930s probably had more to do with lineage than musical achievement. 'Sir Edwin Lutyens, President of the Royal Academy, has a daughter who is making a name for herself as a musician', gushed the gossip columnist of the *Evening Standard* (6 February 1939), and details about the illustrious Lutyens clan continued to seep out into the British press over the years. She was probably justified in thinking that there was an imbalance between her press profile and the calibre of her compositions. Macnaghten recalled that pieces by Lutyens performed at these early concerts lacked the strong sense of identity exhibited in those of her peers. Lutyens, too, was extremely dissatisfied with many of these early pieces, later choosing to withdraw all of them. Insecurity about her technique continued to haunt her at this time and these anxieties prompted her to re-enter the College for a term in September 1932 to take further composition lessons with Darke. There were other issues too. In 1933 Lutyens married the professional singer Ian Glennie and the couple started a family in the mid 1930s: William Sebastian was born in 1934, and the twins Rose and Teresa followed in 1936. She found the demands of juggling family life with a musical career to be difficult and exhausting. Consequently, only five more of her works were performed at Macnaghten–Lemare concerts in the 1930s, the majority of which received a mixed critical reception.[40]

A sense of restlessness and lack of assurance certainly lingers around these early works. With the exception of a string quartet, the majority are settings for voices and chamber ensemble in various combinations – an early indication of

---

'Women's Topics' page, which featured a full page debate on the apparently pressing issue of 'The Shopping Trials of the Housewife: should she phone or go in person?'.

[39] The French composer Cécile Chaminade (1857–1944), author of several popular piano pieces, may have been one of the possible 'ideal' models for the *Herald* critic.

[40] The pieces by Lutyens (excluding arrangements) performed at Macnaghten–Lemare concerts in the 1930s (performance dates given in brackets) were: *Five Songs* for soprano (3 December 1931); String Quartet in one movement (14 December 1931); *The Night is Darkening* for soprano and piano (15 November 1932); *Winter the Huntsman* for chorus and instrumental ensemble (12 December 1932); *Four Songs* for tenor and piano (21 January 1935) and *The Dying of Tanneguy de Bois* for tenor, strings and horns (4 February 1935).

Lutyens's love of the written word. In *Winter the Huntsman* (1932), a setting of three nonsense poems by Osbert Sitwell for mixed chorus, trumpet, horn, cello, double bass and piano, she attempted to join the ranks of the English avant-garde by completing the tribute paid to the Sitwell family by Walton and Lambert – albeit in a somewhat clumsy manner.[41] Her boldness for choosing unusual instrumentation was again apparent in *The Dying of Tanneguy de Bois* (1934), a setting of Austin Dobson's tragic, semi-mystical poem for tenor, four horns and strings. Lambert cruelly exposed some of the work's peculiarities after sitting through the premiere on 4 February 1935:

> Miss Elisabeth Lutyens in her setting of Austin Dobson's very olde worlde poem "The Dying of Tanneguy de Bois" is evidently determined that none of the Morris-wallpaper atmosphere of the words shall be reflected in the music, which is strained, angular and unconvincing. But having chosen that particular text she should at least have paid some slight attention to it and not have obscured its form and meaning by the pointless repetition of phrases.
>
> A formal poem by Dobson cannot be set as if it were a fragment of modern prose. Mr Steuart Wilson struggled manfully with a gauche vocal part in front of him and the very erratic intonation of the strings and four horns behind him. (*Sunday Referee*, 10 February 1935)

As if that wasn't enough, Lutyens's *Four Songs* for tenor and piano (1933–34) – written for, and premiered by, her husband Ian Glennie with the pianist Millicent Silver – was severely criticized a few weeks later for being 'incompletely incubated and inconsequential' (*The Times*, 23 January 1935).[42] In her study of Lutyens's music, Sarah Tenant-Flowers has considered the exploratory nature of these early pieces – in particular, the tendency towards an increased level of dissonance and, in certain works such as *Tanneguy de Bois*, the tentative use of 12-note patterns in places. Even so, Tenant-Flowers concludes that there is nothing connecting these pieces to musical developments in Europe at this stage. As she points out, 'it is only in the later 1930s that Lutyens's rather unorthodox upbringing and exciting musical experiences really begin to bear fruit, enforcing her independence of mind

---

[41] The *Times* critic noted that 'in general these songs were badly written for the voice, Miss Lutyens apparently caring more for the horn, trumpet, and piano of her accompaniment' (16 December 1932). Walton's setting of Edith Sitwell's *Façade* was composed in 1922 and was followed in 1927 by Lambert's setting of Sacheverell Sitwell's *The Rio Grande*. During the 1920s and 30s the three members of the Sitwell family were regarded as being the prime exponents of a distinctively English literary modernism.

[42] The Four Songs were settings of Emily Bronte's 'Stanzas', D.H. Lawrence's 'Thief in the Night' and 'Nonentity', and Shakespeare's 'Feste Song'.

and guiding her away from the more conventional courses and idioms'.[43] While it is certainly possible to discern a natural sense of youthful rebellion in these works – particularly in the use of dissonant harmony and unusual instrumentation – they lack the sophistication, individuality and sense of authority which would characterize later pieces. 'She's got something up her sleeve', Williams told Maconchy in 1935 after hearing *Tanneguy de Bois*, 'but oh it's so carelessly done: that sort of harum-scarum attitude towards composing shouldn't be allowed'.[44] In truth, the impression these pieces generate is of a composer who possessed a raw talent but who was unsure of what she wished to say in musical terms. Lutyens herself was acutely aware of the shortcomings of these pieces and spoke on several occasions about how it took time for her to find her own musical voice.

If Lutyens could be described as a late developer, the opposite was true of Maconchy. The arresting command and technical brilliance of her early orchestral works aroused tremendous expectations in the London musical world, and by the early 1930s she had 'already reached the enviable position in which she can be sure that anything she may say will be listened to with attention' (*The Times*, 7 November 1933). In 1932 her Piano Concertino (Concerto) was broadcast by the BBC and in the following year she won a prize for her Oboe Quintet in the *Telegraph*'s competition for chamber pieces. She also took full advantage of the opportunities for performances provided by the Macnaghten–Lemare concerts. Her String Quartet No. 1, an important work written in response to a request from Macnaghten and first performed at a concert on 6 November 1933, was one of the first exciting new pieces to emerge.[45] The quartet was the first substantial statement in what would soon become Maconchy's favourite genre. She later recalled that at the time of writing this quartet 'at once, I felt that this is something that I enjoyed doing tremendously'.[46]

It was a remarkable debut in many respects. The quartet's first movement is dominated by the heavily accented figure heard at the opening which, with its syncopated rhythmic pulse, disrupts bar lines, regular metre and anything else in its path. Extrovert and fervent in character, the driving intensity of the movement is fleetingly broken by two expansive *tranquillo* sections in 5/4 metre, where a lyrical theme is heard in the first violin above gently undulating chords in violin

---

[43] Sarah Tenant-Flowers, 'A Study of Style and Technique in the Music of Elisabeth Lutyens', PhD dissertation (University of Durham, 1991), p. 48.

[44] Williams, letter to Maconchy, February 1935, as quoted in Jenny Doctor, 'Intersecting Circles: The Early Careers of Elizabeth Maconchy, Elisabeth Lutyens, and Grace Williams', *Women & Music Journal* 2 (1998), p. 101. In her fascinating article, Doctor considers the social, economic and technological changes that had an impact on the three composers' early careers.

[45] Macnaghten had performed Maconchy's Sonata for violin and piano (1927) at a concert in 1932 and was so taken with the string writing that she asked her friend to write a new work for her quartet.

[46] Maconchy, 'Talking About Music' (Radio 3, 1977).

and viola, and sustained fifths in the cello. The pithy scherzo (II) is followed by a bittersweet slow movement (III), its melodic lines stretched by fluid metres, and in which the influence of Vaughan Williams is perhaps most evident. The finale is an ebullient *Presto*, full of humour and high jinx in which, as one critic noted, the composer achieves 'some remarkably original and unexpectedly poetical effects' (*Daily Telegraph*, 8 November 1933).

Example 2.5 String Quartet No. 1 by Elizabeth Maconchy, opening

Source: Copyright © Alfred Lengnick & Co. Ltd. Reproduced by permission of the publisher.

Maconchy's achievement was all the more remarkable given that, by 1932, she had contracted tuberculosis – the disease that had killed her father. The only recommendation that doctors could make was that the patient have plenty of fresh air to clear the lungs – there was no known medical cure for the disease at the time – and she was told that she would have to go to Switzerland to recuperate. Unwilling to forfeit her marriage and her career, Maconchy refused to go abroad, deciding instead to move out of London with her husband to the purer air of the Kent countryside.[47] Although she continued to write music, drastic measures were needed to overcome a very serious illness which succeeded in almost completely ravaging one of her lungs. 'Betty was going to write to you herself', William LeFanu told Williams in August 1932, 'but a week ago she had another attack of

---

[47] Maconchy's younger sister Sheila also contracted tuberculosis at this time, and decided to go to Switzerland to recuperate.

haemorrhage and she has been flat on her back for a week'.[48] During the worst stages of the illness, LeFanu had to place ice on her chest to stop her haemorrhaging blood, and for three years the couple braved the elements in the hope of a cure, living and sleeping outside in an open-air wooden hut in their garden. Gradually, a combination of fresh air and sheer willpower led to a recovery, but years (from 1931 to 1935) of living with the disease drained Maconchy of energy. Although her general physical strength improved, the composer never regained the excellent health she had enjoyed prior to her illness.

Maconchy's poor health effectively prevented her from being able to take part in the cut and thrust of London musical life at a crucially formative stage in her career: Macnaghten remembered her friend as being 'completely *out* of the musical world' at that time.[49] Despite this major setback, she continued to compose and supporters helped to champion performances and broadcasts of her work: a total of 11 pieces were performed at Macnaghten–Lemare concerts in the 1930s, a far higher number than any other composer.[50] Two works in particular reveal that Maconchy was eager both to explore other genres and to expand her musical horizons. Her *Two Motets* for Double Chorus (1931), settings of Donne's 'A Hymn to Christ' and 'A Hymn to God the Father', is a richly intense work which was composed, fortuitously or not, in the same year as the 300th anniversary of Donne's death (1572–1631). Very different in tone from the witty quartet, these lyrical motets underline, with remarkable poise in places, the themes of grief, death and forgiveness in Donne's dramatic religious monologues. *Two Motets* was one of the first choral works by Maconchy to be performed in public, but the piece seemed to be well beyond the capabilities of Iris Lemare's choir at the premiere in December 1933.[51] In his review of the concert – which also included the premiere of Britten's Two Part Songs – Frank Howes noted that the motets 'flouted the conditions of good choral singing' and chastised Maconchy for 'disregarding the *tessitura* of the voices as outrageously as Beethoven' (*The Times*, 14 December 1933). Britten's songs fared little better, although the critic conceded that they were at least 'singable'. 'Have our young English composers in acquiring the wide franchise of instrumental music forfeited their birthright in the great English choral tradition?' Howes fumed.

---

[48] LeFanu, letter to Williams, 23 August 1932 (Grace Williams Archive, NLW).

[49] Macnaghten in 'Elizabeth Maconchy: A Video Portrait' (Channel 4).

[50] The pieces were: String Quintet (14 December 1931); *Fantasy* for children (28 January 1932); Violin Sonata (18 October 1932); 'The Woodspurge' for voice and piano (15 November 1932); String Quartet No. 1 (6 November 1933); Two Motets (11 December 1933); *Great Agrippa* (4 February 1935); Three Songs for tenor and piano (9 December 1935); *Prelude, Interlude and Fugue* for two violins (27 January 1936); String Quartet No. 2 (1 February 1937); *Divertissement* for 12 Instruments (22 February 1937).

[51] Note that in 1930–31 Maconchy had set Gerard Manley Hopkins's *The Leaden Echo and the Golden Echo* for chorus and chamber orchestra but later withdrew the work.

A different side to Maconchy's musical personality was encountered in *Great Agrippa – or The Inky Boys* (1933), a short ballet for five dancers and chamber ensemble which she based on one of the illustrated children's stories in Heinrich Hoffmann's *Struwwelpeter* (1847). The work has the character of a burlesque or pantomime – the story concerns the fate of three rude little boys who, as a result of teasing a 'blackamoor', are made to look foolish by being fully immersed in black ink. The ballet (concert version only) was performed on 4 February 1935 by Lemare's chamber orchestra with the pianist Adolph Hallis, and its percussive, rhythmic drive, witty mood and sharply abrasive style provoked mixed reactions. Lambert praised the work for its accomplished scoring but was unhappy with its general style: 'Miss Maconchy has in her chamber music shown considerable talent', he wrote, 'and it is a pity that in this work she should revert to the conventionally spiky and short-winded manner of post-war ballet music. This grotesque style, though usually attributed to Stravinsky, really owes more to Bartók' (*Sunday Referee*, 10 February 1935). Vaughan Williams thought he spotted 'certain stravynskyesque cliches' [*sic*] in *Agrippa*, and voiced his misgivings in a letter to Maconchy: 'I do feel that you are capable of so much finer thought than that Russian Monkey-brain', he protested, '& that you injure your real self by condescending to use any of his monkey-tricks'.[52] Grace Williams was perturbed by her teacher's comments about *Agrippa* and leapt to Maconchy's defence. 'I am completely baffled by the press & Uncle Ralph too. I don't think any of them really heard [the piece] ... You mustn't bother your head any more, my girl, about writing safe scores', she told her friend. 'It doesn't become you'.[53]

Williams's advice to Maconchy about not writing safe scores might well have applied to herself. Indeed, none of the four chamber pieces she had performed at Macnaghten–Lemare concerts in the 1930s were particularly 'safe'. After returning from Vienna in 1931, Williams had taken up two part-time teaching posts in London – as music lecturer at Southlands College in Wimbledon and music mistress at the Camden High School for Girls – and had continued to focus on her composition. One of the interesting features about the pieces that were performed in London is the way in which they embody a degree of modernity which was absent from other pieces she was writing at the time. Her lean, three-movement Suite for Chamber Orchestra (or Nine Instruments), for example, a piece which was performed in that same 'all-female all-modern' concert, also, like Maconchy's *Agrippa*, betrays a certain 'stravynskyesque' influence.[54] Britten, by

---

[52] Vaughan Williams, undated letter to Maconchy, quoted in Jennifer Doctor, '"Working for her own Salvation": Vaughan Williams as teacher of Elizabeth Maconchy, Grace Williams and Ina Boyle', in *Vaughan Williams in Perspective: Studies of an English composer*, ed. L. Foreman (London: Albion Music, 1998), p. 197.

[53] Williams, undated letter to Maconchy in ibid., p. 196.

[54] Another piece that suggests an awareness of Stravinsky is Williams's *Sonatina* for flute and piano, which was premiered by the flautist John Francis and the composer at a Macnaghten–Lemare concert in November 1933.

now a close friend and supporter of Williams, caught an earlier radio broadcast of the Suite while he was at his parent's home in Lowestoft:

> I heard ... the Suite from the W. Regional [sic], in sections; but really the thing came over so badly that I can't attempt to judge it – all I seem to remember, between grunts and whistles and shrieks is the diminished fifth B–F – But I remember some exciting wind passages in the last movement. It is going to be done at Iris Lemare's show? When? I must definitely come along to hear it.[55]

Although the Suite remains well within the boundaries of tonality, the use of tougher, acerbic harmony and ostinati figures in all movements suggests that Williams was preoccupied with exploring new ways of organizing her material. Furthermore, and in common with some of the other young Macnaghten–Lemare composers, Williams favoured unorthodox and bold instrumental combinations; the Suite is scored for flute, clarinet, trumpet, piano, two violins, viola, cello and double bass. 'I find the whole thing more satisfying than anything else I've done', she told Britten.[56]

When the Suite received its concert premiere in February 1935, Frank Howes praised the work for being 'sturdy, easy to grasp, thoughtful and attractive' (*The Times*, 8 February 1933). He was also one of the few critics to comment on the work's scoring and, in particular, the prominence given to the trumpet. Significantly, the Suite was one of several works Williams wrote at this time in which the trumpet had a star role. Some of these works even had musical themes in common. A trumpet tune, for example, from the first movement of her Sextet (1931) – scored for oboe, trumpet, piano and string trio – was reused in her *Movement* for trumpet and chamber orchestra (1932), a piece that was premiered at a Macnaghten–Lemare concert in January 1933.[57] The bold use of the 'virile' trumpet as the solo instrument in this work probably raised a few eyebrows, but Williams simply chose the trumpet because it was her favourite musical instrument. As she later explained:

> I love the sound of the trumpet, not only for its brilliance in fanfares and processionals; there's the menacing drama of Verdi's trumpets; I'll never forget hearing for the first time the mysterious muted trumpets in Debussy's *Fêtes*; and

---

[55] Britten, letter to Williams, 16 January 1935, quoted in Malcolm Boyd, 'Benjamin Britten and Grace Williams: Chronicle of a Friendship', *Welsh Music* 6/6 (1980), p. 25. The Suite was performed by the Western Studio Orchestra, conducted by Reginald Redman, in a BBC West Regional broadcast on 14 January 1935, three weeks before the work's first concert performance at the Macnaghten–Lemare concert on 4 February.

[56] Williams, undated letter to Britten in ibid., pp. 27–28.

[57] The composer later chose to withdraw the Sextet and it remains unpublished.

it was Wagner who made me realise the trumpet's lyrical potential – that is when I first heard the Prelude to *Parsifal*.[58]

Movement is, in fact, a 'concerto fantasia', its one-movement form encompassing the three distinct sections (fast–slow–fast) of concerto form. The piece opens with a dramatic call to attention by the soloist and orchestra, the sharply syncopated rhythms of the trumpet 'fanfare' theme and orchestral accompaniment dominating much of the ensuing *Allegro Vivace*.

Example 2.6 *Movement* for Trumpet and Chamber Orchestra by Grace Williams, opening

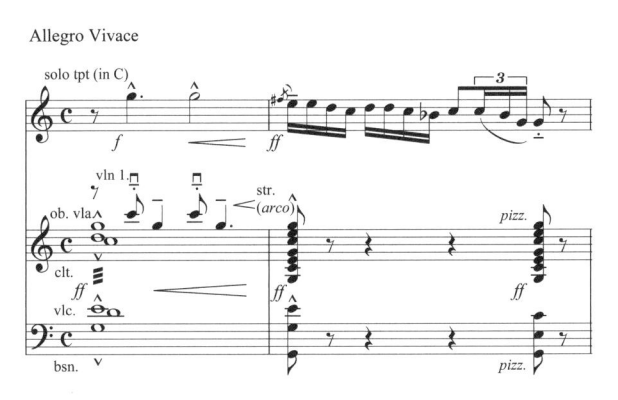

[Some instruments omitted]

Source: Reproduced by kind permission of the Estate of Grace Williams.

The trumpet writing reveals a deftness of touch in that different aspects of the instrument are skilfully exploited. In the opening *Allegro* (section I), brilliant, fanfare-type themes are often contrasted with softer, more lyrical passages where the mute is used. An extended solo trumpet cadenza links the *Allegro* with the mellifluous central *Andante* (section II) which consists of a lyrical dialogue between strings and various woodwind instruments: the soloist's contribution is here kept to a minimum. The trumpet returns in the final *Allegro* (section III), where new themes and variants of those encountered in the previous section are combined, and the work closes with an emphatic final statement of the opening 'fanfare' theme.

Although the piece begins and ends in C major, Williams's handling of the tonality in the piece is often elusive, an ambiguity enhanced by the alternation of major and minor thirds – a feature absorbed from the music of Vaughan Williams – and the use of the tritone or diminished fifth. Interestingly, all these

---

[58] Williams, 'A Self Portrait', *Welsh Music* 8/5, p. 14.

features are present in the octatonic scale, and in the opening *Allegro* section, the trumpet introduces a theme which is entirely based on this scale (Example 2.7). Octatonicism had featured in Williams's scores since her student days and was something which she almost certainly absorbed primarily from the music of Bartók. The scholar Malcolm Boyd has also noted Bartók's influence on Williams's work but adds that the scale 'was simply "in the air" at a time when composers were looking for alternatives to, or refinements of, the major–minor system'.[59]

Example 2.7 *Movement* for Trumpet and Chamber Orchestra by Grace Williams, trumpet theme

Source: Reproduced by kind permission of the Estate of Grace Williams.

Williams's *Movement* was first performed by Richard Walton (trumpet) and the Lemare Chamber Orchestra in January 1933, where it shared the programme with the premiere of Britten's *Sinfonietta* for chamber orchestra. Williams and Britten had had a number of pieces performed together at Macnaghten–Lemare concerts and the two composers soon became friends. 'Look here Benjamin, I'll strike a bargain with you', Williams wrote. 'If you promise to tell me the truth, the whole truth etc. – about my things I'll do the same to you about yours … I'm dead sick of having tactful things said to me'.[60] The friendship deepened during the mid 1930s when the two composers were living very near to each other in Earl's

---

[59] Boyd, *Grace Williams* (Cardiff: University of Wales Press, 1980), p. 79. An octatonic scale consists of eight alternating semi- and whole-tone intervals. There are two possible modes for this scale – one beginning with a whole-tone, the other with a semitone interval (as shown in Example 2.7). Only three transpositions of this scale are possible – beginning on C, C♯ and D. The scale occurs frequently in the music of Stravinsky, Bartók, Scriabin, and is also Messiaen's second mode of limited transposition.

[60] Williams, letter to Britten, January 1935, quoted in Boyd, 'Chronicle of a Friendship', *Welsh Music* 6/6, p. 29.

Court, London. A handful of surviving letters from this period reveal that the two were close musical *confrères*, feeling free to voice candid criticisms about aspects of each other's work:

Dear Benjamin,

Now that [*A Boy was Born*] is a truly remarkable work in many ways. I like best the IIIrd ["Jesu, as Thou art our Saviour"] and the "bleak mid-winter" [variation V] i.e. <u>as music</u>; it's <u>older</u> than the rest. Of course all that <u>skill</u> bowls one over right through – but I can't help feeling that some of it – (about a third of it) – <u>again solely as music</u> – isn't up to the standard of the rest ...

– the 1st ["Lullay, Jesu"], apart from the rather hazy performance, I feel is a bit too reactionary; I know I liked it when I first heard it but now I feel it's too typically English and this same criticism I apply to part of the Finale ...

Now Benjamin aren't you getting angrier and angrier and have you taken up your pen already and dashed off a letter to me "Grace you are talking through your hat and are quite wrong about everything –."[61]

These letters detail the composers' attitudes towards standards of performance in concerts and broadcasts, and also reveal that the two frequently exchanged advice on technical musical details while writing pieces. Williams was largely responsible for persuading Britten to take more of an interest in Wagner's music. He, in turn, appears to have launched a successful counter-campaign on behalf of the then equally unfashionable music of Verdi and Mahler.

A more introspective side of Williams's musical personality is encountered in the poignant *Elegy* for string orchestra, a piece which was written in 1936 and premiered at a Macnaghten–Lemare concert on 22 February 1937.[62] As with *Movement*, harmonic ambiguity and non-diatonic scales feature strongly, but here they are employed to quite different effect. The work opens quietly with a slow melody in violins and violas comprised of three notes B–A♯–C♯ (Example 2.8). It is only with the entry of the first chord, rooted on C♯ and built from the notes of the octatonic scale, that the work's richly chromatic sound palette is

---

[61] Williams, letter to Britten, February 1934, ibid., pp. 13–14. Williams was referring to the first broadcast performance on 23 February 1934 of *A Boy is Born* by the BBC Wireless Chorus and choirboys from St. Mark's Church, North Audley Street, conducted by Leslie Woodgate.

[62] The *Elegy* was actually written in January 1936 in response to a request for a string piece from Idris Lewis, the Music Director of the then newly independent BBC Welsh Broadcasting Region; previously, Wales had been part of the West of England Region. The piece received its first public broadcast on 25 February 1936 on the Welsh Region wavelength.

revealed. Furthermore, although the *Elegy* is only five minutes in duration, the piece possesses an expressive intent that is almost Mahlerian in its intensity. Eryl Freestone, Williams's niece, has suggested that the plaintive character of the work may have been inspired by events relating to the Spanish Civil War, a war which Lutyens described as being 'emotionally the "Vietnam" of our age'.[63]

Example 2.8 *Elegy* for String Orchestra by Grace Williams, opening

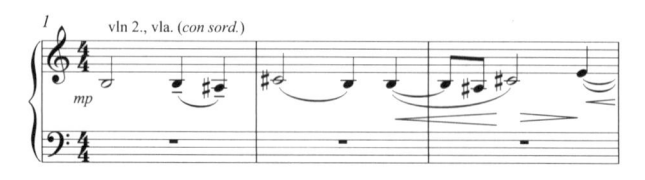

Source: Reproduced by kind permission of the Estate of Grace Williams.

There is a sense that Williams was writing for two different audiences in the 1930s. Pieces performed at the London concert series such as the Suite tended to be abstract, instrumental works which made little direct reference to Wales. These works reflected an awareness of what would have been the latest musical developments – Bartók, Stravinsky – influences which had been assimilated into Williams's music in a natural way. On the other hand, she was also writing music of a more overtly popular bias which drew on traditional Welsh sources and which was intended for Welsh audiences – arrangements of traditional Welsh folk tunes for vocal or orchestral forces. This dichotomy was amusingly summarized in a listing which appeared in December 1934 when Williams's *Two Psalms* was included in a concert broadcast by the BBC Symphony Orchestra. After noting that she was one of the most popular composers of the younger generation, the *Radio Times* went on to inform its readers that 'although most of her works are modern in idiom, she can, at times, be very Welsh'.[64] There was some element of truth in

---

[63] Lutyens, *Goldfish Bowl*, p. 74.
[64] *Radio Times* listing for a broadcast given on 28 December 1934 of Williams's *Two Psalms* for soprano and chamber orchestra, performed by Megan Thomas and the BBC Symphony Orchestra, conducted by Vaughan Williams.

this apparently offhand remark. Although Lambert could argue in 1934 that 'folk songs in England are not a vigorous living tradition',[65] the situation in Wales was rather different. In particular, the establishment of the *Cymdeithas Alawon Gwerin Cymru* (The Welsh Folk Song Society) in 1906 and the subsequent publication of hundreds of neglected Welsh folk tunes effected a sharp revival of interest in Welsh folk music, laying the foundations for the restoration of a living tradition which endures to this day.

Among the earliest of Williams's 'Welsh' works are her striking arrangements of traditional Welsh Dances for chamber orchestra, and Welsh folk songs for voice and piano: six of the vocal arrangements were published by Boosey and Hawkes in 1937 under the title of *Six Welsh Oxen Songs*. In addition, one of the first pieces to bring her to public notice in Wales was the orchestral overture *Hen Walia*, an assured and skilfully wrought medley of Welsh folk tunes.[66] The piece was written in 1930, her Viennese year, and was premiered by the London Symphony Orchestra on 6 August 1931 at the National Eisteddfod which was held in Bangor that year. Williams had been inspired by a performance of the popular Czech folk opera *Švanda Dudák* (Schwanda the Bagpiper) by Jaromir Weinberger (1896–1967), and had originally intended to write a Welsh folk opera, with *Hen Walia* as its overture. As she explained in a letter to the music journal *Y Cerddor* (The Musician) shortly after the overture's premiere:

> I had seen the tuneful folk-opera *Schwanda* and I felt I would like to write a folk-opera. One day, I found myself humming what to me seemed to be a good opening subject for the overture. I wrote it down and soon the whole movement followed. It took me some time to decide on the tunes to use because there were so many good ones to choose from. In the end I boiled them down to "Huna blentyn," "Breuddwyd y Bardd," and "Lliw Gwyn Rhosyn yr Haf" because the three contrasted well and they would be useful in the opera. It took me some time to shape the overture but in the end I believe that the form is good.[67]

Although the folk opera did not come to fruition, *Hen Walia* became one of the first of Williams's orchestral works to receive regular performances and broadcasts in Wales during the 1930s. Indeed, the work became so popular that by 1939 Williams could write to the BBC Welsh Region in Cardiff to make the point that

---

[65] Lambert, *Music Ho!*, p. 124.

[66] Williams named the overture after the 'Hen Walia' district of Caernarfon, North Wales because her father was born there. The name 'Hen Walia' (Old Walls) refers to the surviving walls of a Roman enclosure which is adjacent to the site of Segontium, one of the largest Roman forts in Wales.

[67] Williams, letter to the Editor, *Y Cerddor* (October 1931), p. 338 (author's own translation). *Schwanda the Bagpiper* was premiered in Prague on 27 April 1927 and became one of the most frequently performed operas in the interwar period. Williams probably first heard the work when she was in Vienna or possibly Prague.

'people are beginning – or rather they have been saying it for sometime that ... I've only written one work – it's only Hen Walia all the time. Little do they know that there are stacks of other things which could be played instead'.[68]

In some respects, Williams can be said to have had an advantage over her composer friends because of the interest her music sparked in Wales. The start of her professional career coincided with significant developments for music in Wales. The BBC's creation of an independent Welsh Broadcasting Region (and a Welsh Music Department) in 1936, in particular, opened up new horizons, as did the formation in the same year of a BBC Welsh Orchestra. The BBC in Cardiff had an enlightened policy of performing new works by young Welsh composers, and this gave Williams the opportunity – an unusual one for a British composer of her generation – to focus almost exclusively in the next few decades on writing music for the orchestra. As she later recalled, 'I gained most of my early practical experience in writing for orchestra through trials and errors in the Cardiff studios. Having an orchestra handy is the basic reason for the preponderance of orchestral works in the catalogues of Welsh music'.[69]

Even so, it is interesting to note that while Williams had several pieces performed at Macnaghten–Lemare concerts, she did not receive the same level of recognition in the London press as some of her peers. Indeed, a survey of 1930s critical opinion reveals that Maconchy's profile was far higher. Writing in the *Sunday Referee* (12 November 1933), for instance, Lambert noted that 'there are regrettably few young composers of any personality in England to-day, but in Miss Elizabeth Machonchy [*sic*] and Mr. Benjamin Britten we have two whose future development should be of the greatest interest'. The critic of the *Star* (8 February 1938) went one step further when he praised Maconchy for being *the* outstanding young British composer of her generation with Britten, Berkeley and Lutyens as noteworthy runners-up:

> Who are our young British composers, the young men and women whose work may sway our musical culture a generation hence? ... Pride of place goes to a girl.
>
> **Elizabeth Maconchy** is 27. She left Ireland to study at the Royal College of Music, where she won a travelling scholarship to study in European capitals. The Prague Philharmonic performed her first big work, a piano concerto, and Sir Henry Wood introduced her work "The Land" to his overflowing Proms. Since then her works have been performed from Warsaw to Paris; from New York to Australia ...

---

[68] Williams, letter to Idris Lewis, 1 June 1939 [BBC WAC, WAI/61/2: Williams, Welsh Region Composer, 1938–41].

[69] Williams, 'How Welsh is Welsh Music?', *Welsh Music* (Summer 1973), p. 9.

Benjamin Britten, Lowestoft bred and Gresham taught is only 24. He has twice represented his country at European international festivals (Sienna and Barcelona). Britten wrote 'Our Hunting Fathers' which was cheered by the "county" at the Norwich Festival, and cursed by the critics. He has a great sense of humour, and can "guy" Rossini and Palastrina in his "Variations" which will be played in June at the European Festival in London ...

Lennox Berkeley, quiet, reserved, reflective, is a friend of Somerset Maugham's and, like Maugham, has a certain Gallic turn of mind. He is a product of the Boulanger school, and is to be found as often in Paris as in the East Anglian windmill which he shares with his friend Britten ...[70]

Elisabeth Lutyens ... is slim, dark and sophisticated. She has travelled all over the world, studied at the Royal College of Music, where she played the viola, taken a job as an organist at a country church, and composed a ballet for the Camargo Society.

Lutyens, Maconchy and Williams had been successful in finding public platforms for their work in the 1930s, and this had enabled them to make the all-important transition from music graduate to young, professional composer. During the difficult war years they would pursue quite independent musical paths, often in the face of many obstacles. In the late 1940s each sought to gain recognition as a serious figure in the post-war British music arena.

---

[70] Lennox Berkeley – Appendix.

PART II
1935–1955

If I had a good orchestra and choir at my disposal ... I would give a concert consisting of Purcell's Yorkshire Feast and the last act of Die Meistersinger. Then the public could judge whether Purcell was really a great composer or not, as some people (including myself) assert that he was.

Mr Dolmetsch has taken up an altogether un-English position in this matter. He says, "Purcell was a great composer: let us perform some of his works." The English musicians say, "Purcell was a great composer: let us go and do Mendelssohn's Elijah over again and make the lord-lieutenant of the county chairman of the committee."

Shaw, *Music in London* 1890–94, vol. iii, p. 174

The poor esteem in which English music is held on the Continent is due to a number of causes. Firstly, the debacle of the 19th century. Foreigners are so used to looking upon England as "the land without music" that a town like Paris with 1/10th of the musical activity of London still looks upon itself as the superior musical centre by right of tradition.

Secondly, the fact that the classic period of English music lies too early in musical history to take much place in the general repertoire. We still devote about 99 percent of our programmes to the 19th and 18th centuries (a ludicrous proportion), and the period in which English music really shines still remains in practical obscurity, in spite of all the work of scholars and editors.

Purcell has his followers in Germany, and I once met a Frenchman who had heard of Byrd. But that is about as far as knowledge of the English classics goes.

Lambert, *Sunday Referee* (28 April 1935)

Chapter 3
Lutyens: Music in London

Lutyens may have appeared in the *Star*'s list of 'names to watch' in 1938, but it was not until the 1940s that she began to make her considerable mark on the musical scene. She was one of the first British composers to explore 12-note music, and her engagement with the musical method proved to be an incendiary issue from the start. Her *Three Pieces for Orchestra*, Op. 7, the first of her large-scale works to show an awareness of the method, was premiered on 7 September 1940, the first night of the London Blitz. Consequently, the composer, together with Sir Henry Wood, the performers and the few audience members who had been brave enough to venture out, were forced to spend the night in the old Queen's Hall. 'The next day we learnt that the docks had been hit', Lutyens recalled. 'Whether it was the performance of my work or the German bombers, the Proms temporarily ceased'.[1]

Although the premiere of the *Three Pieces* was somewhat eclipsed by events, the piece did not go entirely unnoticed. In particular, the performance caught the eye of Ernest Chapman, editor of the music journal *Tempo*:

> I did not go [to the concert] and was all the more sorry when I found out from the press reviews that the work was in the 12-tone system! Surprisingly enough the critics were quite kind to it, but how far this was connected with her distinguished father I should not like to say.[2]

Chapman's suspicions were perhaps a little unkind but Lutyens soon discovered that being her father's daughter was the least of her worries. Ever the rebel, she undoubtedly relished the fact that her use of an 'advanced' musical method would be viewed with suspicion by conservatives in British musical life, but even she was unprepared for the critical venom which would be directed at her work during the 1940s and 50s. Critics remained unconvinced by her claim that her interest in writing 12-note music had arisen out of her own musical development and without any awareness of Schoenberg's method. Even so, Lutyens continued to insist throughout this period that her path to new 12-note possibilities had been kindled by her knowledge of sixteenth and seventeenth-century composers – in particular,

---

[1] Lutyens, *Goldfish Bowl*, p. 105.
[2] Chapman, letter to Erwin Stein, 18 September 1940, quoted in *From Parry to Britten: British Music in Letters 1900–1945*, ed. Lewis Foreman (London: Batsford, 1987), p. 236. Chapman (1914–83) worked for the publishers Boosey and Hawkes from 1943–47 and was the first editor of the journal *Tempo*. In the late 1950s he served as Honorary Secretary and Concerts Manager of the Macnaghten Concerts.

insights she had gleaned from her study of the intricate, contrapuntal forms in Purcell's Fantasias for viols (1680). As she stated:

> It was this experience of these works with their independent string part writing, with their English "sensibility" and vitality and wonderful linear counterpoint, coupled with the heavily accented harmonic intervals, which pointed me to new musical possibilities in pursuance of which I developed a serial technique of my own before hearing a note of Schoenberg, Webern or Berg, or being aware of the existence of the expression "12 tone."[3]

Stunned by the combination of radical invention and strict formal discipline in these Fantasias, and the startling level of expressive dissonance generated by string lines moving against each other, she embarked in 1935 on a period of intensive study and reflection. She re-emerged in 1937 with an exploratory Fantasia (in five parts) of her own, a work replete with complex contrapuntal devices governed by a variety of tempi, which ventures into highly dissonant territory in search of heightened expressivity. A succession of pieces for various combinations of string instruments quickly followed in which Lutyens worked through different aspects of the musical discoveries she had made in her Fantasia. Her opus 5 (1937–39), a series of six chamber works, included a Partita for two violins (Op. 5, No. 2), two String Quartets (Nos. 1 and 5) and a String Trio (No. 6). The grouping of pieces of a similar cast in a single opus was a pattern which would recur throughout Lutyens's creative career. As she noted, 'I found it less alarming ... and less pretentious to envisage the writing of several works in the same genre, attempting to solve the problems involved rather than produce the Masterpiece – with a capital M'.[4] The family resemblance between the opus 5 pieces is unmistakable. Each work is written in a richly chromatic (although not atonal) idiom, and displays a preoccupation with contrapuntal devices and Baroque forms. The five contrasting movements of the Partita (1938), for example, are based on Baroque dance forms (overture, two musettes, pastorale and jig), and in common with seventeenth-century practices, drone (tonal) harmony is a feature of one of the musettes. Further interesting features can be found in the First String Quartet (1937–38), which opens with a 'Preludio-Fugato' movement and closes with a finale entitled 'Ricercare sul un tema di Frescobaldi'.[5]

---

[3] Lutyens, unpublished lecture notes (private collection). Lutyens first encountered Purcell's Fantasias in the early 1930s. Anne Macnaghten introduced her to André Mangeot, violinist and leader of the International String Quartet, who was editing and performing these (largely unknown) works at this time.
[4] Lutyens, *Goldfish Bowl*, p. 69.
[5] Frescobaldi was not well known in Britain at this time but Lutyens had been introduced to his music in the late 1920s by Antoine Geoffroy-Dechaume.

Example 3.1 String Quartet No. 1, IV 'tema di Frescobaldi'

Source: Reproduced by kind permission of the Estate of Elisabeth Lutyens.

Tenant-Flowers has drawn attention to a new contrapuntalism in these pieces – notably, a more flexible use of contrapuntal devices and a fluid approach to transposition and rhythm – which she traces directly to Purcell. As she states, 'it is plain to see that [Lutyens's] contrapuntal technique derives more from Purcell than from the Teutonic tradition as represented by Bach, and it signifies, with its denial of rigour and admittance of irregularity, perhaps a typically English solution compared with that of Lutyens's Second Viennese counterparts'.[6] Tenant-Flowers goes on to reach a balanced conclusion about Lutyens's claim to having discovered a serial method of her own as a result of her study of Purcell.

> To be fair, Lutyens's music does to some extent bear out her story. For there is no sudden conversion to serialism which might imply that she had been privy to detailed instructions on the method's technique … However, one must still seriously question whether Lutyens's claim is entirely truthful … [S]he was certainly not prone to thinking theoretically about music; it is extremely hard to imagine that she had the intellectualism or the patience to pursue an abstract, theoretical goal in complete isolation.[7]

Some of the opus 5 pieces also reflect more contemporary influences which were of interest to Lutyens. Her Second String Quartet (1938) shows an awareness of Bartók's highly idiomatic, expressionistic string writing, as does, to an extent, her Viola Sonata (Op. 5, No. 4). The Second Quartet became one of the first pieces by Lutyens to be heard by an international audience when it was selected by the jury of the ISCM for performance at the Society's 1939 festival in Warsaw. The festival also included performances of Webern's String Trio, Op. 20 (1926–27), Luigi Dallapiccola's *Tre Laudi* (1936–37) and Wladimir Vogel's Violin Concerto (1937). Lutyens travelled to Warsaw to attend the premiere of her quartet, and on the return journey home began writing a String Trio, the final work in the opus 5 series and one of the first works to show an awareness of Webern.

By her own account, Lutyens's acquaintance with the music of the Second Viennese School in the 1930s was, at best, sketchy – although opportunities to hear their works in London's concert halls and on the radio certainly existed at this

---

[6] Tenant-Flowers, 'The Music of Elisabeth Lutyens', p. 98.
[7] Ibid., p. 68.

time.[8] There can be little doubt, however, that her discovery of Webern's music was a life-changing experience. In her autobiography she drew attention to a London concert given by the Kolisch Quartet in the mid 1930s that had included a piece by Webern. Although she could not recall *which* piece was performed on that occasion, her musical antennae were immediately tweaked by this new, atomised sound world which seemed to point to new frontiers. 'I shall never forget my excitement', she wrote, 'my certainty that this was the most thrilling music I had heard since the great classics'.[9] Her impression of Webern as a pioneering spirit was strengthened when she attended a performance of his *Das Augenlicht* (The Light of the Eye) for chorus and orchestra at the 1938 ISCM Festival in London:

> The work was received with bated breath and obvious emotion, the audience standing and cheering for minutes afterwards. It was an unforgettable experience and confirmed the earlier impression that here was a composer with a musical mind and an almost Mozartian ear that could only belong to a human being of utter integrity, and that Webern, who had convinced me from the first note of his I had heard, would be a guiding spirit to all future music.[10]

If Webern was the musical catalyst who enabled Lutyens to take essential steps in the search for her own voice, then Edward Clark provided the encouragement she needed at this time. Clark (1882–1962) had studied with Schoenberg in Berlin before the First World War, and became one of the principal architects of contemporary music events in Britain during the interwar years. He worked as a programme planner for the BBC's music department in the late 1920s and, because of his strong links with Europe's musical mainland, was able to persuade continental composers to take part in broadcast performances of their works, either as conductors or soloists. It was largely thanks to him that British audiences had the opportunity to hear Webern conduct three movements from Berg's *Lyric Suite* on 21 April 1933 and Bartók perform his own Second Piano Concerto on 25

---

[8] See Jenny Doctor's analysis of the BBC's performances and broadcasts of the music of the Second Viennese School in *The BBC and Ultra-Modern Music, 1922–1936: Shaping a Nation's Tastes* (Cambridge: Cambridge University Press, 1999).

[9] Lutyens, *Goldfish Bowl*, p. 72. The piece in question was probably Webern's *Five Movements* for String Quartet, Op. 5 (1909) which was performed at a BBC concert by the Kolisch Quartet on 1 December 1933. Grace Williams and Britten also attended this concert. See *Journeying Boy: The Diaries of the Young Benjamin Britten 1928–1938*, ed. John Evans (London: Faber and Faber, 2009), p. 155.

[10] Ibid., p. 76. Edward Clark, the Honorary Secretary of the ISCM, had arranged for Webern to come to London to attend this performance, but the composer was prevented from leaving Austria by the *Anschluss*. The Third Reich ruthlessly suspended all Austrian societies, groups and organizations that were not seen to uphold Third Reich principles. Webern was at this time involved with the Austrian section of the ISCM, one of the organizations which fell foul of the Nazi ruling.

May 1934. In addition, the BBC's British broadcast premiere of Berg's *Wozzeck* on 14 March 1934, for which Clark had vigorously campaigned over the years, became one of the most important highlights of the 1930s musical calendar. After resigning from the BBC in 1936, Clark immersed himself in the contemporary music scene and served as Honorary Secretary of the ISCM.

Lutyens first met Clark in 1938 and was immediately taken with his authority (he was 18 years her senior), and his glamorous reputation as the *éminence grise* of the contemporary music scene. Keen to escape the cramped confines of music establishment thinking, she found his international outlook both refreshing and alluring. As she explained:

> Edward was first and foremost European-minded, with an equal interest in *all* the arts and creative phenomena of all the countries in Europe, not just the small parish of British music. My background, my father, studies in Paris and much travelling around, had given me something of this attitude – without, of course, Edward's erudition …
>
> In that autumn of 1938, having come across him associated with – to me – all the most interesting musical happenings, I was now meeting and getting to know him personally. Was he, perhaps, all I had been seeking for in a man, all I had been seeking for in a musician?[11]

Her rapport with Clark deepened in 1939 when she accompanied him to Moscow on ISCM business after attending the Warsaw premiere of her Second String Quartet. Her relationship with her husband Ian Glennie had been deteriorating for some time and on her return to England the strain of leading a double life took its toll. As the prospect of war loomed closer in the autumn of 1939, Lutyens called an abrupt halt to her six-year marriage and shocked polite society by moving in with Clark, taking her three children with her. 'Edward has given me a confidence by his love which has made me feel reborn', she told her mother. 'He had confidence in me as a composer'.[12]

Many assumed that it was Clark (and not Purcell) who had been Lutyens's main conduit to 12-note music. Indeed, her first real explorations with the method took place when he was becoming an increasingly significant presence in her life. Lutyens never spoke in detail of any influence Clark may have had on her musical development, but it would seem inconceivable that she did not discuss Schoenberg, Webern and Berg with him early on in their relationship: he counted all three composers as personal friends. Furthermore, her trip to the Warsaw ISCM Festival in 1939 had brought her into contact with other young composers who were experimenting in different ways with 12-note techniques in their music.

---

[11]   Ibid., p. 80.
[12]   Lutyens, letter to her mother, quoted in Harries, *A Pilgrim Soul*, p. 110.

Interestingly, Dorothy Gow may also have been a helpful source of knowledge about 12-note music at this time. Although Lutyens did not discuss any influence Gow might have had, she did credit Gow as being responsible for first introducing her to Webern's music when the two had attended that Kolisch Quartet concert in 1933.[13] Gow's own highly original Oboe Quintet in One Movement (1936) is striking in the way in which it reveals a definite awareness of atonal and 12-note music.[14] While it is difficult to be precise about when Gow first encountered music by the Second Viennese School, her musical experience must have been broadened when she lived in Vienna in 1932. Following a recommendation from Williams (who had studied in Vienna in the previous year), Gow had used her College Travelling Scholarship to study with Wellesz. Correspondence between Wellesz and Williams reveals that Gow had been keen to focus on acquiring a knowledge of what Wellesz termed 'the special chamber music stile' (*sic*).[15] On her return to England, Gow had several works performed in London, including her *Prelude and Fugue* for orchestra (1930–31) at a Macnaghten–Lemare concert in 1934, a piece which was later broadcast by the BBC. In spite of these initial successes, however, she was never to receive the kind of public recognition gained by Lutyens, Maconchy or Williams. Extremely self-critical and lacking confidence in her musical abilities, she destroyed works she considered to be immature, leaving only a handful of pieces. Even so, she was held in high esteem by her teachers and her friends. Lutyens later told Gow that she considered her to be 'potentially almost the best composer I've met', adding that, 'it was a struggle in those far off days if one had an unconventional ear, wasn't it?'[16]

Chamber Concerto No. 1, Op. 8, No. 1 (1939–40)

Lutyens may have discussed some aspects of her Chamber Concerto No. 1 for Nine Instruments with Gow, and almost certainly discussed the Concerto with Clark, the piece's dedicatee. Completed in 1940, she described her Concerto as

---

[13] Lutyens, *Goldfish Bowl*, p. 72.

[14] Gow's Oboe Quintet has been recently rediscovered by the oboist George Caird after many years of neglect. The quintet was included in the recording made by Caird, Simon Blendis, Alison Dods, Louise Williams and Jane Salmon (*An English Renaissance*, Oboe Classics CC2009) and was published in 2007 by SPMS Press. These performers gave the first modern-day performances in October and November 2007 in Birmingham and London respectively.

[15] 'I am expecting Miss Gow. Your letter is a good help to understand what she wants to acquire in Vienna and I will try to do my best to bring her in touch with the special chamber music stile'. Wellesz, letter to Williams, 22 October 1932 (private collection). Unfortunately, Williams's side of the correspondence does not seem to have survived.

[16] Lutyens, letter to Gow, quoted in Fuller, *Pandora Guide to Women Composers*, p. 142.

her 'first really serial work', and it represented for her both a purification of her musical language and a bold stride forward in compositional terms.[17] Although exploratory in essence, the most striking features of the Concerto are its purity of musical argument and sense of musical purpose – particularly in comparison with her other works of this period. Compact and concise in structure, the work's four movements are sensitively contrasted, each lasting less than two and a half minutes in performance. While the musical language and gestures are advanced for their time and place, Lutyens uses traditional movement forms and textures in her piece. The opening movement is in the form of a 'Theme and Variations', for example, and is followed by an 'Aria' (II). The tranquil mood and lyrical contrapuntal lines of the 'Aria' are in sharp contrast to the mischievously playful character of the 'Scherzo' (III), and the work concludes with a terse 'Rondo' (IV).

The theme of the first movement presents the principal note row and the ensuing set of lightly-scored miniature variations are governed by this note row. Different instrumentation, rhythm, pitch and texture are used to give each variation, and each transformation of the row, a distinctive profile. Meticulous attention has been given to architectural properties in this movement, with particular, but not exclusive, emphasis on the number three. The principal theme, for instance, is divided into three distinct melodic phrases.

The concern with balance and symmetry is also reflected in the instrumentation, in that the piece is scored for three distinct groups of wind, brass and strings (oboe, clarinet, bassoon / trumpet, horn, trombone / violin, viola and cello). While each instrument has a solo function, it is clear that the piece has been conceived with these groupings in mind. Architectural design together with distinct instrumental groupings continued to be a key focus for Lutyens in her work throughout her life, and many of her mature pieces are characterized by an elegance of overall structure. As the composer stated, 'shape and form remain my major preoccupation, before I even begin the writing of a piece'.[18] Glyn Perrin, one of Lutyens's closest friends in later life, observed that when writing down a new piece, she would always begin with the note rows and then plot the architectural shape of the work in one of her spiral notebooks. 'She never wrote down a piece first in short score', he recalled. 'The full score came first – then the piano reduction. She was confident in her work and entirely professional'.[19]

The comparatively radical language of the Chamber Concerto must have been very much apparent at its first performance in June 1943. The work was premiered at a Boosey and Hawkes contemporary music concert, conducted by Lambert, at the Wigmore Hall in London, where it shared the programme with early works

---

[17] Lutyens, *Goldfish Bowl*, p. 99. Lutyens's description is not entirely accurate as the Concerto contains both tonal and serial elements.
[18] Ibid., p. 267.
[19] Glyn Perrin in interview with the author.

Example 3.2 Chamber Concerto No. 1, I 'Theme and Variations'

Source: Copyright © Mills Music Limited, a Division of Alfred Music Publishing Co., Inc. All rights reserved. Reproduced by permission.

by Bax, Bliss, Ravel and a pastoral Warlock.[20] Instead of provoking enthusiasm, the piece was greeted by polite, muted applause and a few icy press reviews. One critic noted the composer's apparent fascination with 'the experiments of Bartók and Anton Webern', adding that, 'she does not handle the chosen medium with the unquestionable skill displayed by her models, and the result is somewhat crude' (*The Times*, 15 June 1943). Another complained that Lutyens, like 'all good Schoenbergians', had created 'a thin net of spiky, barbed-wire counterpoint'.[21] Lutyens was wounded by this criticism, particularly the insinuation that her Concerto was modelled on Webern's Concerto, Op. 24 (1931–34), a piece also scored for nine instruments. Accusations that she was simply writing cod-Webern would accompany her throughout the years, despite her protests that she had been unaware of his music at the time of writing her own Concerto. Similarities between the style and manner of the two concertos do exist, but the pieces are very distinct. Different instruments are employed – Webern's Concerto is scored for flute, oboe, clarinet, horn, trumpet, trombone, violin, viola and piano – and Lutyens's handling of the note rows is individual, flexible and much more rudimentary than that of Webern. Surrounded by controversy, Lutyens's First Chamber Concerto became, and remains, probably one of the better-known pieces in her *oeuvre*. While it stands as one of the first pre-war pieces by a British composer to embrace 12-note principles, it can also be seen as a powerful critique of the residual conservatism and parochialism of the British musical scene.

Three Symphonic Preludes (1942)

Lutyens followed her First Chamber Concerto with a Second (Op. 8, No. 2 for clarinet, tenor saxophone, piano and strings), several smaller works and *Three Symphonic Preludes* for orchestra (1942).[22] The lush, romantic expressionism of this latter work is in bold contrast to the atomised gestures of the First Chamber Concerto, a disparity of style which reflects the exploratory nature of Lutyens's musical development at this time. As with the Concerto, Lutyens employs traditional formal patterns in her Preludes; the first is in sonata form while the second and third preludes take the forms of a scherzo and a passacaglia. Unfortunately, performances of all these works fell victim to the disruptions of the war years, and to what Jenny Doctor has described as a 'campaign against the

---

[20]   The Chamber Concerto went on to be accepted by the English Selection Committee of the London Contemporary Music Centre and was subsequently conducted by Hugo Weisgall in America, and performed and recorded in Paris by André Girard.

[21]   I.K., *Music & Letters* 29/1 (January 1948), p. 109.

[22]   Although Lutyens claimed not to have heard many of Webern's works at this time, the scoring of her Second Chamber Concerto bears a striking resemblance to his Quartet for violin, clarinet, tenor saxophone and piano (1930).

"ugly" in music' during the late 1930s and early 40s. As Doctor has observed, this campaign

> cannot be interpreted merely as an evaluation of one composer's idiom or a manifestation of sexism, although the output of two prominent women composers of the time, Maconchy and Lutyens, was often described in those terms. In fact, the campaign reflects a larger movement against cerebral and dissonant idioms that was evolving in Britain in the late 1930s, as well as elsewhere in Western society.[23]

After Britain emerged from the war in 1945, it was evident that feelings of suspicion and hostility towards advanced musical idioms had, if anything, intensified. Prior to the start of the 1946 ISCM Festival in London, for instance, Clark felt the need to write an article in *The Listener* in which he defended the Society against accusations that it habitually assaulted its audiences with 'every kind of nerve-racking cacophony or deliberate experimentation'. He went on to highlight some of the new pieces by younger British composers that had been selected for performance (and broadcast), including Lutyens's *Symphonic Preludes* and Alan Rawsthorne's overture *Cortèges*.[24] When discussing the *Symphonic Preludes*, he informed readers that its composer had adopted 'the technique of composing with 12 tones invented by Schoenberg' (*The Listener*, 4 July 1946). Lutyens came to regard this very public statement as marking the start of her many years in the British musical wilderness. The problem was not so much the 'composing with 12 tones' as the fact that the technique had been invented by Schoenberg. As she observed, 'to adopt a technique, like the 12-tone, associated with a German, Schoenberg (albeit that, earlier, I had thought I had "discovered" it myself, from my study of Purcell), was "*mittel*-European", un-English and iconoclastic. I was soon made to feel like a Communist before the Committee for Un-American Activities'.[25]

Several of the reviews of the *Symphonic Preludes*, and of the 1946 ISCM Festival in general, echo Lutyens's comments. *The Times* (8 July 1946) observed that her *Preludes* 'like most atonal music, are logical enough on paper, no doubt, but hardly convey their sense to the ear'. After rather disdainfully describing Lutyens as 'a convert to the 12-tone system', the critic concluded that 'the arbitrariness which Schoenberg introduced into music unfits it for music's normal function as a means of expression and communication'. A similar view was put forward by an irate Dyneley Hussey in *The Listener* (18 July 1946). Hussey accused the ISCM of being 'unrepresentative of the music it was designed to advance', adding that 'at least, one hopes that they are no more representative than is Miss Elizabeth [*sic*] Lutyens of our own abilities'. Only Rawsthorne's *Cortèges*, vividly described by

---

[23] Doctor, 'Intersecting Circles', p. 104.
[24] Alan Rawsthorne – Appendix.
[25] Lutyens, *Goldfish Bowl*, pp. 167–168.

Hussey as being 'like an oasis in the general bewilderness', provided the right note of English sobriety, it would seem. 'Until the Society can bring within its embrace more composers of a similar sanity and accomplishment', Hussey seethed, 'it might be better to leave its mysteries to the private enjoyment of the initiates'.

Hussey's fear that the ISCM was driving Music (with a capital M) into the hands of esoteric coteries was probably directed at Clark, and it is likely that some of the hostility Lutyens experienced at this point in her career was due in part to her association with the ISCM's Honorary Secretary. For although Clark's career was in decline by this time, his public persona, particularly as a zealous champion of the Second Viennese School, remained strong. In a letter to Williams of 1949, for example, Wellesz could refer to what he termed 'the Edward Clark Clique' and the clique's almost religious ardour for 12-note music.[26] Having now publicly backed the wrong Viennese horses, both Lutyens and Clark were effectively banished to a position well outside the boundaries of the British musical mainstream. The result, according to Lutyens, was that 'performances [of my concert music] in England grew fewer and fewer till for some twenty years they were almost non-existent'.[27]

Three Salutes to the United Nations (1941–43)
Music for the Documentary Film *Jungle Mariners* (1944)

Despite these difficulties, Lutyens proved to be a resourceful artist. Life was difficult for her during the war years and, in common with many, time for serious work was severely disrupted. Clark's talents did not extend to managing his personal finances and, with little prospect of a secure job for him in view, Lutyens soon realized that she would have to earn money to keep her family together. The two attempted to initiate some projects in 1940 – Clark hatched the idea for a new promotional organization called the Association of British Musicians, and Lutyens founded a 'Music Bureau for composing, orchestrating, arranging, copying' which briefly traded under the Shavian name of Corno & Co.[28] Both schemes proved to be unsuccessful in a London which was gradually haemorrhaging inhabitants to safer areas in the countryside. In June 1940 Lutyens accepted an offer from her older sister Lady Ursula Ridley of a temporary safe house for herself, Clark and her children at Blagdon Hall, the ancestral Northumberland home of the Ridley family.[29] The extended family gathering proved to be too claustrophobic for all involved, however, and Lutyens and Clark eventually moved into a new house

[26] 'I am in disgrace with the Edward Clark Clique because I am a heretic. You are quite right, one cannot compose in an artificial manner'. Wellesz, letter to Williams, 20 October 1949 (private collection). Wellesz is referring to the fact that he had explored 12-note techniques in some of his early compositions but later came to reject the method.

[27] Lutyens, *Goldfish Bowl*, p. 168.

[28] Ibid., p. 100.

[29] Ursula married Viscount Matthew Ridley in 1924.

in High Callerton, a village close to Newcastle; they moved again to Gosforth, a suburb of Newcastle, a few months after the birth of their son Conrad in August 1941. Clark eagerly threw himself into organizing and conducting concerts (for little financial gain) for the North-East Regional Orchestra (NERO), leaving Lutyens to juggle domestic chores with three small children and a new baby. Somehow, she found time to compose *Three Salutes to the United Nations*, a tonal and overtly popular orchestral work for NERO, and two of these were broadcast by the BBC on 15 February 1945.[30] A startled William McNaught – usually one of Lutyens's most inveterate critical antagonists – was caught off-guard by her colourful Salutes:

> The movements from "Salute" by Elizabeth [*sic*] Lutyens seemed to tell of a broadening and humanising on the part of a composer whose music used to move round in a rather small and cerebral circle. Tunes, shameless tunes, were in the air (a little awkward at times, as if the new mode took some getting hold of); and the shape and growth of the movements spoke more eloquently of an innate gift of composition than the rather narrowly stylised pieces that first brought the name of Lutyens into music.[31]

The *Three Salutes* was one of several light orchestral works Lutyens composed during the 1940s. Shameless tunes can also be found, for example, in the orchestral suite *En Voyage* (1944) and the extrovert overture *Proud City* (1945) – both composed during the Blitz; another fine example of Lutyens's tonal style can also be found in the satirical *Nine Stevie Smith Songs* (1948), composed for the singer and actress Hedli Anderson.[32] Patriotic feelings may well have been the inspiration for some of these works, and Lutyens's ears were also no doubt tuned to the BBC's wartime policy of favouring accessible music to soothe its listeners' jangled nerves. The main pressure, however, must have been financial. Creatively frustrated and exhausted by gas masks and insect-infested air raid shelters, she suffered a nervous breakdown in the winter of 1942. After a difficult period of recuperation, she returned to London permanently in 1943 in order to rebuild a professional career.

For reasons both economic and social, Lutyens was drawn to the London pub society of musicians and writers associated with the BBC in the 1940s; the large amount of incidental music she wrote for radio at this time was commissioned either by the BBC's Drama and Features Departments or, after 1946, by the

---

[30] The two Salutes were performed by the BBC Symphony Orchestra, conducted by Clarence Raybould.

[31] W. McNaught, 'Broadcast Music: Music of the Shires', *The Listener* (22 February 1945). The three Salutes are scored for orchestra (nos. 1 and 2) and for tenor, chorus and orchestra (no. 3, with a text by Milton).

[32] Britten and William Alwyn also wrote songs for Anderson. She married Louis MacNeice in 1942.

Third Programme. Most of the initial ideas for the radio plays at this time were dreamt up over several drinks in *The George* pub in Great Titchfield Street – known as 'The Gluepot' because musicians tended to get stuck there. Located just around the corner from BBC Broadcasting House, old friends such as Lambert, Rawsthorne, Dylan Thomas, Stevie Smith, Louis MacNeice and George Orwell were all familiar figures here, as were BBC radio producers such as 'Bertie' (W.R.) Rogers and 'Reggie' (F.R.) Smith. To a certain extent, Lutyens revelled in the raucous, heavy drinking and smoking culture of so-called 'Fitzrovian' life, with its scurrilous limericks and obscene songs, but found *The George* to be a distracting work environment. Indeed, when she collaborated with Louis MacNeice on the radio play *Enter Caesar* in 1946 (the first of over a hundred radio jobs for the BBC), she found that discussions about the project were fuelled by stupefying amounts of alcohol. While she enjoyed being in regular contact with writers such as MacNeice and Dylan Thomas, she admitted that 'the continual steady drinking involved gradually (with my naturally light head) transformed me into an alcoholic'.[33]

A couple of developments heralded an improvement in her circumstances. Her friend William Walton generously provided her with her first substantial commission (£100 for a concert work of her choosing) and also introduced her to Muir Mathieson, the musical director of a number of film companies. Mathieson offered Lutyens some small jobs and in 1944 she was asked by the film director Basil Wright to write the music for a documentary called *Jungle Mariners* produced by the Crown Film Unit.[34] Lasting 15 minutes in length, this propaganda film is a depiction of the dangers facing eight Royal Marines on jungle patrol in the South East Asia Command. It is 'a war of nerves and terror in the jungle', warns the film's narrator, 'but the cool logic of life must be argued out'. Lutyens's score valiantly follows the soldiers into the Burmese jungle, accompanying their confrontations with bloodsucking leeches, friendly natives and enemy Japanese soldiers. In the opening sequence, a pseudo-oriental melody in D flat major with a 6/8 pastoral lilt accompanies a scene where the marines are seen calmly brewing nice cups of tea in an uncivilized jungle (Example 3.3).

There are a few colourful moments in the film. A theme with a march-like rhythm on the side drum heightens the sense of drama as the soldiers venture into enemy-occupied territory in one of their night patrols, but the first sighting of the Japanese is marked by silence. An armoury of percussion instruments is then deployed to highlight the incidents which follow, including cymbal clashes for exploding grenades and drums for gunfire. The autograph manuscript also records a scene of carnage.[35] The music has been strictly patrolled by sequence

---

[33] Lutyens, *Goldfish Bowl*, p. 169.

[34] Other British composers who wrote music for documentary propaganda films for the Crown Unit during the 1940s included Vaughan Williams, Victor Hely-Hutchinson and Gordon Jacob.

[35] *Jungle Mariners* film score. British Library, Lutyens Collection, BL Add. 64752.

titles and exact timings, conspicuously marked in red pen throughout. Musical sequences have been crudely butchered and numerous insertions, alterations and transformations have been stitched in to ensure that the music is precisely synchronised with the images. The end result was convincing enough. Writing in *Tempo* (September 1946), Ernest Irving reported that he had heard 'some very effective music by Elisabeth Lutyens accompanying our troops through the Burmese Jungle (the music, not Miss Lutyens) which achieved the desired Oriental effect without the use of Ketèlbey clichés. This young lady has ideas and should be watched', he concluded.

Example 3.3 *Jungle Mariners*, introduction theme

Source: Reproduced by kind permission of the Estate of Elisabeth Lutyens.

Having survived the rigorous editing processes in *Jungle Mariners*, Lutyens went on to provide scores for numerous public information films produced by the Crown Film Unit, British Transport Films and Pathé in the following years. She was also approached to write music for feature films. Her first break came in 1948 when she wrote the music for *Penny and the Pownall Case* (Rank), and she later provided the soundtrack for horror films such as *Never Take Sweets from a Stranger* (Hammer Film Productions, 1960), *The Earth Dies Screaming* (Lippert Films, 1965), *The Skull* (Amicus Productions, 1965) and the offbeat sex thriller *My Nights with Susan, Sandra, Olga and Julie* (Scorpio Film Productions, 1975).[36] She approached the writing of film scores with professionalism and a hardheaded understanding of what the film world required from a composer. It was an industry not an art, and film music had to be 'written not only quickly but with the presumption that it will be only heard once', Lutyens stated. 'Its impact must be immediate. One does not grow gradually to love or understand a film score like a string quartet'.[37] While she was always at pains to keep her film work separate from her 'own' compositions, some skills were transferable. The discipline of having to meet extremely tight deadlines improved her general fluency and she later came to feel that the discipline of writing film music greatly enhanced her technique as a whole. A red line was, however, clearly drawn. She was furious, for example, when, after having turned some of the music in *Jungle Mariners* into a suite of orchestral dances, the suite was then selected for performance by Boult and the BBC Symphony Orchestra at one of the 1947 Proms concerts. 'After my last Prom piece under Henry Wood in 1940 and all the works I had written in the intervening seven years, a light suite was hardly representative', she protested.[38]

Interestingly, while 12-note music continued to be regarded with hostility by conservatives in Britain, Lutyens was finding a more sympathetic audience for her work in France at this time. In 1946 she attended a concert of her works in Paris organized by the British Council, and during her visit she met the 12-note composer René Leibowitz, his pupil Serge Nigg and 'a brilliant young French boy' called Pierre Boulez. As she recalled, 'among the young composers in Paris, 12-tone music was, by then, completely accepted so that I lost the sense of utter isolation I had felt in musical England'.[39] The connection with Leibowitz proved to be fruitful. He organized an International Festival of Contemporary Chamber Music in January 1947 during which works by a number of serial composers from different countries (including Lutyens) were performed, as well as pieces by Schoenberg, Webern and Berg. Humphrey Searle (1915–82) was the only other British composer to be featured at this festival. Following studies at Oxford and the Royal College, Searle had studied with Webern in Vienna and first used 12-note

---

[36] I am grateful to Ursula Vaughan Williams for drawing my attention to the existence of this last film.
[37] Lutyens, *Goldfish Bowl*, p. 171.
[38] Ibid., pp. 179–180.
[39] Ibid., p. 165.

technique in his work in the late 1940s. He was frequently paired with Lutyens in discussions about serialism in Britain at this time:[40] Walton affectionately nicknamed them 'the Twelve-Tone Reds'.

O Saisons, O Châteaux!, Op. 13 (1946)

The piece which perhaps should have been included in the 1947 Proms season, and one which certainly would have been more representative, was Lutyens's setting of Rimbaud's ecstatic poem *O Saisons, O Châteaux!* for soprano, mandolin, guitar, harp, solo violin and string orchestra. Completed in 1946, this cantata was commissioned by Gerald Cooper for inclusion in his series of Wigmore Hall concerts, and was premiered in February 1947 by Margaret Hyde-White (soprano) and the Kathleen Merritt String Orchestra, conducted by Violet Merritt. Music came before words in this instance in that Lutyens had already conceived the soundscape of the entire work while still searching for the right words. 'I was hearing a soprano voice', she recalled, 'in a soaring lyrical lament, supported by all variety of string sounds – like an enlarged, amplified guitar'.[41] A chance meeting in a London pub with the writer and literary critic John Davenport brought her frantic search for suitable words to an end. Indeed, it was Davenport who suggested that Rimbaud's vivid and concise poem might prove to be the perfect counterpart to her musical imagery.

O Saisons is one of Lutyens's most powerful and memorable works, a dramatic vocal elegy which is sustained by iridescent string writing of remarkable quality. The work opens quietly with an ascending seventh in the upper register of the first violins. Sustained notes in the violins are joined in ceremonial succession by entries from all the other instruments, creating an accumulative and intense body of sound built from the prime note row of the work. After this dramatic initial statement, an extended instrumental section (I) begins in which the note series (in transposed, inverted and retrograde forms) is presented in different combinations of instruments and textures. The soprano's first entry, an impassioned statement of the prime note row, traces the ascending seventh heard at the opening of the work:

---

[40] Searle also encountered suspicion from sections of the musical establishment because of his affiliations with 12-note music. When he applied for a job at the Royal College in 1949, for example, he was given the minor post of deputy teacher (as opposed to staff member) because the College authorities feared that he might taint the students with ideas about atonality and 12-note music. See Chapter 11 of *Quadrille with a Raven: Memoirs by Humphrey Searle*, available at http://www.musicweb-international.com/searle/lesley.htm.

[41] Lutyens, *Goldfish Bowl*, p. 168.

Example 3.4 *O Saisons, O Châteaux!*, soprano entry

Example 3.4 continued

Source: Copyright © Mills Music Limited, a Division of Alfred Music Publishing Co., Inc. All rights reserved. Reproduced by permission.

It has been suggested that the scoring of *O Saisons* may have been partly inspired by Britten's 1939 setting of Rimbaud's *Les Illuminations* for high voice and strings[42] – although there is certainly nothing Brittenish about Lutyens's music. Yet there is something Bergian about *O Saisons*, particularly in relation to its essentially dramatic gestures, its emotional intensity and occasional tonal inflexions. The work is governed by arch-like, palindromic structures, devices which frequently occurs in the music of both Berg and Webern. The 20 bars or so during which the soprano sings the first seven lines of Rimbaud's poem form the central part (II) of a palindrome. This central section is followed by another instrumental section (III) of some 30 bars in which some of the material first encountered in the first instrumental section I is presented (using contrasting textures) in retrograde. A dramatic section (IV) follows in which the soprano sings the final seven lines of the poem. The piece is brought to a conclusion by a return to source in the final bars when the soprano quietly sings the incantatory phrase 'o saisons, o châteaux!' incorporating the distinctive ascending seventh.

Despite being warmly received at its premiere in February 1947, *O Saisons* failed to secure a broadcast for many years, prompting Lutyens to fear that she had been placed on a BBC blacklist. Indeed, each time Margaret Field-Hyde, the original soprano soloist, attempted to raise the issue of a broadcast with the BBC music department, she was told – somewhat bizarrely – that the work's 'compass made it unsingable'.[43] The Rimbaud cantata may well have been a little too radical

---

[42] Tenant-Flowers, 'The Music of Elisabeth Lutyens', p. 165. The use of mandolin, guitar and harp also suggests that Lutyens may have been familiar with Webern's inclusion of these instruments in his *Five Pieces for Orchestra*, Op. 10 (1911–13).

[43] Lutyens, *Goldfish Bowl*, pp. 177–178.

for BBC tastes at this time but Lutyens's fears of being blacklisted were not entirely justified. Some of her serious concert works did receive broadcasts in the immediate post-war years. She was one of the featured composers, for example, in the Third Programme's 'Contemporary British Composers' series. This series was devised and produced by Searle, who was at the time working as a programme planner for the BBC, and the programme on Lutyens (broadcast on 16 November 1947) included the broadcast premieres of the First Chamber Concerto, the *Five Intermezzi* for piano (1941–42), the *Partita* for two violins and the String Trio.

The Pit, Op. 14 (1947)
Requiem for the Living, Op. 16 (1948)

In that same year, the premiere of the concert version of Lutyens's chamber opera *The Pit* for tenor and bass soloists, women's chorus and orchestra – her response to Walton's £100 'commission' – was broadcast from the Wigmore Hall.[44] *The Pit* is a portrait of a colliery disaster where two men and a boy become trapped underground. Cut off from their rescuers, one of the men (bass) dies, and the father (tenor) and son (non-singer role) confront their fears and prepare for death. The subject had a particular relevance for Lutyens as she had become aware of the intolerable working conditions of miners when she had lived in Northumberland during the war. The suffering of the miners and their families touched a raw nerve in her and Walton's generous offer allowed her to focus on a substantial project worthy of the theme.

The timing and form of this ambitious project was interesting. It was widely accepted at the beginning of the twentieth century that – in spite of the example of Purcell – British opera did not possess a substantial and sustained tradition. Germany could produce Wagner and could boast an opera house in any one of its major cities and towns, but Britain lacked the national operatic institutions to nurture the natural talents of its composers. The operas of English composers such as Thomas Arne (1710–78) and, in the twentieth century, Joseph Holbrooke (1878–1958) – nicknamed 'the Cockney Wagner' – enjoyed popularity and interest from the public in their day, but their operas did not join the *Don Giovanni*s or *Rigoletto*s that were regularly performed at The

---

[44] *The Pit* was performed on 18 May 1947 by Parry Jones (tenor), Norman Allin (bass), the Dorian Singers and the Philharmonia Orchestra, conducted by Edward Clark, as part of a concert presented by the London Contemporary Music Centre. The other works in the programme were Messiaen's *Trois petites liturgies de la Présence Divine* for women's chorus, piano (performed by Yvonne Loriod), ondes martenot (performed by Ginette Martenot), celesta, percussion and strings, Serge Nigg's *Variations* for piano and ten instruments and Henri Sauguet's *La voyante* for soprano and orchestra.

Royal Opera, Covent Garden.[45] In 1945, however, the spectacular national and international public attention ignited by the premiere of Britten's *Peter Grimes* created something of a new dawn for British opera. *Grimes* was followed in July 1946 by the Glyndebourne premiere of Britten's chamber opera *The Rape of Lucretia*, and the extraordinary level of interest generated by these works encouraged other British composers. Eager to explore chamber opera on her own terms, Lutyens asked Dylan Thomas to write a libretto for her – she had recently worked with him on several radio programmes – but he never quite managed to put pen to paper, despite a £50 advance. She then turned to the Belfast poet and BBC producer Bertie Rogers who promptly provided her with the requested libretto.[46]

Both *The Pit* (1947) and the *Requiem for the Living* (1948) for soprano, alto, tenor and bass soloists, mixed chorus and full orchestra, step back from the advanced idiom encountered in *O Saisons* or the First Chamber Concerto. Indeed, the contrast between the laconic, Webernesque gestures in the Concerto and the expressive, but occasionally flabby, phrases in the opera and the *Requiem* (both of which incorporate quasi-tonal material) is marked. Unlike *O Saisons*, the overall forms of *The Pit* and the *Requiem* seem to be very much determined by the texts – Lutyens provided her own words for the *Requiem* – and the scoring in both cases is effective although conventional. Both works, however, represented an advance in the sense that they were the composer's first serious attempt since the early 1930s at writing for larger vocal/choral and orchestral forces. Furthermore, both were designed to be public statements of relevance to their time.[47] The *Requiem* is a work which in a span of some 15 minutes moves from the darkness of war-torn chaos to light and peace: 'And let all that lives be free from pain and sorrow', sings the baritone in the 'Benedictus' (no. 12), 'and let the future's children inherit peace and plenty'. Structure continues to be a core preoccupation for Lutyens here. The chorus refrain (to the words 'breathe in us, life, and breathing let us live') recurs at key points throughout (Example 3.5), and two orchestral sections of similar material (nos. 4 and 7, both entitled 'Confutatis') are used to frame key choral and orchestral sections (no. 5 'Tuba mirum' and no. 6 'Recordare'):

---

[45] The exceptions here were the operettas of Gilbert and Sullivan and ballad opera – particularly John Gay's *The Beggar's Opera* (1728). Both forms were popular with the British public.

[46] The BBC recorded a recitation of Rogers's libretto in April 1947, performed by Dylan Thomas and Reggie Smith, although it seems that this recording was never broadcast. See NSA Cat. No. T11900WR.

[47] Lutyens's biographers have suggested that there are similarities in conception and scale between the *Requiem* and Tippett's oratorio *A Child of Our Time* (1938): Harries, *A Pilgrim Soul*, p. 137. The *Requiem* received its first broadcast performance on 30 September 1952 when it was performed by Margaret Rees (soprano), Maud Baker (alto), Emlyn Bebb (tenor), Stanley Riley (bass), the BBC Chorus and the London Philharmonic Orchestra, conducted by Raymond Agoult.

Example 3.5 *Requiem for the Living*, 2 'Requiem Aeternam', chorus refrain

[Musical notation: Slow, measure 23, pp, four-part chorus (Soprano, Alto, Tenor, Bass) with text "Breathe in us, life, and breath-ing let us live" (Soprano and Alto); "Breathe, Breathe in us, life, and breath-ing let us live" (Tenor and Bass). Instruments omitted.]

Source: Reproduced by kind permission of the Estate of Elisabeth Lutyens.

Lutyens finished orchestrating the *Requiem* in hospital. In the summer of 1948, she suffered another breakdown – brought on by a toxic combination of alcoholism and worries about work, children and Clark – and was treated for depression in an asylum in Southern England. By her own account, one of her first lucid impressions after coming out of hospital was of the premiere in April 1949 of the staged version of *The Pit* at the ISCM Festival at Palermo, Sicily. The work's inclusion in the programme proved to be controversial, however. Clark had succeeded Edward Dent as President of the ISCM in 1947 and accusations of nepotism regarding the selection of works were rife in British music circles. Kenneth Wright, a BBC music producer who attended the Festival, recalled that the reception of *The Pit* in Sicily had definitely been clouded 'by the strong feelings of those who resented the inclusion of a work written by the wife of the Society's President'. In addition, 'the general consensus on it, although acknowledging the interest of the subject, was very luke-warm except for the usual group of devotees of 12-tone music'.[48] Returning to England after the Festival, Lutyens was once again besieged by financial worries – Clark's position as ISCM President was unpaid – and she quickly sought further 'hack' work. In 1949 alone, she worked on eight scores for BBC radio, many of which were produced by Reggie Smith, but wrote little serious music in the next few years. As she recalled, 'I was living through a period of great uncertainty and difficulty which made concentration on my own work almost impossible'.[49]

---

[48] Kenneth Wright, Internal BBC Memo, 30 July 1951 [BBC WAC: Lutyens, Composer, 1940–62]. Reproduced by permission of the BBC Written Archives.

[49] Lutyens, *Goldfish Bowl*, p. 194.

These difficult personal and professional circumstances had a constraining impact on her musical development. The composer Anthony Payne has pointed out that her Third String Quartet, written in 1949, revealed that her style had advanced little over earlier works, despite ten years of using the 12-note method. As he stated, 'rhythmical and textural procedures are identical, and one feels that the composer had been forced by her isolated position to continue by self-contemplation' (*The Listener*, 9 January 1969). With the exception of a vigorous, seven-movement *Concertante*, completed in 1950 and written for the *Pierrot Lunaire* combination of seven instruments (five players), Lutyens admitted that the majority of pieces composed at this time were 'feeble and later scrapped, including two *String Quartets*, a *Lyric piece for Viola and Orchestra* and other bits and pieces'.[50] She continued with her commercial work but it was not until the winter of 1952/53 that she made a significant breakthrough with two works – the Sixth String Quartet and what became known as the 'Wittgenstein' Motet for unaccompanied chorus.

String Quartet No. 6, Op. 25 (1952)
Motet, *Excerpta Tractati-Logico-Philosophici* (Wittgenstein), Op. 27 (1953)

The composition of the Sixth String Quartet was intimately connected to a conversation Lutyens had with the artist Francis Bacon. Regaling each other with tales of artistic life over drinks one cold December evening, Bacon told Lutyens that he always painted very quickly and very instinctively when he wanted to create something which would have a violent impact on the nerves. Excited by this description, she wrote her quartet in one 12-hour sitting, totally immersed in the task at hand. The result is a work of fire and ice, one which exhibits a degree of clarity which had not really been attained in previous quartets. Conceived as a single movement tripartite structure, a central *Adagio* is framed by an impassioned first section and its reprise within a span of about eight minutes. The string writing is adventurous – the individual parts possess a bold independence – and there is, in general, a greater sense of assurance and focus in the writing. The treatment of the note row is interesting and economical. In the opening bars of the tautly argued *Allegro moderato* section ('Primo'), for example, the instruments play the notes of the prime row (P0), and this material is then reflected back on itself in retrograde (R0). Statements of the row in inversion (I0) and retrograde inversion (RI0) follow, leading to a varied restatement of the prime row.

---

[50] Ibid., p. 201.

Example 3.6 String Quartet No. 6, Primo

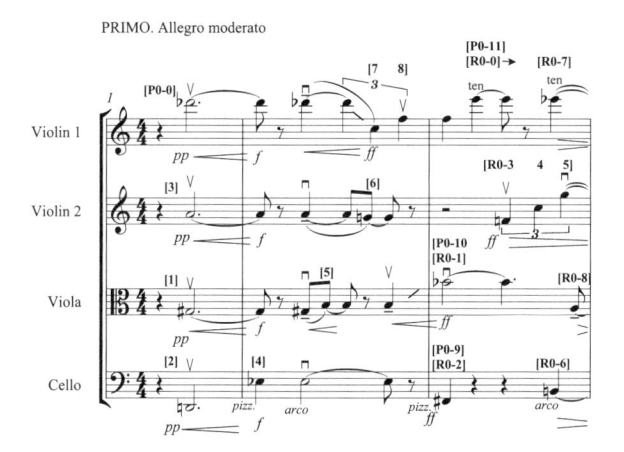

Example 3.6 continued

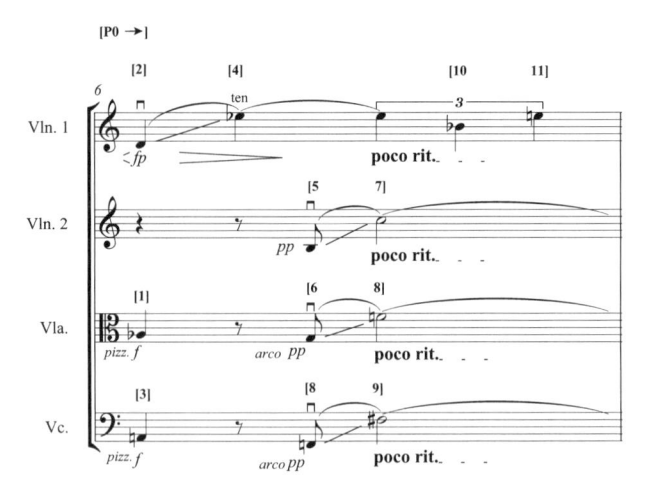

Source: Copyright © 1952 (Renewed) Belwin-Mills Publishing Corp., a Division of Alfred Music Publishing Co., Inc. All rights reserved. Reproduced by permission.

The argument intensifies as the instruments explore forms of the rows in this movement, their fiery and mercurial debate strengthened by the use of a number of distinctive triplet and semiquaver rhythms. In contrast, the temperature cools in the *Adagio* ('Secondo'), where a variety of different transposed rows are used to create a sculpted soundscape, played *senza espressione* (without expression).

Example 3.7 String Quartet No. 6, Secondo

Source: Copyright © 1952 (Renewed) Belwin-Mills Publishing Corp., a Division of Alfred Music Publishing Co., Inc. All rights reserved. Reproduced by permission.

Lutyens's interest in creating objective musical structures was further developed in her Motet, *Excerpta Tractati-Logico-Philosophici* (Wittgenstein), a piece for unaccompanied chorus commissioned by William Glock for the 1954 Dartington Summer School of Music.[51] As with the Rimbaud cantata, music came before words in the motet, the sounds and shapes of the work already crystallizing in Lutyens's mind before she discovered a suitable verse. In search of 'something accurate and impersonal but *not* religious', she mentioned her words dilemma to Clark and the poet and BBC producer Terence Tiller, and they both suggested that she might consider Wittgenstein's philosophical treatise. 'From the first glance [of the *Tractatus*]', she recalled, 'I knew I had found what I wanted, the words and ideas being ideally suited to the already furmulated sound and architecture of the music in my mind'.[52]

Wittgenstein's *Tractatus* (1921) takes the form of seven principal propositions, each consisting of a series of numbered, logically argued statements that are concerned with the logical form of reality and our relationship with the world. According to Wittgenstein, 'the world is the totality of facts' (1.1).[53] A fact is constructed from atomic facts, and an 'atomic fact is a combination of objects' (2.01), and these constituent parts (which in totality make up the world) are linked together in a logical sequence. In order to represent the logical form of the world accurately, Wittgenstein argued, it is necessary to analyse the way in which language works. Language (in its ideal form) also obeys rules of logical formation. Linguistic propositions give expression to facts and create pictures of the world. Propositions can be broken down into their atomic constituent parts and, in this sense, 'the proposition *shows* the logical form of reality' (4.121). If language can be seen to reflect the world, it follows that the ability to describe the world is constrained by the limits of our language. Wittgenstein believed that there were some things that lay beyond the limits of language (death, spirituality, aesthetics and ethics, for example) and concluded his treatise with the enigmatic proposition 'whereof one cannot speak, thereof one must remain silent' (7).

Lutyens extracted 30 statements (from a total of 526) from the *Tractatus* for her Motet text, for the most part preserving the original numbering of the selected propositions. She had originally attempted to set the text in English but,

---

[51] Glock was the founding director of the Music Summer School at Dartington. He invited Lutyens to lecture at the school in 1953.

[52] Lutyens, *Goldfish Bowl*, p. 222.

[53] All quotations from the *Tractatus* are taken from the English translation by David F. Pears and Brian F. McGuinness (London: Routledge, 1961) as presented in the printed score of the Motet (London: Schott Music, 1965). The above summary of the *Tractatus* is intended only as an outline which has relevance to the extracts Lutyens uses in her Motet. Wittgenstein's argument is complex and addresses specific problems within the discipline of philosophy. It is also notoriously difficult to grasp, partly because of its abstract nature but also because it assumes a knowledge of the mathematical model of logic (logical atomism) of Gottlieb Frege and Bertrand Russell.

having failed to find a translation which was also singable, eventually decided to set the original German. Whereas symmetry had played an important formal role in previous works, in the Motet it became a core compositional feature of the basic material. The final hexachord of the prime note row is itself a transposed retrograde of the first hexachord, for example, and the interval sequence of the complete row is palindromic:[54]

Example 3.8 Motet Prime Row with Interval Sequence[55]

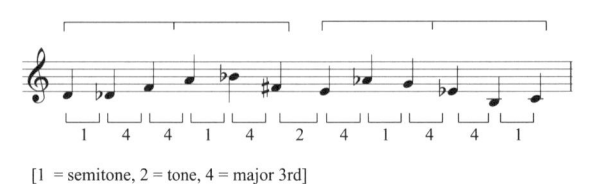

[1 = semitone, 2 = tone, 4 = major 3rd]

By dividing her series into smaller, 'atomic' segments – particularly, hexachords and trichords – Lutyens increases the number of combinatorial possibilities. Such closely integrated basic musical material ensures that the series and its permutations contain many common elements (pitch patterns and intervals) which have the effect of intensifying the overall cohesion of the piece.[56] Furthermore, Lutyens employs contrasting textures replete with palindromes, canons and other contrapuntal forms in this musical realization of Wittgenstein's ideas. The craftsmanship involved in this inventive work is apparent in the opening bars, where some of the key characteristics – such as the emphasis on the hexachord and trichord – are presented. The work opens with the alto's statement of the first hexachord of the prime row, with the second hexachord (presented in retrograde) in the tenor line. These statements are followed by entries in the bass (first hexachord presented as two reordered trichords) and soprano (second hexachord, similarly reordered):

---

[54] A number of Webern's works use derived series, including the Concerto.

[55] The British Library's collection of Lutyens's manuscripts includes her own notated series for the Motet (BL Add. 64789). For a detailed analysis of the Motet, see Laurel Parsons, 'Music and Text in Lutyens's Wittgenstein Motet', *Canadian University Music Review / Revue de musique des universtés canadiennes* 20/1 (1999), p. 85. See also Catherine Roma's discussion of the Motet in Roma, *The Choral Music of Twentieth-Century Women Composers: Elisabeth Lutyens, Elizabeth Maconchy, and Thea Musgrave* (Lanham, MA: Scarecrow Press, 2006), pp. 26–37.

[56] Parsons has described the series as a whole as being 'constituted from a number of musical objects nested within one another and linked by various types of relationships'. Parsons, 'Music and Text in Lutyens's Wittgenstein Motet', p. 86.

Example 3.9 *Excerpta Tractati-Logico-Philosophici*, opening

The world is everything that is the case.
The world is the totality of the facts.
(English Translation by David Pears and Brian McGuiness as reprinted in the score)

Source: Reproduced by kind permission of Schott Music Ltd., London. All rights reserved.

The Motet is one of Lutyens's most economical and rigorously argued pieces, and demonstrates the composer's mastery of modern vocal polyphony. The piece was well received at its premiere in 1954 and was largely responsible for igniting the surge of interest in Lutyens's work in the late 1950s.[57] Glock, the work's dedicatee, later applauded the piece for having achieved an ideal 'balance between its impersonal aspect and its illustrative aspect', and memorably described the music

---

[57] The Motet was premiered by the London Chamber Singers, conducted by Anthony Bernard, at Dartington in August 1954.

as being 'a kind of geometry answering to Wittgenstein's philosophical thought'.[58] Although the Motet's musical significance was recognized, its demanding technical requirements placed it beyond the capabilities of most choirs at this time. Fortunately, the ensuing years witnessed the founding of several professional choirs in Britain which were able to tackle more technically challenging works. In 1962, for instance, the English conductor John Alldis formed a choir from a group of hand-picked, professional singers, and his choir gave the first broadcast performance of the Motet at a BBC Invitation Concert in December 1963. Several more performances and broadcasts followed and the piece was later recorded for the *Argo* label. Alldis was fascinated by the 'lucidity and beauty' of the Motet, and felt the work to be 'a marvellous example of [the] perfect relationship of text and music'.[59] In turn, Lutyens paid Alldis one of the best compliments a performer could have from a composer when she stated that his choir's performance of her Motet was 'as I wrote it'.[60]

Lutyens's transformation from diffident, would-be modernist to pioneering leader of 12-note music during the 1940s and early 50s in Britain had been an arduous and bitter battle. But her own personal use of the method, forged in remarkable works such as *O Saisons, O Châteaux!*, the Sixth String Quartet and the 'Wittgenstein' Motet, brought a distinctive note of conviction to her music. During the war years when recognition of her serious music was negligible, she had succeeded in successfully establishing herself as a composer of music for film and radio. By the early 1950s, however, she began to win some acknowledgement as a ground-breaking force. She gained entry into the hallowed tomes of *Grove's Dictionary* for the first time in 1954 – at the age of 48 – an indication that attitudes towards her work were beginning to change. 'Lutyens has been a pioneer of twelve-note music in England', *Grove* stated, and 'her music commands a high regard among musicians for its integrity, its expressive power and the highly imaginative variety of its conceptions and invention'.[61] The beginning of Lutyens's professional career had been unpromising but she was now becoming mistress of the situation.

---

[58] Glock, 'A Tribute to Elisabeth Lutyens', script of a Radio 3 broadcast of 15 December 1983 [BL Add. 71114, fol. 220].

[59] Alldis, 'Modern Choral Music', *Composer* 33 (Autumn 1969), p. 11.

[60] Lutyens, 'Composer's Portrait' (BBC Third Network, 23 February 1966) [NSA Cat. No. M748R C1].

[61] Colin Mason, 'Elisabeth Lutyens' in *Grove's Dictionary*, ed. Eric Blom (London, 1954), vol. v, p. 448.

Chapter 4
Maconchy: An Impassioned Argument

While Lutyens had lived in a musical no-man's-land in the early years of her career, Maconchy's reputation as one of the most promising British younger composers had continued to flourish. Her music was regularly performed throughout the 1930s both at home and abroad – an entire concert of her chamber music was presented in Krakow in 1937, for example, and performances of her work took place in Budapest, Brussels, Paris, Warsaw, Düsseldorf and Lausanne. Furthermore, at the age of 33, she was one of the few younger British composers (along with Berkeley, Britten and Tippett) to be thought noteworthy enough to merit a couple of columns in the 1940 edition of *Grove's Dictionary*. 'Her artistic creed', *Grove* noted, 'is that music exists for discourse ... and that its method should therefore be in essence contrapuntal'.[1]

The interest in her work enabled Maconchy to settle some old scores. She had been snubbed by the publishers Boosey & Hawkes in the early 1930s when they had refused to consider publishing anything substantial by her on the basis that she was young and female. In 1939, however, came the opportunity to enlighten sceptics. A carefully worded paragraph in the 'Notes and News' section of *The Musical Times* (May 1939) informed readers that Maconchy had decided 'to work in close collaboration with a publisher', and had 'appointed Mr. Max Hinrischen [founder of Hinrischen Edition Ltd.] as her business representative'. Fittingly, one of the first of her pieces to be issued in print by Hinrischen Edition was her formidably bullish Third String Quartet (1938).

It is interesting that although Maconchy had first come into the public eye with a series of high-profile performances of orchestral works such as the Piano Concertino and the suite *The Land*, she had already come to regard the three string quartets she had written up to this point as being her most characteristic works. Composing for a full symphony orchestra offered a composer unlimited possibilities in terms of individual timbre and instrumental blends, but a piece written for four string instruments, four 'individuals', presented different challenges. Maconchy later spoke about her fascination with the string quartet genre:

> I have found the string quartet above all best suited to the expression of the kind of music I want to write – music as an impassioned argument ...

---

[1] Frank Hauser, 'Elizabeth Maconchy' in *Grove's Dictionary*, ed. H.C. Colles (London, 1940) supplementary vol., p. 411.

Dramatic and emotional tension is created by means of counterpoint in much the same way as happens in a play. The characters are established as individuals, each with his own differentiated characteristics: the drama then grows from the interplay of these characters – the clash of their ideas and the way in which they react upon each other.

Thus in a string quartet one has the perfect vehicle for dramatic expression of this sort: four characters engaged in statement and comment, passionate argument, digression, restatement, perhaps final agreement – the solution of the problem.[2]

String Quartet No. 2 (1936)
String Quartet No. 3 (1938)

A comparison of the first three quartets reveals the significant musical distance travelled by Maconchy during the 1930s. Her Second and Third Quartets contain several new features which point towards her mature style and reveal that she underwent a profound rethinking of her whole approach to quartet writing at this time. Contrapuntal textures had featured in her youthful First Quartet (1933), but here the composer had kept counterpoint in its place within the four, relatively independent, movements of the work. The tone and texture of the Second Quartet, however, is strikingly different from that of its younger, high-spirited sibling: in the composer's own words, 'the exuberant energy of the first quartet has given way to a very different kind of work – no less intense, but much more inward, more searching'.[3]

Completed in 1936, the Second Quartet was premiered by the Brosa Quartet at a Macnaghten–Lemare concert in London on 1 February 1937 and went on to be performed by the same group at the 1937 ISCM Festival in Paris – subsequently earning the Haydnesque subtitle of 'the Paris' Quartet.[4] The seriousness of tone and dense contrapuntal textures in this piece seem strongly allied to a desire on Maconchy's part for greater musical integration.[5] The intense *Lento* first movement was her first attempt at creating a monothematic movement and its powerful and compelling argument grows from the quiet viola melody heard in

---

[2] Maconchy, 'The Composer Speaks' (Radio 3, 17 October 1971).

[3] Maconchy, note to String Quartet No. 2, taken from booklet accompanying the CD collection 'Elizabeth Maconchy: Complete String Quartets 1–13' performed by the Hanson, Bingham and Mistry Quartets (Regis Records / Forum, FRC 9301).

[4] The work's premiere received extensive coverage in the press. The *Telegraph*'s review, for example, had the headline 'Notable New Work: Elizabeth Maconchy's Second Quartet' (2 February 1937).

[5] The obvious model for Maconchy here and in subsequent quartets was surely Beethoven: she described his late quartets as being for her 'the very essence of great quartet-writing' (Maconchy, 'The Composer Speaks').

the opening bars. Characteristically, this expressive melody is built from close intervals of tones and semitones, and these intervals are used, as in the music of Bartók, as essential building blocks for the movement. Although the movement can be said to be based around the tonal centre of G, the music is contrapuntal in concept and as such does not follow a formal structure based on key, a feature underlined by the absence of key signatures. While the ensuing scherzo (*Poco presto*), slow movement (*Lento sostenuto*) and *Allegro* finale are closely related, each having their thematic origin in the first movement (see Example 4.1), the only tangible sense of tonal resolution comes in the finale; even then, the music is 'C-centred' rather than being definitively in the key of either C major or C minor. These last three movements are played without a break, a directive which again reveals the composer's concern for movement integration and consideration of the entire shape of the work.

Example 4.1 String Quartet No. 2, opening themes from movements I, II, III and IV

Example 4.1 continued

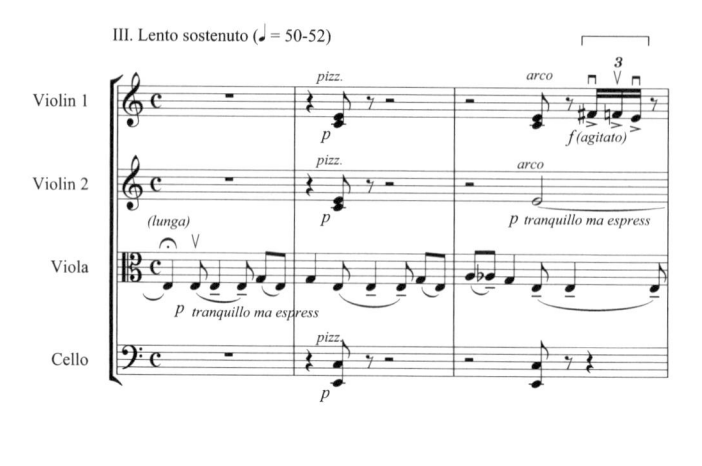

Maconchy's treatment of rhythm in this work is another new feature. Syncopated, pungent rhythms had always featured strongly in her music, but she was now beginning to develop what she described as 'a counterpoint of rhythms' to complement the interweaving of melodic lines. As she explained:

> To crowd new and extraneous notes into existing harmonies may perhaps add a certain colour, but it does not represent any real development. On the other hand the several threads of the music moving in melodic lines can coalesce vertically to create a new harmonic interest. A counterpoint of rhythm exists side by side with melodic counterpoint. By the free movement of several rhythms simultaneously we can hope for more rhythmic development than by any amount of experiment with monodic rhythms.[6]

The Second Quartet contains a number of rhythmic themes which are, during the course of the work, subjected to modification; they appear in augmented, diminished or varied form and are often presented simultaneously. The finale, in particular, includes several animated passages where the instruments engage in what the

---

[6] Maconchy, quoted in Macnaghten, 'Elizabeth Maconchy', *Musical Times* (June 1955), p. 299.

composer described as 'a cross-fire of rhythmic and melodic counterpoints'.[7] This tendency for interlacing rhythmic and melodic ideas is established in the opening movement. Although this movement is dominated by the rhythm of its opening theme, Maconchy develops a palette of variants which are ingeniously used to shape moments of tension and repose. A moment of high tension is reached, for instance, when the original rhythmic theme (a/ in viola and cello) is stated with a diminished variant (b/ in violins):

Example 4.2 String Quartet No. 2, I

Source: Copyright © Alfred Lengnick & Co. Ltd. Reproduced by permission of the publisher.

---

[7] Maconchy, note to String Quartet No. 2. See, for example, bars 42–56 of the finale.

Interestingly, this whole movement is governed by a method of tempo control which outlines a gradual process of intensification and deceleration. The opening *Molto lento* section, for example, has a metronome mark of ♩ = c. 48 ('Tempo 1'), but the pace quickens to ♩ = c. 60 ('Tempo 2') in the ensuing *Lento* passage. After a central *più mosso* section (♩ = c. 86), the pace slows to Tempo 2 (♩ = 60), and the movement ends with a return to the *Molto lento* tempo (♩ = 48) that opened the work. Composers such as Debussy, Ravel and Stravinsky had each sought and achieved a greater degree of rhythmic flexibility in their pieces – at least, in relation to nineteenth-century models – but Maconchy's approach seems to point to another source. Indeed, the control of tempi, the rhythms which avoid regular pulse and the volatile levels of expressive tension in the Second Quartet hint at a special kinship with the music of Berg, even though there is no attempt here at 12-note thinking.

Curiously, the rigorous and concentrated nature of Maconchy's writing prompted some commentators to suggest that the piece was lacking in contrast, a criticism which was often levelled at her works of this period. In the *Monthly Musical Record* (July–August 1938), for example, Frank Howes criticized her generally for creating textures which were 'perhaps, too consistently compact', adding that 'she does not easily relax into the lyrical feeling which Beethoven concentrated into his slow movements and Schubert spilled all over his chamber music'. He went on to discuss the quartet's slow movement, noting that it was 'not song-like but agitated and passionate – a splendid movement but offering no respite to the intense development of the implications of the interval of a second on which her themes are based'. The slow movement is certainly agitated in character – the conflict between its broad melodic lines and brief *agitato* fragments (see Example 4.1, III) recalls, if anything, Janáček's use of such contrasts in his quartets – but Howes seems here to have misunderstood the underlying compositional ethos of this work. Although moments of repose exist, Maconchy's taut integration of the four-movement form is furthered by an overall intensification of mood which is essentially *dramatic* in character. Had she chosen to include a more intimate, song-like slow movement, it would have diluted the work's argument.

The concern for close integration exhibited in the Second Quartet leads naturally to the organic, one movement cyclic form of the Third Quartet, a work which was premiered in October 1938 by the New Hungarian String Quartet at a London Contemporary Music Centre concert at the Cowdray Hall, London.[8] The concentrated nature of the writing is present, as is the dramatic impetus, but here Maconchy allows lighter and more lyrical textures to emerge when teasing out the

---

[8] The (New) Hungarian String Quartet was founded in Budapest in 1935 and became internationally renowned for performances of Beethoven and Bartók. The original members were Sándor Végh (violin 1), Péter Szervánsky (violin 2), Dénes Koromzay (viola) and Vilmos Palotai (cello). In 1937 Zoltán Székely became the new leader with Végh taking on the position of 2nd violin.

potential of the work's central musical ideas. These core ideas – in particular, the major–minor harmonic ambiguity, and the interval of semitone/major seventh – are presented in the work's opening bars:

Example 4.3 String Quartet No. 3, opening

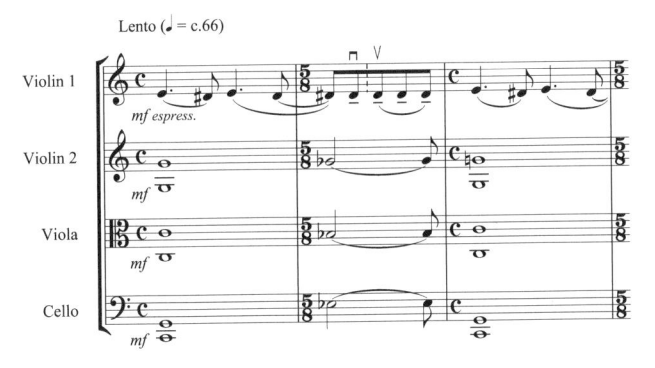

Source: Copyright © Alfred Lengnick & Co. Ltd. Reproduced by permission of the publisher.

While the quartet basks in its thematic single-mindedness, Maconchy achieves variety in her argument by throwing fresh light on her ideas. The contrast between the intense, bittersweet tone of the *Lento*, for instance, and the infectiously playful mood of the ensuing *Presto* section, with its *glissandi* and flashes of humour, is well conceived. The high spirits of the *Presto* give way to an expansive *Andante* section (song-like, this time) before returning for a second time, and the music builds to a restatement of the opening material before reaching the end of its journey in a quiet, reflective coda. Williams wrote to Maconchy after hearing the quartet:

> This is just to say that a second hearing confirmed my impression that Quartet no. 3 is one of your best works if not the best. Apart from its being the real

> stuff of music, & making a lovely sound, it is your most mature work (Dorrie [Gow] agrees with me, too) & is really first-rate quartet writing ... It is grand when a modern work gives one the same sort of wholesome complete feeling that one gets from listening to Mozart or any of the others. But oh what a rare experience![9]

The Third Quartet had been written for (and premiered by) the New Hungarian Quartet but was quickly taken up by other ensembles. The piece caught the ear of the English violinist and conductor Harry Blech and he proposed to include it in concerts given by his quartet in the early 1940s.[10] Unfortunately, these plans were severely affected by the advent of war. Maconchy was in Ireland staying with relatives at the time of the declaration of war in September 1939, and was heavily pregnant with her first child Elizabeth Anna (born in October 1939). Unsure as to what the outcome would be, the family remained in Ireland for a time but returned to Seal Chart, Kent in the spring of 1940. In September of that year, Maconchy wrote a letter to her sister Sheila revealing how the war was beginning to have an impact on her professional life.

> [D]omestic jobs, & gardening ... & 1st Aid lectures & practices keep me quite busy, & I get some work done too. I was to have had my 3rd quartet played at the National Gallery concert to-day – but the viola of the [Blech] quartet was called up for his training as a pilot in the RAF 2 days ago, which was rather sad – but I hope they will do it later on. – I had a preliminary rehearsal of my 'Dialogue' with the orchestra (at Queen's Hall) early in August. The pianist Clifford Curzon is <u>excellent</u> – couldn't be better – and he likes the work very much. The orchestra read it pretty badly – but I think when it has had 2 proper rehearsals it will be allright [*sic*]. It's on Sept 26th – none of the Proms are being broadcast, as you know, which is a pity.[11]

Although the Blech Quartet's National Gallery concert on 4 September 1940 had to be cancelled, a hastily reorganized concert given by the Hirsch Quartet (with a programme that did not include Maconchy's Third Quartet) did take place on that date. The omission of Maconchy's quartet was duly noted by *The Times*, but the critic reported that the Hirsch concert was interrupted by air raid sirens

---

[9] Williams, postcard to Maconchy, 9 October 1938 (private collection). See *The Correspondence between Elizabeth Maconchy and Grace Williams 1927–77*, eds J. Doctor and S. Fuller (Farnham: Ashgate, forthcoming).

[10] The Blech String Quartet was formed by Harry Blech (leader) in 1933 with David Martin (violin 2), Frederick Riddle (viola) and Willem de Mont (cello).

[11] Maconchy, letter to Sheila Maconchy, 4 September 1940 (private collection). Sheila was living in Switzerland at this time. She had contracted tuberculosis at around the same time as Maconchy but, unlike her older sister, had opted to go to Switzerland in search of a cure.

'in B flat' and that players and audience were swiftly ushered to a pre-prepared safe room in the Gallery's basement.[12] Three days later, the full onslaught of the London Blitz brought Sir Henry Wood's 46th Proms season to an abrupt halt, together with the prospect of the premiere of Maconchy's *Dialogue* for piano and orchestra. Wood did not forget about her, however. Her *Dialogue* – a conversation piece between piano and orchestra rather than a concerto – was premiered at the Proms in the Royal Albert Hall on 16 July 1942 by the pianist Clifford Curzon and the London Philharmonic Orchestra, conducted by Basil Cameron.[13] Maconchy came down to London from Shropshire for the premiere. She and her family had been living in Kent in 1940, but in the first few months of 1941 William LeFanu had been charged with overseeing the evacuation of the entire contents of the Royal College of Surgeons' library in London to the safer rural haven of Ludlow in Shropshire. The family was based in England–Wales border country until the end of the war, with Maconchy travelling to attend performances of her works whenever possible.

String Quartet No. 4 (1942–43)

One of the surprising things about Maconchy was the way in which she managed to be as devoted to her family as she was to her music. Composition is a selfish pursuit which demands hours of solitude, and to be able to combine it with being wife, mother, cook and gardener requires boundless energy and skill. The domestic side of Maconchy amused her friends. 'Here was this composer writing this very fiery and exciting music, and yet, she also made jam and bottled fruit and that sort of thing', Ann Macnaghten recalled. 'And I remember her saying that … "if you're a nursing mother, you have to learn to compose between feeds"'.[14]

During the initial years of motherhood and the war, a new quartet, intricate and sinewy in shape and form, began to emerge 'between feeds'. All the musical

---

[12] 'Borodin and the Sirens', *The Times*, 5 September 1940. 'Sirens in B flat *portamento* added an obbligato to the Nocturne of Borodin's string quartet, which the Hirsch Quartet played at the National Gallery yesterday … To hear [the Borodin] was a consolation for missing a quartet by Elizabeth Maconchy which had been announced for performance by the Blech Quartet. Circumstances compelled a change, but we hope to hear Miss Maconchy's third quartet soon'.

[13] The original home of the Proms, the Queen's Hall, was bombed in May 1941, and in that year the Proms moved to its now familiar home, the Royal Albert Hall. In the 1942 Proms season the performances were shared by two orchestras: the London Philharmonic Orchestra (from 27 June to 24 July) and the BBC Symphony Orchestra (from 25 July to 22 August). Henry Wood appointed Cameron as his full-time conducting associate for the Proms in 1940. For further details, see Nicholas Kenyon, *The BBC Symphony Orchestra 1930–1980* (London: BBC, 1981), p. 180.

[14] Macnaghten in 'Elizabeth Maconchy: A Video Portrait' (Channel 4).

characteristics which were present in the previous quartets can be found in the Fourth String Quartet – the taut contrapuntal writing, the preoccupation with themes which use close intervals, and the dramatic and often surprising contrasts within sections – but there is now an even greater concentration in the musical language. Indeed, although the four-movement quartet is succinct (lasting for around quarter of an hour in duration), a great deal of musical terrain is covered in this time, so much so that the impression is of a much more expansive time scale. The serpentine chromatic theme in the cello stated quietly at the opening is the original source.

Example 4.4 String Quartet No. 4, opening

Source: Copyright © Alfred Lengnick & Co. Ltd. Reproduced by permission of the publisher.

The dramatic impetus of each of the four movements is perfectly judged. In the first movement, where two intensely chromatic *Allegro* sections surround a *Lento appassionato* middle section, much of the contrapuntal and harmonic interest focuses on exploring and developing the intervallic and motivic relationships initially stated in the main cello theme. Rhythm and metre also have critical parts to play, as initially suggested by the characteristic fluctuating 5/4, 3/4 metre heard at the work's opening. Rarely flamboyant in expression, the development of the musical material, particularly in some of the more chromatic passages, has a diamond-edged precision about it, with not a note straying out of place. Its motivic structure is a maze of inversion and retrograde patterns, and is established at the outset – the viola entry (bars 4–6), for example, is an inversion of the first bar of the cello theme (see Example 4.4). Interestingly, while this is by no means 12-note music, the use of integrative motivic cells suggests a thorough working knowledge of the method. Maconchy was, indeed, exploring 12-note technique at around this time but, like Britten and Tippett, stopped short of embracing the method as a whole.[15] Already enthralled with the challenge of creating an entire work from one basic idea, or a group of ideas, she felt that strict serial method could only reinforce that tendency whereas what was needed were techniques which would perhaps liberate her in other directions. As she explained, 'I was already an economical composer and for me [the strict use of 12-tone technique] seemed thematically to be an inhibiting rather than a liberating technique, though where tonality and atonality is concerned it has certainly helped me to [develop] a greater freedom'.[16]

The Fourth Quartet is an excellent embodiment of Maconchy's belief that the form of a given work should grow organically from ideas that are unique to a particular work, and all aspects of the quartet can be understood in relation to the pursuit of greater integration. The main theme of the scherzo second movement, for instance, is related to the first movement main theme, and grows, as Maconchy notes, 'directly from the closing notes of the first movement: forthright crotchets are now transformed into extremely fast quavers in 6/8'.[17] Themes from later movements are also derived from the same source.

The ensuing *Lento* movement is a particularly vivid illustration of the composer's idea of the four string instruments as equal partners in an 'impassioned argument'. At the opening, fervent exchanges between first and second violin – rhythmically strong and played with force – are quietly answered by undulating triplets in the viola, the temperature rising as the musical lines lengthen and rhythmic debates intensify. The clash of s*zforzandi* notes, *forte-piano* chords and heavily accented motifs deepens the agitated tone as the music builds dramatically to a series of firecracker climaxes before a reprise of the movement's opening is heard. In contrast, the *Presto* finale (played without a break) sizzles with wit, and diatonic sections (of distinctly Mediterranean colour) are ingeniously weaved with darker chromatic passages.[18] Characteristically, the work ends, as the composer puts it, 'with a bang not a whimper'.

Example 4.5 String Quartet No. 4, themes from II, III and IV

[15] Nicola LeFanu recalled seeing a 1930s textbook on the 12-note method in her mother's study.
[16] Maconchy, 'Composer's Portrait' (BBC Third Programme, June 1966).
[17] Maconchy, notes to String Quartet No. 4, 'Complete String Quartets' CD. All other quotes relating to this quartet are taken from this source, unless otherwise indicated.
[18] Maconchy spoke of the diatonic pizzicato passage (*Meno mosso*) as being suggestive of 'a *sérénade interrompue*', a reference perhaps to Debussy's highly spiced evocation of Spain in 'La sérénade interrompue', Prelude Nine from the first book of *Preludes*.

Example 4.5 continued

Source: Copyright © Alfred Lengnick & Co. Ltd. Reproduced by permission of the publisher.

'They made it sound "grimmer" than it <u>need</u>', Maconchy confided to her sister after the Blech Quartet's European broadcast of the Fourth Quartet in June 1943. 'I wanted much more gaiety in the 2nd and 4th movements – it was all too careful and painstaking and they didn't let themselves go'.[19] Such remarks help

---

[19] Maconchy, letter to Sheila Maconchy, 23 June 1943 (private collection).

to draw attention to an important although often overlooked side of Maconchy's musical personality. Reviews of her music written at this time tended to stress the uncompromising, intellectually vigorous nature of her writing, but failed to mention the wry wit which energized some of her scores. Several of her string quartets contain humorous episodes – the *pizzicato* passage in the finale of the Fifth Quartet, for instance – these elements often serving to diffuse tension, but her gift for expressing lighter moods was also evident in other works. Her *Variations on a Well-known Theme* (1942), written to mark the occasion of Vaughan Williams's 70th birthday, was deliberately conceived as a good-humoured piece. She was one of seven composers – the others were Gordon Jacob, Constant Lambert, Edmund Rubbra, Gerald Finzi, Robin Milford and Patrick Hadley – to be invited by Arthur Bliss, the then Director of Music at the BBC, to write a musical tribute for 'Uncle Ralph's' birthday concert on 12 October 1942. 'It will be a frightfully funny concert, won't it?' Maconchy joked to her sister. 'The others (except Constant Lambert) are all a bit "village pump" – so I must at all costs avoid that'.[20]

In some respects, it is rather remarkable that the *Variations* and the Fourth String Quartet were performed at all given the severe restrictions placed on musical life in war-torn, rationed Britain – a point not missed by the press. 'It takes more than a war to destroy an English tradition', the *Times* critic wrote in May 1943, before adding that 'music in the metropolis has the same function to perform for the national well-being of the art as the hub has for the wheel'. His review of two London chamber concerts (one which had included Britten's First String Quartet, and the other, Maconchy's Fourth String Quartet) was held up as evidence of the plucky British spirit. The bearings might have been damaged, but British composers (namely, Britten and Maconchy) had continued to compose in the face of adversity. Patriotic attitudes notwithstanding, the war created enormous challenges for Maconchy. Stranded in Ludlow she continued to compose, but the separation from friends and other musicians, and the alarming lack of performances of her music, contributed to an attack of depression she experienced at this time. In December 1943 Williams wrote to Kenneth Wright at the BBC voicing concerns about her friend's situation:

Dear Ken,

A word about Betty ... For the last few months her letters have shown that she is terribly depressed about composing. She has never shown any signs of losing heart before – but now she does sound very down-hearted and writes things like "I think that perhaps I am finished as a composer" which isn't a bit like her, but hardly to be wondered at when you consider how consistent the neglect of her music has been ever since war began. A composer just can't carry on indefinitely without contact with players and performances. You know what I think about her

---

[20] Maconchy, letter to Sheila Maconchy, 19 May 1942, ibid.

things and I <u>know</u> I'm right and others will hear them with my ears some day – but don't let it be too late.[21]

Wright responded by asking Williams whether he could show her letter to Bliss, the BBC's Director of Music. He also told her that Vaughan Williams had independently voiced similar concerns about Maconchy to the BBC and that Bliss had resolved to do something about the matter. Unfortunately, events rather took their own course. Bliss resigned from his post in the spring of 1944 in order to concentrate on his composition, and his replacement Victor Hely-Hutchinson hardly had time to get his feet under the desk before London was, once again, under siege – from Hitler's flying 'Doodlebug' bombs. Although the 1944 Proms season from London was temporarily halted on 29 June, the BBC Symphony Orchestra was able to broadcast some of the remaining concerts from their wartime base in Bedford.[22] One of their broadcasts on 5 August 1944 featured an orchestral suite by Maconchy which she had adapted in the previous year from music she had written for the ballet *Puck Fair* (1939–40).[23] Significantly, this piece's inclusion in the Proms was probably the result of Vaughan Williams's efforts on behalf of his former pupil. He wrote to her in February 1944:

> I do feel it very hard that you do not get your stuff done – Have you anything new you could send in to the proms? If so let me know *at once* & I will write to [Wood] …
>
> I fear we must confess that you are not popular – I know though theoretically that is a very noble aspiration practically, it is galling.

---

[21] Williams, letter to Kenneth Wright, undated but 30 December 1943 [BBC WAC, Registry Services Central 1: Williams, Composer, 1939–49].

[22] Following the outbreak of war, the BBC took steps to implement its emergency broadcast plans by moving its major departments out of London. The BBC Symphony Orchestra was moved to Bristol in September 1939 from where it continued to give concerts and broadcasts. Following a series of air raids on the city in the summer and winter of 1940, however, the orchestra was moved to a new, safer base in Bedford (from July 1941), where it remained until the end of the war. See Kenyon, *The BBC Symphony Orchestra*, pp. 155–191.

[23] The ballet was inspired by the traditional Irish 'Puck Fair', an annual street festival held in Killorglin, County Kerry. The music (originally scored for two pianos) was written for the Irish Ballet Club's premiere of the work on 9 February 1941 at the Gaiety Theatre, Dublin. With a script by F.R. Higgins, the ballet was choreographed by Cepta Cullen with sets designed by Mainie Jellett.

> But dearest Betty, you are still young – I was about 30 before I ever heard a *song* of mine done in public ... so push on and one day perhaps the key will turn in the lock.[24]

Maconchy would have been approaching her 37th birthday (19 March) when she read these kind words. Sustained by her own resolve and the support of close friends, she did indeed 'push on', composing, among other things, a three-movement Concertino for Clarinet and Strings in 1945. She also started work on a new Symphony. But the war years marked a particularly low point in Maconchy's professional life.[25] After the end of the war, she and her husband followed the library of the Royal School of Surgeons back to South-East England. Their cottage in Kent had been bombed during the war, so the family moved to Wickham Bishops in Essex.[26]

Concertino for Clarinet and String Orchestra (1945)
Symphony (1945–48)

Maconchy's fortunes improved after the war. The launch of the BBC's pioneering Third Programme in 1946 created new broadcasting opportunities for British composers, and her work began to be taken up again by the contemporary music organizations that had championed her prior to the war.[27] Her Concertino for Clarinet and Strings, for example, her earliest work for the clarinet, was premiered by the renowned English clarinettist Frederick Thurston at the 1947 ISCM Festival in Copenhagen, and received its British premiere broadcast (again, by Thurston) on the Third Programme in November of that year. Maconchy was unable to attend the premiere because she was heavily pregnant (with her second child, Nicola) but was in frequent contact with Thurston before the event. She made him a piano reduction, and he asked his former clarinet pupil Thea King, who was also acting as accompanist for his clarinet classes at the Royal College of Music at this time, to help him learn the piece. 'We went to down to her cottage in Essex to play it to her', recalled King, 'which was a *big* honour for me

---

[24] Vaughan Williams, letter to Maconchy, 18 February 1944, as quoted in Doctor, 'Working for her own Salvation', p. 199.

[25] On a personal note, Maconchy also lost her younger sister Sheila to tuberculosis early in 1945.

[26] I am grateful to Nicola LeFanu for providing me with these details.

[27] The Third Programme was launched on 29 September 1946 (joining the existing BBC national radio networks of the Home Service and the Light Programme) and became the BBC's principal cultural and artistic network. The Third concentrated on broadcasting a wide range of classical music concerts (including specially commissioned works from contemporary composers), plays, poetry readings and talks with leading authors and intellectuals. It was replaced in 1970 by BBC Radio 3.

– to be allowed to meet a real composer'. 'This thing was fiendishly difficult', King noted. It had 'the most awkward runs in it that didn't obey any patterns of major or minor scales or anything, and going up to ferociously difficult high notes which other people didn't write for'. Thurston and King, both celebrated champions of modern British clarinet music, felt that Maconchy was one of the most continentally influenced British composers of the day. 'She did have a feeling for Vaughan Williams', observed King, 'but she was also very interested in Bartók and Messiaen, people that were not so fashionable at the time'.[28] King's memorable encounter with the Concertino and its composer was one of the reasons she, many years later, asked Maconchy to write a new clarinet piece for her, the *Fantasia* for clarinet and piano (1980).[29]

Maconchy's Symphony was composed between the years 1945 and 1948, and it seems significant that she should dedicate it to Vaughan Williams, particularly in the light of his faith and encouragement. In turn, it was Vaughan Williams who persuaded the BBC to give the first performance and broadcast of the Symphony in April 1950.[30] Although the premiere was generally well received, several critics found the work to be forceful and too highly concentrated in terms of both scoring and content. The 'heavily scored symphony ... suggested violence rather than strength' to one critic (*Daily Telegraph*, 28 April 1950), and *The Times* wondered whether 'the time had not arrived, now the composer has come to symphony, for a little relaxation and expansion?' (29 April 1950). *The Listener*'s Dyneley Hussey proposed that 'it sounded like an extraction of all the more forceful passages in the later music of Vaughan Williams', before concluding that 'in the light of this work and of Miss Lutyens' latest Quartet, no one can accuse women composers of being weak, soft, yielding creatures!' (4 May 1950).[31] On a more serious note, however, Vaughan Williams told Maconchy that he had found her Symphony to be 'a little

---

[28]   Thea King, 'Mining the Archive. Time Remembered (3)' (Radio 3, 8 March 1996) [NSA Cat. No. H6675/1]. Maconchy may well have encountered Messiaen's music as early as 1938. She had attended the 1938 ISCM Festival in London where Messiaen performed two movements of his *La Nativité du Seigneur* (1935).

[29]   The *Fantasia* for clarinet and piano (1980) was commissioned by Thea King with funds provided by the Arts Council of Great Britain, and was premiered by King on 12 August 1980 at the International Clarinet Congress in Denver, Colorado.

[30]   Vaughan Williams persuaded the BBC to broadcast a concert of 'new or unknown' pieces (the concert presented by the London Contemporary Music Centre and performed by the BBC Symphony Orchestra, conducted by Adrian Boult, took place at the BBC's Maida Vale Studio on 27 April 1950), and suggested that Maconchy's Symphony should form part of the programme. For further details see Doctor, 'Working for her own Salvation', p. 200.

[31]   Hussey's comments about women composers may well have been influenced by his review of a recent broadcast of Lutyens's Third String Quartet (*The Listener*, 29 April 1950).

too hectic all the way through'.[32] Maconchy seems to have taken her teacher's misgivings to heart and took the decision to withdraw the piece.

Sonnet Sequence (1946–47)
A Winter's Tale (1949)

Interestingly, several vocal works that Maconchy composed at this time reveal that she was writing music of great lyrical range. In 1946 the London concert promoter Gerald Cooper had asked her to write a piece for one of his series of chamber concerts at the Wigmore Hall; he had also commissioned Lutyens's *O Saisons, O Châteaux!* for the same series. Maconchy's response was the elegant *Sonnet Sequence* for soprano and nine instruments, to poems by Kenneth Gee. The work was premiered by Joan Cross (soprano) and players from the Kathleen Merritt String Orchestra on 29 April 1947 – two months after the premiere of Lutyens's *O Saisons* – and so enthralled the audience that it had to be performed twice at the concert.[33] The work is a blend of lyric and dramatic impulses and very much brings Maconchy's innate flair for vocal writing to the fore (see Example 4.6). The poems form a sequence of brief yet contrasting meditations on the seasons and the different stages of life (beginning with winter/old age and moving to summer/youth). Each poem makes striking use of natural imagery and, although obvious use of word-painting is avoided, the emotional intensity of the poetic imagery is captured by music of rousing poignancy.

Maconchy's only other setting of a Kenneth Gee poem was one which the poet dedicated to her. *A Winter's Tale* for soprano and string quartet was completed in 1949 and begins by evoking a winter landscape with a girl standing under a tree in the snow. She remembers her lover who has left her and her feelings are as frozen as the landscape; later, she seems to hear his voice and with it winter melts into spring. The piece remained unperformed for ten years, but was eventually premiered in January 1959 by the soprano April Cantelo and the Amici String Quartet on the Third Programme. 'It is incredible that so attractive a work has not attracted performers until this fortunate occasion', exclaimed Scott Goddard in his *Listener* review (29 January 1959). In fact, the lengthy delay in broadcasting this piece was largely due to the fact that it had been rejected by the BBC's music reading panel in 1950; the chief objection had apparently been the choice of poem.[34] The reading panel had been established in 1934 to review new pieces submitted to the

---

[32] Vaughan Williams, quoted in Doctor, 'Working for her own salvation', p. 200.

[33] Although the piece was originally scored for soprano and nine instruments (flute, oboe, clarinet, bassoon, 2 violins, viola, cello and double bass), Maconchy created another version for soprano and string orchestra. This version was premiered at the Cooper concert in 1947.

[34] See Peter Crossley-Holland internal BBC memo to Richard Howgill, Controller of Music, 30 November 1954 [BBC WAC, RCONT1: Maconchy, Composer, 1951–58].

BBC for broadcast, and had come to be regarded by many established composers as something of an occupational hazard. In the early 1950s, several reputable British composers, including Maconchy, voiced their exasperation about the panel system, arguing that their music was being kept off the air. The BBC listened and, much to her relief, Maconchy was placed on a new BBC list of 'panel-free' composers in 1953. In the following year she attempted to persuade the music department to broadcast *A Winter's Tale*, and this time her request was met with a more positive response.

Example 4.6 *Sonnet Sequence* (piano reduction), opening

Source: Music reproduced by kind permission of the Estate of Elizabeth Maconchy. Music by Elizabeth Maconchy. Words by Kenneth Gee.

String Quartet No. 5 (1948)
String Quartet No. 6 (1950)

The instrumental work which can arguably be said to have most fully achieved a perfect balance between expansive lyricism and taut musical argument is the Fifth String Quartet. The quartet was written in 1948 while Maconchy was staying with relatives in Ireland, and was premiered by the Hurwitz String Quartet at a London Contemporary Music Centre concert in April 1949; the piece also won the Edwin Evans Prize for Composition in the same year. As with Maconchy's other quartets, integration and the concept of thematic and motivic transformation are fundamental to this piece, but a greater contrast is achieved both between and within the four movements, resulting in a work of remarkable individuality.

The quartet opens with a slow ponderous four-part canon which, as the composer notes, 'influences the character of the whole work'.[35] The canon theme comprises several important motivic ideas, the most dominant of which is the interval of a semitone outlined in the cello's first three notes. The theme sparks off the warm, continuously evolving melodic and rhythmic debate between the string instruments in the ensuing *Allegro* section, returning most fully in its impassioned *Lento* guise at the end of the movement. A scherzo (II) follows, its lighter mood very much determined by biting rhythms and sharp, humorous interchanges between the instruments. Again, the scherzo's main theme and its accompanying grace notes are derived from the work's opening (see Example 4.7), but the contrast in terms of mood and texture between the first two movements is well judged. The best is yet to come, however, for the slow movement (III) is a jewel of consummate beauty. Gently undulating chords in the lower strings at the movement's start become the accompaniment to an exquisite song sung by the first violin. The music gradually becomes more impassioned as the instruments reflect on the musical ideas, but the movement ends on a tranquil note with the return of the first violin's elegant song. A robust *Allegro* finale ends the work in which the finale theme (itself derived from the main theme of the first movement) is juxtaposed with the very first three notes of the piece. Williams heard the broadcast of the work's premiere in April 1949 and immediately wrote to congratulate Maconchy:

> I write before the applause has finished – it's grand to hear a manly voice shout encore & I wish [we] could have an encore & many encores of the slow mvt which is perfectly beautiful & about the best thing you've done.[36]

---

[35] Maconchy, note to String Quartet No. 5, 'Complete String Quartets' CD.
[36] Williams, letter to Maconchy, undated but April 1949 (private collection).

Example 4.7 String Quartet No. 5, excerpts from I and II

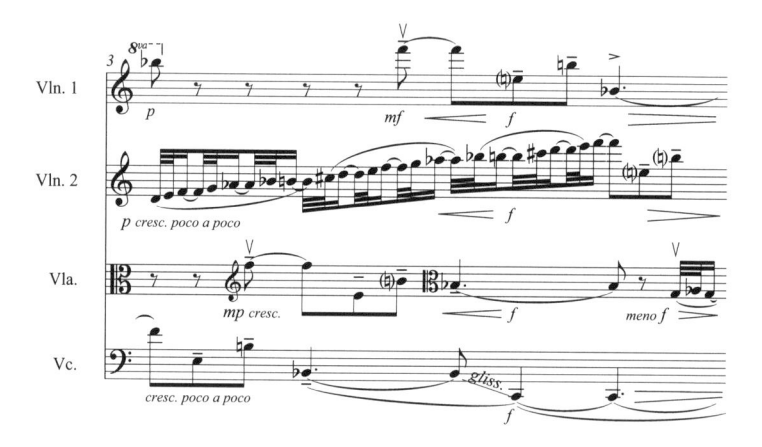

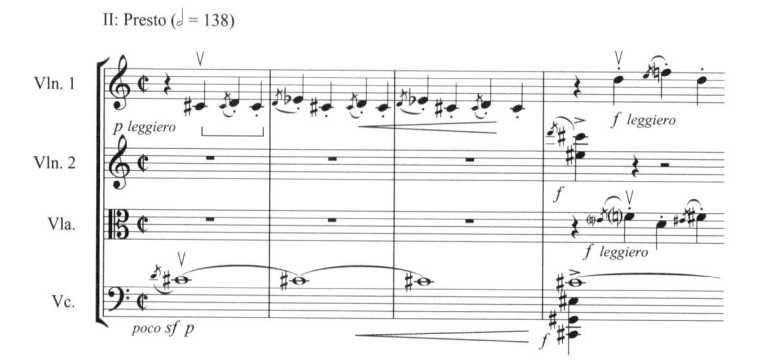

It is fascinating to note this slow movement's musical kinship with Williams's own *Sea Sketches* for string orchestra (1944), a piece which Maconchy admired. The chords used at the beginning of the quartet's slow movement, for example, are the same chords heard in the strings at the opening of the *Sea Sketches*, although the effects achieved are quite different. This intriguing correspondence suggests that the deep friendship enjoyed by these two composers could find expression, perhaps most intimately, in purely musical terms.

Example 4.8 Fifth String Quartet by Elizabeth Maconchy, III

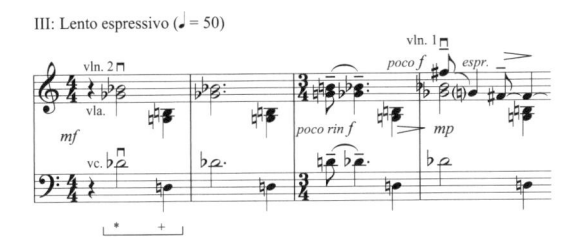

Source: Copyright © Alfred Lengnick & Co. Ltd. Reproduced by permission of the publisher.

Example 4.9 *Sea Sketches* for String Orchestra by Grace Williams, I 'High Wind', opening

Source: 'High Wind' from *Sea Sketches* for String Orchestra by Grace Williams © Oxford University Press 1951. Extract reproduced by permission. All rights reserved.

The warm, expansive lyricism of the Fifth Quartet's slow movement is rather different from the dramatic and often agitated moods encountered in most of the earlier quartets' slow movements, and indicates a move towards a more song-influenced ethos on the composer's part. This lyrical concern is found in other works Maconchy composed at this time, including the String Quartet No. 6 (1950). Although the Fifth and Sixth Quartets are different in character, their musical (thematic) kinship is close. The central idea for the Sixth Quartet is the passacaglia theme stated in the cello at the work's opening (Example 4.10).[37] Although the instruments seldom lose sight of the theme during the course of the first movement (as befits a passacaglia), their debate results in a number of striking and contrasting guises.

Example 4.10 String Quartet No. 6, I, passacaglia theme

Source: Copyright © Alfred Lengnick & Co. Ltd. Reproduced by permission of the publisher.

A robust scherzo (II) follows, its tough-minded argument sparked off by the assertive figure (derived from work's central idea) heard in the first violin. Dramatic contrast comes with the introduction of a *pizzicato* middle section in 5/8 time which builds in intensity as all the instruments gradually enter. Fragments of the violin's original dramatic motif herald a return to the mood of the opening, and the music builds to a vigorous climax. A lyrical slow movement (III) follows which, although distinct in character, recalls the mood of the *Lento* of the Fifth Quartet. The quartet ends with a potent *Allegro* (IV) during which the original passacaglia theme is gradually reintroduced and then restated by all the instruments.

Maconchy's Sixth Quartet was premiered in May 1951 by the Martin String Quartet at a Festival of Britain concert in London. It seems appropriate that this piece – which, in many respects, embodies a spirit of hope and renewed strength – should feature in a national Festival which sought to provide a much needed tonic to a drab nation as it emerged from the ravages of war. The brainchild of the Labour MP Herbert Morrison, the Festival celebrated the very best of Britain's achievements in the contemporary arts and sciences (intentionally echoing the Great Exhibition which had taken place a century before). Music was at the forefront of the celebrations. The premiere of Vaughan Williams's opera *The Pilgrim's Progress* formed part of the Festival's events, together with the

---

[37] Maconchy's use of the passacaglia form was possibly inspired by Vaughan Williams's use of the form in the finale of his Fifth Symphony.

premieres of Britten's opera *Billy Budd* and Lambert's ballet *Tiresias*. In addition, a new national concert hall, the Royal Festival Hall on London's South Bank, was specially built for the occasion and opened in May 1951. The project was managed by the London County Council (LCC) – later the Greater London Council, now the London Assembly – and, following the death of King George VI in February 1952, the LCC launched a competition for a Coronation Overture for the new Queen 'as part of London's contribution to British Music in the Coronation Year'.[38] Maconchy's majestic overture *Proud Thames* won, and the piece was premiered at a special gala concert at the Royal Festival Hall on 14 October 1953.

Proud Thames (1952–53)
Concertino for Bassoon and String Orchestra (1950)
Symphony for Double String Orchestra (1952–53)

'It is rare for the outcome of a competition to be as successful as Miss Maconchy's new overture', the *Daily Telegraph* noted (15 October 1953), while the only slight criticism of *The Times* was that this 'splendid little piece' was far 'too short – a fault as commendable as it is rare' (15 October 1953). The overture is indeed finely judged for the occasion and reveals the very public side of Maconchy's musical personality. Taking its inspiration from the journey of the River Thames from its West Country source to its full tide as London's river, the work begins quietly at first with a simple but striking trumpet motto theme, a call to attention from which the sonorous river springs to life. This river of music is tuneful, capricious and flamboyant in places as it grows in strength and complexity. Themes interweave creating a luxuriant surge of sound which gradually builds towards a final triumphant restatement of the motto theme in timpani and brass. Memories of Prague and of Smetana's *Vltava* were, no doubt, at the back of Maconchy's mind when she was writing this piece.

Around the time of writing the coronation overture, Maconchy completed two other outstanding orchestral works – the Bassoon Concertino and the Symphony for Double String Orchestra. Her exuberant Concertino for bassoon and string orchestra was written in 1950 for the bassoonist Gwydion ('Gwyd') Brooke, a principal member of the famous woodwind section, known collectively as the 'Royal Family', in Beecham's Royal Philharmonic Orchestra.[39] Brooke's musicianship and technical prowess as a bassoonist were legendary, as was his

---

[38] Announcement of the Coronation Overture Prize in *The Times*, 29 September 1952. British composers were invited to submit scores (under anonymous cover) by 1 May 1953, and the judges were Adrian Boult, Edmund Rubbra and Gerald Finzi.

[39] Other members of the RPO's 'Royal Family' included Jack Brymer (clarinet), Terence MacDonaugh (oboe) and Gerald Jackson (flute). The nickname was acquired because these principal wind players were held in great esteem by Beecham. Note that Gwydion Brooke was the son of the British composer Joseph Holbrooke.

ability to produce sounds of great expressive beauty from an instrument which was usually considered to be rather dry and eccentric. It is likely that this latter ability was the direct inspiration for the central slow movement of the Concertino – marked *Lento espressivo, intimo* – in which Maconchy freely explores the expressive range of the bassoon across its whole register (Example 4.11). In contrast, the two outer movements (*Moderato* and a *Presto giocoso* finale) are concerned with exploiting the more extrovert aspects of the instrument's range. In the opening movement, the two contrasting main themes are vigorously debated by soloist and strings, and the finale contains a witty, virtuosic cadenza for the soloist.

Example 4.11 Concertino for Bassoon and String Orchestra, II, opening

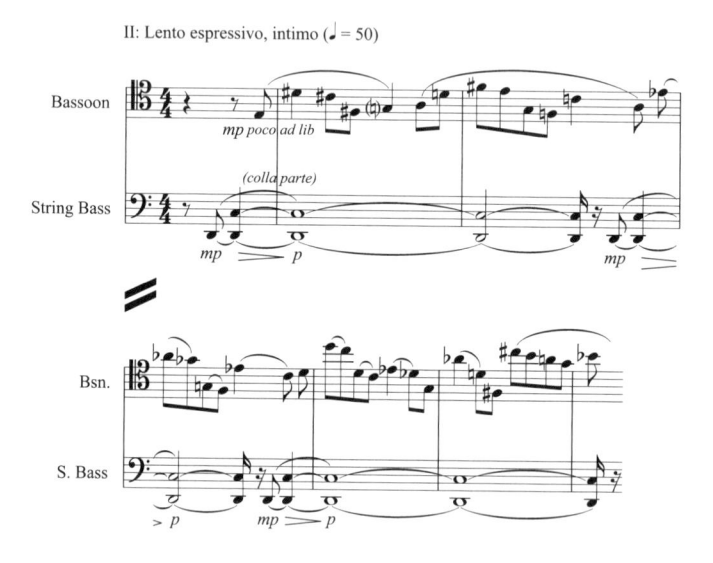

Source: Copyright © Alfred Lengnick & Co. Ltd. Reproduced by permission of the publisher.

The Bassoon Concertino may be described as a character piece, its qualities inspired by insights Maconchy had gained through exploring the bassoon's range with Brooke. In the Symphony for Double String Orchestra, however, the composer created a substantial work which fully exploited the different combinations of instruments offered by a group of massed strings. Eager to explore spatial effects in performance, Maconchy specified that the performers should be seated in a fan-like arrangement on stage. As she stated, 'the strings consist of two separate bodies, arranged in a shallow semi-circle, with the violins of each body on the wings and the double-basses meeting in the middle. Thus the two orchestras can be used antiphonally – as they mostly are – or at times as a single body'.[40] This arrangement allows for a great deal of musical debate between the orchestras but the Symphony also includes several passages for a solo violin, something which initially puzzled commentators. As Donald Mitchell noted, 'a work that pretends to the status of a symphony should avoid the merely rhapsodic or pastoral like the devil. Miss Maconchy's lavish employment of the solo violin not only introduced bouts of rhapsodizing which delayed developmental events but also weakened the work's symphonic character' (*The Musical Times*, January 1955). Keen to avoid any misunderstandings of the work's conception, and possibly to distinguish it in clear terms from Tippett's widely celebrated Concerto for Double String Orchestra (1938–39), Maconchy's defence of her piece was robust and to the point:

> I have called this work a Symphony on account of its weight and serious content, and to some extent its form, though the string writing throughout is consistently contrapuntal – (comparable perhaps to a Brandenburg Concerto) – and so does not conform to the conventional idea of a Symphony, which is harmonically, rather than contrapuntally, organised. But I felt it to be a Symphony when I was writing it, and I still do.[41]

It is tempting to think of this unconventional Symphony as being one which Maconchy might have dedicated to Vaughan Williams, although the piece bears no such dedication. His influence is not apparent on the music's surface – despite occasional glimpses of pastoral elements in the scherzo and a passacaglia finale – yet the work's warm, spacious themes and overall spirit of monumental affirmation, seem to hint at a deep connection with the master. Above all, this work reveals Maconchy's mastery of contrapuntal string writing, combining as it does dramatic, weighty argument with a sumptuous lyricism. This latter quality is captured in one of the composer's finest and most imaginative slow movements (Example 4.12), the opening of which inhabits the same magical world as the slow movement of her Fifth String Quartet.

Although the opening bars of the *Allegro* first movement and the final bars of the passacaglia finale are clearly linked by the use of a dramatic figure (see Example 4.13), thematic interrelations between the four movements are, on the whole, kept in check in order to maximise contrasts of great intensity between movements. The opulent sensuousness of the *Lento*, for instance, is in striking contrast to both the searching, angular themes of the *Allegro* first movement, and to the frenetic argument of the scherzo (III, *Allegro scherzando*) which follows. In the finale, the wistful passacaglia theme appears in a number of different musical

---

[40] Maconchy, note to Symphony for Double String Orchestra in booklet accompanying CD, 'Elizabeth Maconchy' (Lyrita, SRCD.288). The Symphony was premiered on 30 November 1954 by the Royal Philharmonic Orchestra and Walter Goehr (conductor) at the BBC's Maida Vale Studios, London.

[41] Maconchy, ibid.

contexts (including a turbulent fugue). The theme is juxtaposed with the opening phrase of the first movement in a final serene *Lento* section, bringing the work to a close on a note of optimism. 'I've just heard your String Symphony & feel convinced that it is your best orchestral work', Williams told Maconchy in March 1957. 'It's worth growing older if one can write mature music of such quality – deep & vital – more <u>profoundly</u> serious than one's earlier work can ever be'.[42]

Example 4.12 Symphony for Double String Orchestra, II

Source: Copyright © Alfred Lengnick & Co. Ltd. Reproduced by permission of the publisher.

Maconchy had chosen to develop her distinctive musical voice throughout this period mainly, although not exclusively, through the medium of chamber music, and the six string quartets she had composed up to this stage remained

---

[42] Williams, letter to Maconchy, 10 March 1957 (private collection).

Example 4.13 Symphony for Double String Orchestra:
I, opening theme and IV, opening

Source: Copyright © Alfred Lengnick & Co. Ltd. Reproduced by permission of the publisher.

her best-known works. At the beginning of her career, she had been at the very centre of the contemporary music scene, enjoying a position of considerable status in Britain and on the Continent, but during the war years performances and broadcasts of her music went into sharp decline. These were years spent in the wilderness for Maconchy. Certainly, there had been fewer opportunities for performance in general at this time, with many musicians being either called up or moving away from London, but her advanced musical idiom also fell victim to the BBC's wartime policy of favouring accessible music for most of its broadcasts.[43] Maconchy would have to endure several more years of uncertainty, but the success of works such as the prize-winning Fifth Quartet, the popular *Proud Thames* and the Symphony for Double String Orchestra enabled her to regain a foothold in the new post-war British contemporary music scene.

---

[43] For further details of the BBC's wartime policy, see Doctor, 'Intersecting Circles', pp. 104–105.

Chapter 5
Williams: To the Wild Hills

Following the outbreak of war in September 1939, Williams sent the majority of her original manuscripts to a friend in North Wales for safe keeping, and resigned from her part-time post at Southlands Training College. The Camden Girls School was evacuated from London to Uppingham, Rutland at this time, and Williams was one of the teachers accompanying pupils.[1] Conditions in Uppingham proved to be far from adequate and the school moved to Grantham, Lincolnshire within a month, remaining there for two years. After munitions factories in Grantham were bombed, the school moved again to Stamford, Lincolnshire before returning to London at the end of 1943.

Williams was profoundly disillusioned by the war – like Britten, she was a pacifist – and found the unsettling existence of being an evacuee, the demands of her teaching job and the lack of time for serious composition to be exhausting. Her spirits were lifted at the beginning of October 1939, however, when she was informed that her orchestral suite, the *Four Illustrations for the Legend of Rhiannon*, was going to be premiered on the BBC's Home Service later that month:

> I am very glad – and surprised – to hear that "Rhiannon" is to be done so soon … I am pretty certain that it will have more or less the same audience now as it would in normal times because the sort of people who listen to it are not the sort who are now indulging in all the jingoistic rubbish which is being broadcast for the greater part of the day. In fact – I should say more people will listen, because they are so starved of anything which is at all serious that they'll listen to every bar when they do get something in their own line …
>
> I don't feel that there is any real justification for anything connected with this war, because I've no faith in war settling any problems.[2]

The premiere of *Rhiannon* was achieved against the odds. The idea for the piece had come to Williams in the winter of 1938/39 when the BBC Welsh Region

---

[1] Prior to the war, government discussions had taken place concerning the evacuation of civilians from major British cities in order to avoid possible massive casualties from air raids. The evacuation of schoolchildren (code named 'Operation Pied Piper') was a major priority, and the Anderson Committee report (1938) stipulated that children should be evacuated in school parties in the care of teachers.

[2] Williams, letter to Idris Lewis (BBC Welsh Regional Director), 9 October 1939 [BBC WAC, WAI/61/2: Williams, Welsh Region Composer, 1938–41].

commissioned her to write a 20-minute orchestral suite 'on some Welsh subject', for which she was paid the princely sum of 20 guineas (£21). Several attempts by the BBC in Wales to schedule the piece during the summer of 1939 came to nothing, much to Williams's frustration. A firm date was finally set for the autumn, but in September the BBC Welsh Orchestra was disbanded because of the war. It seemed a hopeless situation but several factors now worked to Williams's advantage. In the autumn of 1939 the BBC, now reduced to a single national wavelength (the 'Home Service') as part of its emergency plans, came under fierce criticism from leading musicians because of the vast reduction in its serious music broadcasts.[3] At the same time, a number of Williams's supporters within the BBC – in particular, Kenneth Wright in the London Music Department – felt that the promised performance of *Rhiannon* should go ahead. These factors resulted in the work being broadcast from Bristol in a studio performance by the BBC Symphony Orchestra, conducted by Idris Lewis, on 24 October 1939.[4]

Rhiannon was the most ambitious orchestral piece Williams had composed up to this point. She told her friend Daniel Jones that she had found the writing of this piece to be liberating and far more satisfying than anything she had attempted before. In a fascinating and revealing comment, she also implied that the new sense of creative independence she had experienced at this time had been directly related to her waning friendship with Britten. Britten had been one of Williams's closest College friends but the two drifted apart when he went to America in 1939. When they first became friends in the 1930s, she had immediately spotted his remarkable talent – well before it was generally recognized in the musical world – and she continued to hold his work in the highest regard throughout her life. He had been an engaging and stimulating friend but she confessed that his brilliance had made her feel that her own talent was meagre by comparison. In order to forge her own independent path as a composer, it was necessary for her to move out of the long shadow he cast. As she explained to Jones:

> I learnt a lot from [Britten] – but his musical influence was too overpowering & crippling & I had a permanent inferiority complex – & when we drifted apart I sort of came into my own again & wrote Rhiannon & a few other things which were miles better than anything I'd ever done before.[5]

---

[3] See, for example, 'Music in Time of War: A Plea for Standing Fast' (*The Times*, 26 October 1939, p. 6) in which Thomas Beecham and Hugh Allen raised concerns about the state of British music-making in wartime conditions and the BBC's policy on broadcasting music.

[4] The BBC Symphony Orchestra was moved from London to Bristol in September 1939. See Chapter 4, note 23.

[5] Williams, letter to Jones, 26 February 1940 (Jones Archive, NLW). Williams would no doubt have included two other works in her 'miles better' category. Both the *Magnificat* for soprano and chamber orchestra, and the choral work *Gogonedawg Arglwydd* (Praise the Lord Eternal) were composed in 1939, and will be discussed later in this chapter.

Rhiannon draws from the early myths and folk legends of Wales for its subject. Williams was strongly attracted to the 'curious mixture of barbarism and lyricism'[6] in the *Mabinogion* story 'Pwyll, Prince of Dyfed', and it was her decision to focus on the stronger, more interesting character of his consort Rhiannon.[7] Each of the four contrasting movements in Williams's suite depicts an episode in the life of this Celtic goddess as related in the original tale. The first *Allegro* movement, for instance, is subtitled 'The Conflict', and portrays in musical terms the battle between Rhiannon's mortal suitors Pwyll, the favourite, and the wily Gwawl. Their rivalry is dramatically represented by music which is agitated in character: an *appassionato* theme in the strings driven by restless rhythms and close intervals opens the piece (Example 5.1). In contrast, the music of the second movement (*Moderato largamente*) is more festive in tone, and begins with fanfares which announce 'The Nuptial Feast' held in honour of Rhiannon and the victorious Pwyll (Example 5.2). The music vividly conjures up the sound world of some enchanting ancient pageant, demonstrating Williams's ability for capturing the essence of dramatic events in music.

Example 5.1 *Four Illustrations for the Legend of Rhiannon*,
I 'The Conflict', opening

[Some instruments omitted]

Source: Copyright © Oriana Publications Limited 2010. Reproduced by permission.

---

[6] Williams, letter to Idris Lewis, 22 January 1939 [BBC WAC, WAI/61/2: Williams, Welsh Region Composer, 1938–41].

[7] See the *Mabinogion* – Appendix.

Example 5.2 *Four Illustrations for the Legend of Rhiannon*,
II 'The Nuptial Feast', fanfare theme

Source: Copyright © Oriana Publications Limited 2010. Reproduced by permission.

The royal couple have a son, Pryderi, but on the night of his birth the infant vanishes. Fearing for their lives, Rhiannon's servants accuse her of killing her baby. Williams uses the slow, doleful Welsh hymn tune *Yr Hen Ddarbi* (The Old Derby, Example 5.3) as the main theme of the third movement to illustrate 'The Penance' (III) Rhiannon undertakes for her assumed crime: she is forced to relate her story to all. It transpires, however, that the baby was snatched by a demon which is later killed by Teirion, Prince of Gwent. The child is cared for by Teirion and his wife but they eventually come to recognize his likeness to Pwyll. The *Allegro* finale portrays the dramatic 'Return of Pryderi' (IV) to his real parents, and opens strikingly with a quiet statement in the celesta of the movement's main theme, the traditional Welsh tune *Cainc Dafydd Broffwyd* (David the Prophet's Air), accompanied only by a triangle (Example 5.4).

Example 5.3 *Four Illustrations for the Legend of Rhiannon*,
III, *Hen Ddarbi* theme

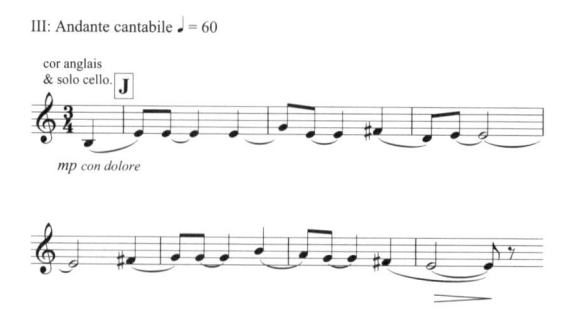

Source: Copyright © Oriana Publications Limited 2010. Reproduced by permission.

Example 5.4 *Four Illustrations for the Legend of Rhiannon*,
   IV, *Cainc Dafydd Broffwyd* theme

Source: Copyright © Oriana Publications Limited 2010. Reproduced by permission.

Rhiannon was one of the first pieces by Williams to receive a national broadcast – previously, her works had been broadcast mainly on the BBC's Welsh Regional wavelength. The work attracted several press notices after its premiere, and one of the more perceptive reviews was penned by the scholar and critic Jack Westrup (*The Listener*, 2 November 1939). After complaining about the 'mass of music written by lesser English composers today which is nothing but a pale reflection of Vaughan Williams', Westrup noted:

> It was pleasant on Tuesday to hear a new work that fitted into no ready-made category – Grace Williams' Symphonic Legend "Rhiannon" – which was well-written and thoroughly confident music. It illustrated, however, how the absence of a national opera can frustrate the natural talents of composers. This work was not really symphonic at all; it was stage music in the concert hall.

Westrup's recognition of Williams's potential for writing opera would, in time, prove to be entirely accurate, but it was her intrinsic (and rare) gift as a musical dramatist, her ability to characterize and to shape dramatic events in sound, that marked her out at this stage of her career. Although Williams honoured the BBC's request for an orchestral suite, the piece took on a distinctly symphonic shape during the process of composition: 'The Nuptial Feast' may be said to correspond to a scherzo, for instance, and 'The Penance' to a slow movement. But *Rhiannon* is neither a symphony nor a suite (nor is it stage music, for that matter), and its stubborn reluctance to fit into any convenient mould may partly explain Williams's indecision over the title. She initially called the work *Symphonic Suite, Rhiannon* when composing it but changed the title to *Symphonic Legend, Rhiannon* for the 1939 premiere. The title was again changed to *Legend for Orchestra, Rhiannon* when a revised version of the work was performed on 27 May 1943 by the BBC Northern Orchestra, conducted by Mansel Thomas, but in subsequent performances the piece became *Four Illustrations for the Legend of Rhiannon*.[8]

---

[8] Mansel Thomas – Appendix.

Williams's indecisiveness was probably also connected with doubts she had about the piece's overall cohesiveness. Reference has already been made in Chapter 2 to the stylistic dichotomy in the music she was writing up to this point – between light, popular works which make use of traditional tunes (such as the overture *Hen Walia*), and more abstract works which were primarily concerned with exploring new musical territory. While *Rhiannon* is more conservative in idiom than, say, either the Suite or the *Elegy*, it was one of the first pieces in which Williams attempted to bring elements from both 'styles' together in a single work. The result was not entirely homogenous. The first two movements were sufficiently well conceived, but she became dissatisfied with the last movements, both of which made use of traditional tunes. 'I don't like the music of [the finale] anymore', she told Maconchy after hearing the May 1943 broadcast of the piece. 'The tune at the beginning is a Welsh tune ... & one tires of it easily. The slow movement tune is also a traditional tune; & somehow, this doesn't have anything like the appeal which it had for me when I wrote the movement'.[9] In fact, the *Hen Ddarbi* theme used in the slow movement seems to have had a particular significance for Williams – she would use it again in her score for the 1949 feature film *Blue Scar* and in her Violin Concerto of 1950. Even so, concerns about her treatment of the traditional material in *Rhiannon* led her to scribble 'perform only I and II' on the front of the autograph manuscript, and in post-war performances the four-movement work was culled to *Two Illustrations for the Legend of Rhiannon*.

Fantasia on Welsh Nursery Tunes (1939–40)

The question of how to marry untapped folk tunes with larger classical forms is a difficult one for a composer, not least because of the disparity between the plain, self-contained structure of folk tunes and the complex demands of large-scale continuity. As Lambert put it, 'the whole trouble with a folk song is that once you have played it through there is nothing much you can do except play it over again and play it rather louder'.[10] Composers as different in style as Stravinsky, Bartók, Janáček, Vaughan Williams and Kodály had discovered possibilities in folk and folk-inspired materials which had liberated their music in new directions. For Williams, the 1940s would primarily be concerned with refining her own personal idiom – reconciling her own distinctly cosmopolitan style with intrinsic Welsh

---

[9] Williams, letter to Maconchy, 7 June 1943 (private collection). Williams had considered two other Welsh subjects for her BBC commission before deciding on the legend of Rhiannon. She sketched two movements of a proposed series of 'Glamorganshire Sketches' (entitled 'Barry Docks' and 'Depressed Areas'), and also started writing a piece based on Shakespeare's Owen Glendower (as depicted in *Henry IV, Part 1*) before revising her plans. Some of the Glendower music was used for 'The Conflict' in *Rhiannon*, and material from the 'Depressed Areas' became Rhiannon's 'Penance'.

[10] Lambert, *Music Ho!*, p. 117.

elements – but at the very beginning of the decade, at least, her music seemed to be continuing to develop stylistically along two paths. Two months after the broadcast premiere of *Rhiannon*, for instance, she composed what was to become one of her best-known works, the *Fantasia on Welsh Nursery Tunes*. She spent Christmas 1939 with her family in Barry and sketched the *Fantasia* in one evening – New Year's Eve, 1939 – completing the full score shortly afterwards. The piece weaves together eight traditional Welsh nursery tunes which are introduced in the following order:

Example 5.5 Williams's annotated list of traditional tunes in the *Fantasia on Welsh Nursery Tunes*[11]

Source: Reproduced by kind permission of the Estate of Grace Williams.

The *Fantasia* was premiered on the Home Service on 29 October 1941 in a studio broadcast from Manchester by the BBC Northern Orchestra, conducted by Warwick Braithwaite. The piece proved to be extremely popular with performers

---

[11] Included in Williams, letter to Kenneth Wright, December 1943 [BBC WAC, Registry Services Central 1: Williams, Composer, 1939–49].

and audiences, and received several performances by the BBC during the war years; it was also recorded by Decca (London Symphony Orchestra, conducted by Mansel Thomas) in the late 1940s. Malcolm Boyd has rightly suggested that Vaughan Williams's *Norfolk Rhapsodies* and his Fantasias on traditional folk tunes 'probably served as models' for Williams, although echoes of Smetana and Dvořák are also present.[12] At the same time, however, the *Fantasia* is also the natural offspring of *Hen Walia* (1930), Williams's older medley of traditional Welsh tunes. Certainly, in its specific use of well-known nursery rhymes, the youthful *Fantasia* appears to have been written with children (of all ages) in mind. 'It's very light and cheerful and not a bit like me', Williams told the BBC's Idris Lewis after putting the final touches to the scoring of the piece, 'but it ought to sound well and perhaps it would amuse people'.[13]

The spirit of fun very much permeates this piece in terms of both mood and structure. It begins and ends in A major but the music in between is coloured by several changes of key as the tunes are introduced. More often than not the tunes are stated in complete form, but Williams often takes advantage of the freer formal parameters of the fantasia form by combining the tunes to create variants. The first half of the original *Deryn-y-Bwn* tune (first stated in the trumpet), for instance, is combined with the second half of *Gee ceffyl bach* (Example 5.6), and motifs from the *Deryn* theme are later combined both with fragments from the opening *Jim Cro* tune and anticipations of *Migildi Magildi*. The score is replete with instances of this kind as Williams plays with her material.

The *Fantasia* also displays an expert's touch in its orchestration. Indeed, the scoring is so clear and fresh that this work could almost be thought of as a type of 'young person's guide to the orchestra'. Naturally, the lion's share of the solos are given to the trumpet, Williams's favourite instrument, but other instruments and, indeed, whole orchestral sections, are given definite characters and frequently interact or converse with each other as the themes are introduced. The *Jim Cro* tune in muted trumpet that opens the work, for example, is soon commented upon by brisk, high woodwind after which the strings join in *con amore* (tenderly) with a broader theme derived from the original tune. This method of scoring is used to great effect throughout and enhances the sense of wit and play that lies at the very heart of the piece.

---

[12] Boyd, *Williams*, p. 22. Boyd also suggests Henry Wood's *Fantasia on British Sea Songs* (1905) as another possible model. See Boyd, notes accompanying 'Grace Williams' CD (Lyrita, SRCD.323).

[13] Williams, letter to Idris Lewis, 11 August 1940 [BBC WAC, WAI/61/2: Williams, Welsh Region Composer, 1938–41].

Example 5.6 *Fantasia on Welsh Nursery Tunes*

[Musical score excerpt showing measures 30-33 with "Deryn-y-Bwn" and "Gee ceffyl bach" themes, marked with solo tpt. (in C, muted), vln. 1 & 2, vla., vlc. pizz., and solo ob.]

Source: *Fantasia on Welsh Nursery Tunes* by Grace Williams © Oxford University Press 1951. Extract reproduced by permission. All rights reserved.

'Gee ceffyl bach' (complete)

[Musical notation of the complete 'Gee ceffyl bach' melody in 6/8]

Intriguingly, although Williams liked her 'little *Fantasia*', as she called it, she had mixed feelings about the piece's reception and popularity. When the piece was performed in Cardiff by Adrian Boult and the BBC Symphony Orchestra in June 1942, for instance, the BBC's programme note inadvertently described it as being Williams's 'most mature work'. This prompted a swift reaction from the composer:

> Please the *Fantasia* isn't my most mature thing. I tossed it off (i.e. the sketch of it) in one evening whereas I've spent months on other things I've written during

the last few years. It was <u>never</u> meant to be taken seriously. I like the little work well enough – lovely Welsh tunes – but, but, but - - - .[14]

Although her name became indelibly linked over the years with the *Fantasia* in the perception of the public – and remains one of her most popular pieces today – she was acutely aware of the dangers of being labelled as a composer/arranger, however exemplary those arrangements might be. As she explained, 'I do realize that when people see my name attached to folk song arrangements and Fantasias for children it is so easy for them to forget that I also write full scale serious works'.[15]

Sinfonia Concertante for Piano and Orchestra (1940–41)

Williams was certainly disappointed that her Sinfonia Concertante, a piece marked by a total absence of traditional folk tunes, never achieved the popularity of the *Fantasia*. She had been planning to compose a large-scale work for piano as early as 1934 – at that stage, she had had in mind a Sinfonia Concertante for piano and chamber orchestra with herself as soloist[16] – but serious work on the piece did not begin until 1940. Completed in June 1941, the piece was written in Grantham (where she was based with the Camden School) and in Barry during the holidays. It is typical of Williams that once she had started the piece (now conceived as a Piano Concerto) she should invest such a great deal of energy in ensuring that the piano writing in the work's three movements was of the very highest quality. She even sought advice from some of the leading pianists of the day. In the summer of 1942, for instance, she sent the completed score to the pianist and composer Michael Mullinar for his comments.[17] She had previously shown the work to another pianist who had suggested that she completely rewrite the piano part to make it more 'pianistic'. Mullinar, however, suggested only a few practical changes and advised Williams to leave the piano part as it was. 'I feel that your lay-out and piano-writing are exactly right for what you have to say', he told

---

[14] Williams, letter to Idris Lewis, 30 June 1942 [BBC WAC, WAI/61/3: Williams, Welsh Region Composer, 1942–48].

[15] Williams, letter to Richard Howgill, BBC Music Controller, 20 September 1954 [BBC WAC, RCONT1: Williams, Composer, 1950–62].

[16] Williams wrote to Sam Jones, BBC West Regional Director, in June 1934 outlining a list of her compositions, including the new Sinfonia Concertante for piano and chamber orchestra. Williams, letter to Jones, undated but June 1934, [BBC WAC, WAI/61/1: Williams, Welsh Region Composer, 1934–37].

[17] Michael Mullinar – Appendix.

her, and he also recommended that the title of the work should be changed from 'Concerto' to 'Sinfonia Concertante'.[18]

The change of title is entirely appropriate because it is clear from the nature of the writing that Williams was far more preoccupied with developing a dramatic argument or conversation between piano and orchestra than adding yet another confrontation between soloist and orchestra to the repertoire: in the words of the pianist Eiluned Davies, 'the piano part is a strand, albeit a dominant one, in the orchestral web'.[19] Passages of *bravura* writing for the piano certainly exist – particularly in the *Alla Marcia* finale – but the instrument rarely dominates the arena. The fine balance achieved between soloist and orchestra is intimately connected to the romantic ethos which pervades the work as a whole. Although the work opens assertively with an angular theme in orchestra, the music of the first movement as a whole is lyrical and wistful with several of the main themes being given to the orchestra. Lyricism is given full reign in the central *Lento* movement, which is characterized by unfolding melodic lines, and in the march finale, the piano part is often complemented with layers of contrapuntal lines in the orchestra. The richly romantic gestures in this finale, and in the work as a whole, have prompted commentators to note the debt Williams owed to Rachmaninov in terms of piano writing (see Example 5.7).[20]

The Sinfonia Concertante was to be Williams's only major work for piano and orchestra, and it was premiered on 7 January 1943 on the BBC's Home Service by Margaret Good (piano) and the BBC Symphony Orchestra, conducted by Clarence Raybould. Although Williams felt that the performance suffered from a lack of adequate rehearsal time, the broadcast did much to enhance her reputation as a composer of full-scale serious works. The *Radio Times* (7 January 1943) described her as being 'one of the most distinguished Welsh composers', and she received many enthusiastic letters and telegrams from listeners who tuned in. The broadcast caught the ear of *The Listener* (15 January 1943), although the reviewer William McNaught had some reservations:

> The career recently beginning of Grace Williams will be worth watching. On the showing of her Sinfonia Concertante she is a gifted composer who is inclined to protest too much. The music was over-voiced and over-expressed in relation to its content. That tragic climax in the second movement was very fine; but there hasn't been all that tragedy to set it going. However, the stuff of the work was interesting throughout.

---

[18] Mullinar, letter to Williams, 9 August 1942, as quoted in Eiluned Davies, 'A Pianist's Note on Grace Williams's *Sinfonia Concertante*', *Welsh Music* 5/9 (Summer 1978), p. 23. Davies was the soloist in the second performance of the Sinfonia which was given on 30 September 1947 by the BBC Welsh Orchestra, conducted by Mansel Thomas.

[19] Ibid., p. 26.

[20] See, for example, Boyd, *Grace Williams*, p. 23.

McNaught had, in fact, previously encountered Williams and her work in 1935 when he had attended a Macnaghten–Lemare concert as music critic of the *Evening News*. On that occasion he had criticized her (together with Lutyens and Maconchy, who also had pieces featured in the concert) for writing music which was 'too formidably clever'. Williams probably read his review of her Sinfonia with a wry smile.

Example 5.7 Sinfonia Concertante for Piano and Orchestra, III

Example 5.7 continued

[Some instruments omitted]

Source: Reproduced by kind permission of the Estate of Grace Williams.

Symphony No. 1 (1942–43)

By the time the Sinfonia was broadcast early in 1943, Williams was close to finishing a piece which she described as being her 'first big attempt at symphonic form'.[21] She was the first Welsh composer to respond to the challenge of composing a symphony, and for this she turned to Welsh narrative sources. If the *Mabinogion*-themed *Rhiannon* could be described as a type of wordless, covert opera, then Williams's gift as a musical dramatist was even more evident in her First Symphony. The piece was directly inspired by tales of Owain Glyndŵr, the aristocrat who led a fierce rebellion for Welsh independence in the fifteenth century. A celebrated figure in Wales, existing accounts of Glyndŵr present him as something of an enigma in that although events in his historic rebellion are well documented, details about the man himself remain elusive. He was a brilliant strategist and his successes against the Crown, both on the battlefield and elsewhere, led his enemies to believe that he possessed magical powers, including the ability to control the weather. Although his battle for Welsh independence ultimately failed, he was never captured by the English and in common with other fabled figures his final resting place still remains a mystery.

---

[21] Williams, letter to T.M. Whewell (organizer of the Home Service Tuesday afternoon programmes), 13 March 1952 [BBC WAC, RCONT1: Williams, Composer, 1950–62].

Glyndŵr is probably better known beyond Welsh borders as Shakespeare's Owen Glendower in *Henry IV* and *Henry V*, and it is interesting that it was the fictional Glendower who provided the spark of inspiration for Williams's symphony: she specifically entitled the piece 'Symphony no. 1 in the form of Symphonic Impressions of the Glendower scene in Henry IV, Part I'. As she explained to her friend Enid Parry:

> That wonderful scene in Henry IV, Part I (Act III, Sc. I) always made me want to write something called Owain Glyndŵr. My father has supplied me with a lot of additional data – & now I suppose I ought to read the new book Owen Glendower by John Cowper Powys. Still, the Shakespeare was the real inspiration. The "wanton rushes" paragraph is one of the loveliest bits of Shakespeare, I think – & such a contrast to the fireworks at the beginning of the scene.[22]

Gerald Cockshott, another friend of Williams's, recalled a lively discussion he had had with her in the 1940s about the way in which Shakespeare portrayed Glendower in *Henry IV*. 'I thought then', he stated, 'that Shakespeare was making fun of the Old Wizard and meant us to laugh at him; but Grace would have none of this, and we argued the point in letter after letter'.[23] In keeping with her theme, Williams shaped the first three movements of the symphony into musical impressions of different aspects of Glendower's character as presented by Shakespeare in his play. The *Allegro con fuoco* first movement, for example, is a depiction of 'Glendower the warrior', and is prefaced in Williams's original manuscript by his dramatic description of his own birth from Act III, scene 1 of Shakespeare's play:

> At my nativity
> The front of heaven was full of fiery shapes,
> Of burning cressets: and at my birth
> The frame and huge foundation of the earth
> Shaked like a coward.[24]

Williams wanted the opening to be, in her words, all 'fire and brimstone & pageantry'.[25] The work begins in suitably belligerent mood with a stark semitone (C–D flat) in strings which outlines the tonal area of D flat while also preparing for the intensely agitated section which follows (Example 5.8). Brass fanfares and turbulent chromaticism give way to a more reflective middle section which is dominated by a theme played on the trumpet (Example 5.9). Although original,

---

[22] Williams, letter to Parry, 27 February 1942 (Williams-Parry Collection, Bangor University Archive). Enid Parry – Appendix.

[23] Gerald Cockshott in 'Williams Symposium (Part 1)', pp. 27–8.

[24] All excerpts from Shakespeare's *Henry IV, Part I* are taken from the original manuscripts of Williams's *Symphonic Impressions* (Williams Archive, NLW).

[25] Williams, letter to Maconchy, 7 June 1943 (private collection).

the theme possesses characteristics which can be found in traditional Welsh tunes – in particular, the presence of the rhythmic motive ♪ ♩. and a certain modal colouring.[26] The theme is stated in full and accompanied by static chords in strings over an E pedal, after which it is repeated twice in slightly varied form with added countermelodies in strings and woodwind. The theme and its treatment are of interest because it contains elements that Williams would develop more extensively in her *Penillion* for orchestra (1955) and other later works. The fireworks of the opening briefly return in the short recapitulation, but the violence quickly dies away and the movement ends with a brooding *misterioso* passage for strings and high woodwind. Williams vividly described the recapitulation as 'snatching at the feeling of the opening, but never bursting forth on it & gradually giving out: rather like old Owen himself, in fact'.[27]

Example 5.8 Symphony No. 1, opening

Source: Copyright © Oriana Publications Limited 2007. Reproduced by permission.

---

[26] The rhythm is sometimes referred to as the 'Lombard' rhythm or 'Scottish Snap' (commonly associated with close intervals) and is found in abundance in the Robert ap Huw manuscripts, the oldest existing collection of Welsh instrumental music. See Boyd, *Williams*, p. 82 and *Robert ap Huw Studies*, volume 3 (1998) of *Welsh Music History / Hanes Cerddoriaeth Cymru*, eds Sally Harper and Wyn Thomas.

[27] Williams, letter to Maconchy, 7 June 1943 (private collection).

Example 5.9 Symphony No. 1, I, trumpet theme

Source: Copyright © Oriana Publications Limited 2007. Reproduced by permission.

The drama of the first movement is in contrast to the tranquillity of the *Andante liricamente* movement (in B major), which is a musical impression of Glendower 'the dreamer'. The movement is prefaced with Williams's favourite passage from the play – Glendower's translation of his Welsh-speaking daughter's appeal to her husband Edmund Mortimer:

> She bids you upon the wanton rushes lay you down,
> And rest your gentle head upon her lap,
> And she will sing the song that pleaseth you,
> And on your eyelids crown the god of sleep,
> Charming your blood with pleasing heaviness,
> Making such difference 'twixt wake and sleep,
> As is the difference betwixt day and night
> The hour before the heavenly-harnessed team
> Begins his golden progress in the east.

Although the movement contains passages of lyrical beauty, Williams felt it to be the weakest in terms of its overall aim. 'I don't like the middle music of this mvt', she confessed to Maconchy:

> I think it is descriptive (if played properly) of the "pleasing heaviness – – twixt wake and sleep" – but whereas there is a wonderful beauty in the way

Shakespeare describes this state – there just isn't any beauty in my music (except that I think the opening theme <u>cd</u>. make a lovely <u>sound</u>.)[28]

She had no such qualms about the hotspurred scherzo (III). Marked *Barbaro e Segreto* (savagely and secretively), this movement is a musical depiction of Glendower 'the magician' and is inspired by the protagonist's assertion that he is able to 'call spirits from the vasty deep ... [and] to command the devil'. The ensuing scene where Hotspur mocks and sneers at Glendower's boasts is portrayed in musical terms by quick-fire exchanges in the orchestra, and the whole movement sparkles with wit and rhythmic energy. The scherzo is followed by a weighty Epilogue (IV) which, in contrast to the first three movements, is the composer's own 'retrospective impression of Owain Glyndŵr, great figure of Welsh history'.[29] In the manner of a grand Mahlerian funeral march, the movement opens with muffled timpani and side drums accompanying a passionate and delicately ornamented theme in strings (Example 5.10). The movement's monumental subject and elegiac character suggests that Williams may well have drawn from Welsh literary forms for inspiration, an inclination which would become more conspicuous in her later pieces. Indeed, the movement can be said to share an affinity with a *marwnad*, a Welsh poetic form found in the sixth-century writings of Taliesin and later medieval Welsh poets, in which the bard composed an elegy or lament for a dead lord or prince.

The First Symphony was an ambitious symphonic debut and it contained elements that foreshadowed the music of Williams's maturity. Ever the perfectionist, however, the composer had serious reservations about the work's overall structure. She was acutely aware, for example, of the work's reliance on dramatic-narrative considerations rather than 'classical' symphonic schemes, something which is implicit in her wordy title – *Symphony No. 1 in the form of Symphonic Impressions*. Indeed, she seems to have felt that the formal idiosyncrasies of some of the movements fell short of the requirements of a 'proper' symphony. These misgivings she shared with Maconchy, the work's dedicatee:

---

[28] Williams, letter to Maconchy, 6 April 1950 (private collection). Boyd has commented on the 'retrospective' style of the movement's central section, and has suggested that it may have been written 'some time before the other three'. Boyd, *Williams*, p. 25.

[29] Williams, note in the manuscript of *Symphonic Impressions* (Williams Archive, NLW). Although Williams used Shakespeare's anglicized spelling of Owen Glendower in the work's title and for the first three movements, she used his original Welsh name (Owain Glyndŵr) when discussing the final movement. She also included in her programme note a guide to the correct Welsh pronunciation of his name: 'pronounced <u>O</u>wine Glind<u>oo</u>r ("oo" as in soon – final "r" to be sounded)'.

About its form – Betty I really don't know – this [first] movement shaped itself, somehow: one thing grew from another & yet somehow it fulfilled what I wanted ... My last movement – an Epilogue – hasn't the proportions of a finale of a Symphony proper, yet it is big and broad enough, I hope.[30]

Example 5.10 Symphony No. 1, IV, opening

[woodwind omitted]

Source: Copyright © Oriana Publications Limited 2007. Reproduced by permission.

Williams would go on to address formal symphonic concepts more fully in her Symphony No. 2 (1956) – a work which does not follow a specified programme – but although she made a number of revisions to her First Symphony, she remained dissatisfied with it as a whole. 'I've got very mixed feelings about my old Symph. [*sic*]' she told Kenneth Wright after the work was premiered by the BBC Welsh Orchestra and Mansel Thomas (conductor) in March 1950. 'It's good in patches – but doesn't hang together as a vital consecutive whole – I expect because it was written in snatches when I had time off from teaching'.[31] Although the piece

---

[30] Williams, letter to Maconchy, 7 June 1943 (private collection).
[31] Williams, letter to Kenneth Wright, 6 April 1950 [BBC WAC, RCONT1: Williams, Composer, 1950–62].

went on to receive two more performances in its complete form, she eventually withdrew it with the exception of the scherzo.[32]

Sea Sketches for String Orchestra (1944)

Towards the end of 1943, Idris Lewis at the BBC in Wales had been in discussion with Barry Music Club about a possible concert and broadcast of chamber music by Welsh composers. Williams accepted an invitation from the Club to contribute to the proposed concert but was reluctant to write the new piano trio that Lewis had suggested. 'I've got a bee in my bonnet about Piano, Violin and Cello', she told him, 'and can't bear the ensemble'.[33] She did, however, have the idea of writing something for a small string orchestra. 'I myself feel that I must now write something specially for the Club and have in mind a short suite of pieces connected with Barry – three (or 4 or 5) seascapes perhaps'.[34] Although plans for the Barry concert and BBC broadcast fell through, Williams continued to work on her new *Sea Sketches* throughout the spring and summer of 1944. Believing that the worst of the Blitz was over, she had returned to London with the Camden School at the end of 1943. She rented a flat in Willow Road, Hampstead and it was here in August 1944 that she finished her suite while Hitler's doodlebug bombs flew overhead and rained down on the capital:

> There was a crash on the Heath at breakfast time last Wednesday ... – The blast extended as far as our corner of Willow Road so we had a very lucky escape ... We are not nervous wrecks yet, & things could be much worse even though one is sometimes inclined to look back on pre-flying-bomb London as a sort of Elysium ...
>
> I must have some tea & then get on with the scoring of my final sea piece – yes, at last I've finished the sketch of it & shan't be long before I've scored it & copied it out.[35]

---

[32] The second performance (of the complete Symphony) was given in April 1952 by the BBC Scottish Orchestra, conducted by Clarence Raybould, and the third in September 1952 by the BBC Welsh Orchestra, conducted by Arwel Hughes. More recently, a new edition of the work by Graeme Cotterill (published by Oriana Publications) was performed by the BBC National Orchestra of Wales, conducted by Owain Arwel Hughes, at the BBC's St. David's Day concert in 2008, and broadcast on Radio 3 on 3 March 2008.

[33] Williams, letter to Lewis, 1 November 1943 [BBC WAC, WAI/61/3: Williams, Welsh Region Composer, 1942–48].

[34] Williams, letter to Lewis, 2 November 1943, ibid.

[35] Williams, letter to Maconchy, undated, but August 1944 (private collection).

Despite the horrors of war, Williams succeeded in producing one of her finest works. She dedicated the piece to her 'parents who had the good sense to set up home on the coast of Glamorganshire', and the piece was almost certainly composed with a touch of nostalgia for the sea views which lay a short walk away from her house in Barry. She often admitted to friends at this time that her ideal life would be to live near the sea and compose. 'I never tire of looking at [the sea], and listening to it', she later stated, 'and I like to think that it's had some influence on my music. There's my fondness for long undulating melodic lines and flowing rhythms, particularly in works that were directly sparked off by the sea'.[36]

One of her favourite haunts was the wild, stony beach in Barry known as Cold Knapp. From this beach it is possible to see straight across the Bristol Channel over to Weston-super-Mare and the Somerset hills beyond, and this breathtaking vista probably provided the inspiration for the five contrasting and poetic portraits which make up the *Sea Sketches*. The first sketch 'High Wind' opens with a whirling ♪ figure in violins and violas, above which a fanfare-like theme in *divisi* violins rises and falls like waves in rough sea (see Example 4.9, Chapter 4). These opening bars recall the beginning of Britten's *Les Illuminations* (1939) but the movement as a whole has a character of its own. The fanfare theme is based upon adjacent major triads (G and F♯) – a characteristic of many of Williams's themes – and is paired with a descending chromatic figure with a distinctive triplet rhythm. These figures are extensively developed, their blustery argument enhanced throughout by a weak sense of tonality. Significantly, the clear C major tonality which is reached at the end of the movement occurs only after the winds have subsided.

The second sketch, 'Sailing Song', is a charming *Allegretto* in C major, and here boats are gently rocked by a tamer sea – captured in a gently undulating figure stated initially in violas. The third sketch, 'Channel Sirens', evokes a ghostly nocturnal scene where boats tentatively travel through heavy fog and mist. The *Lento* movement is marked *misterioso*, a direction frequently encountered in Williams's scores, and contains some of the most striking writing for strings, including the use of *glissandi*. It opens quietly with the sound of a distant foghorn in muted violas and cellos, accompanied by stark chords in upper strings (Example 5.11). The material in these opening bars is built from notes of the octatonic scale which has the effect of blurring any clear sense of key. Even when later the fog begins to lift, as briefly suggested by the brighter D-centred harmony, the tonality is shrouded by chromatic chords in upper strings (Example 5.12). The eerie tone and dramatic gestures of this movement again recall Britten – although, in this instance, it is the Britten of *A Midsummer Night's Dream*, composed in 1959–60, 15 years after the *Sea Sketches*.

---

[36] Williams, 'Self Portrait', *Welsh Music* 8/5, p. 13.

Example 5.11 *Sea Sketches* for String Orchestra, III 'Channel Sirens', opening

Source: *Sea Sketches* for String Orchestra by Grace Williams © Oxford University Press 1951. Extracts reproduced by permission. All rights reserved.

Example 5.12 *Sea Sketches* for String Orchestra, III

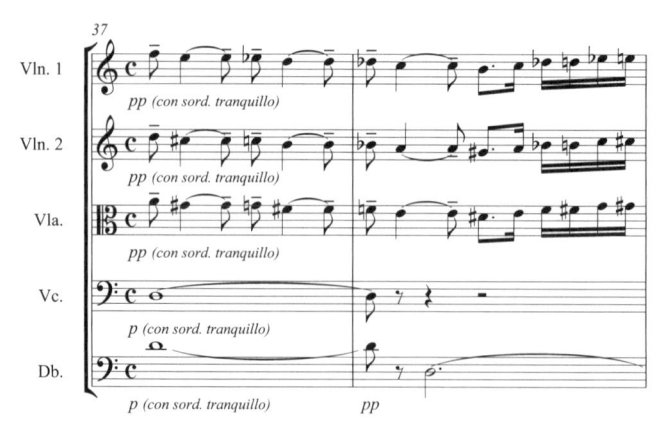

Source: Sea Sketches for String Orchestra by Grace Williams © Oxford University Press 1951. Extracts reproduced by permission. All rights reserved.

The fourth sketch, 'Breakers', an edgy *presto* in D major, is a vivid depiction of waves breaking on the shores, teeming with vigorous arpeggiated themes and chromatic scales. In contrast, the final sketch, 'Calm Sea in Summer', is an *Andante* of profound intensity. Here, opulent string textures bask in the rich, sultry harmonies of late Romanticism foreshadowing the sensuous sound world of her *Fairest of Stars* for soprano and orchestra (1973).

Example 5.13 *Sea Sketches* for String Orchestra,
V 'Calm Sea in Summer', opening

Source: Sea Sketches for String Orchestra by Grace Williams © Oxford University Press 1951. Extracts reproduced by permission. All rights reserved.

The radiance of the final sketch belied the fact that Williams had reached an extremely low point in her life at this time. The strain of combining a demanding teaching job with composition had taken its toll on her health, and she frequently felt over-stretched and exhausted. Letters to friends and colleagues reveal that Williams had experienced periods of ill health as early as the mid 1930s, although more often than not she would attempt to make light of these incidents. 'There wasn't anything seriously wrong at all', she told Idris Lewis after attending a medical check-up in the spring of 1939, 'but my doctor, seeing one look so lousy, swore there was. When I told him I was sure it was only an excess of composing, he treated me with the sort of sympathy one doles out to poor things suffering from delusions'.[37] Health problems continued to plague Williams during her evacuation, and when she returned to London with the Camden School in 1943, matters simply got worse. Towards the end of 1944, she was diagnosed with exhaustion and spent nearly two weeks in a London hospital. After making a partial recovery, Williams took the momentous decision to give up composing entirely. Her decision was almost certainly encouraged by her lover Zenon Sliwinski, a Polish factory worker whom she had first met in Grantham during the war. The two had quickly become very close, and when Williams moved back to London, Sliwinski followed. Although he clearly meant a great deal to her – she seriously considered marrying him at one point – it seems that he was unable (or unwilling) to understand the importance of music in her life. Williams dedicated her Polish Polka (1948), orchestral variations on the Polish tune 'Husia Susia', to him, and their relationship came to an end when he left for South Africa in the late 1940s.

True to her word, Williams composed nothing of consequence between 1944 and 1947. She continued her schoolteaching for a while, but a combination of restlessness, homesickness and a boredom with dingy London school buildings prompted her to begin applying for a number of full-time music jobs. Her (unsuccessful) application for a music lectureship at Cardiff University in 1945 was certainly inspired by a desire to swap grimy Kentish town for the bracing salt sea air of Barry. Opportunities for full-time employment in Wales were scarce at this time, however, and in May 1946 she accepted the position of Music Assistant within the BBC's Schools Broadcasting Department in London. The job involved writing scripts about music, arranging music (particularly folk songs), visiting schools and occasionally being an accompanist for live schools broadcasts. She excelled at all these tasks – if anything, she was rather overqualified – and impressed colleagues with her professionalism. But the health problems persisted and within a couple of months she was forced to start thinking about alternative career paths:

> I'm not sure as to what my future plans are going to be – there is the possibility that I might give up my job and try free-lancing ... The new job is so nice – but ... there's an awful lot of running around in it & after a couple of months it got me down completely. A quiet life with long stretches near the sea, and free-lancing, is <u>very</u> tempting – but precarious financially perhaps – I don't know.[38]

---

[37] Williams, letter to Lewis, 11 May 1939 [BBC WAC, WAI/61/2: Williams, Welsh Region Composer, 1938–41].

[38] Williams, letter to Lewis, 28 November 1946 [BBC WAC, WAI/61/3: Williams, Welsh Region Composer 1942–48].

Two weeks later, Williams handed in her resignation to the BBC. Her doctors had advised a complete rest, and in February 1947 she moved out of her London flat and returned home to the wild, rolling hills and spectacular coast of Glamorganshire. Complete rest, however, was not on the agenda for Williams. 1947 was quite a healthy year in the professional sense with a number of premieres and other performances taking place. The most important of these was the March premiere (and broadcast) of the *Sea Sketches* by the strings of the BBC Welsh Orchestra and conductor Mansel Thomas. These clever *Sketches* captivated the audience at its premiere and soon came to rival the popularity of the *Fantasia on Welsh Nursery Tunes*, another piece to be heard on the airwaves that year. In addition, two of the *Rhiannon Illustrations* were performed and broadcast from the National Eisteddfod in August, and the Welsh premiere of the Sinfonia Concertante was given by the pianist Eiluned Davies and the BBC Welsh Orchestra in September. It was hardly the 'quiet life' she had originally envisaged!

Music for the Feature Film *Blue Scar* (1949)

Although still officially 'retired' from composing, Williams took on a number of different musical jobs in the late 1940s which enabled her to establish a freelance career in Wales. The BBC's Schools Department still continued to provide her with work, and the majority of her earnings at this time came from writing scripts and folksong arrangements for children's programmes such as 'Adventures in Music' and 'Rhythm and Melody'. One of the more interesting projects to emerge was *The Merry Minstrel*, a piece for narrator and orchestra based on one of the Grimm's *Fairy Tales* ('Der wunderliche Spielmann') which was first broadcast on 'Children's Hour' on 6 August 1949.[39] Intended as an introduction for young children to all the instruments of the orchestra, the merry minstrel charms the wolf, fox and hare he encounters in the forest by playing every orchestral instrument with skill and imagination. Williams also provided the incidental music for *Hannibal*, a three-part radio play about the post-war years of the Carthaginian general, written and produced by Robert Gittings. The play was broadcast on the Third Programme in June 1947 and was the first of several for which Williams provided music. In June of the following year, for example, she provided a score for Gittings's production of Henry Treece's *The Dark Island*, a dramatic poem about Caractacus and ancient Britain. The richly imaginative incidental music was singled out by *The Listener*'s drama critic for being 'unusually successful' in enhancing the poem's dramatic impact (*The Listener*, 10 June 1948). And in 1949, Williams became the first British woman

---

[39] The piece was performed by John Darran (narrator) and the BBC Welsh Orchestra, conducted by Mansel Thomas.

composer to write music for a feature film when she provided the score for *Blue Scar*, a film written and directed by Jill Craigie.[40]

Set in 1946, *Blue Scar* focuses on the social, economic and political tensions within a small mining community in the South Wales valleys and, unusually for its time, has a bold socialist agenda. Filmed on location in the village of Abergwynfi, near Port Talbot, Craigie was keen to counter the romanticized views of Wales presented in films such as *How Green Was My Valley* (John Ford, 1941) through the incorporation of documentary-type scenes which focused on the realities of post-war mining life. In addition to professional actors, Craigie drew from the Abergwynfi miners for her cast, and her film tackled issues which were of pressing relevance to the community such as the nationalization of the mines. These episodes are juxtaposed in the film with events in the relationship between a young miner, Tom (played by Emrys Jones) and his girlfriend Olwen (Gwyneth Vaughan).

Williams was approached to write the music for *Blue Scar* because it was felt that her musical style, particularly those pieces which used traditional tunes, would complement the film's subject and images of the Welsh valleys. Her score for *Blue Scar* uses a number of well-known Welsh tunes – including *Mae Nghariad i'n Fenws* (My Love is like Venus), *Y Gwydd* (The Loom) and the popular rugby song *Sosban Fach* (Little Saucepan) – and these themes are linked with specific aspects of the drama: Tom's bond with his mining community, for instance, is represented in musical terms by the tune *Y Gwydd*.[41] Some aspects of working on the film clearly puzzled Williams, however, and while in the middle of writing her score, she sought the advice of Vaughan Williams:

> It seemed to me that some of the film director's demands were quite unrelated to music. "Just think," I said, "I'm expected to write music for a football rolling down a mountain side; what on earth has that got to do with music?" "I can beat that," confessed V.W., "I've had to write music for foot and mouth disease," and he rounded off the remark with a terse chuckle.[42]

As soon as the film score was completed, Williams felt the urge to return to original composition and began sketching a new Piano Concerto in which she used material

---

[40] Jill Craigie – Appendix.

[41] Williams also used the hymn tune *Yr Hen Ddarbi* in one scene but both music and scene were scrapped from the film. An analysis of Williams's use of the traditional themes which were included in *Blue Scar* is provided in Jan G. Swynnoe, *The Best Years of British Film Music 1936–1958* (Woodbridge: Boydell Press, 2002), pp. 110–118.

[42] Williams, 'Vaughan Williams: a Tribute', *RCM Magazine* 55/1 (1959), p. 37. Williams solved her problem in that there is a scene in *Blue Scar* where a football rolls down the mountain to the accompaniment of the tune *Sosban Fach*. Vaughan Williams's film scores include *The 49th Parallel* (Ortus Films, 1941), *Scott of the Antarctic* (Ealing Studios, 1948) and *The England of Elizabeth* (British Transport Films, 1957).

from both her *Blue Scar* and *The Dark Island* scores; she also turned some of the music of *The Dark Island* into a four-movement suite for string orchestra. The *Dark Island* suite was completed in 1949 (and dedicated to the Kathleen Merritt String Orchestra), but Williams abandoned her concerto, completing only one movement in rough score. The real problem here for her was a combination of financial pressures and insufficient time. She did not have the luxury of private means, and income was a constant worry for her. With the exception of the *Rhiannon Illustrations*, none of her larger-scale works had been commissioned, she did not have a publisher, and the income she received from Performing Rights Society (PRS) royalties for broadcasts and performances of her works was certainly not large enough to live on.[43] She continued to earn money from scriptwriting and writing music for films and radio, but her freelance activities broadened to include copying work for various music publishers and a part-time teaching post at the new National College of Music and Drama in Cardiff.[44]

A new opportunity appeared to present itself in February 1949. Flushed by the success of Britten's *Peter Grimes* (1945), the Arts Council of Great Britain launched a national opera competition with a view to commissioning a limited number of full-length operas for the 1951 Festival of Britain. Although the outcome of this competition (and the four winning operas) was to prove to be something of a disaster, the organizers were initially flooded with proposals for over a hundred operas.[45] In the summer of 1949, Williams submitted an outline to the Arts Council of a three-act opera which was based on the life of the Welsh folk hero Richard Lewis, better known as Dic Penderyn. Penderyn (1808–31), a well-known champion of worker's rights, was executed by the English authorities for allegedly stabbing a soldier during the Merthyr riots in the summer of 1831, although many suspected that the authorities had sought to make an example out of him because they feared the emergence of workers' power in industrial Wales. The choice of subject of the opera is interesting because Williams had for some time wanted to write a 'Welsh' opera. Her *Hen Walia* (1930) had originally been conceived as an overture for a Welsh folk opera, and although the opera did not come to fruition, she had continued to delve into Welsh history and culture for interesting subjects over the years. In the late 1930s, for instance, she had briefly contemplated writing a one-act comic opera using some of the satirical plays or 'interludes' of the Welsh poet Twm o'r Nant (1739–1810). Again, however,

---

[43] The first of Williams's works to be published by Oxford University Press (OUP) was her *Polish Polka* (two piano version) in 1950. Other works taken up by OUP (listed here with year of publication) include the *Sea Sketches* (1951), *The Dancers* (1953), the *Fantasia on Welsh Nursery Tunes* (1956), *Penillion* for orchestra (1962), and *Ave maris stella* for mixed chorus (1975).

[44] See the Welsh College of Music and Drama – Appendix.

[45] For a full account of the ill-fated competition, see Lewis Foreman, 'Alan Bush, Arthur Benjamin, Berthold Goldschmidt, Karl Rankl, Lennox Berkeley and the Arts Council's 1951 Opera Competition', *British Music Society News*, Issue 100.

the project was never realized and this was also to be the fate of *Dic Penderyn*. Williams wrote to Enid Parry in 1949 just after she had been informed that her outline had been declined by the Arts Council:

> I still feel that it's a fine opera story – though now I doubt whether it's right for <u>my</u> music. The last scene (the one I tried out in vocal score) was O.K. – but the first act might find me writing in my folk-song Fantasia style, and my two distinct styles ... might crop up in the same work and that would be confusing.[46]

Had Williams had the time and the opportunity, she almost certainly would have attempted to resolve the potential stylistic fracture she identified in *Dic Penderyn*. But bearing in mind her reticence about being labelled as a composer of Welsh folk songs and *Fantasias*, the desire to write a folk-inspired opera may not have burned as brightly as it had in the past.

Violin Concerto (1950)
***The Dancers* (1951)**

Given that further work on the opera was now out of the question, it seems natural that Williams's thoughts should turn to an instrument which is nearest to the human voice. Her three-movement Violin Concerto was written for the violinist Granville Jones, and first performed on 30 March 1950 by Jones and the BBC Welsh Orchestra, conducted by Mansel Thomas: the concert also included the premiere of her *Symphonic Impressions*.[47] One of the most striking features of the Violin Concerto is its profoundly lyrical and romantic impetus. Unusually for Williams, the work opens with a slow movement which is in the nature of a leisurely extended rhapsody, where the soloist is given long melodies to sing above rich harmonies and orchestral textures (Example 5.14). The movement's novelty is further heightened by an overall cohesion of mood: it is marked *liricamente* and there are few sharp contrasts of texture. Indeed, it is almost as if Williams used this concerto to express the songs or arias she did not write in her opera.

This extended song is followed by another – a central *Andante sostenuto* movement which uses the hymn tune *Hen Ddarbi* as its main theme. Williams was particularly drawn to this tune, and had used it in two previous works where it had been associated with themes of penitence and anguish. 'Queer how I cling to that tune', she told Parry shortly after the Concerto's premiere. 'I used it in the slow mvt of *Rhiannon* (which I have now scrapped ...) & I used it in a bit of *Blue Scar* which also got scrapped. Third time lucky!'[48] The opening phrase of the hymn tune is first stated in the oboe at the beginning, and soloist and orchestra comment

---

[46] Williams, letter to Enid Parry, 21 September 1949 (Williams/Parry Collection, BU).
[47] Granville Jones – Appendix.
[48] Williams, letter to Enid Parry, 3 April 1950 (Williams/Parry Collection, BU).

Example 5.14 Violin Concerto, I, solo violin theme

Source: Reproduced by kind permission of the Estate of Grace Williams.

on and improvise around it throughout the movement. The use of pedal points is significant as is the inclusion of improvisatory-type textures – both are features of Williams's late style. The concerto ends with a brisk *Allegro con spirito* finale which incorporates a virtuosic cadenza for the soloist.

The intimate and concentrated expression of the concerto revealed a marked shift towards a more song-influenced ethos on the part of the composer, and this lyrical concern is seen in works such as the choral suite *The Dancers* (1951) and the songs *Flight* for tenor and piano (1949) and *When Thou Dost Dance* for high voice and piano (1951). Although Williams had concentrated on orchestral pieces during the 1940s, she did compose two short vocal works just before the war. The first to be written (September 1938) was *The Song of Mary*, a rapturous setting of the *Magnificat* for solo soprano and a chamber orchestra of oboe, two trumpets, three trombones, harp and strings. Related in genre to Williams's two earlier settings for solo voice and orchestra, *Tuscany* and *Tarantella*, the concise *Magnificat* displays a maturity in the intensity of the soprano's declamation, in the layering of chromatic textures in the accompaniment and in the delicacy of the scoring.

The work was followed in June 1939 by *Gogonedawg Arglwydd* (Praise the Lord Eternal), a short setting for chorus and orchestra of a Welsh religious poem taken from the thirteenth-century manuscript *The Black Book of Carmarthen*. This hymn of praise is Williams's first known setting in the Welsh language, and the exultant nature of the words is effectively brought to the fore by choral writing which is dramatic and declamatory in style – the directive *declamando* is specified in the score. Williams wrote the piece with a view to getting it performed at the National Eisteddfod, but initial discussions were abandoned because of the outbreak of war. Ironically, although the piece was performed (in English translation) by the BBC Singers and Leslie Woodgate (conductor) in 1945, it was never performed in Wales during her lifetime. Even so, Williams seems to have put the piece to one side while she concentrated on writing other works for voice. While her renewed interest in writing for voices from the 1950s onwards primarily arose as a natural consequence of her development, it was also linked to her awareness of a gradual improvement in vocal standards in the Welsh choral scene at this time. She addressed this very issue many years later when she asked 'for a singing nation, why aren't there more choral works?'

> The simple answer is that until recently Welsh choirs, with very few exceptions, just weren't interested in contemporary pieces and were indeed incapable of singing anything in an advanced idiom ...
>
> However, in recent years the choral scene has improved – from the composer's point of view at any rate. One fully-fledged professional chorus and several small semi-professional choirs have been formed ... That there is a higher standard of musical intelligence in these choirs goes without saying, and they are able to cope much more easily with new works.[49]

Williams's choral suite *The Dancers* was composed in 1953 and was the first of several substantial works for voices that she would write during the 1950s and 60s. With a duration of some 20 minutes, the work is scored for solo soprano, three-part women's chorus (SSA – soprano, soprano, alto), harp and string orchestra.[50] The suite consists of five songs each set to a different poem on the theme of dance. The songs are convincingly built into the whole, and Williams varies her forces with imagination. The opening song, 'Gather for Festival' (to words by H.D. – Hilda Doolittle), for solo soprano and orchestra, is in the nature of a graceful, stylized dance where the soloist invites us to join her in a festival of dance and song. The melody (stated first in the violin and then by the soprano) is not extensively developed in the song, but is restated (albeit in different harmonic guises) at the beginning of each verse, something which reinforces the stately and formal mood of the song. Strings weave delicate counterfigures around the melody, and rapidly shifting modal harmonies add colour and vibrancy to the music. Williams uses a traditional 6/8 tarantella metre in her zesty choral setting of Belloc's 'Tarantella' (II), varying the metre only to incorporate the rapid, shifting rhythms within the verse. The mood darkens in the central section, a setting of Thomas Chatterton's 'Roundelay' (III), where chorus and soprano join forces to sing a beautiful lament for a lost lover. One of the most striking features is the soprano's haunting refrain

---

[49] Williams, 'How Welsh is Welsh Music?', *Welsh Music* (Summer 1973), p. 9.
[50] *The Dancers* was premiered in November 1954 by a young Joan Sutherland, the Penarth Ladies Choir and members of the BBC Welsh Orchestra, conducted by Arwel Hughes.

which is heard at the end of each choral entry, and which recurs unaltered (although in different keys) throughout.

Example 5.15 *The Dancers*, III 'Roundelay'

Example 5.15 continued

Source: 'Roundelay' from *The Dancers* by Grace Williams © Oxford University Press 1953. Extract reproduced by permission. All rights reserved.

A mood of defiance is introduced in the fourth song, 'Lose the Pain in the Snow' (to words by May Sarton) for chorus only, where dance becomes a metaphor for experience in love, life and death. The chorus sings a rising figure of hope at the beginning of each verse, and is delicately accompanied by harp and strings. Echoes of the first movement of the *Sea Sketches* are heard, particularly at the end of the song in violas and cellos, and the link with the earlier piece is further strengthened in the final song, a setting of Kathleen Raine's 'To the Wild Hills' for soprano and chorus.

Despite being looked on favourably by the BBC during the war, it had taken Williams noticeably longer to make an impact in the musical world than some of her peers – Britten, Maconchy or Lutyens. Although the challenges of establishing a freelance career as a composer in the Wales of the late 1940s were not to be underestimated, by the early 1950s she had acquired a deserved reputation as a highly gifted composer worthy of attention. 'Her outlook is essentially cosmopolitan', *Grove* observed in 1954, and her 'serious music reveals a certain independence of character, and is carried out with invention and resource'.[51] With the seascapes of the Glamorganshire coast in sight as she composed, Williams was now poised to embark on the most exciting phase of her creative development, one that would have far-reaching consequences for Welsh music.

---

[51] Peter Crossley-Holland, 'Grace Williams' in *Grove's Dictionary* (1954), vol. ix, p. 306.

Example 5.16 *The Dancers*, V 'To the Wild Hills'

Source: 'To the Wild Hills' from *The Dancers* by Grace Williams © Oxford University Press 1953. Music reproduced by permission. All rights reserved. Words by Kathleen Raine reproduced by permission of the Estate of Kathleen Raine.

PART III
1955–1994

Three things I covet from a man composer:

1. His larynx. I like to sing when I write for voices and I'd dearly love to be able to run the gamut from basso profundo through counter-tenor to falsetto soprano. To be given a starting point halfway up is a maddening handicap.

2. His ability to eat a good square meal immediately before a performance. Composers' wives, observing my inability to do this, are apt to whisper, "My dear, you're just like us!"

3. His freedom to write a *molto barbaro* movement and have it regarded as just part of his nature and not in any way abnormal.

Williams, 'A Short Symposium of Women Composers',
Composer 6 (Spring 1961)

"Women's Music": the subject which has dogged – or should I say "bitched" – me all my life.

Lutyens, *Divide and Misrule*, 1972

Chapter 6

Lutyens: *And Suddenly It's Evening*

Lutyens had attained a new level of technical assurance in such pieces as the Sixth String Quartet (1952) and the 'Wittgenstein' Motet (1953), but neither piece, nor any of her other works, had received the level of attention they deserved. Indeed, like Williams, only a handful of her concert works had actually been commissioned up to this point. The challenges confronting Lutyens in the 1950s were, however, of a different nature to those facing Williams, and part of the problem lay with the shifting perspectives of the immediate post-war musical climate in England. Whilst the hostile attitudes of the war years towards continental and dissonant compositional styles gradually became less flagrant, there were still diehard conservatives who were 'trying to keep England free of the moderns, free for Elgar, the Three Choirs Festival, England and St. George'.[1]

The situation at the BBC in London was also complicated. Although contemporary music concerts had been a regular feature on the airwaves prior to the war – a policy largely initiated by Edward Clark – a new battlefront opened out on the issue of listener ratings after the war. In April 1948, for instance, an internal BBC report noted that 'the Third Programme audience has diminished considerably and is now so small that it represents only a fraction of those who showed an early interest'.[2] In the face of rapidly diminishing audiences, planners sought to broaden the appeal by introducing what were thought to be more popular programme formats – a series of Light Music Concerts beginning in November 1948, for example – and contemporary music (in the broadest sense) was one of the casualties of this process. Although new works by 'safe' composers such as Vaughan Williams, Bliss, Rubbra and Walton could regularly be heard, the situation for composers such as Lutyens, Searle and the Hungarian-born Mátyás Seiber was far less secure. When Seiber enquired in March 1949 whether the Third would be interested in broadcasting a performance of his Second String Quartet, for instance, he was bluntly told by Herbert Murrill, the BBC's Head of Music, that they could only broadcast 'a very little of music so

---

[1] John Amis, *Amiscellany* (London: Faber and Faber, 1985), p. 156. Amis was referring to the insular outlook of some of the more senior (unnamed) music critics writing in the 1940s and 50s.

[2] As quoted in Humphrey Carpenter, *The Envy of the World: Fifty Years of the BBC Third Programme and Radio 3 1946–1996* (London: Weidenfeld and Nicolson, 1997), p. 80.

radical as this'; the reason given was that 'the audience to whom it would appeal is, as you know, extremely small'.[3]

Lutyens was immensely frustrated by the lack of support for her music from the BBC at this time, and made her feelings known in a succession of increasingly bitter letters. As her biographers have stated:

> Between 1952 and 1956 she conducted a running battle with the renamed Music Division. She protested at the terms in which her compositions were rejected (with an undeniably terse standard letter declaring them simply "unacceptable for broadcasting"). She deplored the BBC's penchant for playing music which was thoroughly untypical of her output; *En Voyage* was featured in a Festival of Light Music "with Max Jaffa and The Lot," while the Music Division busied itself rejecting her chamber concertos.[4]

When Richard Howgill, the BBC's new Music Controller, published a letter in *Musical Opinion* (August 1953) stating that a number of 'established' composers (including Maconchy) had been granted 'panel-free' status, Lutyens wrote to the Music Division pointing out that although she was thought to be 'established', she still had difficulty in getting her serious music broadcast. Her complaint was passed to Howgill who replied directly to her. His letter contained the statement that 'your work for documentaries and features is much appreciated and possibly is more the real Elizabeth [*sic*] Lutyens than that of your music which shows you as a disciple of Schoenberg'.[5] This sentence said a great deal about Howgill's own musical tastes, as well as the provincial horizons of his Music Division. The BBC's neglect of British-based serial composers was not, however, an isolated case. Little interest was also shown in some of the adventurous musical developments taking place abroad, with the result that the music of Messiaen, Boulez, Karlheinz Stockhausen and Elliott Carter was largely ignored. As William Glock recalled, broadcasting on the whole 'still gave the impression that contemporary music was led, for example, by Samuel Barber in the United States and by Poulenc in France'.[6]

In contrast, Glock had been conducting a 'campaign of insurrection' against the musical establishment on behalf of contemporary music. In August 1948, as the Director of a new summer school of music in Bryanston, Dorset, he took the initiative of inviting musicians such as Nadia Boulanger, Paul Hindemith

---

[3] Murrill, quoted in ibid., p. 95. Seiber (1905–60) was born in Budapest but had lived and worked in England since 1935.

[4] Harries, *A Pilgrim Soul*, p. 186.

[5] Howgill, quoted in Carpenter, *The Envy of the World*, p. 148. Richard Howgill became the new Controller of Music (as the job was now termed) in 1952. He succeeded Herbert Murrill who had been the BBC's Head of Music between 1950 and 1952.

[6] Glock, *Notes in Advance* (Oxford and New York: Oxford University Press, 1991), p. 58. All subsequent Glock quotations are taken from this book unless otherwise indicated.

and Boris Blacher to give lectures and composition classes (on both traditional and contemporary repertoire), much to the disapproval of many reactionaries in Britain. When the school moved to Dartington Hall, Devon in 1953, Glock retained the wide-ranging scope of the programmes but again raised the blood pressure of the musical establishment by increasing the number of performances and lectures on contemporary music. In that same year he invited Lutyens to present a composition masterclass, the first of many she would give at Dartington.[7] In this, she joined the ranks of an illustrious group of composers associated with the School, including Luciano Berio (1925–2003), Morton Feldman (1926–87), Harrison Birtwistle (1934–) and Peter Maxwell Davies (1934–).

Although Lutyens would have to endure a few more years in the wilderness, her work was beginning to receive a more sympathetic hearing in some circles. Glock's support, in particular, was important to her at this time: 'Life would be very grim without your help and good will', she told him.[8] He published her Sixth String Quartet in *The Score*, and made a point of arranging performances of her music whenever there was an appropriate opportunity.[9] The two briefly served together on the music committee of the Institute of Contemporary Arts (ICA) in the early 1950s. After Lutyens resigned from the committee in 1954, Glock (as newly appointed ICA Chair) commissioned an organ work from her (*Sinfonia*, Op. 32).[10] Both her song cycles *The Valley of Hatsu-Se* (1965) and *Akapotik Rose* (1966) would be 'Dartington' pieces, the former commissioned by Glock, the latter commissioned by the Arts Council for first performance at Dartington. Glock's support of her work continued after he was appointed BBC Controller of Music, and his tenure at the BBC (1959–73) coincided with the period of Lutyens's greatest critical success.[11]

Even so, her precarious financial situation in the mid 1950s dictated that the pleasures of being a 'Dartington' composer had to be balanced with other types of work. She was now becoming a figure of some fascination for younger composers who were attracted to serialism, and she began to accept private composition students. One of her first was Malcolm Williamson (1931–2003) who studied with her during the 1950s; she later became a mentor to, among others, Richard Rodney Bennett (1936–), Alison Bauld (1944–), Brian Elias (1948–) and Robert Saxton

---

[7] Although initially a nervous speaker, many who attended Lutyens's classes regarded her as an inspirational teacher. She, in turn, came to relish contact with like-minded musicians, particularly younger composers such as Brian Elias, who first attended her classes in 1965. Elias subsequently became one of her private composition students.

[8] Lutyens, letter to Glock, quoted in Harries, *Pilgrim Soul*, p. 164.

[9] Glock founded the new music journal *The Score* in 1949 and served as editor until 1961.

[10] The *Sinfonia* was premiered by Ralph Downes at London's Royal Festival Hall in April 1956. The ICA also commissioned Lutyens's chamber opera *Infidelio*, Op. 29 (1954).

[11] Glock served as both Controller of Music (1959–72) and Controller of the Proms (1960–73).

(1953–). Teaching commitments were combined with as much commercial work as she could find. In 1954 alone, for instance, she provided the music for five radio programmes and six documentary films. One score in particular seems to highlight the widening chasm between her commercial work and her own composition. In *The Heart of England* (1954), a documentary film made by British Transport Films, images of cows, Cotswold villages and agricultural shows are accompanied by the modal strains of English pastoralism. The music is pure pastiche (with the exception of a few moments that recall sections of Lutyens's own *En Voyage*) and bears the sure touch of a seasoned film composer. But this certainly was not the 'real Elizabeth Lutyens' referred to by Richard Howgill.

Music for Orchestra I, Op. 31 (1953–55)

While Lutyens's battles with the BBC were reaching epic proportions, she was embarking on an adventurous phase in her serious work. Some of her finest, most ambitious, works date from the late 1950s and early 60s, and include the *Musics for Orchestra I* and *II* (1953–55 and 1962), the cantata *De Amore* (1957) and *Quincunx* (1959–60) – all uncommissioned pieces. These are works conceived on a substantial scale, and considerably modify the label of post-Webern miniaturist that has sometimes been applied to Lutyens. *Music for Orchestra I* was the first of four pieces in the *Music for Orchestra* series, which, as a group, were composed between the years 1953 and 1981. Written for full symphony orchestra, the piece recalls, in places, the lush, almost Bergian gestures found in earlier works such as the *Three Symphonic Preludes* (1942). Although framed in one continuous movement, the work's four sections (*Allegro ma non troppo*; *Poco Adagio*; *Allegro*; *Lento, Allegretto–Allegro*) follow a symphonic pattern. Important thematic and rhythmic ideas are presented in the opening *Allegro* and, in common with the 'Wittgenstein' Motet, extensive use is made of canonic organization. The slow section (II) is a web of deftly crafted, chamber-like textures (reminiscent of Webern), and the scherzo section (III) contains passages for percussion only which foreshadow the more extensive percussion section in the later *Quincunx*. The final *Lento–Allegro* opens with a theme and set of variations, a form which Lutyens would employ again in the finale of her *Music for Orchestra III* (1964).

Music for Orchestra I was certainly symphonic in overall design, if not in title.[12] Lutyens probably chose the title in order to avoid the diatonic processes associated with the symphony, but she may also have been aware of Constant

---

[12] Anthony Payne has argued that Lutyens reserved the title *Music for Orchestra* for 'important artistic statements' and that all four pieces in this series 'occupy a place in her work similar to that of symphonies in other composers'. Payne, introduction to the broadcast premiere of *Music for Orchestra IV* (City of London Sinfonia/Richard Hickox) (Radio 3, 15 December 1983) [NSA Cat. No. T6360BW C3].

Lambert's colourful, one-movement *Music for Orchestra* of 1927. She counted Lambert among her dearest friends and was shattered by his untimely death from undiagnosed diabetes in August 1951. Although her *Music for Orchestra I* does not bear any dedication, it is possible that the work may have started life as a discreet tribute to a greatly admired, absent friend: 'I miss him to this day', she later stated.[13]

Music for Orchestra I remained unperformed until June 1961 when it was premiered in a studio broadcast by the BBC Symphony Orchestra, conducted by Bruno Maderna. Lutyens became dissatisfied with the piece, however, and later rejected it for being too old-fashioned: she scribbled 'ocuous' (rather than innocuous) in large letters across the front of her autograph manuscript.[14] Conscious of the work's reliance on traditional features, she described the piece as being her 'first and last attempt at employing what Stravinsky has called the "anachronistic orchestra for anachronistic composers"; the eighteenth- and nineteenth-centuries' orchestra being a straitjacket for twentieth-century ideas'.[15]

Lutyens's unhappiness with *Music for Orchestra I* seems to have been linked to a more general restiveness with both the general tempo of her life and her musical development. By her own admission, time spent on the handful of serious pieces she wrote at this time (many of which she later withdrew) had to be fitted around family life, commercial deadlines and work for the Composers' Concourse.[16] Her husband's poor heath was also a concern for her, and she stood loyally at Clark's side throughout the ugly public spectacle of his High Court slander case against the composer Benjamin Frankel in June 1955.[17] It was not until 1956 that she was able to pause and take stock. She now underwent a period of intensive self-examination during which she reappraised the events of her life and the direction of her music. *Quincunx* and the *6 Tempi for 10 Instruments* were, according to her own account, the first fruits of this important phase of creative renewal, but two choral/vocal works of this period also suggest new beginnings. Indeed, the

---

[13] Lutyens, *Goldfish Bowl*, p. 202. Interestingly, the opening movement of *Music for Orchestra I* makes occasional use of syncopated, jazz-type rhythms, something of a rarity in Lutyens's serious music as a whole. Lambert had previously provided Lutyens with several titles for pieces. He suggested the names 'Adumbration', 'Obfuscation' and 'Peroration' for her *Three Improvisations* for piano (1948), a piece she dedicated to him. He also suggested *Aptote* (an anagram of teapot) for her solo violin variations (1948). Each of the six variations in *Aptote* is dedicated to a friend; variation five is dedicated to Lambert.

[14] Autograph manuscript of *Music for Orchestra I* (British Library – BL Add 64491).
[15] Lutyens, *Goldfish Bowl*, p. 232.
[16] Composers' Concourse – Appendix.
[17] Clark's Presidency of the ISCM was challenged by a group of delegates in 1952. Faced with accusations of embezzlement, Clark took Frankel, the leading complainant, to court in 1955. The jury cleared Frankel of slander but also cleared Clark of any deliberate misconduct. For a detailed account of the case, see Harries, *Pilgrim Soul*, pp. 172–181.

choral work *The Country of the Stars* and the cantata *De Amore* are marked by the combination of a new fluency of technique and a warm, sensual expressiveness which had not really been encountered in previous works.

The Country of the Stars, Op. 50 (1956–57)[18]
De Amore, Op. 39 (1957)

Lutyens had always been stimulated by poetry and her reading of Chaucer in the summer of 1956 provided the inspiration for both pieces. She took the words of the evocatively titled *Country of the Stars* from Chaucer's translation of Book IV (metre VI) of the sixth-century philosopher Boethius's treatise *The Consolation of Philosophy*.[19] Echoing perhaps Boethius's classification of the music of the spheres (*musica mundana*), her choral work is a lyrical meditation on the philosopher's notion of the harmony of the cosmos, and the way in which the preordained course of the celestial bodies reflects the motion of the seasons and all life cycles on earth.[20] Set for unaccompanied chorus, Lutyens blends passages for solo voices with *divisi* choral sections, and there are moments of inspired and poetic word-setting and word-painting. As with the earlier 'Wittgenstein' Motet, *The Country of the Stars* is a fine example of a balanced relationship between music and words, the shape and pattern of the music reflecting, in this instance, the restrained passion of Chaucer's poetic translation (Example 6.1).

One of the interesting features of the series used in this work (and also that of *De Amore*) is the relatively high number of thirds Lutyens included in her note rows. It is perhaps not coincidental that one of the characteristics of medieval English polyphony was a marked preference for intervals of thirds and sixths, this practice contributing to the rise of 'a peculiarly English sonority'.[21] Certainly, the

---

[18] Although *The Country of the Stars* was composed in 1956–57, several accounts give the year of the work's premiere as the date of composition. The motet was premiered by the John Alldis Choir at Holy Trinity Church, Kensington on 20 March 1963.

[19] In *The Consolation of Philosophy*, Boethius argued that although our lives seemed to be determined by the whims of fortune, philosophy could teach us to look beyond the immediate and to perceive a higher (Platonic) reality. Love and goodness were the essential constants which bind all together in an ordered harmony.

[20] Boethius's *De institutione musica* divided music into three categories: *musica mundana* (music created by harmonious movement of stars and the seasons), *musica humana* (music created by harmony of human soul and body) and *musica instrumentalis* (music created by musical instruments and the human voice). For further details, see 'Boethius' in E. Fubini, *The History of Music Aesthetics*, trans. M. Hatwell (London: Macmillan, 1990), pp. 72–77.

[21] Donald Grout, *A History of Western Music*, 3rd ed. (London and Toronto: W.W. Norton, 1983), p. 148.

sweetened sonority in *De Amore* is a characteristic feature and acts as a striking complement to Chaucer's sunny verse (Example 6.2).

Example 6.1 *The Country of the Stars*, opening

Source: Music by Elisabeth Lutyens. Words by Boethius as translated by Chaucer. Copyright © 1963 Novello & Company Limited. All Rights Reserved. International Copyright Secured. Reprinted by Permission.

Example 6.2 Prime note row for *De Amore*

De Amore consists of nine distinct sections in which Lutyens sets extracts from Chaucer's *Troilus and Criseyde*, *The Parliament of Fowls* and *The Prologue to the Legend of Good Women*. Scored for soprano and tenor soloists, chorus and orchestra, this alluring piece is, as its title suggests, an exploration of different aspects of human love. In the lyrical second section, 'Pastorale' for tenor and orchestra, for example, the soloist delights in the coming of spring, while in the following section 'Pleynte' he sings of the torment and sense of vulnerability that love can sometimes bring. Two 'Invocations' and two entrancingly beautiful 'Night-Spels' follow, each more intense in mood than its predecessor, and the work is brought to a haunting close by two sections ('Lenvoy' and 'Apotheosis') which draw on full vocal and orchestral forces. Throughout, Lutyens employs her series with fluency, and her stress on particular intervals and marked use of repetition endow the piece with a memorable freshness and vigour. Unfortunately, *De Amore* had to wait some 16 years to be heard in public. 'Shame on everyone', commented Alan Blyth in his review of the work's Proms premiere, 'for letting us wait so long to hear such a subtle, unfashionably straight-forward piece'.[22]

The 40-minute *De Amore* was one of the most elaborate (and longest) works Lutyens had written up to this point. In the early years of her development, she had chosen to forge her own style mainly through the medium of chamber music, and her fondness for writing smaller-scale works continued in her maturity. Now, however, she showed a greater interest in writing larger-scale instrumental works, as well as vocal music encompassing short songs to operas. Her desire to extend her artistic range was connected to the new confidence that can be detected in pieces composed in the 1950s. Indeed, Payne has argued convincingly that the 'immediacy of nervous impact' achieved in the Sixth String Quartet (1952), a piece which Lutyens wrote at speed in one sitting, is one of the key pointers to the style of her maturity.

> The style which she subsequently evolved and refined, and which is seen to perfection in *Quincunx* ... has much to do with this immediacy of nervous impact, whether it be violent or otherwise. It is a style which above all enables her to compose with great speed. The result, as in a good improvisation, is that we feel the closest possible contact with the initial creative activity, and this does lend her best work considerable directness and vitality. The compositional technique used is an exact analogy of her stream of musical consciousness, and places great reliance on what could broadly be called a continuously evolving monody. (*The Listener*, 9 January 1969)

---

[22] *The Times*, 8 September 1973. *De Amore* was premiered at the Royal Albert Hall on 7 September 1973 by Jane Manning (soprano), Philip Langridge (tenor), the London Choral Society and the BBC Singers Women's Chorus (directed by John Poole), and the BBC Symphony Orchestra, conducted by Leon Lovett.

Quincunx, Op. 44 (1957–60)

Lutyens's style continued to evolve in interesting directions during the 1960s, but important fingerprints are present in all the major works of her maturity. Chief among these was her lifelong preoccupation with architectural design and balance, a concern which manifested itself in the complex, elegant structures of pieces such as *And Suddenly It's Evening* (1966) and *Driving Out the Death* (1971). The interest in structure was allied to precise usage of orchestral/instrumental and vocal colour; indeed, structure and colour were an integral part of the musical conception in each composition. This approach was clearly exemplified in *Quincunx*, a piece which Lutyens began sketching in 1957 immediately after her period of self-analysis.[23] Scored for baritone, soprano and an exceptionally large orchestra, the piece was inspired by her reading of Sir Thomas Browne's *The Garden of Cyrus* (1658), a mystical treatise concerned with the higher geometry of nature, art and the universe through the symbol of the 'quincunx' pattern – a shape of five parts, one at each corner (forming a rectangle) and one in the centre. The piece's elegant ninefold structure reflects the idea of the quincunx in that five full (tutti) orchestral sections enclose four soli sections where woodwind, strings, percussion and brass are featured in turn:

Tutti 1	—	Soli 1 (woodwind)
Tutti 2	—	Soli 2 (strings)
	Introduction: Baritone solo	

But the Quincunx of Heaven runs low, and 'tis time to close the five ports of knowledge; we are unwilling to spin out our waking thoughts into the phantasms of sleep, which often continueth precogitations; making cables of cobwebs and wildernesses of handsome Groves.[24]

Tutti 3 (Soprano solo, wordless)

Soli 3 (percussion)	—	Tutti 4
Soli 4 (brass)	—	Tutti 5 Coda – Finale

Lutyens had used a very large orchestra in her *Three Symphonic Preludes* (1942) but these forces were dwarfed by those required for *Quincunx*. In command of a gargantuan orchestra, she created a monumental, 20-minute work which is compelling in its use of instrumental colour and emotional intensity. The opulent scoring of the five tutti sections is skilfully balanced with the chamber-music clarity

---

[23] The composition of *Quincunx* was interrupted by other work commitments and was not completed until February 1960.

[24] Thomas Browne, *Garden of Cyrus*, chapter v, quoted in the score of Lutyens, *Quincunx*, introduction to Tutti 3 (University of York Music Press). The ordering of the sections is Lutyens's own as indicated in the score. Interestingly, she had originally wanted the quincunx idea to be reflected in the arrangement of the instruments on stage but this proved to be impractical because of the size of the orchestra.

of the soli sections. The delicate, sensuous sonorities of Soli 2 (for mandolin, guitar, harp and strings) recall the heady atmosphere of *O Saisons*, while the exhilarating Soli 3 – scored for pitched and unpitched percussion (including piano, tubular bells, bongos and whip) – shows off Lutyens's mastery of percussion writing to brilliant effect. Both sections surround Tutti 3, the weightiest section of the work (as is appropriate for the centre of a quincunx). The quotation from Browne's *Garden of Cyrus* is heard in an introduction to Tutti 3, and is sung by the baritone in the manner of a recitative without accompaniment. The passage dwells on the shadowy state between wakefulness and sleep, rational thoughts and dreams, and has the effect of preparing the listener for a central movement which is intensely lyrical in character. The entry at this point of the wordless soprano – a Debussy-inspired *Sirène* perhaps? – is in contrast to the song with words encountered in the unaccompanied baritone introduction.[25] The absence of words allows the soprano to become another orchestral colour in a movement which seems to echo Browne's nocturnal imagery in musical terms (Example 6.3).

When *Quincunx* was premiered at the Cheltenham Festival in July 1962, the work's eloquent design and voluptuous scoring clearly took some critics by surprise.[26] 'Miss Lutyens's *Quincunx* after Sir Thomas Browne towers over all other new music of this fortnight', wrote J.F. Waterhouse. 'Never before, not from Schoenberg, not from Berg have I heard 12-note music embody such luxuriance of full-orchestral sound'.[27] In contrast, others felt that the great array of instruments had 'come first', and that 'the music was an answer to the question "What can we give them to do?"'.[28] Interestingly, although Lutyens felt that a rich palette of instrumental colour was essential to the ethos of the piece, she also admitted that the chamber-like clarity she was able to draw from her enormous forces was partly a reaction against the existence in contemporary music of (in her own words) 'so much "pointillist" orchestration'.[29] Although she did not elaborate on this point, she may well have in mind the vogue in the late 1950s and early 60s for employing what was more often than not a standardized use of Webern-inspired textures in pieces for ensembles. On a more fruitful note, it is possible that Lutyens was aware of Boulez's *Le Marteau sans maître* (1952–54, rev. 1957), a piece which had a similar number of movements to *Quincunx* and

---

[25] Debussy employed a wordless female chorus in 'Sirènes', the final movement of his orchestral suite *Nocturnes* (1897–99).

[26] The performers were Joseph Ward (baritone), Josephine Nendick (soprano) and the BBC Symphony Orchestra, conducted by Norman del Mar.

[27] J.F. Waterhouse review, press cutting (source unknown) in Lutyens's private collection.

[28] Jeremy Noble, *The Musical Times* (June 1964). Noble reviewed the London premiere of *Quincunx* which took place on 2 May 1964.

[29] Lutyens, draft biography in unpublished Notebook dated 1964 (private collection).

Lutyens: And Suddenly It's Evening 167

Example 6.3 *Quincunx*, Tutti 3

[Score in C. Brass omitted]

Source: Copyright © University of York Music Press. Reproduced by permission.

which was also concerned with instrumental and vocal nuance.[30] Widely admired for both its formal elegance and its exploitation of unusual instrumental and vocal expression (including speaking and *bouche fermée*), *Le Marteau* was hailed by leading figures in British contemporary music as 'the flagship of the avant garde'.[31]

Lutyens was genuinely fascinated by Boulez and was encouraged to take an interest in his work by Clark, Williamson, Rodney Bennett and others close to her at this time.[32] She had first encountered him in Paris while attending a British Council concert of her works in the late 1940s and had sensed brilliance in the 'young boy'. But the excitement generated in British contemporary music circles by a new piece from the latest, heavily promoted composer was in stark contrast to the reception of her own work, and there are enough acidic references to 'new musical Messiahs' and 'aural Boulestin(s)'[33] in her autobiography to suggest that she probably found the experience irritating. Naturally, her musical antennae had been attuned to experiments with total serialism (where serial principles were applied to rhythm and dynamics as well as pitch) but she had not been tempted to follow. From the First Chamber Concerto (1939) onwards, she had adopted a *sui generis* approach to serial composition, and it was simply not her style to prepare for her own pieces the 'pages of pre-compositional diagrams, arrows in all directions, *blocs sonores* and other scaffolding' that she saw in the rooms of her younger colleagues.[34] 'I let the young go down the [total serialism] cul-de-sac', she later stated in full regal tone. 'They came back with some interesting things which I could take advantage of because we can all use principles but not private mannerisms'.[35]

6 Tempi for 10 Instruments, Op. 42 (1957)

In contrast to the pre-compositional 'scaffolding' adopted by some composers, Lutyens's music had become increasingly free of conscious calculation. Indeed, when speaking of her *Music for Orchestra II* (1962) she could draw attention to

---

[30] *Le Marteau* consists of a series of nine interpenetrating settings and commentaries on three René Char poems, and is scored for contralto, alto flute, viola, guitar, vibraphone, xylorimba and unpitched percussion.

[31] Alexander Goehr, quoted in Carpenter, *The Envy of the World*, p. 202.

[32] Rodney Bennett studied with Boulez in Paris, as did the pianist and writer Susan Bradshaw.

[33] Lutyens, *Goldfish Bowl*, p. 306. French-born Marcel Boulestin (1878–1943) became well known in Britain as a chef and restaurateur. His book *Simple French Cooking for English Homes* (London: W. Heinemann, 1923) triggered a vogue for French cuisine, and he became the first 'TV celebrity chef' when he appeared on the BBC's *Cook's Night Out* in 1937.

[34] Lutyens, *Goldfish Bowl*, p. 248.

[35] Lutyens interview (Radio 3, 5 July 1971).

the fact that 'there was no preconception in the composition or envisaged plan, the form becoming apparent to me only in the writing'.[36] She felt that her reliance on instinctive compositional processes and her ability to compose at speed enabled her to avoid sinking into a routine or mechanical approach to composition, thereby keeping her 'ear' fresh. The improvisatory, gestural style encountered in *Quincunx* and *Music for Orchestra II* was one of the features of her new confidence, but another work to signal a new beginning was the *6 Tempi for 10 Instruments*, the first of several mature works that specifically set out to explore the nature of musical time. Each of the divertimento-like six movements has a fixed time signature and duration of around two minutes but Lutyens crafts contrasting portraits of 'music in time' by varying her metres and textures. Both the first and second movements open, for example, with statements of the prime row (Example 6.4), but in movement one, '3/8, ♪ = 144' (Example 6.5), the row is presented as a quick, mercurial melodic line threaded through the ensemble, while in movement two, '7/4, ♩ = 44' (Example 6.6), colours which are entirely different in effect are generated by slower, more static music, played *con sordini* (muted). This use of contrasting tempi and textures had a precedent in the first two movements of the Sixth String Quartet, a work with which the *6 Tempi* is intimately connected.[37]

Example 6.4 *6 Tempi for 10 Instruments*, Prime note row

Although the work's somewhat abstract title is well chosen (and reflects the objective quality and precise nature of the music), the music critic and composer Bayan Northcott has suggested that the piece also contains elements of 'a more traditional style of musical character-piece'.[38] The elegiac fifth movement, '3/2, ♩ = 46', for example, takes the form of a miniature funeral march, and the other movements also take on personalities of their own. At the same time, the work might be described as a set of variations – common musical elements are present in all six movements – echoing the brief but exquisite set of six Variations for Solo Flute, Op. 38, a piece Lutyens also completed in 1957.

---

[36] Lutyens, programme note to *Music for Orchestra II* (private collection).
[37] See my discussion of the Sixth String Quartet in Chapter 3.
[38] Bayan Northcott, note to *6 Tempi* in booklet accompanying NMC CD 'Elisabeth Lutyens' (NMC D011).

Example 6.5 *6 Tempi for 10 Instruments*, I: 3/8, ♪ = 144 – opening

[Score in C]

Source: Copyright © Mills Music Limited, a Division of Alfred Music Publishing Co., Inc. All rights reserved. Reproduced by permission.

Lutyens: And Suddenly It's Evening 171

Example 6.6 *6 Tempi for 10 Instruments*, II: 7/4, ♩ = 44 – opening

[Score in C]

Source: Copyright © Mills Music Limited, a Division of Alfred Music Publishing Co., Inc. All rights reserved. Reproduced by permission.

Stravinsky was particularly fond of the *6 Tempi*: 'That is the music I like!' he told Lutyens after hearing Robert Craft play through the work on the piano in the autumn of 1959.[39] She had been aware of Stravinsky's genius since her early days in Paris and had since come to share many of his views on music, in particular the idea of music as 'simply organized sound'.[40] His influence became more pronounced after her first meeting with him in May 1954, when he came to London to conduct a concert of his ballet music.[41] She and Clark (who had known Stravinsky since 1911) attended the first rehearsal and spent a memorable evening with the composer at the Savoy Hotel afterwards. Undoubtedly, her friendship with him was one of the highlights in her life. Affectionate accounts of intermittent meetings with him thread their way through her writings, and her descriptions of him were always personal and revealing:

> Stravinsky himself is instantly recognizable in his many changing moods: ... the intellectual curiosity; the all-absorbing eyes, the wit – with every nail hit squarely on the head; the sly remark of great astuteness, and the skilful – sometimes gentle – malice ...

> Musicians are so often extremely dull, and dullness and Stravinsky do not go together. But with all the parade of the "great" there is no trace of the "holy cow." On the contrary, he was unbelievably humble before his gifts. He sought interest and stimulus from interesting and stimulating people, giving as good as he got.[42]

When she heard that he was recovering from a stroke in the autumn of 1956, she sent him a 30-bar orchestral piece to speed his recovery. The *Chorale for Orchestra* (1956) is a series of six miniature canons and chorales for wind, brass, harp, three violins and three cellos, which are based on fragments from the opening

---

[39] Stravinsky quoted in Lutyens, *Goldfish Bowl*, p. 264. The American conductor and writer Robert Craft was Stravinsky's biographer and devoted amanuensis.

[40] 'Music is simply organized sound, and if it is well organized it may have the power to produce emotions in the listener, but those emotions are not inherent in the music itself'. Lutyens in R. Murray Schafer, *British Composers in Interview* (London: Faber and Faber, 1963), p. 107. 'The phenomenon of music is given to us with the sole purpose of establishing an order in things ... its indispensable and single requirement is construction ... It is precisely this construction, this achieved order, which produces in us a unique emotion having nothing in common with our ordinary sensations and our responses to the impressions of daily life'. Stravinsky, *An Autobiography (1903–1934)* (New York: Simon and Schuster, 1936; London: Boyars, 1990), p. 54.

[41] Stravinsky conducted the Royal Philharmonic Orchestra at the Royal Festival Hall on 27 May 1954. The programme included performances of *Orpheus* (1947) and *Petrushka* (1910–11).

[42] Lutyens, review of Craft, *Stravinsky: The Chronicle of a Friendship 1948–1971* in *Tempo* 105 (June 1973), p. 46.

bars of the slow movement of Beethoven's A minor Quartet, Op. 132. Lutyens adapted Beethoven's own heading for his movement ('Hymn of Thanksgiving to the divinity from a convalescent, in the Lydian mode') to 'Hymn of Thanksgiving to the divinity for the recovery of the master Igor Stravinsky' in her score. 'Dear Friend, nothing could give me more pleasure than your precious "Homage"', Stravinsky wrote after receiving her *Chorale*.[43]

Symphonies, Op. 46 (1960–61)
Wind Quintet, Op. 45 (1960)

Associations with 'the master' were deliberately invoked in her *Symphonies* for Piano, Wind, Harps and Percussion, a piece which was commissioned by Glock's forward-looking BBC Music Division for the 1961 Proms season.[44] As its Stravinskyan title and scoring implies, the piece is primarily concerned with the exploration of different instrumental combinations (new 'soundings together'). At the same time, however, there is perhaps a hint of self-conscious modernity in the work's concern with unusual seating arrangements and the diffusion of sound in acoustic space. The piece is scored for solo piano, 24 wind and brass instruments, two harps, timpani and six percussion players, and in order to fully realize some of the balanced antiphonal and stereophonic sound effects, players were arranged into four 'groups' on stage, radiating from the piano like the ribs of a fan. The work is cast in the form of a palindrome (a favoured form for Lutyens), the instrumental textures becoming more complex as the music moves to a dramatic central climax which is then followed by a reversed reprise. This form had initially been suggested to Lutyens by the shape of the Albert Hall dome, but the venue's ungrateful acoustic – unfettered by sound-diffusing 'mushrooms' at this time – played havoc with the finer details of the scoring in performance. As she recalled,

> the performance ... was a complete flop ... The piece was unrecognizable to me and not helped by a percussion player dropping his triangle, which provoked some laughter ... Under these conditions the party I gave afterwards, at which Luigi Nono was one of the guests, was for me a wake.[45]

---

[43] Stravinsky letter quoted in Lutyens, *Goldfish Bowl*, p. 247.

[44] One of Glock's first initiatives as BBC Controller of Music involved raising the profile of British contemporary music largely through new commissions for the Proms, the BBC's Invitation Concerts and for the Cheltenham Festival. Established composers such as Malcolm Arnold were commissioned as well as the younger generation including Williamson, Rodney Bennett, Maxwell Davies and Birtwistle. Lutyens received eight commissions from the BBC between 1961 and 1971 – more than any other British composer – and this considerably boosted her profile as a composer of significance. For further details, see Glock, 'The BBC's Music Policy', *Notes in Advance*, pp. 200–213.

[45] Lutyens, *Goldfish Bowl*, p. 269.

The *Symphonies* was one of two works requested by BBC in 1960. The first was the Wind Quintet, written for the launch of the newly formed BBC Chamber Music Ensemble (later the Leonardo Ensemble) and premiered at a BBC Invitation Concert on 26 January 1961. Unaccustomed at this stage to working to commission as far as her serious works were concerned, Lutyens recalled the conditions under which work began:

> I know that a Wind Quintet was the *last* thing I was wishing to write at the time, being immersed in a piece of different character – *Catena* for Soprano, Tenor and Instruments. However, I had to put this to one side and it took me three days to transform my aural reluctance into the one and only thing I wanted to do ... I even looked up the movement of Beethoven's String Quartet with its prefaced motto theme: "Muss es sein? – Es muss sein! Es muss sein!" which so expressed my mood that at one stage I contemplated taking these notes as my *donné* for the quintet. I discarded this tentative idea as other ideas, shapes and sounds began to emerge and my initial indecision became transformed into an opening, a kernel of deliberate and definite decisiveness.[46]

Lutyens produced a sinewy, tautly argued quintet, replete with inventive passages in its four compact movements. Scrupulously objective in tone, it is as if she was using the precision of timbre and articulation of her wind instruments to, in Stravinsky's words, 'render a certain rigidity of form'.[47] Indeed, shape and form remained central preoccupations for her at this time, and it is interesting that in common with her *Symphonies*, she made use of palindromic form in some of the Quintet's movements. Furthermore, the experience of writing the work probably influenced her choice of instrumentation for her *Symphonies*.

Music for Orchestra II, Op. 48 (1962)
Music for Orchestra III, Op. 56 (1964)

The gradual process of refinement achieved by Lutyens in works of the late 1950s and early 1960s reached a new level of sophistication in *Music for Orchestra II*. Cast in a single movement, the tempestuous and uncompromising argument of the *Allegro* is brought to a dramatic and surprising close by a sparsely orchestrated 16-bar coda (*Adagio*) which is intensely elegiac and serene in character. The work calls for an unconventional orchestra which includes prominent parts for alto flute, alto saxophone, double-bass sarrusophone, as well as a substantial percussion section, and the scoring is integral to the piece's overall form. The music does not proceed in a smooth, flowing line but rather in a series of sharp, angular undulations

---

[46] Ibid., p. 267.

[47] Stravinsky, 'Some Ideas about my *Octuor*' reprinted in E.W. White, *Stravinsky: The Composer and His World* (London: Faber and Faber, 1979), p. 574.

of different size and shape which are derived from the series upon which the work is based: Lutyens used the analogy of a series of fountains when speaking about the piece.[48] These gestural undulations are coloured by a mixture of carefully selected instrumental groupings and solo entries, a use of instruments which foreshadows the distinctive groupings in *And Suddenly It's Evening* (1966) and other later works. The grouping of three B-flat clarinets doubled with violins in the piece, for instance, functions as a type of timbral *l'idee fixe*, featuring prominently throughout the vigorous *Allegro* (see Example 6.7). Robert Saxton has suggested that Lutyens used orchestral colouring or groups of sounds 'rather in the manner of mixtures on the organ' in this piece. The instrumental colouring, Saxton argues, is 'inseparable from the harmonic palette, which itself is inseparable from the *jets d'eau* concept of the overall form'.[49]

Lutyens dedicated *Music for Orchestra II* to Edward Clark, who died before the work was completed. Poignantly, the moment of Clark's passing was recorded in the manuscript of Lutyens's piano score (bars 184–85). When the work eventually received its British premiere by the New Philharmonia Orchestra and Ole Schmidt (conductor) at the Royal Festival Hall on 6 November 1975 – 13 years after its world premiere[50] – critics were keen to interpret the chorale ending as being a heartfelt tribute to Clark. Lutyens loathed the notion of self-expression in music and was keen to point out that the chorale had been planned well before Clark's death. Even so, she never denied that the piece had a special emotional significance for her and admitted that when she listened to the first performance she 'waited for bar 185 with clenched fists'.[51]

The Second *Music for Orchestra* was followed by a Third, which was commissioned by the BBC for the 1964 Cheltenham Festival and first performed there by the BBC Symphony Orchestra and Antal Doráti (conductor). In accepting this commission, Lutyens may well have savoured the irony that she could now refer to herself as a 'Cheltenham' composer, a title which, in the past, would have been a term of abuse for her. During the 1950s, the Cheltenham Festival (or 'Festival of Contemporary British Music' as it was known until 1961) had become something of a joke within contemporary music circles because of its taste for conservative music – in particular, a breed of commissioned orchestral piece known as the 'Cheltenham symphony'. Towards the end of the decade, however, there was a distinct change of mood – largely influenced by Glock's BBC appointment – and in the early 1960s the Festival became more adventurous

---

[48] Lutyens stated that the music was not heard 'as a left to right horizontal movement in a direction but as a fountain ejects water, in a continuous vertical movement'. Lutyens, *Goldfish Bowl*, p. 272.

[49] Saxton, programme note for *Music For Orchestra II*, BBC Proms booklet (4 August 1976, Proms premiere).

[50] *Music for Orchestra II* was premiered in Strasbourg by the Strasbourg Radio Orchestra, conducted by Charles Bruch, in September 1962.

[51] Lutyens, *Goldfish Bowl*, p. 284.

in its choice of new works. Although not a Cheltenham commission, Lutyens's *Quincunx*, for example, had received its premiere at the 1962 Festival, and *Music for Orchestra III* followed two years later.

Example 6.7 *Music for Orchestra II*

[Score in C. Some instruments omitted]

Example 6.7 continued

Source: Reproduced by kind permission of Schott Music Ltd., London. All rights reserved.

Given this context, one of the surprising features about this 14-minute piece is its romantic tone; indeed, Payne can state with justification that *Music for Orchestra III* 'occupies territory somewhere between [*Musics for Orchestra*] I and II'.[52] Each of the three movements draws from traditional forms, but the

---

[52] Payne, introduction to *Music for Orchestra IV* (Radio 3, December 1983).

overall structure is characterized by a typical concern for architectural balance. In the first movement, a rhetorical 'introductione' is followed by an *adagio* 'tema' section in which the core material of the work is presented, and the movement concludes with a dramatic 'cadenza' section for full orchestra. The second movement, a scherzo and trio, is followed by the finale which takes the form of a set of eight free variations. The final three variations are based on the 'cadenza', 'tema' and 'introductione' of the opening movement, and the work closes quietly with a brief coda which reflects on the original 'tema'. The piece is scored for (in Lutyens's words) 'a normal symphony orchestra'[53] – an unexpected feature given her earlier attitude towards 'anachronistic' orchestras. The instrumentation was probably dictated by the commission but it may well also have been that she was keen to avoid a repeat of the disastrous performance of her *Symphonies*, the only other large-scale orchestral work the BBC had commissioned up until this point. For whatever reason, stereophonic effects and complicated seating arrangements are absent from *Music for Orchestra III*. Much of the musical argument is articulated in terms of timbre, the melodic line passing from one instrumental group to another, although the distinct instrumental groupings which played a vital role in the Second *Music for Orchestra* are less prominent in the Third.

Catena, Op. 47 (1961)

Taken as a musical entity, *Music for Orchestra III* belonged, along with works such as the *Fantasie-Trio*, Op. 55 (1963) and the String Trio, Op. 57 (1964), to a period in which the technical advances Lutyens had made during the 1950s were consolidated and refined in a sequence of largely abstract, instrumental/orchestral works. All these pieces are characterized in varying degrees by a potent mixture of precision and the 'nerve-tingling' quality that had invigorated her music since the composition of the Sixth String Quartet. Yet she was now on the point of writing some of her most inspired vocal music – in particular, an important series of vocal cycles with mixed ensembles. The first of these cycles to be written was *Catena* for soprano, tenor and instrumental ensemble (22 players), completed in 1961. It seems telling that Lutyens should choose to dedicate this piece to her friend Luigi Dallapiccola, a composer for whom the modern vocal cycle had a special significance.[54]

Catena is the Latin word for chain or series and this idea is fundamental to the piece's shape. Lutyens sets ten different, predominantly British, poetic texts (ranging from Dryden and Donne to Joyce and Theresa Tanner), which are linked

---

[53] Lutyens, programme note to *Music for Orchestra III* (private collection).
[54] Luigi Dallapiccola – Appendix.

Example 6.8 *Catena*, 2a 'Hachi No Ki'

Source: Reproduced by kind permission of Schott Music Ltd., London. All rights reserved.

by their allusion to particular seasons.[55] The work is divided into three main parts and each part consists of a number of alternating vocal and instrumental sections. These sections function as links in a chain with the final motive or

---

[55] The themes of renewal and the cycle of seasons recur frequently in Lutyens's *oeuvre* and seem to have had a profound significance for her.

cadence of each becoming the starting point of the following. Part One consists of a total of seven sections, all of which are themed with references to spring. Each section has a different instrumentation with some scored for s soloist and a few instruments and others for fuller ensemble.[56] The work opens, for instance, with a brief setting of lines from Dryden's *Astraea Redux* (1660) for soprano, flute, violin, bassoon and horns (section 1), and is followed by an instrumental section for oboe, bass clarinet, trumpet, guitar and double bass (1a). The second section (2) is for flute, oboe, bassoon, violin, viola, trumpet, harp, percussion and piano, and is linked to the ensuing vocal section (2a) by the notes C and C♯: the final notes of section 2 and the first notes of the next section, 2a. This delicate and highly atmospheric section for soprano, viola, percussion, celesta and piano (Example 6.8) is a setting of lines from the Japanese Noh play *Hachi No Ki* by Seami (translated by Arthur Waley), and is only 36 bars in length.

The Valley of Hatsu-Se, Op. 62 (1965)
Akapotik Rose, Op. 64 (1966)

Lutyens turned again to Japanese poetry and the theme of the seasons in her celebrated song cycle *The Valley of Hatsu-Se* for soprano and chamber ensemble, a work conceived along similar lines to Stravinsky's *Three Japanese Lyrics* (1912–13). Commissioned by Glock for the Dartington Summer School, *Hatsu-Se* was premiered there by the soprano Jane Manning and the Vesuvius Ensemble in August 1965. Prior to accepting the commission, Lutyens had come across a collection of early Japanese poems in phonetic transcription and had been mesmerized by the *sound* of some of the poems. The eight compact poems that make up *Hatsu-Se* are set in the original language, with particular attention given to the nuances and accents of the words. The vocal line is strictly notated throughout and great care has been taken to ensure that each syllable is articulated in a clear and controlled manner.[57]

---

[56] The idea of links or chains also governs the seating arrangement for *Catena*, as detailed in the autograph manuscript (full score, BL Add. 64644). Conductor, vocal soloists and individual players are arranged on stage in a series of ornate circles, triangles and other shapes radiating from a central celesta. The arrangement bears a passing resemblance to a sacred mandala or magic circle which might be used by some Hermetic mystical order.

[57] *Hatsu-Se* was the first of several important vocal works that Lutyens would write for Jane Manning. These include *Akapotik Rose* (1966), *A Phoenix* (1968), *Lament of Isis on the Death of Osiris* (1969), *Islands* (1971), *Requiescat* (1971) and *Variations – Winter Series: 'Spring Sowing'* (1977). For insights into Lutyens's vocal writing, see Manning, *New Vocal Repertory* (Oxford: Oxford University Press, 1986), pp. 207–211.

Each poem is sensitively sketched in musical terms. The first four poems are concerned with the imagery of spring while the final four are reflections on autumnal/wintry scenes. The interplay between soprano and instruments is beautifully conceived, and the work contains many imaginative instances of delicate word-painting. One of the most striking examples is heard at the end of the first poem 'Fuyu-komori' where a lyrical song of the nightingale is played by the flute before the soprano sings the lines 'Hatsu-se no ya, Konure ga shita ni, Uguisu naku mo' (And the nightingale sings in the trees of Hatsu-Se). This passage is repeated at the end of the work, heralding the return of spring.

Example 6.9 *The Valley of Hatsu-Se*, I 'Fuyu-komori'

Example 6.9 continued

Source: Copyright © University of York Music Press. Reproduced by permission.

Phonetic texts of a very different kind provided the inspiration for *Akapotik Rose*, Lutyens's next song cycle. In 1965 she had provided the music for *Kakafon Kakkoon*, a film made by the artist and sculptor Eduardo Paolozzi about his series of *As Is When* prints. At the time, he had been immersed in writing a book of phonetic poetry, free association words and collage, and he gave Lutyens the freedom to arrange the words and phrases of several of his poems to suit her musical purposes. *Akapotik Rose* consists of seven free association 'sound poems' for soprano and ensemble with titles which include 'Blue-print, for a clock of straw', 'Koncert contorted' and 'Layers of Paradox'. Lutyens exploits the aural nuances of these sound poems and the resulting vocal part is spectacularly virtuosic. Words are often elongated into separate syllables with different vocal effects (trills on one note and *glissandi* at different speeds) required for each syllable. Other vocal techniques used include *bouche fermée*, freely spoken passages and singing through a loudhailer.[58] 'Each word or phrase', noted Lutyens, 'had for me its evocation, creating a definite if constantly changing musical "meaning"'.[59]

---

[58] It has been suggested that Lutyens's inclusion of a loudhailer may have been inspired by Maxwell Davies's *Revelation and Fall* for soprano and ensemble where the soloist is asked to scream into a loudhailer. This is misleading because although Davies wrote *Revelation and Fall* in 1965–66, the piece was not actually premiered until February 1968, some 18 months after *Akapotik Rose*'s premiere (August 1966) and first broadcast performance (Third Programme, 20 December 1966).

[59] Lutyens, notes on *Akapotik Rose*, undated Notebook (private collection).

> SILABONG FIRE eaters high priests.
> King Lockatoo costumed in SUN CLAWS
> Head long into peacocks
> Steel bells hammered tins – glimpse of swamp
> traumatic cadence
> is that the
> RACOONS LAUGH or the KAKAFON KAKKOON[60]

The frivolous, theatrical character of *Akapotik Rose* may well have been partly conceived by Lutyens as an attempt to debunk the quasi-religious ambience sometimes associated with the concert hall: she frequently complained to friends that the sanctimonious sitting-in-rows at concerts reminded her of the dull church services she had attended as a child. Yet the work was also very much of its time. The composer George Mowat-Brown remembered the excitement *Akapotik Rose* generated when it was premiered by Manning and the Vesuvius Ensemble at Dartington:

> The class at the 1966 Summer School included people who had just been to Darmstadt like Roger Smalley and Brian Dennis and this piece seemed like appropriately modern music to them. It also seemed to many of us to capture the exuberant, irreverent attitude of 1960s Britain in a way that had not really been achieved before.[61]

Mowat-Brown has argued that the work's flamboyant nature prepared the ground for the expressionist theatricality of works such as Maxwell Davies's *Eight Songs for a Mad King* (1969) and pieces written by Davies in the late 1960s for his chamber ensemble, the Pierrot Players (later, The Fires of London).[62] Significantly, Lutyens traced *Akapotik Rose*'s roots to 1920s Dadaism, dedicating the work to her friend the composer Virgil Thomson in 'recognition of his association with Gertrude Stein and the Dada movement'.[63]

---

[60] Paolozzi, 'Kakafon Kakkoon' as reproduced in the score of *Akapotik Rose* (University of York Music Press).

[61] George Mowat-Brown, interview with author.

[62] Lutyens was certainly an influential figure for the younger generation of British composers at this time. She had encouraged Davies, Birtwistle and Goehr when they first came to London in the 1950s, introducing them to useful contacts in the musical world. They, in turn, admired her musical radicalism.

[63] Lutyens, *Goldfish Bowl*, p. 298. Thomson first met Stein in Paris in 1925 and the two artists collaborated on a number of projects.

Example 6.10 *Akapotik Rose*, III 'Kakafon Kakkoon'

Source: Music by Elisabeth Lutyens reproduced by permission of the University of York Music Press. Words by Eduardo Paolozzi reproduced by permission of the Paolozzi Foundation.

Time Off? Not a Ghost of a Chance, Op. 68 (1967–68)

The reference to the experimental modernism of Stein is interesting, and links *Akapotik Rose* to the stage work *Time Off? Not a Ghost of a Chance*. Described by Lutyens as 'a charade in four scenes with three interruptions', the composite nature of *Time Off?* – which includes pop songs, jazz, prerecorded material and film excerpts – is complemented by a libretto (the composer's own) which mixes Steinesque word play, word associations and riddles with a liberal sprinkling of quotations from a variety of different authors.[64] In common with the plays of Stein, 'plot' in the traditional sense is absent. Instead, the four scenes (entitled 'Tempus', 'Fors', 'Aetates' and 'Spectra') explore the idea of Time from a number of different angles, dwelling on time itself, chance, as well as the different periods of life such as youth and old age. In her presentation of these ideas, Lutyens adopts the spirit of Rabelaisian buffoonery and something perhaps of the irreverence of the Greek comedies of Aristophanes.[65] Serious, often profound, ideas are mixed with irreverent burlesque, and the main argument is articulated through the verbal sparring of the two main characters – the thoughtful, poetic Harold (baritone) and his satirical *alter ego* Stooge (actor).

HAROLD	Where are the snows of yesterday?
STOOGE	Well, where are they? Where – bloody well – are they?
HAROLD	(with CHORUS) Melted … snow melts … wax melts …
	Moons wax … moons wane … Can you hear me? Wax out your ears!
	Where are the snows of yesterday? Echo parlant …
	They are THEN. THEN was now once … then – then
	That yesterday looked to now – THEN tomorrow
STOOGE	Tomorrow never comes.[66]

Although completed in 1968, *Time Off?* was not staged until March 1972 when it was produced at the Sadler's Wells Theatre, London by Anthony Besch and performed by John Gibbs (baritone), Barry Foster, the New Opera Chorus and New Opera Orchestra, conducted by Leon Lovett. The work won Lutyens new admirers and was generally well received in the press. For some, however, the verbal puns and references to 'farts' clearly went too far. 'What was one to make of this farrago of a libretto', fumed Alan Blyth, 'in which a maze of quotations, a jumble of verbal styles, and a host of schoolgirl puns are thrown together with reckless regard to any kind of sense or form?' (*Opera*, April 1972). In fact, the use of modern colloquialisms (the majority of which are spoken rather than sung) and the capricious, conversational effect of the writing, were all quite deliberate. 'I wrote the libretto in about two days in a stream of consciousness kind of way',

---

[64] It is perhaps not coincidental that Lutyens's 'four scenes with three interruptions' shares a delight in irreverent wordplay and 'stream of consciousness' writing with the Thomson/Stein opera *Four Saints in Three Acts* (1934). Lutyens is known to have discussed *Four Saints in Three Acts* with Brian Elias at the time of writing *Time Off?*

[65] Lutyens set an extract (part of 'The Ringing Island') from the fifth book of Rabelais's *Gargantua and Pantagruel* in her *Islands* for narrator, soprano, tenor and ensemble (1971).

[66] Extract from *Times Off?*, scene 1 (Tempus), printed libretto [Lutyens Collection, British Library, BL Add. 64457].

Lutyens stated in an interview before the premiere.[67] 'I have ... a crossword-puzzle mind and I wanted to write quickly, so that it was simply like a free association'. All these literary choices, together with the blend of different musical styles from pop to serial, ultimately seemed allied to a desire on Lutyens's part to create a stage work which was immediate in impact and which brought the 'action' on stage closer to the audience.[68] As she argued:

> [I]n any work which is theatre, whether it's radio, films or opera, there's another factor, the audience. When you write a string quartet, you don't say "ah, I'm going to surprise the audience." But if you're in the theatre, the audience is like another character, a sort of reactor, and there's an ingredient in the theatre which calls for instantaneous reaction.

Interestingly, the creative compulsion for writing *Time Off?* and the other two uncommissioned stage works which date from this period – *The Numbered* and *Isis and Osiris* – seem to have been intimately linked with Lutyens's experience of writing theatre music. Her career in the theatre had started in earnest when she was invited to write the music for a 1959 production of *The Bacchae* at the Oxford Playhouse by the charismatic Greek director Minos Volanakis.[69] She relished the challenges of working in this new environment, and found the experience of working as part of a professional team to be a welcome contrast to the solitude and loneliness of the composer's world. 'Above all, I prefer writing for the theatre', she told a journalist in 1960. 'I would dearly love to be attached permanently to a theatre company – like the Oxford Playhouse, for example. But what theatre these days can afford a full-time composer?'[70]

---

[67] Lutyens in '*Time Off?* and *The Scene Machine*' (Stephen Walsh in conversation with Lutyens and Anthony Gilbert about their new operas), *The Musical Times* 113 (February, 1972), p. 137. All subsequent quotations by Lutyens in this section are taken from this source, unless otherwise indicated.

[68] Indeed, at the end of scene 1, the front row of the audience changes places with the characters on stage.

[69] Lutyens's other collaborations with Volanakis at the Oxford Playhouse included productions of Aeschylus's *The Oresteia* (1961) and Ben Jonson's *Volpone* (1966). The music she composed for *The Oresteia* provided the point of departure for her *Présages: Recitative and Variations for Solo Oboe*, Op. 53 (1963) – a 'recitative and variations on Cassandra's lament from the *Oresteia*', written for the oboist Janet Craxton.

[70] Lutyens, unnamed newspaper cutting, 26 October 1960 (private collection). Lutyens described Volanakis as 'the person who means most to me (though twenty years younger) outside my family'. *Goldfish Bowl*, p. 258.

The Numbered, Op. 63 (1965–67)

The idea for *The Numbered* was sparked by a conversation Lutyens had with Volanakis about his earlier production of Elias Canetti's *Die Befristeten*; the play had been premiered in English as *Their Days are Numbered* at the Oxford Playhouse in 1956.[71] Mesmerized by Volanakis's description of the play, Lutyens became intrigued by the possibilities it seemed to offer as the basis for an opera. The play draws on concepts that were central to Canetti's work as a whole – in particular, the behaviour of crowds and the dynamics of power. The characters all know in what year they will die – they are named by the state government according to their lifespans (Fifty, Seven, Ten, etc.) – although they do not know precisely when and how. This knowledge has a profound effect on their personal morality and social standing. Those who are given a higher number at birth, for instance, are privileged in this society while those with a lower number are second-class citizens. The people are also vulnerable to manipulation by those in power. They carry their own number in a sealed capsule worn around the neck, opened only at death by a keeper or high priest to confirm the date. When Fifty, the main character, discovers that nothing is contained in these capsules, and that the whole system is part of an elaborate lie perpetrated by the authorities, the ordered state descends into confusion and chaos.

Lutyens started composing *The Numbered* in December 1965, completing it in November 1967.[72] Although she had previously written two chamber operas, *The Pit* (1947) and *Infidelio* (1954), she saw *The Numbered* as her first 'real' opera (or 'music-drama' as she preferred to describe it).[73] Her response to powerful themes of death, time and power in Canetti's play was a two-and-a-half-hour, two-act music drama which used 13 soloists, two trebles, three male speakers, mixed chorus and a vast orchestra (including electric guitars): 'it's got everything', she noted, 'like all first operas'.[74] *The Numbered* draws much from Greek drama. The work opens, for example, in the tradition of Greek tragedy, with a spoken Prologue which serves to establish the key themes and context of the opera. Despite having a battalion of vocal and orchestral forces available, most of the opera's 20 scenes (11 in Act 1 and 9 in Act 2) take the form of delicately scored dialogues between no more than two characters. These dialogues are interspersed with choral passages where, as in Greek drama, the chorus comments and reflects on the drama while remaining detached from the central actions. Indeed, Richard Rodney Bennett and Susan Bradshaw have argued that the chorus 'is always used as in Greek

---

[71] Elias Canetti – Appendix.

[72] Volanakis provided the libretto for *The Numbered*.

[73] For a comprehensive analysis of the work, see Laurel Parsons, 'Elisabeth Lutyens's Music Drama *The Numbered*: A Critical-Analytical Study', PhD dissertation (University of British Columbia, 2003).

[74] Lutyens, 'Talking about Music 201: Elisabeth Lutyens at 70' (Radio 3, 1976) [NSA Cat. No. 1LP0201961 S1 BD3 BBC TRANSC].

drama' in Lutyens's stage works. 'The chorus of waiting wives in *The Pit*, the changing persona of the crowd in *Time Off?* ... and the specifically Greek-chorus role allotted to the chorus in *The Numbered* are examples of this approach'.[75]

And Suddenly It's Evening, Op. 66 (1966)

Lutyens found work on *The Numbered* to be immensely stimulating, but was nevertheless drained by the sheer physical labour of writing. As she stated:

> In my opera, owing to the nature of its subject, there is a beginning, middle, end – a drive, in time, a propulsion from one thing to another. I was feeling exhausted by the work on this, its sheer length and the necessity of keeping all the necessary drive. I was longing, as a composer, just to stand still – and sing, to get out of 'time' and its momentum.[76]

Two works for voice and mixed ensemble composed during the 18-month period of writing *The Numbered* provided a welcome and necessary contrast with opera work. The first to be composed was *Akapotik Rose*. The second was *And Suddenly It's Evening*, a work commissioned by the BBC for the inaugural concert opening of the new Queen Elizabeth Hall at London's South Bank Centre on 3 March 1967.[77] Unusually for Lutyens, who more often than not began a work with a musical idea which dictated the form and orchestration, the idea of *And Suddenly* began with a search for the right instrumentation. The BBC had requested a choral work and Lutyens's initial response was the idea of a modern madrigal for chorus and brass drawing from the tradition of Monteverdi and Gabrieli. She considered setting Elizabethan verse, but came to discard the idea when she 'found her head full of [the perfect Elizabethan settings] of Dowland and the English madrigalists'.[78] At the same time, she had been reading the poetry of the Sicilian Nobel Literature Prize winner Salvatore Quasimodo, and was immediately captivated by the powerful mixture of unsentimental nostalgia and intense imagery in his work.[79] She chose four of his poems (in Jack Bevan's English translation), and decided to set the work for solo voice and ensemble.

---

[75] Bennett and Bradshaw, 'Elisabeth Lutyens's Stage Works', *Tempo* (March 1977), p. 48.

[76] Lutyens, undated notes for Dartington lectures (private collection).

[77] The work was premiered by the BBC Chamber Ensemble and Herbert Handt (tenor and conductor).

[78] Gerald English, note for *And Suddenly It's Evening*, BBC Proms booklet (10 August 1967, Proms premiere).

[79] Lutyens later turned again to Quasimodo when she composed two different settings of his poem 'Dialogo'. The first setting, written in 1972, is for tenor and lute, while her second (of 1981) is an aria for soprano and orchestra.

As with *Quincunx* and *Catena*, the striking architectural elegance of *And Suddenly* is linked with the scoring. The work is scored for tenor and 11 instruments, and Lutyens divides her instruments into three distinct groups: a 'coro di strumenti' of two trumpets, two trombones and double bass; and two ritornelli trios consisting of celesta, harp and percussion (ritornello 1), and violin, horn and cello (ritornello 2). These groupings – which suggest an acquaintance with both Gabrieli's instrumental *cori spezzati* (separated brass choirs) and Stravinsky's use of instrumental groups in late works such as *In Memoriam Dylan Thomas* – are used both to accompany and frame the four settings.

    Ritornello 1
1. Tenor and Coro di strumenti   'On the Willow Boughs'
    Ritornello 1

    Ritornello 2
2. Tenor and Coro di strumenti   'In the Just Human Time'
    Ritornello 2

    Intro: Coro di strumenti
3. Tenor and ritornelli   'Almost a Madrigal'
    Coda: Coro di strumenti

    Antiphon 1: Ritornelli
4. Tenor solo   'And Suddenly it's Evening'
    Antiphon 2: Ritornelli
    Coda: Coro di strumenti

The balanced structure alludes to the recurring instrumental sections used by Monteverdi in his operas, and other elements of early Italian Baroque style are also present in the vocal line. The tenor, for instance, is asked to 'trill on one note', a characteristic of Baroque vocal style and, indeed, of Lutyens's own vocal style. Fascinating, too, is the way in which Lutyens writes for voice and instruments. In the first poem, 'On the Willow Boughs', the tenor's statements are punctuated by hieratic, chordal repetitions from the brass choir (Example 6.11). Interestingly, while the piece as a whole is filled with inventive and contrasting material, the writing is characterized by an effective use of repetition (whether direct as in the example below, or through use of palindromic form in the ritornelli sections) which serves to introduce a ritualistic element into the settings.

The structural elegance, sensitivity to timbres and the emotional immediacy of *And Suddenly* appealed to audiences and critics at its premiere. Described by *The Times* (4 March 1967) as 'something altogether out of the ordinary' and 'one of the composer's most moving works', the piece was also praised by Roger Smalley for its 'unmistakable originality' and 'restrained and lyrical expression' (*The Musical Times*, December 1971). Self-effacing when praised, Lutyens

Example 6.11 *And Suddenly It's Evening*, I 'On the Willow Boughs'

Source: Music by Elisabeth Lutyens. Words by Salvatore Quasimodo in English translation by Jack Bevan (*Quasimodo – Selected Poems*, Harmondsworth: Penguin Books Ltd., 1965). Music reproduced by kind permission of Schott Music Ltd., London. All rights reserved.

claimed that the sectionalized structure and use of repetition in the piece had been dictated by exhaustion – the result of concentrated work on *The Numbered*. Yet *And Suddenly* represented a new phase in terms of her stylistic development. As Payne has remarked, 'the less complex harmony, the simple gestures and the block structuring' employed in this piece provided 'a strong contrast with the fluid lyricism of previous works',[80] and these elements were retained and refined further in subsequent works. Payne is certainly right to suggest that the new flexibility and simplicity of style was prompted in part by 'the special needs' of the vocal music she composed in the 1960s – although some of these features (particularly a less rigid approach to serial manipulation and the use of repetition) were present in raw form in *De Amore* (1957). Lutyens's interest in the music of Stravinsky, one of the principal exponents of block-form composition, may also have had some impact on works composed at this time. Although she did not speak in detail of any influence he may have had on her creativity, it is interesting to note that both composers were, in the context of their own stylistic developments, moving towards greater simplification in the mid 1960s: Stravinsky in works such as *Introitus (Requiem aeternam)* (1965), and Lutyens in *And Suddenly* and the vocal cycle *Essence of Our Happinesses*. Admittedly, she was sometimes ambivalent about the way in which he used 12-note methods – she had resented the fact that his *Canticum Sacrum* (1955) in its marriage of serial and tonal elements had been described as 'serialism without tears'.[81] Even so, she may have felt that the sparseness and concentrated expression in his *Requiem Canticles* (1965–66), a work she profoundly admired, resonated with the greater economy of style which characterizes her late works – although she would probably have argued that arthritis in the hands was the reason.[82] In the end, however, her connection with Stravinsky was deeply personal. When she heard of his death in April 1971, she experienced 'a feeling of cold as if a fire that has warmed and cheered me had gone out'. Her *Requiescat: In Memoriam Igor Stravinsky* for soprano and string trio, commissioned by the music journal *Tempo* as one of a series of musical tributes to Stravinsky, is a masterly setting of words taken from Blake's *Couch of Death*.[83] Although the mould is miniature – the work is only five minutes in length – the material is intense in its emotional feeling. As Lutyens eloquently stated, her *Requiescat* was a sincere 'expression of grief – and hope – for a person much treasured; a frail, vibrant, and never, never dull old man whom I had come to love and for whom I felt lonely'.[84]

---

[80] Payne, 'Elisabeth Lutyens', *The New Grove Dictionary of Music and Musicians*, ed. S. Sadie (London: Macmillan, 1980), vol. 11, p. 376.

[81] Lutyens, quoted in Harries, *A Pilgrim Soul*, p. 158.

[82] Lutyens noted that composers 'seem to get much more economical with age' and cited Stravinsky as a prime example of this tendency. '[Is it] a phenomenon of age that one gets very economical? Or physical inability? With arthritis in the hands, I just can't write a lot of notes'. Lutyens, 'Talking about Music: Elisabeth Lutyens at 70' (Radio 3, 1976).

[83] Other composers contributing to *Tempo*'s 'Canons and Epitaphs in Memoriam Stravinsky' included Berio, Berkeley, Birtwistle, Blacher, Boulez, Copland, Carter, Denisov, Goehr, Maw, Maxwell Davies, Milhaud, Schnittke, Sessions, Tippett and Wood.

[84] Lutyens, *Goldfish Bowl*, p. 312.

Essence of Our Happinesses, Op. 69 (1968)

Emotional directness and simplicity of style are features of *Essence of Our Happinesses*, a work which explores the relationship between mystical and musical concepts of time. According to Lutyens, the inspiration for the piece arose during a talk she gave to a group of Royal Academy of Music students who claimed only to be interested in the music of 'now'. After returning home, she re-read Donne's *Devotion XIV* and was particularly drawn to the following passage:

> Before you sound that word, *present*, or that *Monosyllable*, *now*, the present, and the *Now* is past. If this *Imaginary halfe-nothing*, *Tyme*, be of the Essence of our *Happinesses*, how can they be thought *durable*? *Tyme* is not so; how can they be thought to be?[85]

The passage led her to reflect further on the nature of time, and on experiences of timelessness – particularly the religious trances and states of ecstasy considered in R.C. Zaehner's book *Mysticism, Sacred and Profane* (1957). Inspired by these sources, Lutyens chose texts by three authors from different times and traditions which seemed to her to best illuminate these experiences: extracts from *The Mi'raj* (ascension) by the ninth-century Islamic philosopher Abu Yasid, Donne's *Devotion XIV* and Rimbaud's poem *Enfin, ô Bonheur*. Each setting is followed by a dance-like orchestral movement:

1. *The Mi'raj of Abu Yasid* – Tenor and Orchestra
   Choros 1 (Mystikos) – Orchestra
2. *Their Criticall Dayes* by Donne – Tenor, Chorus and Orchestra
   Choros 2 (Chronikos) – Orchestra
3. *Enfin, ô Bonheur* by Rimbaud – Tenor and Orchestra
   Choros 3 (Manicos) – Orchestra

The work opens with an evocative portrait of Abu Yasid's experience of eternity attained in a state of mystical ecstasy. The use of slowly changing harmonic clusters of different intensity and colour in brass and strings to accompany the tenor's statements has the effect of suspending the listener's sense of time.

The impression of timelessness is sustained in the ensuing orchestral *Mystikos*. Described by Lutyens as 'a short dance movement',[86] its argument is underscored by the intensely hypnotic ♩ pulse of a *pianissimo* tam-tam. The second setting, the work's main movement, is an extended meditation on the transient nature

---

[85] Words taken from Donne's *Devotions XIV* as reproduced in the score of *Essence of our Happinesses* (University of York Music Press). The work was commissioned by the BBC and first performed at the 1970 Proms by Richard Lewis (tenor) and the BBC Symphony Orchestra and Chorus, conducted by Norman del Mar.

[86] Lutyens, note to *Essence of Our Happinesses* (private collection).

Example 6.12 *Essence of Our Happinesses*, I 'The Mi'raj of Abu Yasid'

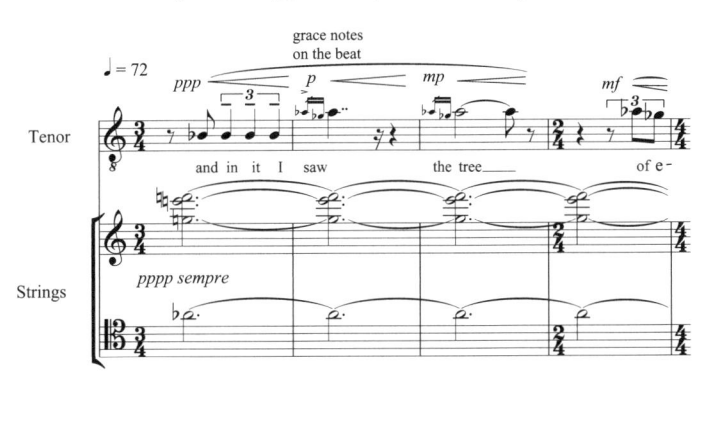

Example 6.12 continued

[Score in C]

Source: Copyright © University of York Music Press. Reproduced by permission.

of '*Tyme*'. Extracts from Donne's *Devotion* are presented in a series of eight antiphonal statements for unaccompanied chorus and tenor with orchestra, and both choral and solo tenor sections have their own contrasting musical material which is repeated extensively during the course of the movement.[87] A second orchestral dance (*Chronikos*) follows which, as Lutyens explained, places 'emphasis on metric time in the form of a clock-like ostinato on marimba and harp against which the orchestra plays'.[88] The third movement is a highly atmospheric setting of an introduction and two short verses from Rimbaud's *Enfin, ô Bonheur*, in which the poet expresses his ecstatic vision of eternity. In the introduction, the tenor is accompanied by percussion only, and the harmonic colouring of the ensuing two verses is enriched by the addition of sustained chords in wind, brass and strings. In contrast, the final dance for orchestra (*Manicos*) is a frenzy of agitated fragments and forceful rhythms which are scattered at high speed throughout the orchestra before coalescing into a dramatic, final tutti chord.

Essence of Our Happinesses is, in the broadest sense, a work of incantation. The work was written at a time when Lutyens was preoccupied with concepts of

---

[87] The movement consists of a total of four choral statements interspersed with four statements for tenor and orchestra.

[88] Lutyens, note to *Essence of Our Happinesses*.

philosophical and mystical time, and ancient rites reflecting the struggle between Life and Death. 'I have come to the conclusion and now *personally* believe that music and art are more allied to religion and magic', she later stated, 'meaning neither creed nor voodoo, than elementary arithmetic or science (so often inaccurately aped by composers), which has a different function'.[89] Other works inspired by these concepts quickly followed. In 1969–70, for example, she composed the lyric drama *Isis and Osiris*, a realization of the legend of Osiris based on the first-century writer Plutarch's version of the *Egyptian Book of the Dead*: here, the death and resurrection of the corn god Osiris symbolized the cycle of natural decay and revival of life. She took the title of her oboe quartet *Driving Out the Death* (1971) from an ancient Thüringian ceremony which represented the ending of winter (a period of death and hardship) and the beginnings of new life in spring.[90] And in *Counting your Steps* (1972) for mixed chorus, flutes and percussion, she set six West African songs/chants which were concerned with the important stages of life, from birth to death.[91] While Lutyens had always favoured universal themes in her work, one of the particularly interesting features of works written at this time is the correlation between these themes and the broadening of her expressive range and simplification of her musical style. Indeed, her use of repetition and of simpler gestures tends to reinforce the ritualistic ethos of all these pieces.

Driving Out the Death, Op. 81 (1971)
Isis and Osiris, Op. 74 (1969–70)

Concepts of ritual and sculpture lie at the heart of *Driving Out the Death*. The work, written for Janet Craxton and the London Oboe Quartet, is divided into six sections (played without a break), each of which is associated with ceremonies of Death and Life from Thüringia and ancient Greece.

1. Carrying out of Winter	–	2. Pantomimos
3. Carrying out of Summer	–	4. Euché
5. Driving out the Death	–	6. Dithyrambos

Lutyens stated that the *donné* or basic musical idea from which the work was derived – in this instance, the three note figure F♯-E-F♯ stated by the oboe at the

---

[89] Lutyens, *Goldfish Bowl*, p. 305.

[90] Traditionally, the 'Driving out the Death' ceremony took place in some villages in Thüringen, Germany at the beginning of March and involved young people building a straw figure of Death, carrying it out and throwing it into the river. For further details, see Jane Harrison, *Ancient Art and Ritual* (Oxford: Oxford University Press, 1913, rev. 1948), pp. 67–68.

[91] The texts were taken from Cecil Maurice Bowra's collection, *Primitive Song* (1962).

opening – presented itself to her as a piece of sculpture, an object complete in itself. Each section is dominated by this figure and/or its variants.

Example 6.13 *Driving Out the Death*, opening

Source: Copyright © University of York Music Press. Reproduced by permission.

Lutyens achieves great variety between sections. In 'Carrying out of Winter', the strings form a unified 'chorus' in response to the oboe's invocatory-type statements. In the ensuing 'Pantomimos' (Gk: 'all imitator'), however, the spirit of movement, mime and dance is captured by the strings' mimicry of the oboe's line and the intricate rhythmic interplay between the instruments. In contrast, the fourth section 'Euche' (Gk: 'prayer' or 'vow'), described by Lutyens as a sculptured prayer of winter, is characterized by quiet, slow-changing harmonies.

Repetitive gestures are a marked feature of *Isis and Osiris*, a two-hour lyric drama for eight voices and chamber orchestra, and these elements strengthen the ritualistic, hieratic events in the piece. Eager to explore the possibilities of opera further, Lutyens wrote her own libretto for the work, describing the Osiris myth as 'a perennial ritual of the seasons, life and death, as pertinent today as it was thousands of years ago'.[92] In the opera, the Egyptian King Osiris teaches his people how to cultivate grain and irrigate the Nile. Revered throughout Egypt, he travels the world to convey this knowledge to others, leaving Isis, his sister and consort, to govern his kingdom. His success arouses the jealousy of his brother Seth who wants Isis and the crown of Egypt for himself. When Osiris returns from his travels, Seth tricks him into lying down in a chest which is then sealed with lead and dumped into the sea. After searching the earth, the distraught Isis eventually finds the chest and hides it. But Seth discovers the chest and cuts Osiris's body up into 14 pieces, scattering them throughout Egypt. To avenge Osiris's murder, Isis collects each part of his body that she finds, and makes models of each part to place in local temples for people to worship. One 'precious part' is missing, but she makes a model to serve as an eternal symbol of fertility. Osiris is eventually reborn and resurrected as God of the Underworld.

Isis and Osiris was staged at Morley College in November 1976 and was one of the events marking Lutyens's 70th birthday year. Produced by Mike Ashman and with a set design by Ellen Graubart, the piece was performed by Anna Bernardin (Isis), Michael Lewis (Osiris), Richard Wigmore (Seth) and the Morley Musica Viva Ensemble, conducted by Michael Graubart. Unfortunately, the production (nicknamed 'Crisis and Osiris' by the College production team) was hampered from the start by a microscopic budget and lack of adequate rehearsal time. Despite the performers' best efforts, the work was not well received. Most critics felt that the monumental themes in the opera were not convincingly realized in musical (or literary) terms. Paul Griffiths described it as being 'like a tomb painting brought to life, but only just', and noted that the production looked like '*Aida* done on the cheap' (*The Times*, 29 November 1976). Furthermore, certain events on stage produced unintentionally comic effects on the opening night. Osiris's reconstructed 'precious part', for example, intended as a centrepiece in one of the scenes, was missing in the performance and the audience was treated to the sight of a hapless cast member rushing onto the stage clutching a colossal replica penis!

Lutyens was bitterly disappointed with the whole production. Having unsuccessfully attempted to interest Covent Garden and Glyndebourne in staging the work, she now showed a spectacular lack of interest in the Morley College production. Attempts by the producer to engage her in detailed discussion about the opera's staging and set design came to nothing and, according to her biographers, she refused to attend the first dress rehearsal because 'she did not want to miss

---

[92] Lutyens, *Goldfish Bowl*, p. 300.

the third episode of *I, Claudius*'.[93] Such indifference, certainly as far as her stage works were concerned, was not characteristic and probably hid a multitude of misgivings she had about the work. Yet although her appetite for composing works for the stage resulted in a series of shorter dramatic works including *Linnet and the Leaf* (1972), *The Waiting Game* (1973), *One and the Same* (1974) and *Like a Window* (1976), *Isis and Osiris* was to be her final large-scale opera.[94]

In the early 1970s Lutyens had made little attempt to hide her bitterness about the fate of her (at that stage) unperformed operas. As she told Stephen Walsh, 'there's one thing I'm rather jealous of Britten about, and that is that he knows where he's writing for and who he's writing for' (*The Musical Times*, February 1972). Britten was not the only composer to provoke Lutyens's envy. One fascinating item in her private papers is a photocopy of a *Western Mail* article entitled 'How Grace Williams wrote her opera with hire-purchase piano. Welsh woman finds her musical forte'. The article's presence is intriguing as it is the only article about another composer in Lutyens's meticulously ordered collection of reviews of her own music. It seems unlikely that she kept this article simply because she belonged to the 'Lutyens-Maconchy-[Imogen] Holst-Williams era', as the *Western Mail* put it. A better clue is perhaps provided by the article's subject and date – opera and 10 June 1971. Five years earlier, Williams had been commissioned by Welsh National Opera to write an opera, and *The Parlour* had been unanimously praised by critics when it was premiered in 1966. In contrast, Lutyens had written three uncommissioned operas/stage works between the years 1965 and 1969 and none of these had been staged by June 1971. Despite performances of *Time Off?* and *Isis* in the 1970s, the scandalous neglect of *The Numbered* was, understandably, to be a source of extreme bitterness and disillusionment for Lutyens.

Frustration over the fate of *The Numbered* (which still awaits a first performance) was probably one of the factors which contributed to the crisis of confidence she suffered in the early 1970s. Now approaching 70, she was suffering from serious health problems – in particular, arthritis in her spine and hands which made the process of composing agonizingly painful. She was also plagued by vicious attacks of depression (her cocktail of prescribed pills included antidepressants), which tended to amplify toxic feelings of anxiety, bitterness and isolation. 'My confidence has temporarily seeped away and left an arid uncertainty', she confessed to Brian Elias.[95] Although a respected figure in the contemporary music world, she sensed that she was out of step with the musical climate and complained to friends that she had passed 'from avant-garde to old hat overnight'.[96] Indeed, Susan Bradshaw

---

[93] Harries, *Pilgrim Soul*, p. 258. In 1976 the BBC adapted Robert Graves's novels *I, Claudius* (1934) and *Claudius the God* (1935) into the 13-part TV series *I, Claudius*.

[94] The exception was the uncommissioned ballad opera *A Goldfish Bowl* (1975) which Lutyens withdrew.

[95] Lutyens, letter to Elias, November 1970, quoted in Harries, *Pilgrim Soul*, p. 238.

[96] Lutyens, in ibid., p. 214.

could claim in 1971 that Lutyens had 'been dogged by the misfortune of always having been an "unfashionable" composer':

> Mocked for being far ahead of her time in the 1930s and 40s, her works made little impact on a musical public conditioned to regard any deviations from tonal harmony as somehow un-English and not quite nice. Having, with the passage of time, become part of the "establishment," her works now fail to qualify for inclusion in avant-garde programmes: so important has fashion in music become that the newness of outlook of the works themselves is all too often overlooked. (*The Musical Times*, July 1971)

Plenum I–IV, Opp. 87, 92, 93, 100 (1972–74)

Although Lutyens's profile began to wane in the final decade of her life, her creative fertility remained undiminished. Among the most intriguing works of this period are the four *Plenum* pieces, static soundscapes scored for different instrumental combinations. As the series title suggests – *plenum* is Latin for 'a filled space' – each work is an exploration of the idea of space and/or silence filled with sound. In *Plenum*, written in 1972 for the pianist Katherina Wolpe, Lutyens employs her favoured palindromic form, dispenses with bar lines and experiments with brief pauses between statements. The performer is also asked to play notes which are 'stopped and played' and 'stopped and plucked'. *Plenum II* (1973), premiered in June 1974 at the Queen Elizabeth Hall by Janet Craxton and members of the London Sinfonietta, is also remarkably free of bar lines. The score presents a series of sonorous events which are separated by pauses and written for different instrumental groupings. Whole chunks of silent bars are left out completely, thus enabling the central idea of silence and sound to be represented graphically as well as aurally (see Example 6.14). In addition, Lutyens does not specify any tempi in the piece, stating instead that 'the tempi and duration of pauses between groups is dictated by the reaction of soloist and the conductor to notation (i.e. 𝒐 = slow, ♪ = quick)'.[97]

The idea of silence and sound is once again graphically represented in the score of *Plenum IV* for organ duet (1974), a piece which was commissioned by Stephen and Nicholas Cleobury. The work is extremely economical in texture, its sparseness graphically highlighted by an absence of annotated rest signs. A number of stops are suggested (including flute, trumpet, and soft reed), and the tempo is determined by the approximate durations indicated for each bar of the piece (e.g. 2 seconds, 4 seconds, etc.). The impression is of a duet of sonorous events embedded in silence. Notated bars return in *Plenum III* (1972), a piece which was premiered by the Chilingirian String Quartet in May 1974. The string writing is extremely precise and the intensity of the work is much enhanced by

---

[97] Lutyens, note taken from the score of *Plenum II* (University of York Press).

moments of silence. It is a work which actualizes Lutyens's vision of 'silence filled, emptied, and refilled with sound'.

Example 6.14 *Plenum II*

Source: Copyright © University of York Music Press. Reproduced by permission.

Mare et Minutiae, Op. 107 (1976)

Several of these ideas are encountered again in *Mare et Minutiae* for string quartet – in particular, the sensitive use of silence throughout, the occasional absence of annotated rest bars and time signatures, and the use of specified durations for certain sections. In contrast, however, to the abstract idea which inspired the *Plenum* series, *Mare et Minutiae* has a more pictorial theme. Indeed, the work can be described as a series of sea sketches, conceived as dramatically contrasting sections within a single movement. Three static 'Mare' sections, all associated with the oceans in different ways ('Tranquillus', 'Tempestas' and 'Undulatus'), are interspersed with eight fragmentary 'Minutiae' sections which are identified with the sand, pebbles, flotsam and jetsam found on the seashore. According to Lutyens, the piece had been inspired by 'the times when the sea metamorphosed all into beauty, and was not built on. Now – oil rigs, tar, plastic and French letters ... Pity'.[98]

Mare et Minutiae was written for and premiered by the Medici String Quartet. Lutyens had formed a particularly close relationship with this quartet when they were 'in residence' together at York University in 1976. The performers proved to be superb and enthusiastic interpreters of her work, and she went on to compose three more quartets for them in the last five years of her life. Her *Doubles*, Op. 125 (pronounced as in the French) was written in 1978 and, like its Medici predecessor, is in single movement form. The piece consists of three main sections together with their respective 'doubles', Lutyens deliberately drawing from the style and form of Bach's Partitas. She turned again to a pictorial theme for her *Diurnal*, Op. 146 (1980), in that the three main sections of the piece, each divided into subsections, follow the span of a single day, from sunrise to nightfall. Her series of 'Medici' pieces was completed in 1981 with her String Quartet XII, Op. 155, but she also composed a piece for solo viola, *Echo of the Wind*, Op. 157 (1981), for the Medici violist Paul Silverthorne.

Dialogo, Op. 142 (1980)
Music for Orchestra IV, Op. 152 (1981)
Triolets I and II, Opp. 160a and b (1983)

Four works written in the early 1980s summed up many of Lutyens's preoccupations in her last years. The first to be composed was the concert aria *Dialogo* for coloratura soprano and orchestra, commissioned by the City of London Sinfonia. Here, Lutyens returned to Quasimodo (the poet of her *And Suddenly It's Evening*) for a poem which blended elements of Orpheus's loss of his lover Eurydice with the modern, brutal imagery of the devastation wrought by war. Directly inspired by the dramatic arias of Mozart – Lutyens wanted her *Dialogo* to have something of the quality of the 'Queen of the Night' throughout – the high, virtuosic soprano line and richly complex orchestral textures are impassioned and turbulent in character.

---

[98] Lutyens, letter to John Patrick Thomas, 29 January 1976, as quoted in Harries, *Pilgrim Soul*, p. 263.

She returned to sparser textures in *Music for Orchestra IV*, her last major piece for orchestra. She was almost crippled by arthritis by this time, and the contorted accidentals, gnarled stems of notes and crooked bar lines found in the original sketches and manuscript of the work show a drastic deterioration in the legibility of her notation. The physical fragility of the sketches is, however, in contrast to the positive character of the piece. Indeed, from the first three opening chords to the end (where the same chords are repeated in reverse order), the piece seems to embody a mood of vitality and even defiance. The work is scored for chamber orchestra (without violins) and is in one continuous movement. Throughout, one is aware of the imaginative quality of the writing and the sensitivity to instrumental colour. The orchestration is bold, economical and translucent, the composer drawing both on solo instruments and distinct instrumental groups to achieve imaginative (and often stark) sonorities. As in other works of the 1970s and early 80s, moments of silence become a core structural feature, and are frequently used to separate fragmentary and contrasting musical sections.

Frustratingly, health problems and a series of accidents (including a fire in her ground-floor flat which had left her badly burned in 1981), dictated that Lutyens had to spend much of the final two years of her life either in a wheelchair or a hospital bed. Finding her in a depressed frame of mind during hospital visiting hours on one occasion in 1982, Brian Elias suggested that her mood might lift if she focused on composing 'a string of short self-contained pieces, independent but related' – something along the lines of Schumann's *Papillons*, a piece they both admired.[99] Both *Triolet I* (for clarinet/bass clarinet, cello and mandolin) and *Triolet II* (for cello, harp and marimba) consist of nine tautly structured sketches, with each 'sketch' lasting less than two minutes. Almost illegible in manuscript form – a result of painful, arthritic hands – the completed *Triolets* had to be transcribed by Susan Bradshaw with the aid of a magnifying glass. Sadly, Lutyens did not live to hear the piece performed: she passed away on 13 April 1983. But she knew that 'Death which must come, cometh nobly, when we give our wealth and life and all to make men live'.[100] Her *Triolets* were premiered in London on 4 December 1984 – fittingly, at a New Macnaghten Concert, the same organization she had helped to found in 1931.

---

[99] Elias, quoted in ibid., p. 271.

[100] From the *Hitopadesha* (collection of ancient Sanskrit fables) as quoted in Lutyens, *Goldfish Bowl*, p. 318.

Chapter 7
Maconchy: *My Dark Heart*

Maconchy had found herself isolated during the war years, and had found the lack of contact with players or performances to be immensely discouraging. In common with many creative artists, she was vulnerable to attacks of depression or 'moments of silence', as she put it, and had seriously considered giving up composing at this time. The urge to compose, however, returned – as compulsive and all-consuming as ever – and in the immediate post-war years her work gradually began to gain broader recognition and attract new supporters. In the spring of 1955, the BBC broadcast a series of concerts on the Third Programme in which all six of her string quartets were heard in sequence. The series came as a timely reminder to many of Maconchy's mastery of the quartet genre. As Scott Goddard noted in *The Musical Times* (May, 1956):

> [T]he complete series, so far, of Elizabeth Maconchy's string quartets was broadcast [last year] and so one was able to watch the development of her remarkable talent. But perhaps development is the wrong term, at least as regards talent, for she appears, on the evidence of these six works, always to have possessed a talent for original thinking. It has not been so much talent as technique in expressing her thought that has developed. Her mind, one of the most interesting among the mature composers working in this country at present, has come to express itself with increasing ease.

Maconchy may well have been generally regarded as an interesting, 'mature' composer at this time, but her professional situation was still far from ideal. The majority of her pieces were nearly all uncommissioned, and there was a gaping disparity between the apparent respect of critics and the intermittent performances of her music. It is little wonder that she found this situation frustrating. 'You are right to feel dejected at lack of performances', Williams wrote in 1957, '& wrong too because the all important thing is that you composed all these truly original & fine works & there must come a time (I'm sure it will come suddenly) when they will be recognized for what they are worth'.[1] Recognition of Maconchy's achievements did not come suddenly, however. While the post-1945 musical scene in Britain differed from that of the interwar years, she may well have reflected on some aspects of her professional circumstances with a fleeting sense of *déjà vu*. Her suite *The Land* had attracted lavish critical praise when it was premiered at the Proms in 1930, but that success had not been followed up by any commissions,

---

[1] Williams, letter to Maconchy, 10 March 1957 (private collection).

grants or immediate further performances. In moments of exasperation, it may well have crossed her mind that the situation for a composer in 1950s Britain had hardly improved since the 30s. Some of these issues may well have prompted her to accept an invitation in 1954 to serve on the Executive Committee of the Composers' Guild of Great Britain, an influential organization which represented and promoted the artistic and professional interests of British composers.[2] She proved to be an exceptionally capable committee member and was elected as the Guild's first woman chairman in 1959.

String Quartet No. 7 (1956)

One issue which must have been discussed at Guild Committee meetings was the reduction made to the Third Programme's music broadcasts in September 1957. Prompted by dwindling listener figures, it was proposed that the nightly six hours of the Third (broadcasting from 6 p.m. to midnight) be reduced to three hours per night (from 8 p.m. onwards), and that the two-hour evening slot from 6 p.m. to 8 p.m. be filled by Network Three, a new service which would concentrate on adult education programmes. When the new reduced schedules were published in the autumn of 1957, John Morris (Controller, Third Programme) had to admit that music would be 'the chief victim' of the cuts.[3]

As the novelist and BBC producer Rayner Heppenstall wryly noted, one of the consequences of the cuts to the Third Programme's schedules – described by *The Times* as the 'diminished Third' – was 'the lack of string quartets with the first gin at six o'clock'.[4] The broadcast premiere of Maconchy's Seventh String Quartet was affected by these schedule reductions, although other factors contributed to the delay of its first performance. She had composed her quartet in 1955 for the Hungarian String Quartet, and the piece had been promised a broadcast by Richard Howgill, the then Controller of Music. Although a number of potential dates for the performance were considered in 1955 and 1956, the players were unable to commit to a specific date due to their heavy schedule.[5] Maconchy was initially reluctant to give the premiere to another quartet because she had the Hungarian

---

[2] Founded in 1944, the Composers' Guild of Great Britain published the journal *Composer* from 1958 to 1987, and established the British Music Information Centre in 1967.

[3] Morris, quoted in Carpenter, *Envy of the World*, p. 176. Early in 1958, the Sound Broadcasting Society issued a report which claimed that the cuts to the Third included a 37 per cent reduction in serious music broadcasts as a whole, with contemporary music broadcasts being reduced by 41 per cent (ibid., p. 185).

[4] Heppenstall in ibid., p. 184.

[5] For a full account of the events leading up to the broadcast premiere of Maconchy's Seventh String Quartet, see J. Doctor, 'Maconchy's String Quartet No. 7 and the BBC', *Musical Objects* 1 (1995), pp. 5–8.

Quartet's phrasing in mind when she wrote it.[6] When it became clear in the summer of 1957, however, that a performance by the Hungarian Quartet was not on the horizon, she offered the premiere to the Aeolian String Quartet, who duly accepted. Although the reduced schedules of the Third made it more difficult to find a suitable placing for Maconchy's quartet, the BBC did honour its promise. Listeners were finally able to hear the premiere of her Seventh String Quartet (with the second or third gin?) at eight o'clock on 8 January 1958.

The Seventh Quartet was, in many respects, a culmination of Maconchy's extensive exploration of the quartet genre up to this point. The characteristic concern with dramatic contrapuntal writing is evident, as is the use of organic form and thematic and textural contrasts both between and within movements. Here, however, the composer's desire to venture into new musical territory and fascination with connections between motivic development and overall structure takes her in a new direction. In contrast to its predecessors, the Seventh Quartet possesses a Bartókian arch-like, symmetrical design which extends over its five contrasting movements.[7] A deeper aspect of arch form is revealed in the motivic relationships between movements. The atmospheric central *Lento, tempo libero* (III) – described by the composer as 'the central *massif* of the quartet'[8] – is framed by two brief scherzos (II and IV). These pungent scherzos are closely related thematically, yet contrasting in tone and texture: the *pizzicato* theme of the second, for example, is a variant of the first scherzo theme (see Example 7.1). The vigorous four-note theme of the finale is derived from the material of the opening movement. In the course of its argument, the finale theme is combined with new ideas before a final coda which brings the work's central ideas together. The intricate relationships between movements, and between the four instruments, are never static. Indeed, this is music which is in a continuous state of regeneration.

The compelling conviction of this work captured the ear of the critic Dyneley Hussey when it was first broadcast. 'This new quartet', he declared, 'is yet another manifestation of [Maconchy's] remarkable ability as a composer and her complete mastery of her chosen medium'. Hussey also took the view that Maconchy's engagement with writing chamber music had, thus far, 'prevented her from gaining the high place in public estimation that is really her due' (*The Listener*, 23 January 1958). This was an interesting point. The string quartet was a genre which had come to be associated with intimate expression, intricate craftsmanship and,

---

[6] Maconchy, letter to Howgill, 1 July 1955 [BBC WAC RCONT1: Maconchy, Composer, 1951–58]. Maconchy's Third String Quartet had been premiered by the Hungarian Quartet in 1938.

[7] Bartók's Fourth and Fifth String Quartets (1928 and 1934) both employ five-movement arch forms. The Fourth Quartet is the most likely model for Maconchy in that it has a central slow movement which is framed by two thematically related scherzos (the second of which is a *pizzicato* movement – the first of its kind in the quartet genre). Note that Tippett employed a five-movement form in his Third String Quartet (1945–46).

[8] Maconchy, note for String Quartet No. 7, Maconchy: Complete String Quartets CD.

particularly in the hands of Beethoven and Bartók, the exploration of new musical territory. While the advent of broadcasting offered new opportunities for hearing string quartets outside the concert hall, audiences for string quartets in the 1940s and 50s tended to be smaller than those for choral or orchestral concerts – as is the case today. One of the reasons for this discrepancy lies in the concentrated nature of the quartet medium itself. As Maconchy noted, 'it is music stripped down to its essentials, to line rhythm and form without the distractions of colour and dynamic contrast afforded by the orchestra'.[9] Listening to a string quartet requires a different level of aural attention than that for an orchestral piece. Indeed, an audience is invited to 'listen in' to a string quartet, to join a private conversation between four individuals.

Example 7.1 String Quartet No. 7, themes from II, III and IV

Source: Copyright © Alfred Lengnick & Co. Ltd. Reproduced by permission of the publisher.

Hussey's implication was that Maconchy's focus on chamber music had prevented her from writing larger-scale works which might have had wider appeal – a *Belshazzar's Feast* perhaps, or, indeed, a *Fantasia on Welsh Nursery Tunes*. In fact, Maconchy had written larger works but pieces such as *The Land*, *Proud*

---

[9] Maconchy, 'Talk on the String Quartet' (Radio 3, 9 October 1976).

Thames and the Symphony for Double String Orchestra were entirely absent from British orchestral programmes at this time; the issue for Maconchy – and for many other British composers – was not the first performance, but the second and third. Nicola LeFanu has suggested that her mother's lack of 'modishness – for saying the right things to the right person, or for being in the right place at the right time' might partly explain why 'her music was not taken up by music impresarios or orchestras in a big time way'.[10] Yet LeFanu has also argued that the under-representation of her mother's works in concerts at this time was linked to a systematic discrimination against women composers by British musical institutions. In a musical establishment which privileged patriarchal values, women composers' contributions were considered to be less 'important' than those of their male counterparts:

> What constitutes "importance"? This was the question that used to disturb me all through my childhood. Why was the music of William Alwyn, Arthur Benjamin, Benjamin Frankel and Edmund Rubbra played more than that of my mother? Or Constant Lambert, Alan Rawsthorne, Humphrey Searle: why were they preferred over her? How did these men come to be regarded as more "important"?[11]

Maconchy's profile during the 1950s supports this notion. Although her work tended to attract favourable reviews in the press, and her achievements were mentioned in the context of other women composers,[12] she seems not to have received the level of recognition or performances of some of her male peers. Nor for that matter did any other woman composer. In the introduction to an article about Lutyens's music in *The Listener* (21 September 1960), for example, Colin Mason noted that

> in spite of the general acceptance of their right to be taken seriously in this field as in any other, women composers, unlike women writers, have remained few – and are seemingly becoming fewer …
>
> Whether because the women composers active between the wars were a few crucial years younger than their male contemporaries or competitors, or because their talent was not so strong, or because "parity of esteem" became a reality only after the Second World War (as the First World War was needed to bring

---

[10] LeFanu in a feature about her mother's life and work on 'Woman's Hour' (Radio 4, 6 May 2002). 'My mother was never a pushy person', LeFanu added. 'She had a shy temperament and had no time for modishness'.

[11] LeFanu, 'Master Musician: an Impregnable Taboo?' in *Contact: A Journal of Contemporary Music*, vol. 31 (August 1987).

[12] Writing about the music of Phyllis Tate, for example, Mosco Carner noted that Tate was one of 'three British women composers who have achieved prominence in recent years'. The other two were Lutyens and Maconchy (*The Listener*, 3 November 1953).

male capitulation over the vote), their achievement has been overshadowed by that of the exceptionally numerous and gifted men of the same generation – which includes Tippett, Walton, Rawsthorne, Rubbra, Berkeley, Bush and the younger Britten.

In what seems to be a direct response to Mason's argument, Maconchy challenged the whole premise of placing composers into separate male and female boxes. Drawing from her own experiences, she made the point that one of the reasons that relatively few women composers had established themselves in the profession was because of the commitment involved in raising a family:

> It is not impossible to write music if one has children – though difficult enough: but rearing them comes just at the time when one ought to be making a career, and it is almost impossible to combine the two, if one takes one's children seriously ... Unfortunately, the experience and stimulus of performance are an essential part of the growth and development of a composer – it is not only a matter of "getting known".
>
> This, and not inferior capacity, accounts I believe for the relatively small number of women composers who have so far established themselves.
>
> I think myself that it is a mistake to divide composers into men and women – as if the music they write is necessarily different ... Can any honest and intelligent listener who does not know already tell which it is?[13]

The Sofa (1956–57)
The Three Strangers (1957–58)
The Departure (1960–61)

Maconchy experienced a type of musical emancipation in the mid 1950s. She continued to juggle composing and other professional commitments with family life, but now underwent a reassessment of the direction her music would take. 'I felt I got a bit stuck – that I'd been writing the same sort of forms for too long', she later recalled. 'So I made a break away from chamber music and abstract music in general and wrote my three one-act operas. This was something quite new for me and it was very stimulating'.[14] While the reasons behind Maconchy's new beginning were personal, it is interesting to note that both Lutyens and Williams also underwent serious reappraisals of their music in the mid 1950s. Significantly, although very different in terms of creative ends, these reassessments coincided

---

[13] Maconchy, 'A Short Symposium of Women Composers', *Composer* 6 (Spring 1961), p. 20

[14] Maconchy, 'Composer's Portrait' (Third Programme, 15 June 1966).

with the beginnings of a change of direction in contemporary music and a rise in the profile of a younger generation of British composers.[15] Serialism was in the air at this time and it may well be that these factors prompted the three composers to reevaluate their own positions within British music.

Opera might have been 'quite new' for Maconchy at this point in her career, but she had shown an interest in writing for the stage much earlier. When her *Comedy Overture* was broadcast by the BBC in 1934, for instance, the *Radio Times* noted that the overture was 'written as a prelude to a comic opera'.[16] No doubt, Maconchy's plans for a comic opera were thwarted by the miserable lack of performance opportunities for British opera in at this time. Indeed, the situation had been so dire that when Vaughan Williams first approached the writer Harold Child for a libretto for his ballad opera *Hugh the Drover* (1909–14, rev. 1924, 1955), it was with the caveat that there was 'hardly any chance of an opera by an English composer ever being produced, at all events in our lifetime'.[17] By the mid 1950s, however, the situation had improved. Two events, in particular, had had a galvanizing impact on the fortunes of contemporary British opera. The first was the opening in 1931 of the new Sadler's Wells Theatre, a venue which hosted performances of ballet and opera. The second was the premiere (at Sadler's Wells) of Britten's *Peter Grimes* in June 1945, an event which the composer himself later admitted 'broke the ice for British opera'.[18] *The Sofa*, the first of Maconchy's chamber operas, was premiered at Sadler's Wells in December 1959 by the New Opera Company, one of several enterprising opera companies formed in the wake of Britten's success.[19] The company specialized in contemporary opera, and its first seasons (1957/58) included productions of Stravinsky's *The Rake's Progress*, Arthur Benjamin's *A Tale of Two Cities* and Vaughan Williams's *Sir John in Love*. Maconchy's *The Sofa* was paired with the London premiere of John Joubert's one-act opera *In the Drought* in the company's 1959 season.

The plot of Maconchy's opera revolves around the various sexual intrigues which take place on a single piece of furniture. The story is based on the satirical novel *Le Sopha* (1740) by the French dramatist Crebillon *fils*, and Maconchy asked

---

[15] Maxwell Davies, Birtwistle and Goehr in England, for example, and Mathias and Hoddinott in Wales.

[16] *Radio Times*, 28 December 1934. The overture was performed by the BBC Symphony Orchestra (section C), conducted by Vaughan Williams, in a programme that also featured the broadcast premiere of Grace Williams's *Two Psalms* for soprano and orchestra. The manuscript for Maconchy's opera does not survive. Note that Williams's *Hen Walia* (1930) was originally intended as the overture to a folk opera but the opera was never realized. See Chapter 2.

[17] Vaughan Williams, quoted in *The New Penguin Opera Guide*, ed. A. Holden (London: Penguin Books, 2001), p. 971.

[18] Britten in interview with Alan Blyth, *Gramophone* (June 1970).

[19] The New Opera Company – Appendix.

Ursula Vaughan Williams to provide her with a verse libretto.[20] Significantly, just prior to this request, Ursula Vaughan Williams had been engaged in supplying a new dialogue for her husband's 'romantic extravaganza' *The Poisoned Kiss* (1929, rev. 1956–57), a light opera with which *The Sofa* shares much in terms of mood and tone: both could reasonably be described as a combination of farcical plot and clever music. In *The Sofa*, Dominic, a louche young prince, hosts a ball at his Parisian palace and is caught with capricious Monique *in flagrante delicto* on a sofa by his overbearing grandmother. In a fit of fury, grandmamma casts a spell on him, transforming him into a sofa, and informs him that only someone successfully making love on him can break the spell and return him to human form. As the party progresses, various scenarios occur. Three party girls sit on the sofa (Dominic) and are eventually approached by three young men. Two of the couples leave to dance, but Lucille remains on the sofa with her admirer: 'so far so good', comments the upholstered Dominic, a line apparently contributed by Vaughan Williams himself. Instead of attempting to seduce her, however, the young man merely proposes to her, much to Dominic's exasperation. The couple leave and Monique now flirts with Edward, an old flame, on the sofa. Monique's seduction breaks the spell and she is shocked by the mysterious and, from her point of view, ill-timed, reappearance of the real Dominic.

The Sofa must have come as a surprise to those who had viewed Maconchy primarily as a composer of uncompromising string quartets; indeed, it is difficult to imagine how her complete 'break away' from abstract chamber music could have been better achieved. Scored for eight solo singers, chorus and chamber ensemble, her irreverent, high-voltage score is filled with original tunes and rhythmic dynamism, the music underlining and enhancing the improbable twists and turns of the plot with ease. There are several affectionate winks at the established operatic repertoire, from witty grand opera parodies to allusions to Offenbach, and the blend of duets for the leading characters and set pieces for vocal ensemble are cleverly balanced. The melodramatic posture and spectacular vocal gymnastics of the enraged grandmother (the opera's own 'Queen of the Night'?) are particularly memorable, as are the pastiches of Strauss-inspired waltzes and polkas which create a party *ambiance* throughout the opera. And, as the critic Edmund Tracey noted, the opera included 'the only attempt I have ever seen to present of the act of copulation on the public stage' (*The Observer*, 20 December 1959).

In choosing to score *The Sofa* for chamber forces, Maconchy contributed to a genre which had attracted several other British twentieth-century composers,

---

[20] Before deciding on *The Sofa*, Maconchy had briefly considered basing her libretto on the play *Life Is a Dream* by the Spanish dramatist Pedro Calderón de la Barca (1600–81). According to Ursula Vaughan Williams, the idea of basing the opera on *Le Sopha* came from William LeFanu. See *Paradise Remembered: An Autobiography by Ursula Vaughan Williams*, eds R. Buckley and J. Kennedy (London: Albion Music, 2002), p. 188.

including Holst, Vaughan Williams, Britten and Lutyens.[21] Chamber opera offered a composer the opportunity of avoiding the ostentatious style of presentation required in 'grand opera' and, for practical reasons, too, an opera conceived on a smaller scale had a greater chance of being staged and/or of being toured. Maconchy again employed chamber forces in her next opera *The Three Strangers* (1957–58) – in this instance, 12 solo singers, chorus and chamber orchestra. She turned to the English countryside and to folksong for her setting, and wrote her own libretto, basing it on Thomas Hardy's bucolic play *The Three Wayfarers*, with additional poems by Hardy and his Dorset contemporary William Barnes.

The Three Strangers opens on a stormy night in a Dorset cottage, where a shepherd, his family and friends have gathered to celebrate the christening of a baby. During the evening, three strangers appear at the cottage. The first, an affable young man, is invited to take shelter from the storm and to join the party. He is asked for news of the imminent public hanging in Casterbridge of a clockmaker who has been convicted of theft, but appears ignorant of the event. As the guests start to sing and dance, another stranger appears. The shepherd's wife takes a dislike to this arrogant, sinister character and after a while the group realize that he is the hangman who is due to execute the convict in the morning. Another knock at the door marks the appearance of the third stranger who nervously asks for directions and then abruptly leaves. The distant boom of the prison gun is heard signalling the escape of a prisoner. The hangman is convinced that the third stranger is the escaped convict, but when the magistrate appears with the (now apprehended) third man, it soon becomes apparent that he is innocent. He confesses that the real escaped convict (the first stranger who has slipped away undetected) is his brother Timothy Summers, and that his crime of sheep-stealing was motivated by a need to feed his family. The guests' sympathies are firmly with Summers, and as the party continues they delight in the way that he has managed to make a fool of both the hangman and the law.

The dramatic musical idiom of *The Three Strangers* possesses an immediacy of tone which highlights the bold contrasts in the plot and mirrors the unexpected events of the night: things are not quite as they seem. The dark, tempestuous orchestral prelude which opens the work is suggestive of the threatening, rain-lashed countryside, and is contrasted with the cosy, fireside scene within the cottage where guests sing and dance to celebrate the christening. Maconchy's use of folk material (inspired by English folksong) is specifically allied to dramatic ends. The folk-inspired themes of the songs and dances of the revellers effectively help to create a sense of time and place in the drama – whilst also echoing Hardy's

---

[21] Holst's *Savitri*, Op. 25 (1908–09), Vaughan Williams's 'pastoral episode' *The Shepherds of the Delectable Mountains* (1921–22), Britten's *The Rape of Lucricia* (1946) and Lutyens's *Infidelio* (1954) all employ chamber forces. Holst specified that his *Savitri* was to be termed a 'chamber opera', and it is the first known twentieth-century British opera to be designated as such. See Grout and Williams, *A Short History of Opera*, 4th ed. (Columbia: Columbia University Press, 2003), p. 710.

own love of the music of his native Dorset. The most dramatic moments in this engaging black comedy are reserved for the encounters at the party between Summers and his executioner (who remains unaware of Summers's real identity).

Some might have felt that this tale of bucolic life was an intriguing choice for a composer who had remained fiercely independent from associations with English pastoralism. Even so, the composition of *The Three Strangers* nevertheless enabled Maconchy to develop and extend the particularly rich musical vein, and profound identification with the English countryside, she had revealed in *The Land*. Indeed, there seems to be a special musical resonance (in terms of mood and character) between the early suite and the opera despite the 20 years' distance between their composition. It also seems significant that Maconchy wrote her chamber opera at around the same time that Vaughan Williams was preoccupied with his Ninth Symphony (1956–57, rev. 1958), a work which drew inspiration from Hardy's *Tess of the D'Urbervilles*. One imagines teacher and former pupil engaged in fervent discussions on the merits of Dorset's finest novelist and poet.

The Three Strangers was composed out of creative compulsion rather than in response to a specific commission, and consequently the work had to wait several years for its first performance. The opera was premiered in June 1968 by the Opera Group at Bishop's Stortford College for Boys where it was performed alongside Maconchy's *The Birds* (after Aristophanes), a specially commissioned one-act 'extravaganza'.[22] By the time these works were premiered, Maconchy had completed her third one-act chamber opera *The Departure*, to a libretto by the poet Anne Ridler.[23] This opera was first performed in a workshop production by the New Opera Company at Sadler's Wells on 16 December 1962 where it was heard with Buxton Orr's one-act opera *The Wager*.[24] Sparingly scored for two singers, off-stage chorus and chamber ensemble (14 players), *The Departure* is a haunting tragedy which explores themes of love and tragic loss. The opera focuses on a strange encounter between Julia (mezzo-soprano) and her lover Mark (baritone). Julia is alone in her bedroom waiting for Mark to return when she hears the distant strains of a funeral march and sees him with their friends. She calls to him but he does not hear her. He comes into the bedroom, distraught with grief, but appears not to be aware of her. Gradually, she realizes that she has been watching her own funeral. Mark thinks that he can hear her voice, and implores her to stay with him and with their young son who survived the car crash that claimed her life. The couple reflect on their life together, and question why they decided to go for a

---

[22] The performance was given as part of the centenary celebrations of Bishop's Stortford College. Both Maconchy pieces were conducted by Ernest Warburton and produced by John Cole.

[23] Ridler also provided the libretto for Maconchy's masque *The Jesse Tree* (1969–70) and her children's opera *The King of the Golden River* (1975–76).

[24] *The Departure* and *The Sofa* were revived by Independent Opera at Sadler's Wells in autumn 2007 to great acclaim. More recently, both operas (performed by Independent Opera) have been recorded by Chandos (CHAN 10508).

drive that day, but the time for Julia's departure is fast approaching. The encounter enables Julia to prepare for death, and the opera ends with her words 'depart – depart – depart' receding into the distance.

Example 7.2 *The Departure*

Example 7.2 continued

Source: Music by Elizabeth Maconchy. Libretto by Anne Ridler. Copyright © by Chester Music Limited. All rights reserved. International Copyright Secured. Reprinted by Permission.

The strength of this 30-minute, psychological drama lies in the subtle exploitation of the ambiguity of the characters' situation.[25] At the start of the opera, for instance, we are simply presented with a woman waiting for her lover to return, and yet everything is already implicit in the music. The lyrical lines of Julia's monologue grow directly from the funeral theme stated at the work's opening and later by the chorus, hinting that there is a direct, but as yet unspoken, connection between the two (Example 7.2).

Maconchy's music gives expression to the intense, inner turmoil of both principal characters. Julia's realization that she has been watching her own funeral – a point which occurs nearly halfway through the opera – is spine-tingling in effect, its dramatic impact having been expertly prepared by music which gradually builds in intensity, mirroring her agitated state of mind. Although it is unclear whether Mark is able to see and/or hear the ghostly Julia in the drama, the two are united musically in a love duet of compelling power. Their memories of happy past times are interrupted by the sounds of an off-stage choir chanting Latin words from Psalm 120, a reminder that Julia must depart.[26] As her time nears, the strains of the funeral march heard in the opera's opening bars return.

Reflections for Oboe, Clarinet, Viola and Harp (1960)
Serenata Concertante for Violin and Orchestra (1962)

Maconchy's engagement with operatic forms seems to be intimately connected to the greater concern with timbre and sonority, and the more spontaneous modes of expression which feature in many of her instrumental and vocal works of the 1960s. Although a lyrical quality was evident in earlier works, a new song-influenced ethos can be heard to instigate the heightened musical expressivity characteristic of these mature works. The *Lento* third movement of her *Reflections* for oboe, clarinet, viola and harp, in particular, is an essay in rhapsodic form where long contrapuntal lines are combined with improvisatory-type textures in viola and harp. All four contrasting movements of this concise, delicately scored piece 'reflect' on their origin in the sense that they are derived from material stated in the slow introduction to the first movement.

Reflections was written at the request of Glock's BBC Music Division, and was premiered by the Melos Ensemble at a BBC Invitation Concert on 27 April 1961.[27] Maconchy was on good terms with Glock and, following his appointment as BBC

---

[25] The ultimate model for Maconchy – and for most twentieth-century composers interested in exploring psychological drama in music – was surely Bartók's *Bluebeard's Castle*.

[26] Psalm 120: *Levavi oculos meos in montes, unde veniet auxilium mihi* ... (I have lifted up my eyes to the mountains, from whence help shall come to me ...).

[27] The performers were Peter Graeme (oboe), Gervase de Peyer (clarinet), Cecil Aronowitz (viola) and Osian Ellis (harp).

Controller of Music in 1959, was in regular contact with him on matters relating to the Composers' Guild. Even so, she was never a 'Dartington' composer; nor was she one of the key British beneficiaries of his policy of 'creative unbalance' at the BBC. In contrast to Lutyens, who received eight BBC commissions during Glock's tenure, only two Maconchy pieces were commissioned by the BBC in the 1960s. It is difficult to say with any certainty quite why her profile was not higher, in that, although Glock's policy sought to champion the most advanced music of the day, non-serial composers were not ignored. The change in the direction of contemporary music which took place at this time, however, did have the effect of polarizing attitudes in the musical world. Interviewing Maconchy in 1990, the broadcaster Michael Hall noted that serialism had become a sort of *lingua franca* for the younger generation of composers in the 1950s and early 60s: 'it was automatically assumed that you were going to be a serialist', he recalled, 'that you would step in line with Webern, Boulez and Stockhausen'.[28] It was simply not Maconchy's style to step in line with any school of composition, musical *-ist* or *-ism*. She had remained fiercely independent of musical fashions from the very start of her career, choosing instead to focus on refining and advancing her own musical idiom and vision. As a consequence, commentators often found her work difficult to pigeonhole. Certainly, from the perspective of the post-war avant-garde, her music would have seemed largely irrelevant to their vision of musical progress. But then most diatonic-based music by established British composers, including that of Britten and Tippett, was deemed to be outdated by progressives at this time. Indeed, if Britten's *War Requiem* (1961) could be criticized by some for being too accessible, what chance was there for a folk opera such as *The Three Strangers*?

Maconchy may well have been regarded as unfashionable, and yet fascinating and subtle changes were occurring in her style. Core fingerprints such as a concern with concentrated thematic motives, contrapuntal writing and an organic concept of structure remain, but her mature works reveal a loosening (but not abandonment) of ties with tonality, and a range of fresh approaches to instrumental texture and sonority. All these features are present in her Serenata Concertante for violin and orchestra, a work commissioned by the Feeney Trust and first performed at Birmingham Town Hall on 17 December 1963 by Manoug Parikian (violin) and the City of Birmingham Symphony Orchestra, conducted by Hugo Rignold.. While the title might suggest a work which is light in character, this substantial 20-minute piece balances dramatic expression with, as befits a concertante work, a transparency of instrumental texture. Though not a full-scale concerto, the soloist is, the composer noted, 'given considerable scope for display' in a work that 'is in chamber-music style rather than in the grand orchestral manner'.[29]

---

[28] M. Hall, interview with Maconchy, 'Third Ear: Elizabeth Maconchy' (Radio 3, 29 March 1990).

[29] Maconchy, 'Serenata Concertante' in *British Contemporary Composers*, p. 51.

The opening 24 bars of the first movement alone demonstrate Maconchy's skill as a musical portraitist in that the group of themes presented here, from which all material in the work's four movements evolves, are clearly delineated in terms of character and instrumental timbre. The work opens with a *fortissimo* call to attention in the trumpets which functions as a type of motto theme in the work as a whole.

Example 7.3 Serenata Concertante, opening

[Score in C]

Source: Copyright © by Chester Music Limited. All rights reserved. International Copyright Secured. Reprinted by Permission.

This dramatic fanfare is followed by a contrasting *Andante* section which possesses a gentler, 'almost pastoral character', and during which several more important themes are introduced: an undulating melody in 9/8 for solo harp which is followed by two interlaced themes in oboe and horns respectively. The solo violin enters at this point with a richly expressive theme, clearly derived from preceding material, which extends from the lowest to the highest registers of the instrument. The section ends with a return of the opening fanfare theme, cast this time as a debate between the soloist and fuller strings, which leads directly to the first movement's main *Allegro* section. Brooding and restless in tone, the *Allegro*'s initial argument is driven by hallmark Maconchy accented rhythms and alternating metrical bars (4/4 and 5/8). There are many threads to this unfolding drama and their elaboration and development are complex and absorbing, but the argument is always balanced by a delicacy of texture. Particularly striking is a sparingly accompanied dialogue between solo violin and xylophone, with asides from solo timpani.

Example 7.4 Serenata Concertante, I

[Score in C]

Source: Copyright © by Chester Music Limited. All rights reserved. International Copyright Secured. Reprinted by Permission.

The scherzo second movement (in 5/8) has an edgy, satirical tone which brings to mind Bartók and, to a lesser extent, perhaps the biting *con malizia* (with malice) Presto of Walton's First Symphony. The barbed tone is tempered by a central trio section which is more reflective in character, and an impassioned cadenza for the soloist links the trio to the reprise of the scherzo section. Maconchy's most eloquent musical statement is reserved for the slow movement, a richly expressive *Andante* which recalls the radiant sound world of the slow movements of the Fifth and Sixth String Quartets and of the Symphony for Double String Orchestra. The movement opens with slowly alternating chords in *pianissimo* brass and a *pizzicato* ostinato figure in lower strings, above which the soloist plays an exquisite melody of long lines. The work ends with a rondo (*Allegro vigoroso*) in which a continuously inventive thematicism is ingeniously alternated with recollections from previous movements.

Clarinet Quintet (1963)
Variazioni Concertante (1964–65)

The Serenata was, in many ways, a watershed work in Maconchy's output. Nicola LeFanu has argued that the piece successfully reestablished her mother's orchestral voice at a time when many still associated her almost exclusively with chamber music. Indeed, although it is very difficult to separate musical ideas from the way in which they are presented, much of the work's freshness and vitality arises from the consistently inventive textures and adventurous scoring employed. This concern with varied textures, the ingenious thematic interconnections and sheer range of different moods – from the 'almost pastoral' to wildly astringent and/or richly sensuous – indicates the composer's desire to encompass a very wide range of expression. In this respect, it is possible that she turned for inspiration not to contemporaneous composers such as Boulez or Stockhausen, but to Mozart, the master of lyric and dramatic expression. Even the title 'Serenata Concertante' seems Mozartian in flavour, and it is interesting that two of the pieces Maconchy wrote after completing the work were intended as companion pieces to specific Mozart works. Her Clarinet Quintet, for instance, was commissioned in 1963 by Timothy Reynish, the then Director of the Minehead Music Club, to provide a balance to Mozart's Clarinet Quintet, K. 581.[30] Again, one of the most striking features of this Quintet is the sheer range of expression covered in the work's modest, 15-minute span. The vital and extrovert aspect of the piece is partly dictated by the character of the clarinet which, while totally integrated with the strings, consistently takes the lead. The *Allegro* first movement is characterized by sharp, jazz-inspired rhythms

---

[30] See T. Reynish, 'Forty Years of Commissions', *Winds* magazine (available at http://www.basbwe.org/articles/02winter_commissioning40.pdf). Reynish also commissioned Lutyens to write an oboe quintet (*The Fall of the Leafe*, 1967) as a companion piece to Mozart's Oboe Quartet.

and playful interaction between the instruments. The exuberant tone continues in the scherzo in which the clarinet and strings humorously explore a theme in 11/8 time. In contrast, the ensuing *Lento* is a movement of contrasts – of fervent declamatory statements and lyrical, improvisatory-type melodies. The finale is an energetic *Allegro*, for most of the time played *con forza*, which includes a dramatic cadenza for the clarinet and recollections of the ideas heard at the beginning of piece. All the music grows from a group of ideas heard in the opening bars – a series of seconds in the three upper strings, and clarinet fragments answered by the cello.

Example 7.5 Clarinet Quintet, opening

Source: Copyright © 1985 Chester Music Limited. All rights reserved. International Copyright Secured. Reprinted by Permission.

By the time the Clarinet Quintet was premiered in March 1964 by Gervase de Peyer and the Dartington String Quartet, Maconchy had already started work on a new piece for the BBC's 1965 Proms season. Although the BBC gave her the freedom to choose whatever she wanted to write for this commission, the idea for her *Variazioni Concertante* was sparked by a discussion she had with Glock. Their conversation had turned to Mozart and he had suggested that she might write a companion piece to Mozart's *Sinfonia Concertante* for solo wind instruments and orchestra.[31] Maconchy found the idea irresistible and responded by creating a piece which employed similar forces – oboe, clarinet, horn, bassoon and strings – and which also seems to have drawn from the form of the *Andantino con variazioni* (third movement) of Mozart's *Sinfonia*.[32] Maconchy's own *Variazioni* is a series of eight beautifully coloured variations. The variations are preceded by an introduction which contains all the germinal ideas for the work – a series of string *divisi* chords, decorative phrases for oboe, clarinet and horn, and a dialogue between oboe and bassoon. These ideas are extensively explored in the first three contrasting variations (*Andante con moto*, *Presto* and *Molto Moderato*) in which Maconchy achieves great delicacy in the play of her instruments. The fourth variation is a lively four-part fugue and it is followed by an expressive *Andante, tempo libero* (V), an *Allegro* scherzo (VI) and an *Andante* (VII), the latter described by the composer as 'a sort of serious conversation piece between the wind soloists in which the string soloists soon join'.[33] The eighth and final variation (*Allegro vivo*) is in Maconchy's favoured 5/8 metre, and the work is brought to a conclusion by the return of the material heard in the introduction.

Music for Brass and Woodwind (1965)
Nocturnal for Unaccompanied Choir (1965)

Stimulated by the experience of composing a concertante work with wind soloists, Maconchy actively sought to write music for new instrumental combinations in the following years. In 1965, for example, she accepted a commission from the Thaxted Midsummer Festival to write a piece for an instrumental grouping she had not tackled before. The resulting *Music for Brass and Woodwind* was specifically

---

[31] See Maconchy, letter to Miss Evans (secretary to William Glock), 24 May 1964 [BBC WAC RCONT12: Composer, Maconchy, 1963–67].

[32] A question mark hangs over the authenticity of Mozart's *Sinfonia Concertante* for solo winds and orchestra K. 297b (K. Anh. C14.01). For further details, see Daniel N. Leeson and Robert D. Levin, 'On the Authenticity of K. Anh. C. 14.01 (297b), a Symphonia Concertante for Four Winds and Orchestra', *Mozart Jahrbuch* 1976/77, pp. 70–96.

[33] Maconchy, note to *Variazioni Concertante*. The piece was premiered at the Proms on 10 August 1965. The performers were Terence Macdonagh (oboe), Jack Brymer (clarinet), Geoffrey Gambold (bassoon), Douglas Moore (horn) and the strings of the BBC Scottish Symphony Orchestra, conducted by James Loughran.

written with the grand architectural proportions and rich acoustic of Thaxted Church ('the Cathedral of Essex') in mind.[34] At the work's premiere in June 1966, members of the Morley College Wind Ensemble were placed at various points in the Church in order to 'fill' the physical space with music. Fittingly, the music embodies a certain grandeur in its use of ceremonial-type themes – particularly the chant-like rising and falling theme in the trombones which opens the work – and contrasting sections (including a central scherzo and lyrical slow section) build in intensity, creating arresting sound structures.

Interestingly, Graham Treacher, the conductor for that performance, had, weeks before, directed the Morley College Choir's premiere of Maconchy's *Nocturnal* for unaccompanied mixed chorus at the Cork International Choral Festival. For this piece she linked three different poems – 'Come!' by William Barnes, 'Will you come?' by Edward Thomas and Shelley's 'To the Night' – in a continuous musical structure. The common theme of anticipation in the poems, emphasized by the gentle refrain of 'will you come?', finds its musical counterpart in the intricate thematic interconnections between the settings. As the composer explained, 'I have treated these three poems like the three panels of a triptych – three contrasted pieces which are one at the same time linked by the subject matter and by technical means'.[35]

Nocturnal signalled Maconchy's return to the *a cappella* medium after a gap of some 30 years, and the piece initiated a phase of renewed interest for her in writing choral and vocal works. Some of her finest works for voices date from the mid to late 1960s and include the witty *Propheta Mendax* (The Lying Prophet), commissioned and premiered by the Vienna Boys' Choir in 1966.[36] The experience of writing both *Nocturnal* and *Music for Brass and Woodwind* seems to have informed her setting of Dylan Thomas's *And Death Shall have no Dominion* for chorus and brass ensemble, a 1969 Three Choirs Festival commission. The composer wrote that when she was setting the poem, she 'had in mind the high spaces of [Worcester] cathedral, writing music whose reverberations are intended to hang in the air'.[37] Similarly, Maconchy almost certainly had the high, resonant spaces of Salisbury Cathedral in mind when she chose to set Gerard Manley Hopkins's 'Pied Beauty' and 'Heaven-haven' for chorus and brass in 1976. One of

---

[34] The Thaxted Music Festival was originally founded by Gustav Holst in 1916.

[35] Maconchy, note to *Nocturnal*. Excellent discussions of several of Maconchy's choral works, including *Nocutral*, can be found in Roma, *The Choral Music of Twentieth-Century Women Composers: Elisabeth Lutyens, Elizabeth Maconchy, and Thea Musgrave*.

[36] The Vienna Boys' Choir also commissioned Britten's *Golden Vanity* in the mid 1960s. The Choir gave the first performance of Britten's work at the 1967 Aldeburgh Festival in a concert which also included a performance of *Propheta Mendex*.

[37] Maconchy, note to *And Death Shall Have No Dominion*. The piece was premiered in Worcester Cathedral at the Three Choirs Festival in August 1969 by the three Cathedral choirs and members of the Birmingham Brass Ensemble, conducted by Christopher Robinson.

several Hopkins settings composed by Maconchy in the 1960s and 70s, the piece was premiered in July 1976 at the Southern Cathedrals Festival by the combined three cathedral choirs (Salisbury, Winchester and Chichester) and the Philip Jones Brass Ensemble.

Three Settings of Poems by Gerard Manley Hopkins (1964–70)
The Leaden Echo and the Golden Echo (1978)

Poetry had always been a potent source of inspiration for Maconchy – whether in a vocal setting or employed as a stimulus for an orchestral work such as *The Land* – but Hopkins's poetry seemed to strike a particular chord within her. She spoke eloquently about how she came to choose a particular poem:

> In searching for words to set every composer stumbles upon a magic moment of recognition: this is it, this is what I've been looking for – a sort of love at first sight reaction. It may not in fact be one's first sight of the poem but suddenly there's an instinctive sense of possession. The poem becomes as it were part of oneself. That for me in any case is how the writing of song starts, or a choral work or any setting of words. This initial impulse starts the piece going, and the sense of complete identification with the words continues to grow as the work takes shape and persists to the end.[38]

Two pieces, in particular, are important in understanding Maconchy's love of the poet 'who meant more to me than any other'.[39] The first is a setting of Hopkins poems for soprano and orchestra. She set 'The Starlight Night' and 'Peace' in 1964 for the soprano Mary Wells, and the two settings were premiered at Chelmsford Cathedral in October 1964 by Wells and the Jacques Orchestra, conducted by Philip Ledger.[40] Feeling that a triptych was a more satisfying shape, however, she added a new setting of 'A May Magnificat' to the group in 1970, and all three were first performed together in Norwich on 29 May of that year by Robert Tear (tenor) and the English Chamber Orchestra, conducted by Philip Ledger.

In 'The Starlight Night' (I), the poet speaks of his exhilaration as he contemplates the beauty of a night sky. Maconchy opens her setting with highly atmospheric glimmering tremolos in *divsi* strings which support the soprano's incantatory call to 'look at the stars!' The beautiful imagery, sheer colourfulness

---

[38] Maconchy, introduction to 'Settings of Poems by Hopkins' performed by Noelle Barker and the Orchestra of St. John's, Smith Square, conducted by John Lubbock (Radio 3, 15 March 1977) [NSA Cat. No. M7030BW C1].

[39] Ibid.

[40] Maconchy dedicated these settings to Wells and her husband Philip Ledger. Ledger was Master of Music at Chelmsford Cathedral at this time.

and sense of movement in the poem are suggested in the music by atmospheric means and sensitive use of word-painting.

Example 7.6 Three Settings of Poems by Gerard Manley Hopkins,
    I 'The Starlight Night'

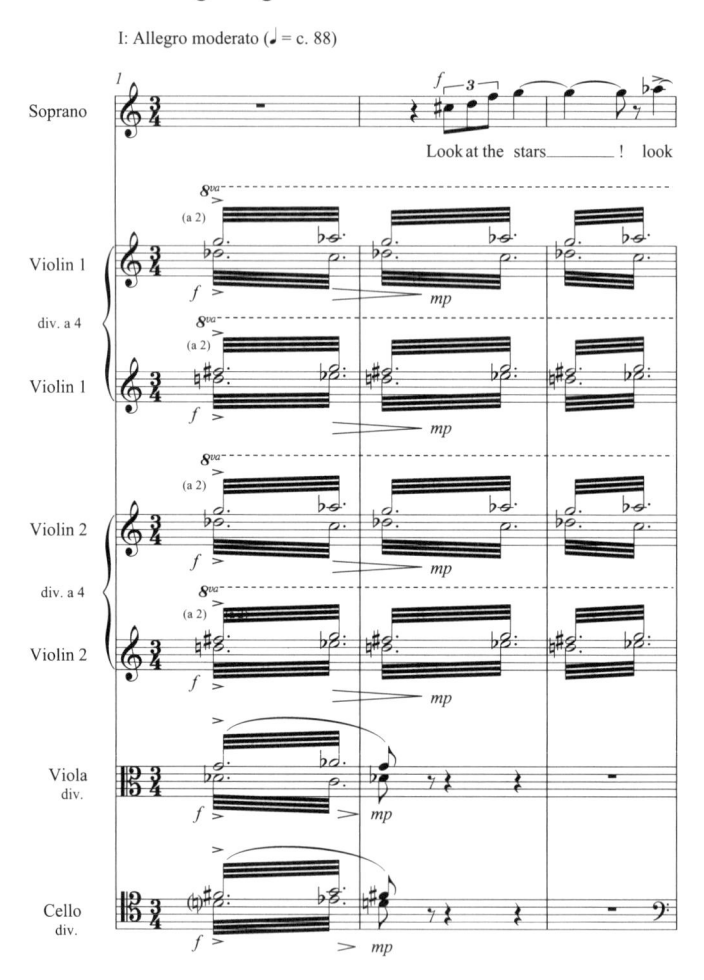

Example 7.6 continued

Source: Copyright © by Chester Music Limited. All rights reserved. International Copyright Secured. Reprinted by Permission.

'Peace' (II) is portrayed by the poet as a 'wild wood-dove' with 'shy wings shut' (a metaphor, perhaps, for the Holy Spirit), and Maconchy captures the atmosphere of an Arcadian scene with slow, shifting chords in strings, an undulating melody in cor anglais, and a duet for two horns – the latter intended as the song of the wood-doves. Her *Allegramente* setting of 'A May Magnificat' (III), a euphoric celebration of Mary and her month of May, captures the pulse of spontaneity in the evocative descriptions of spring in Hopkins's joyous poem, with their richly chiming consonants and lithe rhythms.

Example 7.7 Three Settings of Poems by Gerard Manley Hopkins, III 'A May Magnificat'

Source: Copyright © by Chester Music Limited. All rights reserved. International Copyright Secured. Reprinted by Permission.

Maconchy's love affair with Hopkins's poetry had started early in her career. In 1930 she had composed a setting of his *The Leaden Echo and the Golden Echo* for chorus and chamber orchestra, but her misgivings about the piece as a whole had prompted its swift withdrawal. After a gap of nearly 50 years, she turned again to the same poem, composing a new setting for mixed chorus and instrumental ensemble. Maconchy spoke about how she had been mesmerized by this poem from the first moment.

> [O]f all his poems the one that has haunted me most vividly, and which seems to me to cry out for music, is "The Leaden Echo and the Golden Echo." When Stephen Wilkinson asked me for a work for his William Byrd Singers, it was a welcome opportunity to make a setting of it for voices with alto flute, viola and harp.[41]

Hopkins himself had retained a special fondness for this poem, describing it as being one of his most musical. He had originally intended the poem to be sung as the maiden's song in a larger drama about St. Winifred, but the project was never completed.[42] His poem falls into two parts. 'The Leaden Echo' is concerned with feelings of despair about the loss of youth and physical beauty on account of age and death, but the mood becomes more revelatory in 'The Golden Echo' where eternal, spiritual beauty is contemplated. Throughout, the idea of an echo is vividly actualized by Hopkins through the sound and rhythms of words, and this idea is central to Maconchy's conception of the music. As she stated:

> The St. Winifred's Well of Hopkins's poem is, I am sure, one with a spring bubbling up into a little pool (not a bucket–and–chain affair). The watery music of the spring and the echoes sounding from the rocks round the well have suggested the musical ideas: as in the poem, the echoing of voices chimes all through the piece. "The Leaden Echo" introduces these two elements at once – the watery sounds and the echoing of the women's intertwining voices.[43]

Maconchy's elegant treatment of the colour, movement and inherent music within the poem is extraordinarily effective. She was particularly fascinated by what she described as 'the variety of pace – of tempi' within the poem, the prosodic contrast between accelerating lines of alliterative pyrotechnics and slower passages of drawling syllables. She perhaps sensed an affinity here with her own penchant for rhythmic counterpoints in her music, and several passages in this setting capture

---

[41] Maconchy, note to *The Leaden Echo and the Golden Echo*. Maconchy enjoyed a particularly fruitful professional relationship with Stephen Wilkinson, who was also chief conductor of the BBC Northern Singers for many years. Other works written for him include *Creatures* for unaccompanied mixed chorus (1979), *O Time Turn Back* for mixed chorus, wind quintet and cello (1983–84), and *On St. Stephenses Day* for women's chorus (1989), written to mark Wilkinson's 70th birthday.

[42] St. Winifred is the patron saint of virgins and her remains are enshrined in Shrewsbury Abbey.

[43] Maconchy, note to *The Leaden Echo and the Golden Echo*. For a detailed analysis of this work, see Roma, *The Choral Music of Twentieth-Century Women Composers*, pp. 88–95.

Example 7.8 *The Leaden Echo and the Golden Echo*, 'The Leaden Echo'

[Harp omitted]

Source: Music by Elizabeth Maconchy. Words by Gerard Manley Hopkins. Copyright © 1981 Chester Music Limited. All rights reserved. International Copyright Secured. Reprinted by Permission.

these two qualities simultaneously – something which, as she noted, 'music can do that words alone cannot'. In 'The Leaden Echo', for instance, the lightness and echoing effect of the women's staggered entries on the words 'Be beginning' are juxtaposed with the slower pulse of the men's more ponderous line, 'And wisdom is early to despair' (Example 7.8).

A fascinating example of free writing occurs later in 'The Golden Echo' where Maconchy ingeniously illustrates Hopkins's verbal cascade of sounds – 'winning ways, airs innocent, maiden manners, sweet looks, loose locks, long locks, lovelocks' – to dramatic effect.

Example 7.9 *The Leaden Echo and the Golden Echo*, 'The Golden Echo'

Source: Music by Elizabeth Maconchy. Words by Gerard Manley Hopkins. Copyright © 1981 Chester Music Limited. All rights reserved. International Copyright Secured. Reprinted by Permission.

230   *Lutyens, Maconchy, Williams and Twentieth-Century British Music*

String Quartet No. 8 (1967)
String Quartet No. 9 (1968)

Maconchy's use of free writing was not unusual in the context of her mature works as a whole. A particularly striking example of this technique occurs in the slow movement of her Eighth String Quartet in which sections of long, braided melodic lines for all four instruments are played *tempo libero, senza misura*. Lutoslawski's use of similar techniques in his String Quartet of 1965 may have had some influence on Maconchy at this time but, equally, her use of this method in the quartet medium can also be seen as a natural extension of the freely sung *senza misura* bars contained in *The Departure* and other vocal works of this period.

The composition of the Eighth and Ninth String Quartets saw Maconchy's return to the quartet medium after a break of over ten years.[44] She had considerably expanded her compositional range in the intervening years, but in the mid 1960s she felt 'an urgent wish to write another quartet'.[45] Her Eighth String Quartet was premiered by the Aeolian Quartet in London at a Macnaghten Concert in April 1967, and was the first of five outstanding quartets she would compose between 1967 and 1984. These last five quartets continue to be dominated by the desire for a greater unity and integration of material, but each achieves this goal in different ways. At the same time, the quartets reveal an expansion of musical and expressive means, particularly in their avoidance of stable tonal regions and their multi-thematic interconnections within broader areas of textural contrast.

All these features are apparent in the Eighth Quartet, a bracing work which ventures into more radical harmonic territory than its predecessors. The opening *Lento* of the Quartet begins with increasingly insistent statements of a chord (two perfect fifths superimposed at a distance of a tritone), and the musical argument of the ensuing *Allegro* is developed from this core idea in terms of both melodic and harmonic motifs. Maconchy's controlled approach to tempo enables the movement's dramatically contrasting textures – from vigorous and fiendishly quick contrapuntal passages to gentler, more expansive lines – to hold the ear without any loss of continuity. While much of the writing has a powerfully abrasive edge, the work nevertheless contains a great deal of lyrical material in both the *Allegro* first movement and the finale, and also in the *tranquillo* central section of the scherzo, described by the composer as being 'rather like a musette in character'. The *Lento* third movement is a fine example of Maconchy's art of 'impassioned argument' and, as the composer states, is 'written out in long unfolding lines (not divided into bars)'.[46]

---

[44] The exception here was a light, four-movement *Sonatina* for string quartet, composed in 1963.

[45] Maconchy, note to String Quartet No. 8 in 'Maconchy: Complete String Quartets' CD.

[46] Ibid.

A similar concern for freedom of melodic lines (marked *tempo libero*) recurs in the slow (third) movement of the Ninth Quartet. Related thematically perhaps to the slow movement of the Seventh Quartet, this weighty 'threnody or lament' is the work's emotional crux, its elegiac intensity being directly inspired by the Soviet occupation of Prague in August 1968.[47]

Example 7.10 String Quartet No. 9, III

Source: Copyright © by Chester Music Limited. All rights reserved. International Copyright Secured. Reprinted by Permission.

This slow lament is preceded by two succinct movements which are uncompromising in character. The opening movement displays the composer's fondness for concision and balanced construction, and although the movement contains changes of tempi and moods, there is a stark quality to the writing.

---

[47] Maconchy, note to String Quartet No. 9, ibid.

Similarly, the jagged, fragmentary nature of the ensuing scherzo is brought to full effect by remarkably light scoring. A forceful *Allegro* finale, replete with percussive *martellato* effects, wild rhythms and reflections on ideas from previous movements, brings this work to a close with a ferocious bite.

Ariadne for Soprano and Orchestra (1970–71)
Oboe Quartet (1972)
String Quartet No. 10 (1972)

Maconchy's Ninth Quartet was one of the winning entries in the 1969 Radcliffe Music Award Competition, and the piece had its first public performance by the Allegri Quartet at the Wigmore Hall, London on 15 January 1970.[48] While this prestigious award confirmed her stature as the leading string quartet composer of her day, her exploration of other genres continued in the 1970s. Three works in particular were important to the evolution of her mature style. The first to be written was the dramatic monologue *Ariadne* for soprano and orchestra, a work which was premiered at the King's Lynn Festival in July 1971 by Heather Harper (soprano) and the English Chamber Orchestra, conducted by Raymond Leppard. Maconchy was drawn to the richly dramatic possibilities offered by Greek mythology's most famous castaway, and used an abridged version of Cecil Day Lewis's poem *Ariadne on Naxos* (1959) for her words. In this dark lament, Ariadne's fury at her abandonment, her sense of isolation on Naxos and feelings of revenge for her lover Theseus, are vividly conveyed in a vocal line which is declamatory and highly expressive in scope. While passages for full orchestra are used to dramatic effect, the vocal line is more often than not balanced by finely spun instrumental writing which recalls the transparent textures of the Serenata Concertante. The sensuous orchestration has the effect of amplifying the extraordinary range of moods expressed by Ariadne as she moves from vicious anger to gentler recollections of love-making with Theseus, and memories of the innocence of her childhood. Yet Maconchy's luxuriant, nocturnal sound world also reflects the fact that Ariadne's experience of pain leads to forgiveness and self-knowledge, enabling her to rise above her isolation and anger. Free from her obsession with Theseus, Ariadne finally embraces the celestial 'bridal crown' offered to her by the god Dionysus.

Maconchy's Oboe Quartet and the Tenth String Quartet took up *Ariadne*'s thread. The Oboe Quartet, written for and dedicated to Janet Craxton and the London Oboe Quartet, may well have started life as an idea for a companion piece

---

[48] There were four finalists in the 1969 String Quartet Competition, and the jury (Britten, Thea Musgrave and Humphrey Searle) decided that the prize money should be shared equally. The other winning entries were Sebastian Forbes's Quartet No. 1, Robert Sherlaw Johnson's Quartet No. 2 and Peter Sculthorpe's Quartet No. 8. All four quartets were performed by the Allegri Quartet at the Radcliffe Award ceremony which was held at Sussex University in November 1969.

to the Mozart Oboe Quartet. Craxton and the Quartet were renowned interpreters of the Mozart, and were also at this time eagerly commissioning new works for their ensemble: one notable addition to their repertoire was Lutyens's *Driving Out the Death* (1971). In four finely etched movements, Maconchy's Quartet possesses a unity of mood which has a resonance with the dramatic, haunted soundworld of *Ariadne*. Indeed, the oboe's angular, declamatory phrases in the first movement of the Quartet (*Poco Lento, tempo libero*) seem intimately connected, in expressive terms, with the instrument's plaintive 'duets' with the voice in the monodrama. The driving rhythmic motifs and repeated pitch themes of the scherzo (II) generate a restless volatility which is not tempered by the anguished slower sections which thread their way through its structure. The *Lento* slow movement (III) is a type of 'arioso dolente', a dramatic lament of scorching intensity replete with anguished, rhapsodical passages for the oboe. Even the lighter tone and quicker tempi of the Finale cannot entirely lift the lingering mood of tragedy and lament which lies at the heart of this work. Indeed, it is as if the composer wished to explore further the emotional aspects of her monodrama in purely musical terms, a notion supported by Nicola LeFanu's description of the oboe's character in this work as being a kind of 'Ariadne' figure.

The spirit of *Ariadne* also haunts the Tenth String Quartet. Commissioned by the Cheltenham Festival and premiered there by the University of Alberta String Quartet in July 1972, the Tenth Quartet is a darkly hued work of contrasting sections which is cast in a single span. It seems significant that Maconchy should feel the need, at this point, to return to the one-movement form she had used in her Third String Quartet (1938). In that instance, her choice of overall form had been a natural consequence of her quest for greater musical integration, a preoccupation which had first become perceptible in the Second String Quartet (1936). In the Tenth Quartet, however, structural coherence is taken to a new level of sophistication. The Quartet's labyrinthine structure consists of a number of fluidly alternating sections (three fast sections interspersed with three slower episodes, all framed by *Lento* sections), and each section is distinguished by contrasting use of rhythm and texture. As with the majority of Maconchy's quartets, all the musical material is derived from core ideas heard in the opening – in this instance, a chain of static chords which emphasize tritonal intervals and a sinuous melodic fragment played *quasi sotto voce* by the viola (Example 7.11). Through the alchemical-like process of motivic and thematic transformation, these quiet chords and the initially unassuming viola fragment transmute into the lyrical variants of the slower sections, and the more boisterous, robust manifestations in each of the *Allegro* sections. The family resemblance is always there, but the character and mood of the work subtly alters at each turn.

Example 7.11 String Quartet No. 10, opening

Source: Copyright © 1975 Chester Music Limited. All rights reserved. International Copyright Secured. Reprinted by Permission.

Epyllion for Solo Cello and Strings (1975)

Another work to be commissioned by the Cheltenham Festival was *Epyllion*, a piece which was premiered there in July 1975 by the cellist Kenneth Heath and the Academy of St. Martin in the Fields Chamber Orchestra. As was the case in the Serenata Concertante, the ensemble in *Epyllion* has an important, multifaceted role: the strings are employed as soloists as well as a group, and the solo cello functions 'as the leading character in the cast rather than as a regular concerto soloist'.[49] The underlying compositional ethos of *Epyllion* is, however, quite different from that of the earlier work. *Epyllion* is the Greek word for 'little epic', and Maconchy chose the title 'to suggest that like an epic poem, this piece consists of [musical] events of a widely varied character'.[50] The title is extraordinarily apt. Vivid contrasts of textures and character are present both within and between the work's four main sections but, like an epic poem, the whole piece is infused with a spirit of ritual and personal odyssey. These qualities are dramatically suggested in the work's opening bars where plangent, tolling chords, widely deployed throughout the string ensemble, seem to summon both ancient gods and modern mortals to lend their ears to events of significance. Piercing *glissandi* in harmonics for the violins are gradually added in preparation for the first statement of the solo cello which, against a sustained *pianissimo* string chord, freely outlines the tritonal intervals which make up the opening chords (Example 7.12).[51]

An extended central episode follows in which the cello ruminates freely in improvisatory-like phrases on the core musical ideas, its argument highlighted by dialogue with the ensemble (used both as soloists and as a group), and contrasting passages of free writing for strings (Example 7.13). The section ends with the return of the chiming chords heard at the opening.

---

[49] Maconchy, introduction to the first broadcast performance of *Epyllion* by Christopher van Kampen (cello) and the Orchestra of St. John's Smith Square, conducted by John Lubbock (Radio 3, 14 March 1978) [NSA Cat. No. NP3137BW C1]. Note that the Kenneth Heath was also the cellist in the London Oboe Quartet, for whom Maconchy had written her Oboe Quartet (1972).

[50] In classical scholarship, the term 'epyllion' has come to refer to the shorter epic poems of authors such as Virgil and Ovid.

[51] Nicola LeFanu has stated that the idea for *Epyllion*'s opening came to her mother while she was in Venice. 'She said the wonderful sound early in the morning of ... all the deep, deep sounding bells, and then the screaming of the swifts as the birds flew high in the sky ... got into her ears, and you can hear the orchestral strings being the deep bells and the cellist, very high with harmonics – the screaming swifts'. LeFanu in 'Composer of the Week: Maconchy', programme 5 (Radio 3, 23 March 2007).

Example 7.12 *Epyllion* for Solo Cello and Strings, opening

Example 7.12 continued

Example 7.13 *Epyllion* for Solo Cello and Strings, I

Source: Copyright © by Chester Music Limited. All rights reserved. International Copyright Secured. Reprinted by Permission.

The ensuing scherzo section (II) is more puckish in tone. Fleet *ostinati* figures in *pizzicato* strings, propelled by rapidly changing metres, are combined with the cello's more extended lines, and the argument throughout is extremely finely spun. The *Lento* (III) is intensely lyrical and contains free writing for the strings and some of the most rhapsodical *ad lib* passages for solo cello. The finale begins with a dramatic rising figure in trills for the strings, itself a variant of the work's opening chords, and after several episodes where material from previous sections is contemplated, the work ends with a reiteration of the opening chords.

The clarity of musical thought, formal elegance and sheer inventiveness of sonority in *Epyllion* were widely praised by critics, although some were surprised by the work's use of free writing techniques. 'So Elizabeth Maconchy, who is one of the senior composers on the British music scene, still has ears and a mind open to new sounds', Gerald Larner noted, a little patronizingly, in his *Guardian* review (15 July 1975). In fact, Maconchy had always kept her ear attuned to new compositional developments, but had succeeded in absorbing the new techniques which interested her within her own personal idiom without any loss of musical integrity. Her ability to surprise and to remain open-minded were qualities that endeared her to a younger generation of British musicians: although she never taught composition, composers such as Jeremy Dale Roberts, Thea Musgrave and Richard Rodney Bennett sought her advice and guidance. Furthermore, her public work on behalf of British composers through organizations such as the Composers' Guild and the Society for the Promotion of New Music, and the numerous positions she held on advisory panels for the BBC, the Arts Council and other associations, won her the admiration of the musical profession as a whole. In 1976, at the age of 69, she succeeded Britten as President of the SPNM, a fitting appointment for a composer who had, throughout her career, sought to improve conditions for her colleagues and her profession. Her leadership qualities and remarkable compositional achievements were publicly recognized when she was awarded a CBE in the 1977 Honours List.

String Quartet No. 11 (1977)
String Quartet No. 12 (1979)

Public work in the 1970s and 80s was combined with the composition of a number of important works, all premiered by leading performers of the day. Both her Eleventh and Twelfth String Quartets were written for the Lindsay String Quartet, performers who were particularly revered for their interpretations of string quartets by Beethoven and Bartók, kindred musical spirits for Maconchy. The Eleventh Quartet was commissioned by the City Music Society to mark the 650th anniversary of the granting of the royal charter to the Worshipful Company of Goldsmiths, and was premiered by the Lindsays in December 1977 in the magnificently opulent Goldsmiths' Hall, London. Cast, like the Tenth Quartet, in a single movement, the many vivid and varied thematic shapes in this piece grow from a handful of ideas (including the motif B-D♭-C and the interval of a seventh) stated at the work's opening (Example 7.14). Although the spirit of rhapsody encountered in both the Tenth Quartet and *Epyllion* is very much present in the Eleventh Quartet, *ad lib* or *senza misura* passages are eschewed in the interest of a more concentrated process. Significantly, Maconchy described this work as 'the most integrated of my quartets – rather like a piece of woven material with contrasting patterns and colours running through it, which is yet "all-of-a-piece"'.[52]

Example 7.14 String Quartet No. 11, *Lento*

Source: Copyright © 1977 Chester Music Limited. All rights reserved. International Copyright Secured. Reprinted by Permission.

Contrast between sections is maximized by sensitive use of texture, tempo and mood. The opening is followed by a vigorous scherzo-like movement which contains a contrasting central *lento* section of profound lyrical quality where the instruments play long *cantabile* lines; several references are made to this section during the course of the piece. After an abridged restatement of the scherzo, the lyrical mood returns in the ensuing *Moderato* section (here, in more impassioned

---

[52] Maconchy, note to String Quartet No. 11 (Complete Quartets CD).

guise) which also contains references to music from previous sections. A fiery *Vivo* leads to a closing *tranquillo* section which directly recalls the work's opening.

In contrast to the single-movement structures of the previous two quartets, the musical argument of the Twelfth Quartet is presented in four independent, although thematically related, movements. First performed at the Crucible Theatre, Sheffield on 21 October 1979, this is very much a work of friction and extreme contrasts, where turbulent, forceful passages collide with quieter, more reflective, sections, both within and between movements. In the opening *Allegro*, for instance, the tension generated by the agitated main theme with its incessant dotted-note rhythm is dramatically allayed by two brief passages of sustained chords (which recur in subsequent movements). The scherzo, in 5/8 time, is delicately scored with *pizzicato* writing and magical *glissando* harmonic effects but is still insistent in tone, and it is followed by an ardent, elegiac slow movement composed of extended, interlacing lines. The work's inner tensions erupt in the finale's opening bars in what Maconchy describes as 'a sort of challenge' – a series of loud, triple-dotted, *glissando* chords in all instruments. These chords unleash a movement of ferocious energy where urgent, restless themes are powered by dotted-note rhythmic figures. The mood is briefly suspended by a brief restatement of the *pianissimo* chords first heard in the opening *Allegro*, but the finale's unrelenting themes return, reaching a climax in a series of *fortissimo* double-stopped chords in all four instruments. The Quartet ends dramatically with a forceful restatement of the opening 'challenge' chords.

Example 7.15 String Quartet No. 12, IV 'challenge' chords

Source: Copyright © 2007 Chester Music Limited. All rights reserved. International Copyright Secured. Reprinted by Permission.

Sun, Moon and Stars (1976–77)
Heloise and Abelard (1976–68)

Although the string quartet formed the backbone of Maconchy's *oeuvre*, she continued to be drawn to vocal writing in her later years. The cycle *Sun, Moon and Stars* for soprano and piano, for instance, was written for Jane Manning and Richard Rodney Bennett, and consists of four contrasting songs to words taken from the poems and meditations of the English mystic Thomas Traherne (c.1636–74).[53] The first setting 'Sun, Moon and Stars' is a mystical invocation to the Infant Christ, in which Maconchy invokes the sense of wonder and rapture in the poem with radiant vocal lines that encompass soaring leaps to high notes. The words for the second song are taken from the poem 'The Hill', and the setting's brisk tempo and dance-like rhythms suggest a spirit of youthful quest and exuberance. In contrast, 'Solitude' (III) is tragic and impassioned in tone, and the soprano's dramatic lines here are coloured by melismas, 'echo tones' and other vocal techniques. The final song 'Clothed with the Stars' (IV) begins without a break and is a slow, serene setting of a poetic fragment shaped into long, arching phrases for the soprano. While the intoxicating, mystical character of the poems and sensuous lyricism of the music suggest a natural affinity with Maconchy's Hopkins settings, and with *Morning, Noon and Night* for solo harp (1976), the cycle as a whole is marked by an acute sensitivity to the poetic nuances of the chosen texts and an elegance of structural balance and design. As Manning noted, 'audiences are bound to fall under the spell so subtly woven by this most distinguished composer at the height of her powers'.[54]

Maconchy was now on the point of composing *Heloise and Abelard*, one of her most ambitious, large-scale works. The piece was commissioned by the Croydon Philharmonic Society and was premiered at the Fairfield Hall, London in March 1979 by Hannah Francis (soprano), Philip Langridge (tenor), Tom McDonnell (baritone) and members of the Croydon Philharmonic Society (mixed chorus and orchestra), conducted by James Gaddarn. Although described by the composer as a 'dramatic cantata', *Heloise and Abelard* is semi-operatic in concept: with a duration of 75 minutes, it is more than twice the length of any one of her three chamber operas. Underlining the work's significance in Maconchy's output, Anthony Burton has argued that although she 'never had the opportunity to write a full-scale opera … the gap is to some extent filled by *Heloise and Abelard*'.[55]

---

[53] The piece was premiered in Hong Kong by Manning and Rodney Bennett in February 1978. Manning and Rodney Bennett also commissioned Lutyens to write a song cycle for them. Her *Winter Series – Spring Sowing*, Op. 115 (to words by Ursula Vaughan Williams) was premiered at the Royal Northern College of Music in February 1979.

[54] Manning, *New Vocal Repertory*, vol. 1, p. 242.

[55] Burton, 'Maconchy: Intense But Disciplined', article for The Contemporary Music Centre, Ireland (available at http://www.cmc.ie/articles/article-maconchy.html).

In detailing this well-known love affair between Peter Abelard, the famous twelfth-century philosopher and theologian, and his brilliant student Heloise, Maconchy scrupulously avoided existing scholarly and fictional accounts. Her libretto draws exclusively from primary sources – in particular, Abelard's *Historia Calamitatum* (*The Story of my Misfortunes*) and letters exchanged between the two lovers. Maconchy also highlights Abelard's ability as a poet and composer by imaginatively incorporating some of his own hymns and verses into her work. Abelard's skill as a composer was, according to Heloise, one of the features which made him so irresistible to women, and the cantata opens with a Latin setting of one of his Easter hymns, *Veris grato tempore* (In the pleasant springtime). This beautiful opening chorus is the first of nine sections, and it is followed by a section entitled 'In the Cloister of Notre Dame' (II) which is scored for the three soloists and orchestra. Heloise has been listening to Abelard's lecture to his students, and afterwards tells him that she wishes to study philosophy, a desire which is gently rebuffed by the philosopher. But Canon Fulbert, Heloise's uncle, tells Abelard of his niece's widely admired intellectual gifts, and begs him to tutor her at home with a view to making her a renowned scholar. Singing together, the three characters express their differing views on the proposal: Abelard thinks of his fee, Fulbert of his reputation and Heloise of her love for Abelard. Abelard accepts the challenge and also becomes a lodger in Fulbert's house, the scene of the cantata's third section. As Heloise and Abelard begin their tutorial, his students (chorus) are heard in the distance singing the seductive, medieval love song *O admirabile Veneris idolum*. The two become distracted, and declare their love for one another in a passionate love duet which is framed by luxuriant orchestral textures. Their duet is followed by a short orchestral interlude.

One of the many interesting features of this cantata is the way in which the character of Heloise is developed. In Maconchy's score, Heloise is given all the best tunes, so to speak, and is presented as a much stronger and ultimately more interesting personality than Abelard. This is very apparent in the fourth section (entitled 'In Brittany') which takes up the tale after the birth of Heloise and Abelard's son, Astrolabe. In order to protect his honour and Heloise's name, Abelard proposes that they marry, a suggestion which appalls the young woman. As she famously declares, 'I prefer love to wedlock, and freedom to chains … God is my witness that it would be dearer and more honourable to me to be called your harlot than to be Empress'. Abelard pleads with her and she reluctantly relents. But, she warns, 'we shall both be destroyed … All that is left to us is suffering as great as our love has been'.

Heloise's words prove to be the pivotal point in the drama. In the fifth section, an incensed Fulbert (who had earlier agreed to the marriage) now becomes convinced that Heloise will be abandoned, and takes his revenge by ordering the castration of Abelard. Abelard survives the brutal and humiliating assault, but his lamentable fate scandalizes medieval Parisian society. The remaining four sections of the cantata take place some time after this event. Both Abelard and Heloise have now entered religious life: Heloise is the Abbess of the Paraclete, an oratory located in the Champagne region of France. In 'At the Convent' (VI), the novices' joyful praise of their Abbess is dramatically juxtaposed with Heloise's anguished lament: 'Abelard, why have you forsaken me?'. The final three sections of the cantata reflect on Abelard's death. After a moving choral statement of the hymn *O quanta qualia* (VII), the work ends with an elegiac setting of Abelard's *Planctus* (VIII), and a 'Naenia' or funeral chant (IX) where chorus and Heloise lament his death.

My Dark Heart (1981–82)
Music for Strings (1982–83)
String Quartet No. 13 (*Quartetto Corto*) (1984)

The theme of lost love is again encountered in Maconchy's song cycle *My Dark Heart* for soprano and instrumental ensemble – in this instance, the poet Petrarch's unrequited love for his Laura. Commissioned by Maconchy's *alma mater*, the Royal College of Music, to mark its centenary anniversary, the cycle is a setting of some of J.M. Synge's modern prose translations of Petrarch's Sonnets – 'poetic prose with a recognizably Irish cadence', as the composer described them.[56] In the first sonnet, 'Life is flying from me', the poet speaks of the utter desolation he feels at Laura's death, and compares himself to a rudderless ship with broken masts and ropes. The work opens with the sound of funereal bells – repeated chords in the ensemble which by their emphasis and tritonal outline recall the opening of *Epyllion* and the Tenth String Quartet. These chords are intimately linked with the sonnet's emotional aura of darkness and loss, and serve both to frame the entire setting and to accentuate the bleakest expressions of anguish in the song. After their initial statement, a delicately scored passage for the ensemble introduces other important motifs and the soprano enters echoing a melodic fragment in the oboe (Example 7.16). The vocal line is perfectly balanced with the ensemble throughout, the music as a whole both reflecting on and reacting to the shape and rhythms of the words.

The song is followed by a radiantly lyrical setting of 'The South Wind is Coming Back'. In brighter mood, the soprano's description of the coming of spring is coloured by the sounds of spring in the ensemble – in particular, a flute melody interlaced with delicate countermelodies and supported by undulating harmonies. Although the setting is, in the composer's words, 'fresh and happy', it is interesting to note that the opening figure of the flute melody recalls the dark viola fragment heard at the opening of the Tenth Quartet (see Examples 7.17 and 7.11). The resemblance may be coincidental, but this instance of self-referentiality (whether conscious or not on the composer's part) has the effect of underlining the poignant emotional implications of the verse: the coexistence of

---

[56] Maconchy, note to *My Dark Heart*. The work was premiered at a special College concert on 19 March 1982 in celebration of Maconchy's 75th birthday.

love and despair the poet experiences because Laura is not there to share his joy at the coming of spring.

Example 7.16 *My Dark Heart*, I 'Life is Flying from Me'

Example 7.16 continued

[Score in C]

Source: Music by Elizabeth Maconchy. Traditional Words. Copyright © by Chester Music Limited. All rights reserved. International Copyright Secured. Reprinted by Permission.

Example 7.17 *My Dark Heart*, II 'The South Wind is Coming Back'

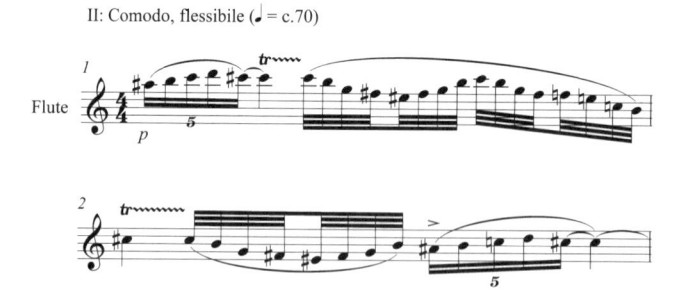

Source: Music by Elizabeth Maconchy. Traditional Words. Copyright © by Chester Music Limited. All rights reserved. International Copyright Secured. Reprinted by Permission.

Maconchy shapes verses from three different Petrarch/Synge sonnets into an integrated whole for her final song, the longest in duration. In the opening brief evocation of summer ('If the birds are making a lamentation'), the soprano's expressive lines are elegantly coloured by the woodwind (in particular the plaintive sound of the cor anglais in low register) and strings. The mood changes in the ensuing *con moto* section ('The eyes that I would be talking of') where recollections of Laura's beauty in the vocal line are heard above slowly changing harmonies in the strings. The poet's desolation returns, however, a moment dramatically emphasized by the restatement of the repeated tritonal chords heard at the work's opening. Recollections of the gently undulating harmonies of the second sonnet are heard as the music moves to the final *Poco Lento* section, 'But I am going after her'. As the poet anticipates his meeting with Laura 'in the Heavens', beautifully flowing vocal lines interspersed with countermelodies in the wind and lush low harmonies in strings bring this most poignant work to a serene end.

Example 7.18 *My Dark Heart* and *Music for Strings*

Source: Copyright © by Chester Music Limited. All rights reserved. International Copyright Secured. Reprinted by Permission.

The sombre chords heard at the end of *My Dark Heart* become the starting point of Maconchy's *Music for Strings*, a work commissioned for the 1983 Proms and premiered by the strings of the BBC Philharmonic Orchestra, conducted by Edward Downes. In four contrasting movements, much of the material in the piece is coloured by these poignant opening chords. In the first movement, for instance, recurrent statements of the chords are intermingled with contrasting passages of intricate contrapuntal lines for solo strings as well as full ensemble. The chords are also central to the impassioned argument of the third movement, *Mesto* (sad), where a mesh of expressive lines in the ensemble is framed by evocative melodies for solo viola. The arguments of the scherzo (II) and finale are, in contrast, lighter and much more extrovert in mood. Lithe, *pizzicato* figures scattered throughout the strings compete with the striding 5/4 theme in violins in the scherzo, and the final movement is filled with rhythmic ambiguities, surprising returns (the scherzo main theme) and an abrupt, unexpected ending which leaves the audience unsure of when to applaud.

Maconchy's final string quartet *Quartetto Corto* is also a work of surprises. Composed as a finalists' test piece for the 1985 Portsmouth String Quartet Competition (later the London International String Quartet Competition), the work grows from the formidable, *Epyllion*-like chords announced in the opening bars, and is cast in three contrasting, thematically related movements (all played without a break). Two highly charged *Allegros* surround an intensely eloquent *Lento* movement, the most substantial movement in the piece, which is in the nature of an extended song. There are no sharp contrasts of texture in this haunting central movement – which in essence recalls the sound world of *My Dark Heart* – its interlacing solo lines requiring considerable expressive qualities from performers. In contrast, both *Allegros* are energized by volatile rhythms and rapid shifts of tempo and texture (including *pizzicato* and *ad lib* episodes). The ending of the work returns to source with a varied and strident reiteration of the work's chiming opening chords. Although the form is compact – Maconchy frequently referred to it as her 'little quartet' or 'Quartet No. 12½' – the eight minutes of music in this piece contain some of the most challenging writing for a string quartet in the modern repertoire.

Maconchy's remarkable contribution to British musical life was publicly recognized once again when, in her 80th year (1987), she was awarded a DBE in the Honours List; the only other British woman composer to be made a Dame of the British Empire had been Ethel Smyth in 1922. She continued to compose throughout the 1980s, adding, amongst other things, a memorable setting of Edith Sitwell's *Still Falls the Rain* for double chorus (1984), the popular carol for mixed chorus *There is no Rose* (1984) and a *Life Story* for string orchestra (1985) to her extensive output. Her final years were, however, darkened by serious illness. A few years before her death in November 1994 she experienced what was to be her final 'moment of silence', and took the decision to give up composing completely. As she explained, 'the reason I stopped was because the ideas weren't coming any more. I could have gone on writing on technique, but I didn't want to do that'.[57] Ever the professional, Maconchy had no desire to write music that might not have been up to the standard of her other work. She had once stated that 'the object of all technical means, of all the art I can muster, is to achieve a more concentrated expression of the emotion implicit in the musical ideas themselves'.[58] For Maconchy, then, this was to be 'the end of my songs of love'.[59]

---

[57] Maconchy, quoted in interview with Stephen Johnson, *Gramophone* (November 1989), p. 11.
[58] Maconchy, 'Talk on the String Quartets' (Radio 3, 9 October 1976).
[59] From Synge's prose translations of Petrarch, 'Life is Flying From Me', the first setting of *My Dark Heart*.

Chapter 8
Williams: *My Last Duchess*

Williams had experienced her own 'moment of silence' when, between 1944 and 1947, bad health and exhaustion had forced her to almost give up composing completely. Her decision to move back to her native Barry in the late 1940s had been primarily determined by health reasons, but the Wales she returned to was different in many ways from the one she had left earlier for the Royal College. Although rich in terms of folk culture and choral tradition, the 1920s Welsh musical scene had been conspicuously lacking in the professional orchestras, opera houses and other musical institutions that were taken for granted in most European countries. The founding of an independent BBC Welsh Regional Service and the BBC Welsh Orchestra (both in 1936) had been key developments, and Williams had directly benefitted from the new Cardiff-based Music Department's policy of performing and broadcasting works by Welsh composers. As was the case with other regional orchestras, the BBC Welsh Orchestra was disbanded in wartime, but the orchestra was then reformed in 1946 under the new direction of Williams's gifted contemporary Mansel Thomas. There were other signs of expansion in Wales during the immediate post-war years. In 1945 the Arts Council of Great Britain created a Welsh Committee, responsible for advising on music policy in Wales, and both the Welsh National Opera Company and the National Youth Orchestra of Wales came into existence at this time. Furthermore, important festivals such as the Swansea Music Festival (established 1948) began to spring up, offering yet another new dimension to musical life in Wales.

These new developments promised improvements in Wales's musical health, but Williams had still taken an enormous risk in launching a freelance career in the late 1940s. Nearly all of her original works had been uncommissioned up to this point, and time for serious composition had to be slotted around 'earning' jobs such as writing radio scripts, film music and, from 1950, part-time teaching at the (Welsh) College of Music and Drama in Cardiff. Letters to friends detailed her general frustration at the lack of time for original composition and fears about becoming a 'snippets' composer – 'writing snippets of this, that and the other'.[1] By the autumn of 1954 her financial situation had become so difficult that she took the decision to become a full-time copyist simply to make ends meet:

> Copying isn't as bad as I thought ... & I've earned more at it than I expected (thanks to Musician's Union rates). I copied the full score of Dent's version of [the] Beggar's Opera for O.U.P. [Oxford University Press] in just over three

---

[1] Williams, letter to Daniel Jones, 2 April 1950 (Daniel Jones Archive).

weeks & got £52.10 for it!! ... I can't see myself ever making time for composing again. Just can't afford it. ('The Dancers' took months to do i.e. composing & seeing through the press – during which time I earned nothing.[2]

Despite these financial concerns, Williams was poised to embark on the most significant chapter of her musical life. Some of her finest works date from the 1950s onwards and include her Second Symphony (1956), the one-act opera *The Parlour* (1960–66) and the *Missa Cambrensis* (1968–71). The first piece to signal a phase of creative renewal was an orchestral suite entitled *Penillion*. She had been in the middle of doing some 'soul destroying' orchestrations of Victorian ballads for the BBC in September 1954 when the idea for the new work came to her. The pressure of job deadlines made it impossible for her to explore her idea, but an unexpected Christmas present from the Performing Rights Society (a generous cheque for American performances of her *Fantasia*) enabled her to forgo immediate copying and orchestration work for a time. Work began on the new piece in the early months of 1955.

Penillion for Orchestra (1955)

Williams's four-movement suite is an imaginative and highly original adaptation of some of the characteristics of the Welsh tradition of 'penillion singing' (*canu penillion* or *cerdd dant*).[3] *Pennill* is the Welsh word for stanza or verse (plural, *penillion*), and penillion singing is the traditional way of setting Welsh poetry to music where the poet/singer improvises a countermelody to a traditional harp air. With roots in the oral culture of the medieval Bardic period, and possibly earlier, it is a style that is inextricably bound to the Welsh poetic tradition and the Welsh language. Williams would almost certainly have heard penillion singing at the Eisteddfodau she had attended in her youth, but her fascination with the form from a compositional perspective probably dated from the 1940s. It is possible to detect raw elements of the style, albeit in instrumental form, in the First Symphony, but her misgivings about her Symphony as whole, and lack of time for composition, meant that such issues could only perhaps be fully thought through after her return

---

[2] Williams, letter to Enid Parry, 23 November 1954 (Williams/Parry Collection).

[3] *Cerdd Dant* translates as 'craft of the string' and refers to the harp in its traditional accompaniment role in *penillion*. For an excellent account of the origins of *cerdd dant*, see Sally Harper, *Music in Welsh Culture before 1950: A Study of the Principal Sources* (Aldershot: Ashgate, 2007). An insightful summary of the later developments of *cerdd dant* can be found in Meredydd Evans and Phyllis Kinney, 'Welsh Music: *Cerdd Dant*', in *Celtic Culture: A Historical Encyclopedia*, vol. 1, ed. J.T. Koch (Santa Barbara, USA and Oxford: ABC-Clio, 2005), p. 1767. See also *Canu penillion* or *cerdd dant* – Appendix.

to Wales.[4] Shortly after completing her new orchestral suite in 1955, she admitted that she had been 'ruminating on penillion' for years, but that she had encountered difficulty when searching for the right words:

> I got the desire to write *Penillion* [for orchestra] a few years ago when I suddenly got "penillion" on the brain & kept inventing them. And felt frustrated. Because having always thought of it being a vocal style, I knew I'd never find words to fit what I was creating. And then it dawned on me that if this music couldn't be sung, it could be played.[5]

Although orchestral instruments replace voices in *Penillion*, Williams does not attempt to adhere to the strict rules governing the traditional form. Rather, the suite is a very free and highly original adaptation of some elements of penillion style for the composer's own creative purpose. Williams neatly sidestepped the thorny issue of what Schoenberg identified as 'the discrepancy between the requirements of larger forms and the simple construction of folk tunes' by omitting any traditional Welsh tunes – normally the bedrock of *cerdd dant* – from the work's thematic palette.[6] Instead, original melodic lines become the source for the suite's intricate contrapuntal layers, although each of the four movements retain 'the narrative style, stanza form, and many melodic and rhythmic characteristics of traditional Penillion'.[7] The opening *Moderato* movement, for instance, is structured in the form of five 'stanzas' consisting of a statement and four successive and varied statements of the main melody, heard first on the trumpet. Introduced by a brief figure in woodwind, and accompanied by soft, expressive chords centred on F major in strings and harp, the melody's wistful, improvisatory quality and unexpected turns of phrase convey the impression of a freely unfolding line. Its vocality is quite deliberate. Marked *declamato*, the trumpet melody incorporates certain melodic and rhythmic patterns which are characteristic of traditional penillion singing – in particular, the use of stepwise movement and thirds in the melody, and rhythmic motifs which reflect the inflections and cadences of the Welsh language.

The presence of the 'Lombard' rhythm (♩♩ ♩), based either on repeated notes or close intervals, is significant, and is a pattern that, in this context, would be recognizable to a Welsh speaker. The rhythm duplicates the disyllabic endings

---

[4] See, for example, my discussion of the folk-like theme in the first movement of the First Symphony, Chapter 5.

[5] Williams, extract from an undated letter as quoted in 'Grace Williams: A Portrait', BBC Wales TV documentary, produced by Vincent Dowdall (1978).

[6] Schoenberg, 'Folkloristic Symphonies (1947)' in *Style and Idea: Selected Writings of Arnold Schoenberg*, ed. L. Stein, trans. L. Black (London: Faber and Faber, 1975), p. 163.

[7] Williams, note in the printed score of *Penillion* (Oxford University Press).

found in the language and is frequently encountered in Welsh folk songs, particularly, although not exclusively, at the end of phrases.

Example 8.1 *Penillion* for Orchestra, I

[Score in C. Brass and timpani omitted]

Source: *Penillion* by Grace Williams © Oxford University Press 1953. Extracts reproduced by permission. All rights reserved.

The texture becomes more intricate in subsequent sections. Although the main theme is clearly perceptible, different countermelodies achieve equal prominence as they are added to the melos. When the main melody is repeated in the second stanza (in horn and cellos), for example, it is interlaced with countermelodies based on both the melody itself (second trumpet) and on the accompaniment (first violins passing to violas and then woodwind), both of which introduce new ideas. The remaining three movements of the suite also employ stanzaic structures. In the *Allegro con fuoco* (II), boisterous statements of the principal theme, again initially heard in trumpets, are punctuated by a brief, emphatic ritornello with syncopated rhythms in 2/4 and 3/4 metres. As in the first movement, the texture becomes more elaborate in each stanza through the addition of countermelodies and with varied orchestration. The third movement, an *Andante con tristezza*, is plaintive in tone and takes the form of a *marwnad* (lament), with each subsequent stanza increasing in intensity. In contrast, the rumbustious rhythms of the opening bars and of the main violin theme of the *Allegro* finale were inspired, as Williams confessed, by 'the rhythms of the old Welsh *hwyl* … I heard from the pulpit several times when I was a child'.[8]

Example 8.2 *Penillion* for Orchestra, Finale, 'hwyl' rhythms

---

[8] Williams, letter to Daniel Jones, 13 February 1972 (Daniel Jones Archive). The Welsh word *hwyl* has a number of different meanings but Williams here uses it to convey the sense of religious fervour or passion in the orations of the Welsh preachers.

Example 8.2 continued

[Woodwind, brass and percussion omitted]

Source: *Penillion* by Grace Williams © Oxford University Press 1953. Extracts reproduced by permission. All rights reserved.

Penillion was, for a number of reasons, a crucial work in Williams's development. In the past, she had been acutely conscious of the disparity between her two distinct styles – 'my folk song *Fantasia* style and the other true me that's a bit different', as she put it. In *Penillion*, however, a process of subtle yet ambitious transformation resulted in a piece that drew from both 'styles' without descending into self-conscious or sentimental gestures. Undoubtedly, the work was, on one level, the result of a deeply held need to create a more integrated and personal musical language; it is no coincidence that, as Boyd has noted, 'not a single original work written after 1954 uses a Welsh folksong'.[9] The declamatory style and improvisatory-type textures heard in *Penillion* now became core characteristics of Williams's mature style, featuring in works as different as the Trumpet Concerto (1963) and *Ballads* for orchestra (1968). There were, however, other reasons behind the complex flowering of Williams's creative maturity. Certainly, the new direction and self-confidence in her music seems to be inextricably linked in both time and place to the realization of her long-held wish to live in Wales. Indeed, in spite of the harsh reality of forging a freelance career as a composer in the 1950s, she suggested that the changes this brought to her work routines offered a greater degree of flexibility than she had enjoyed in the past. She shared some of her reflections with Enid Parry:

> [Three] years of free-lancing have taught me a lot – in the old days, composing cd. [sic] only be done in snatches of free-time from teaching – & now I can have long consecutive stretches at it (though not often on non-commissioned works!)

---

[9] Boyd, *Grace Williams*, p. 36.

& that makes one much more professional – & that, alas, is what few composers can ever afford to become, real professionals.[10]

It also seems significant that Williams wrote her *Penillion* for the National Youth Orchestra of Wales (NYOW). Founded in 1945, the NYOW had the distinction of being the first national youth orchestra in the world, and it was to Williams that the orchestra turned for one of their first commissions to mark their tenth anniversary. The piece was first performed in Llangefni, Anglesey on 30 July 1955 by the orchestra, conducted by Clarence Raybould, and further performances took place during the orchestra's short tour of Wales in August.[11] The piece was also included in the NYOW's concert at the Edinburgh Festival on 3 September 1955 – significantly, the first concert to be given by the NYOW outside Wales.[12]

All these factors suggest the energy of youth and new beginnings, and it seems appropriate that Williams would wish to create a work that drew inspiration from the rich cultural heritage of Wales. In title, at least, *Penillion* proudly displays its Welsh credentials, but it is more difficult to say to what extent the music can be regarded as 'Welsh'. Daniel Jones certainly felt the heady combination of lyrical and improvisatory-type features, particularly in the 'rhapsodic, bardic' opening of work, to be 'recognizably Welsh'.[13] Even so, *Penillion* was never intended to be a nationalist work. As Williams noted:

> I didn't deliberately set out to write Welsh music – but my state of mind in planning it was full of Welsh contrasts of temperament – oratory – poetry – medieval legends of the Mabinogion. So when I got started and concentrated wholly on the music all that was reflected in what I wrote. The style is narrative, but what is being reflected is anyone's guess. I feel it is a genuinely Welsh work (but, of course, there are so many other influences, too, as in all composers' works).[14]

In contrast to the obvious Welshness of the traditional tunes used in the *Fantasia*, a more sophisticated and profound concept of nationhood is at work in *Penillion*.

---

[10] Williams, letter to Enid Parry, 3 April 1950 (Williams/Parry Collection).

[11] The choice of composer for the NYOW's first commission was, no doubt, partly initiated by Raybould, who was already an admirer of Williams's work. See, for example, his comments on Williams's work in Raybould, 'Modern Welsh Composers' in ed. Alwyn D. Rees, *Yr Einion / The Welsh Anvil*, vol. 5 (Cardiff: University of Wales Press, 1953), pp. 34–36.

[12] *Penillion* was also the first piece by Williams to be heard at the BBC Proms. It was performed at the Royal Albert Hall on 13 August 1958 by the London Symphony Orchestra and Basil Cameron (conductor).

[13] Jones in a memorial tribute to Williams (BBC Radio Wales, 10 February 1977).

[14] Williams, letter to Esther Warkov, 28 January 1977, quoted in Warkov, 'Traditional Features in Grace Williams's *Penillion*', *Welsh Music* 7/1 (Summer 1982), p. 24.

It is as if Williams's experiences to date allowed her to reabsorb native influences at an entirely different, more detached, level. Her approach was certainly informed by the example of Bartók, Kodály, Janáček and Vaughan Williams, and in this company *Penillion* may seem to be a rather late entry.[15] Even so, it is an original one. Certainly, nothing quite like it seems to have existed in Welsh music before. Wales possessed neither the educational and professional musical resources, nor the gifted composers capable of producing original work of this kind before the twentieth century.

Symphony No. 2 (1956)

The musicologist and critic Arnold Whittall has noted that one of the fascinating features of *Penillion* is 'the bridge it builds between the far from mutually exclusive concepts of suite and symphony'.[16] *Penillion* is to some extent symphonic in concept and overall design but it is worth noting that Williams had been busy building bridges long before this time. Her earlier suite *Rhiannon* (1939) had also taken on a distinctly symphonic shape during the process of composition –the composer had even toyed with the idea of entitling the work 'Symphonic Legend'. In that instance, *Rhiannon* had been followed by the First Symphony (1943). This pattern was repeated in the mid 1950s when, after completing *Penillion*, Williams started work on her Second Symphony. The Symphony was written in response to a commission from the Arts Council's Welsh Committee, and was premiered at the Swansea Festival on 8 October 1957 by the Hallé Orchestra, conducted by George Weldon.

In contrast to the First Symphony, Symphony No. 2 does not have a specific programme connected with Welsh sources. Williams had had reservations about her 'Owain Glyndŵr' Symphony – withdrawing all but the scherzo movement – and her avoidance of poetic quotations or general programme in favour of a more abstract structure in the Second was almost certainly the result of a decision to do things differently. Unusually, Williams also went to the trouble of providing a lengthy programme note for the work in which the main arguments of each of the four movements were itemized in spartanly musical terms. For some, the apparent contrast between the soft mould of the freely poetic *Penillion* and the more classically etched Second Symphony was puzzling. Arguing that Williams's creativity found 'its most congenial expression in poetic or narrative forms', for instance, Boyd suggested that the Symphony gave 'the impression that the composer ... responded to symphonic form as a challenge rather than turned to it

---

[15] As Williams noted, 'in my treatment of the tunes there are lots of extraneous influences – Bartók and Kodály especially – but the Welsh rhythms so often resemble Hungarian. Goodness knows why, but they do'. Williams, extract from an undated letter as quoted in 'Grace Williams: A Portrait', BBC Wales TV documentary.

[16] Whittall, 'Grace Williams 1906–1977', *Soundings: A Music Journal* 7 (1978), p. 20.

as the natural vehicle for what she wished to express'.[17] Certainly, the symphony, with all the burden of history and philosophy the genre carried with it, was going to be a challenge for any twentieth-century composer. Yet the dramatic–lyrical contrasts in Williams's Second Symphony are convincingly wrought, even though she may have chosen to use the sharp edge of a chisel in places. The piece undoubtedly ranks among her major achievements, and she succeeded here in building a strong bridge with the established symphonic tradition without sacrificing any of her individuality.

Taken as a whole, this powerful work – one of Williams's more introspective, darkly hued pieces – represented a significant step forward in creative terms. Although the *Allegro marciale* first movement begins in the region of A flat, the character of the music is quietly seditious in its refusal to adhere to any clear sense of key. Its aggressive tone is defined by the stark, chromatic trumpet theme which opens the work (Example 8.3).

Key features of interest are the imaginative touches and attention to detail in the scoring. After the trumpet theme is explored in the orchestra, the tension abates slightly, and a brief *misterioso* bridge passage introduces the second subject (in 6/8). Gentler in character, although still agitated, Williams uses delicately sketched chamber-like textures to present this woodwind theme, accompanying it only with contrapuntal threads in the first desks of the strings. Both first and second subjects are enterprisingly developed and expanded in the ensuing development section, their varied treatment made more compelling by the unsettling harmonic ambiguity which pervades the movement as a whole. Shostakovich's influence seems close to hand – particularly in shrill passages for high woodwind, and also more generally in the bitter, aggressive drive of the movement.[18]

The mordant tone of the *Allegro* gives way to the more reflective mood of the *Andante* second movement (in G major). Interestingly, the modal oboe theme heard at the opening – sparingly accompanied by a sustained open G string on the violins and occasional harp chords – possesses rhythmic characteristics which the composer described as being 'distinctly Welsh'.[19] As the musical line freely unfolds, the theme's affinity with some of the lyrical sections from *Penillion* becomes apparent. During the course of the movement, this theme is stated in muted trumpet above which the oboe plays a penillion-like melody (Example 8.4).

The mood established by the *Andante* is shattered by the brute force of the *Allegro scherzando* (III), a movement described by Williams as being 'a bit of an ugly duckling'.[20] The scherzo opens *misterioso* (mysteriously) in one of her

---

[17] Boyd, *Grace Williams*, p. 83.

[18] Vaughan Williams's Fourth and Sixth Symphonies have also been suggested as possible models. Ibid., p. 44.

[19] Williams, note to Symphony No. 2 (private collection).

[20] 'Now I've finished the sketch [of the scherzo] I think it adds up logically and sounds alive even if it is a bit of an ugly duckling'. Williams, letter to Maconchy, 6 February 1956, quoted in Boyd, *Grace Williams*, p. 45.

258 Lutyens, Maconchy, Williams and Twentieth-Century British Music

Example 8.3 Symphony No. 2, opening

[Score in C]

Source: Copyright © Oriana Publications Limited 2008. Reproduced by permission.

Example 8.4 Symphony No. 2, II, main theme

[Cor anglais, bassoon, harp, tam-tam omitted]

Source: Copyright © Oriana Publications Limited 2008. Reproduced by permission.

favourite keys – C♯ minor – but there is little kinship between this movement and earlier pieces (such as the *Elegy*) that had formally employed this key. Instead, the music recalls the combative tone of the opening movement, its relentless progress only slightly eased by an austere *Andante* trio section. After a return to the scherzo material, the movement ends with a fiery coda and an emphatic statement of the opening theme. In contrast, a richly elegiac tone is established at the beginning of the *Largo* finale.[21] The movement opens with a solemn fugato (Example 8.5) in what the composer described as 'a mixture of D major and D minor'.[22] After the fugato melody is extensively developed, a new theme is introduced, and the ensuing thematic tussle is brilliantly deployed throughout the orchestra. The debate anticipates the return of the first movement's trumpet theme – at first, stated quietly as if 'coming from the distance' but gaining strength at each subsequent restatement. Towards the end of the movement, the jagged trumpet theme is interwoven with more rhapsodic passages, but the final bars of the work burn with pounding *fortissimo* chords (in E major), played *con forza* in full orchestra.

Example 8.5 Symphony No. 2, IV, opening

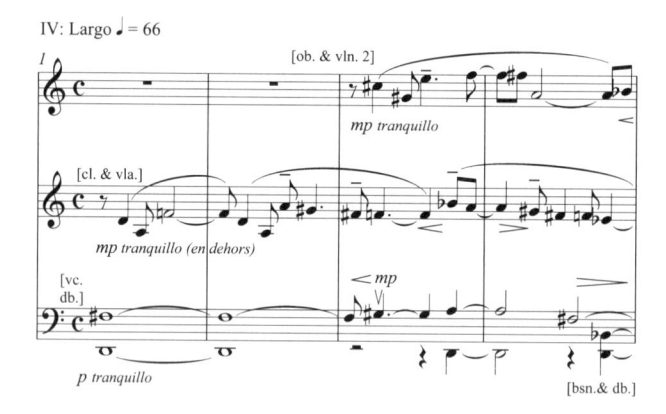

Source: Copyright © Oriana Publications Limited 2008. Reproduced by permission.

Williams provided her most cogent and personal solution to the issue of dramatic contrast to date in her Second Symphony and it is regrettable that she did not go on to write a Third. Her reluctance to write another symphony, however, may well have stemmed from the circumstances surrounding the symphony's premiere at the Swansea Festival in October 1957. Although the work was, by

---

[21] Whittall has observed that the Largo finale 'has material which seems generically Mahlerian' and has also noted that the completion of the Symphony in 1956 coincided with 'the discovery and acceptance of Mahler as the supreme "early modern" symphonist' in Britain. Whittall, *Soundings*, p. 21.

[22] Williams, note to Symphony No. 2.

all accounts, extremely well received – Williams was given a standing ovation by the audience – few present at the concert would have been aware of the traumatic events that had occurred before the work's first public performance. After the first rehearsal of the work in August 1956 – to which Williams was not invited – the conductor George Weldon demanded that she make large cuts in the slow movement, something which the composer was, understandably, reluctant to do. A distressed Williams wrote to Enid Parry two days after the premiere:

> [Weldon] told me he'd found two places where I could cut easily, showed me them and said, "You'd better make up your mind now." I told him that was quite impossible – I'd have to consider the cuts in the context of the movement as a whole & that could take a few days. He hummed and hared about little technicalities for three hours – not a word about the interpretation of the music – he didn't ask me to play a note ... My last words to him were "And if I refuse to cut?" & he replied "The orchestra & I will be very displeased."[23]

Weldon's attempt to blackmail Williams into making cuts in her symphony was deplorable, and it is little wonder that her initial response was to offer to withdraw the work entirely. Her reaction prompted what she described as a 'volte face' from Weldon, however, and, mindful of her obligation to both the Arts Council and the Swansea Festival, plans for the premiere were not abandoned. Having decided that his cuts 'made nonsense of the music', she reluctantly made two of her *own* from the slow movement. The amended symphony was duly rehearsed and performed, but the whole appalling incident left Williams badly scarred. 'I expect the general feeling at the outset was: we've got to do this damned work by this obscure Welsh woman to please the Festival Committee', she told Parry, 'hence the arrogance – which really was quite cruel. I could never go through such an experience again', she added, '& I look forward now to writing nothing but songs & partsongs – & perhaps very short orchestral works – but never another symphony'.

Six Poems by Gerard Manley Hopkins (1958)
All Seasons shall be Sweet (1959)

True to her word, Williams did not compose a substantial orchestral work in the immediate years following the completion of her Symphony. An opportunity to write songs did, however, present itself when she was asked by the BBC to compose a song cycle for the 1958 Cheltenham Festival. Energized by this fresh challenge, she initially pondered setting Welsh poems or English poems by a Welsh poet, and discussed several candidates with Mansel Thomas. None seemed right for the task, however, and it was Thomas who suggested that she should

---

[23] Williams, letter to Enid Parry, 10 October 1957 (Williams/Parry Collection). All subsequent quotes about the Symphony are also taken from this letter.

consider the poetry of Gerard Manley Hopkins. A re-reading of Hopkins's work confirmed to her that the 'Celtic imagery' and 'Welsh characteristics of rhythm & rhyme'[24] in his ornate verse was precisely what she needed. Williams selected six contrasting poems for her Hopkins cycle and chose to score the work for contralto and string sextet. The piece was premiered in Cheltenham on 14 July 1958 by Helen Watts (contralto) and the Allegri String Quartet with Cecil Aronowitz (2nd viola) and Terence Weil (2nd cello).

Whittall has rightly drawn attention to the 'unselfconscious' quality of these settings, noting that they go 'straight to the heart of the deep feeling which lies beneath the complex surfaces'.[25] One of the most striking features about the cycle is the way in which Williams approaches the complicated metres and syntax of Hopkins's idiosyncratic style. Indeed, the freshness and spontaneous flow of her six settings are convincingly integrated into a whole, concealing the fact that this poetry is notoriously difficult to set to music. The work opens and closes with three of Hopkins's Welsh sonnets – 'Pied Beauty', 'Hurrahing in the Harvest' and 'The Windhover' (nos. 1, 5 and 6 in the cycle) – which were written during the poet's short residency at St. Beuno's Jesuit College, near St. Asaph in North Wales. Williams's joyful, quick-paced setting of 'Pied Beauty' begins with the ringing sound of string fanfares which prepare for the contralto's entry, and the flowing vocal line and supporting sensuous textures are well matched to the natural imagery and religious fervour of the verse. The second setting, 'Peace', introduces a more haunted, contemplative mood with its arching lines, and it is followed by a lighter, scherzo-type setting of 'Spring and Fall', replete with sinuous solo lines and delicate pizzicato accompaniment. The impassioned and dissonance-laden argument of the fourth setting, 'No worst, there is none ...' is a harrowing depiction of grief which is only partly dispelled by the autumnal 'Hurrahing in the Harvest'. The cycle closes with an emotive setting of 'The Windhover' in which the vocal line glides above impassioned string textures like Hopkins's 'dapple-dawn-drawn Falcon'.[26]

Another opportunity to write for voices came in 1959 when Williams was commissioned by the BBC in Wales to write the choral suite *All Seasons shall be Sweet*. As Boyd has observed, this piece is very much the natural successor to the earlier *The Dancers* (1951): the two works employ almost identical forces (soprano, women's chorus and chamber orchestra and/or piano), and both testify to Williams's skill at selecting suitable poems.[27] *All Seasons* brings together nine English poems – ranging from Shakespeare and Thomas Heywood to Blake – which are linked by their allusion to a particular season. The work opens with

---

[24]   Williams, letter to Enid Parry, 20 May 1958 (Williams/Parry Collection).

[25]   Whittall, *Soundings*, p. 22.

[26]   Note that Maconchy set several of Hopkins's poems, including 'Peace' (for soprano and orchestra in 1964) and 'Pied Beauty' (for chorus and brass in 1976).

[27]   See Boyd's discussion of this work in *Grace Williams*, p. 56. See also Whittall, *Soundings*, pp. 22–23.

a setting of Coleridge's 'Frost at Midnight' in which gentle, soft chords in the orchestra set up a rocking motion in 5/8 time as the choir sing to the cradled child to whom 'all seasons shall be sweet'. Two settings by Blake follow which allude to spring. The beautiful, lilting 'Song of Spring' (II) is scored for solo soprano, while the choir's rippling scales in 'When the Green Woods Laugh' (III) capture the joy of springtime. Summer is represented by a more languid solo soprano setting of Oberon's speech 'I know a bank' from Shakespeare's *A Midsummer Night's Dream* (IV), and by a choral setting of 'To Phoebus' from Thomas Heywood's *Love's Mistress* (V). Heywood's 'Praise of Ceres' from *The Silver Age* (VI) is concerned with harvesting the grain in autumn, and it is followed by contrasting settings of two 'Winter' poems: James Thomson's 'The Wintry Waste' from *The Seasons* (VII) and Shakespeare's 'When icicles hang' from *Love's Labours Lost* (VIII). The cycle ends with a bittersweet setting of Robert Southwell's 'Times go by Turns' which heralds the return of spring.

The Parlour (1960–66)

Williams was in the middle of writing *All Seasons* in the summer of 1959 when she was approached by the Arts Council's Welsh Committee with the offer of a commission to write a one-act opera. The Committee's original intention was to commission Williams and Daniel Jones to write two operas which could be performed as a double bill by the Welsh National Opera Company (WNOC). Although both commissions were fulfilled, plans to perform the operas together fell through. Jones's *The Knife*, completed in 1961, went on to be premiered by the London-based New Opera Company at Sadler's Wells in December 1963. And Williams had the distinction of being the first woman in Wales to write an opera when *The Parlour* was first performed in May 1966 by the WNOC together with Puccini's *Il Tabarro*.[28]

After suffering years of thwarted ambition, Williams might have been expected to realize her long-held desire to write an opera on a Welsh subject. She had certainly considered several possible scenarios in the past, including a one-act comic opera based on the satirical plays of the eighteenth-century Welsh poet Twm o'r Nant, and an opera based on the Welsh folk hero Dic Penderyn.[29] Yet *The Parlour* is not a folk opera; neither is it Welsh in any sense at all. Indeed, when the opportunity to write a new opera finally presented itself in 1960, Williams turned not to native writers for her libretto, but to the French satirist Guy de

---

[28] WNOC had shown interest in performing *The Knife* separately but this idea was never realized. Williams joked with Jones that she should have called her opera 'The Fork' to go with his 'Knife'. Williams, letters to Jones, 7 October 1965 and 10 May 1966 (Daniel Jones Collection).

[29] Note that *Hen Walia* (1930) was also originally intended as an overture to a folk opera. See Chapter 2.

Maupassant.[30] His savagely funny short story *En Famille*, in which the apparent demise of an obnoxious matriarch reveals the greed of family members – a sort of 'Granny Schicchi', as one quipster put it[31] – offered the rich, sardonic vein she needed at this time.

Williams wrote her own libretto for *The Parlour*, brilliantly elaborating Maupassant's story for her own purposes, and her story reveals her formidable technical skill and innate understanding of musical theatre. Structured in two scenes, the drama focuses on a day in the life of an 'ordinary' Victorian family who live in an English coastal town. Papa, a Navigation clerk, and his wife, Mamma, live frugally, but life is coloured by Louisa and Augusta, their two lively daughters, and by Grandmamma, who delights in terrorizing the neighbours. When the old lady is found lying flat on the floor one lunchtime, the family is thrown into turmoil and sends for her doctor. Dr Charlton initially thinks that the 'old rascal' is 'up to her tricks' again, but after examining her he announces that 'it's the end'. In a state of shock, the family and doctor sit down to a meal but it is not long before grief gives way to more practical matters. 'Tell me, did your mother make a will?' Mamma asks Papa when they are alone as she eyes her mother-in-law's elegant furniture. She has toiled for years in the house but it is his indolent sister Genevieve who is to inherit half of the furniture. Or perhaps not. Mamma argues that all the best furniture should be theirs, and the first scene ends as she and Papa start to exchange their faded furnishings for Grandmamma's more deluxe belongings.

Genevieve's arrival at the start of the second scene coincides with that of the doctor and the undertaker, and all are ushered into the now sumptuous parlour. Mamma and Papa now find themselves in a hopelessly compromised position when Grandmamma appears at the top of the stairs in the middle of the funeral preparations. It transpires that she has been in a temporary coma but has heard everything. She pointedly asks Genevieve to accompany her to her room to help her to make a will. A furious quarrel breaks out and Grandmamma acidly tells Mamma and Papa to return all her belongings to their original places. Mamma is distraught and Papa suddenly remembers that he has not informed his boss about his absence from work. A furious Mamma rushes away and the opera ends as Papa drags his mother's sofa towards the stairs.

---

[30] It may well be the case that Williams's avoidance of native themes was influenced by the fact that the WNOC already had Welsh-themed operas in their repertoire. The company had commissioned only two 'Welsh' operas at this stage, both by Arwel Hughes, who for many years had conducted company productions. His *Menna*, a three-act tragedy based on a Welsh folk story (libretto by Wyn Griffith), was premiered by the WNOC in Cardiff on 9 November 1953. The premiere of Hughes's three-act comedy *Serch yw'r Doctor* (libretto by Saunders Lewis after Molière's *L'amour médecin*) followed in 1960. See Arwel Hughes – Appendix.

[31] Eric Mason, *The Parlour* review (*Daily Mail*, 6 May 1966). Mason was referring to Puccini's *Gianni Schicchi* (1917–18).

Some might have claimed that in choosing a Maupassant comedy Williams was simply cadging an idea from Britten. His *Albert Herring* (1947, with libretto by Eric Crozier) was based on the Maupassant story *Le rosier de Madame Husson*, and Williams was well aware that her decision to use *En Famille* would invite comparisons:

> I didn't forget that another composer – and an illustrious one – had chosen a Maupassant story for one of his operas, and for obvious reasons I hunted high and low for a story from another source. But there was always a snag, and at last, in sheer desperation, I stretched out my hand to one of my bookshelves, and within five minutes I was re-reading *En Famille*.[32]

Although both *The Parlour* and *Albert Herring* have a presumed death as a denouement and can be described as musical satires with serious undertones, the two are quite different in conception. With a duration of 75 minutes, Williams's opera is roughly half the length of Britten's comedy, and, consequently, the dramatic tempo of *The Parlour* is more compressed. Indeed, the opera moves at speed from the very start, beginning in C major and swiftly passing through a succession of keys as the drama unfolds: as the composer put it, 'there is quite a lot to say in a short time'.[33] The wording throughout is very effectively confined to colloquial, everyday conversation and, in keeping with the swift pace of twists and turns in the story, the succinct arias, ensembles and choruses are seamlessly integrated into the whole. The dividing of the opera into two main scenes allows for some excellent examples of comic and dramatic timing for the principal characters – not least, Grandmamma's 'resurrection' in the second scene. Although she is confined to a state of (off-stage) suspended animation for much of the opera – she appears 'in person' at the start of scene one, and at the climax of scene two – her musical presence is felt throughout the drama by means of a recurrent motif.

Example 8.6 *The Parlour*, Grandmamma's theme

Source: Reproduced by kind permission of the Estate of Grace Williams.

---

[32] Williams, 'The Parlour' radio script in 'A Self Portrait', *Welsh Music* 8/5, p. 9.
[33] Ibid.

The music fits the action perfectly in this tightly controlled score, and one is constantly aware of Williams's deftness of musical characterization and mood. The charming innocence and freshness of the duet between the two young daughters when they are first introduced early in scene one, for example, contrasts sharply with the worldly disenchantment of their squabbling parents, and the swaggering pronouncements of the medical quack Dr Charlton are portrayed with considerable wit. Williams also makes clever use of the structure to highlight the chorus who assume the role of the neighbours. At the opening of the opera, for instance, Grandmamma is seen screaming abuse at them from an open window of the house while Mamma struggles to keep the peace. The irony is not lost when, half an hour later at the opening of the second scene, the neighbours struggle to conceal their jubilation at the old lady's passing as they offer hollow condolences to the family. This situation is anticipated by the inclusion of a mock-solemn funeral march as the neighbours are initially ushered into the parlour – with a musical wink towards the Marche Funèbre of Chopin's Piano Sonata No. 2, one of several knowing references to established repertoire in the opera.

When *The Parlour* was first performed by the WNOC in 1966, the work's success took the Welsh musical establishment and the opera world by surprise. Indeed, Williams's skill as a musical portraitist and natural sense of theatre suited the genre so well that many found it hard to believe that it was her first attempt at opera. Writing in the *Western Mail* (7 May 1966), Alun Hoddinott noted that

> there can be no doubt that Miss Williams has brilliantly solved the technical problems of opera, and this in a first opera is no mean achievement. The performance was not only a notable event for the WNOC, it was also a step forward for Welsh music. The opera was a huge success with the audience and performers and composer received a sustained ovation.

The opera had several performances during WNOC's 1966 season in Cardiff as well as one performance in North Wales, but was dropped from the company's schedule in 1967 because of poor ticket sales. Williams herself was both delighted and surprised at the critical success of her opera, but was typically philosophical about its reception as far as the public was concerned:

> Next week *The Parlour* is being done at Cardiff – Tuesday and Thursday – & I'm afraid these will have to be the final performances because bookings are so bad ... I knew all along that only a limited number of people would be interested & they all came in May ... I can't blame anyone. They have the choice between Mozart, Rossini, Smetana, Donizetti, Rossini – & me, & not even Puccini as bait can draw them in & can one really wonder?[34]

---

[34] Williams, letter to Parry, 6 October 1966 (Williams/Parry Collection).

Opera had proved to be an entirely natural medium for Williams but, regrettably, *The Parlour* was to be her only opera. Although she considered several more ideas for opera subjects, none were ever realized.[35]

Four Mediaeval Welsh Poems (1962)
Trumpet Concerto (1963)
***Severn Bridge Variations* (1965)**
***Carillons* for Oboe and Orchestra (1965/73)**

By the time *The Parlour* was premiered in May 1966, Williams had completed several smaller pieces. The first to be composed was her Four Mediaeval Welsh Poems for contralto, harp and harpsichord, which she set in the original language.[36] The piece was written in response to a request from the BBC in Wales to compose songs specifically 'in penillion style' for a Festival of Welsh Music in 1962. The text of the first song 'Stafell Gynddylan' (Cynddylan's Hall) dates from the ninth century, and Williams uses the sparse, thorny textures of harp and harpsichord to accompany the contralto's lament for the murdered prince Cynddylan.[37] In keeping with elements of traditional penillion style, the harp begins with a statement of a theme (an original melody stated with chords in the harpsichord) after which the singer enters over the theme's restatement with a declamatory countermelody. Welsh 'Lombard' rhythms are employed extensively, matching the rhythms of the verse, and the inspired use of jagged, wide intervals in the vocal line has the effect of intensifying the grief-laden tone of the setting (Example 8.7).

---

[35] When WNOC's *The Parlour* season came to an end, Williams was in discussion with the BBC producer Cedric Messina to write a TV opera. After briefly considering Vercors's *Le Silence de la mer* as a subject, she proposed an up-to-date adaptation of Maupassant's *Boule de Suif* but the idea was turned down. She also went on to make a few other suggestions (including Balzac's *El verdugo*), but the proposed commission didn't come to fruition. Interestingly, while in discussions with the BBC, Williams had the idea of composing a full-length stage opera based on Chekov's *Uncle Vayna*. However, lack of funding and other composing commitments seem to have prevented her from developing this idea any further.

[36] Williams had long had a fascination with the complex sonority and syntax of Welsh medieval verse – the sound of its rhythms, cadences, and inflexions – and held David Vaughan Thomas's settings of medieval poems, *Saith o Ganeuon* (Seven Songs) of 1922, in particularly high regard.

[37] Williams's unusual but always skilful choice of instrumental ensemble for her vocal/choral settings continued throughout this period. Her *Carmina Avium* (Song of Birds), for example, a choral setting of three Latin texts (medieval and Roman), written in 1967 for the Cardiff Festival of Twentieth-Century Music, is scored for viola d'amore and harp.

This forbidding song is followed by the gentler 'Hwiangerdd' (Lullaby) in which a mother rocks her child to sleep – a feature captured in the lilting vocal line – with tales of his father's hunting skills. The song retains, for the most part, the basic penillion pattern (melody, in this instance, stated in the harpsichord, and countermelody in voice), as does the third song 'Boddi Maes Gwyddno' (the Drowning of Gwyddno's Land). Agitated, dramatic and delivered in *declamando* style, this song tells of the submersion of a mythical land, and is the most complex of the four in terms of musical themes and textures. Dry land is reached in 'Claddu'r Bardd' (the Bard's Burial), where a poet speaks of the flowers he would like to be laid around him on his grave. Starker, leaner textures for harp and harpsichord provide an excellent counterpart to the vocal line in this final, sombre setting.

Example 8.7 Four Mediaeval Welsh Poems, I 'Stafell Gynddylan'

Example 8.7 continued

[Musical notation for Alto, Harp, and Harpsichord, 3 bars starting at measure 9, with text "Wyl-af wers, taw-af we-dy."]

Stafell Gynddylan ys tywyll heno,
Heb dân, heb wely;
Wylaf wers, tawaf wedy.

Cynddylan's Hall is dark tonight,
without a fire, without a bed;
I will weep for a while then I will fall silent.

Source: Copyright © Oriana Publications Limited 2010. Reproduced by permission.

Shortly after completing her Welsh settings, Williams received a fan letter from Bram Gay, principal trumpeter of the Hallé Orchestra, informing her about a recent Hallé performance of her *Penillion*. 'I don't know how you came by the happy knack of writing for my instrument so well', he stated, 'but it's true to say that your handling of the trumpet and, indeed, the whole brass, is a delight to us who play it'.[38] Williams's fondness for the trumpet had been blatantly apparent in all of her orchestral works – she earned the nickname 'Williams the Trumpet' in orchestral circles – and it was perhaps only a matter a time before she would come to write a concerto for her favourite instrument. The request duly followed, and Williams's new Trumpet Concerto was premiered by Gay and the Hallé Orchestra, conducted by Charles Mackerras, in Rhyl on 8 March 1964, the first of three concert performances given by the Hallé in North Wales. Williams wrote to Maconchy to tell her about some comments she had received after the performances:

> Today I heard from William Mathias (a most gifted musician & very promising composer) who'd been at the Bangor concert & at last he gave me the truth. The

---

[38] Bram Gay, letter to Williams, quoted in 'Composer of the Week: Grace Williams', programme 3 (Radio 3, 9 August 2006).

performance was not satisfactory. Orchestra competent technically – but hadn't got to understand it well enough – or to grasp the relationship bet: tpt. & orch. 'I am convinced [he said] that despite its clear idiom it is not a work which yields up all its subtleties at one hearing; it appears to be direct – but isn't – I feel there is much in the work which is very important to you & personal –' which is far better than I hoped to hear – & I know Wm M is honest and wouldn't write what he didn't mean.[39]

As Mathias implied, there are indeed a number of unconventional features in this three movement concerto. One might expect, for instance, a brilliant *Allegro* opening movement with much virtuosic display for the soloist but, as with the Violin Concerto, Williams opens her concerto with an *Andante* movement. The movement as a whole is lyrical and enigmatic in tone and the solo trumpet is skilfully blended with the orchestral texture in a way which defies the Romantic confrontational concerto. The work reveals its close kinship with both *Penillion* and the inflexions of the Welsh language from the very first bars: indeed, the declamatory A major trumpet theme at the work's opening (Example 8.8) has an identical pitch outline to the opening motif of the suite – although the rhythms and keys are different. This theme contains rhythmic and melodic features which are extended and developed in the first movement by both soloist and orchestra.

Example 8.8 Trumpet Concerto, opening

Source: Copyright © Cyhoeddiadau Curiad / Curiad Publications. Reproduced by permission.

The central *Lento* movement is in the form of a passacaglia. While the music is, for the most part, in the key of C, its main theme, stated in cellos and basses (Example 8.9), draws from 12-note technique in its construction: all 12 notes of

---

[39] Williams, letter to Maconchy, 14 April 1964 (private collection).

the chromatic scale are used and the second phrase is an exact inversion of the first. Above this highly chromatic theme – which is restated 14 times in different instruments during the course of the movement – the solo trumpet plays elaborate, improvisatory-type lines, almost in the manner of a penillion. This central movement is followed by a lively, syncopated *Allegro con brio* finale in which the more familiar, extrovert side of the trumpet's range is fully exploited.

Example 8.9 Trumpet Concerto, II, passacaglia theme

[Some instruments omitted]

Source: Copyright © Cyhoeddiadau Curiad / Curiad Publications. Reproduced by permission.

While Williams's employment of a 12-note row for the passacaglia theme of her central movement was unusual in the context of her work as a whole, this was not an attempt on her part to write atonal or 12-note music. She had little sympathy for the music of Schoenberg, although she greatly admired that of his pupil Berg. As she stated, 'when a composer [Schoenberg] exerts such a powerful influence on musical thought, then naturally one wants to respond to him, if not as a composer then at least as a listener; and that, alas, I've never been able to do'.[40] A much more likely source of inspiration for Williams, and one which was much closer to home,

---

[40] Williams, 'A Self Portrait', *Welsh Music* 8/5, p. 15.

probably came from Britten's pen. In the operas *The Turn of the Screw* (1954) and *The Midsummer Night's Dream* (1960), Britten had shown that passacaglia and/or variation form and 12-note themes could be employed within a broader tonal framework to highly original effect. Williams knew these works well, and although the trumpet's distinctive, penillion-like declamations in her concerto's central movement makes this particular sound world very un-Brittenish, her formal choices alone suggest an intriguing kinship.

Williams was, of course, well aware that her compositional style and tonal idiom would have been considered to be horribly unfashionable by 1960s progressives in Britain. As she stated, 'to continue composing in the post-war years without capitulating to Schoenberg's serialism was like being left behind in a backwater, when everyone else was swimming ahead with the tide'.[41] She often voiced feelings of musical isolation to friends, and of feeling out of touch with the musical explorations of not just a younger generation of composers, but also with her own. Her attitude, for example, towards Lutyens's music was interesting. She was genuinely fond of 'Liz', often referring to her as 'one of us' (i.e. from the same generation of RCM women composers), but had mixed feelings about her music. When she heard that Lutyens had been awarded a CBE in 1969, she wrote a carefully worded letter of congratulations to her. 'The actual congratulations will be ... really sincere', she told Maconchy, 'because [Liz] has worked & is a kind soul; it's going to be difficult to avoid mentioning her music which I'm afraid I can't like at all ... (I well know what she'd say about the likes of me so I'll beg her not to reply)'.[42]

It would be wrong, however, to assume that Williams remained aloof from contemporary developments in music. She maintained a lively interest in the music of her day and, according to her sister Marian Glyn Evans, would regularly scan the *Radio Times* for concerts and broadcasts of new music. Although her reactions were not always positive, there was invariably something which struck her as interesting, be it in pieces by younger Welsh colleagues such as Mathias and Hoddinott, or in the music of Birtwistle, Feldman, LeFanu and, indeed, Lutyens. 'I feel when [Liz] composes she puts on an act', she confessed, '<u>except</u> that the song from the new opera ... ['Isis's Lament' from *Isis and Osiris*] ... <u>is</u> rather lovely in a way'.[43] Furthermore, in 1972, at the age of 66, Williams attended a course in Electronic Music at the Glamorgan Summer School at Barry because she wished to explore new ways of integrating the sounds and rhythms of the sea into her music. Even so, Williams was not prepared to compromise on some things. Pre-compositional diagrams and 12-note matrixes were alien to her musical vision, and she had long since (happily) accepted that the chances of her ever being

---

[41] Ibid. Williams added that 'one's only comfort was, there was *some* resistance in high places in this country, and of course in Russia'. The resistance fighters she was referring to were Britten and Shostakovich.

[42] Williams, letter to Maconchy, February 1969 (private collection).

[43] Williams, letter to Maconchy, September 1970 (private collection).

invited to either Darmstadt or Dartington were about as unlikely as her travelling to the moon. 'I have avoided things which were wrong for me, such as serialism', she explained, 'because it was not melodically suitable. But remember, every composer has his own series of notes which form his own idiom, though it does not obey the semitonal rules of serialism itself ... we've all got a "series", or there would be no style'.[44]

Williams's own 'series' was heard alongside those of five other British composers when she was asked in 1965 by the BBC (West) to contribute to a composite piece celebrating the opening of the Severn Bridge. Malcolm Arnold provided the theme and first variation to the *Severn Bridge Variations*, while Hoddinott, Jones, Tippett, Maw and Williams each contributed a single variation to the suite. Williams chose to pen a choral prelude (no. 5 in the series) based on the well-known Welsh hymn tune 'Braint'. Her prelude took the form of an anguished elegy and was directly informed by the profound sense of grief she experienced on hearing of the horrific accident at Aberfan, South Wales in October 1966.[45] The *Severn Bridge Variations* was premiered by the BBC Training Orchestra at a special concert in Swansea on 11 January 1967, and as one critic noted, the piece as a whole 'surpassed expectation by producing a contrast rather than a conflict of styles' (*The Times*, 13 January 1967).

Williams continued to explore instrumental forms when, in 1965, she accepted a commission from BBC Wales to write a short work for a Welsh radio programme. Although the programme never materialized, the resulting *Carillons* for oboe and chamber orchestra was premiered on 1 March 1967 by Philip Jones (oboe) and members of the BBC Welsh Orchestra, conducted by Rae Jenkins. In this succinct and charming piece, Williams paid tribute to her favourite wind instrument, and chose to call the work *Carillons* 'because the chiming of bells influenced the orchestration and to some extent the character of the music'.[46] The work is scored for oboe, brass, strings and percussion, and these forces are imaginatively used to invoke a variety of bell-like sonorities in each of the work's four movements. It is clear from the opening bars of the work, however, that this is very much a Celtic Carillons. The lissom, improvisatory-like lines of the oboe soar above the orchestra, and the music throughout contains the by now unmistakable imprint of Williams's Welsh rhythms and modal sonorities. The work was originally written as a three-movement piece, but when Williams came to revise the work in 1973, she added a brief cadenza-like movement leading into the *Allegro* finale.[47]

---

[44]   Williams, 'Views and Revisions', *Welsh Music* 10/9–10, p. 14.

[45]   A large coal tip subsided and crushed the Aberfan Junior School and much of the village below. One-hundred-and-forty-four people lost their lives in the disaster, the majority of whom were schoolchildren under the age of 10.

[46]   Williams, 'A Self Portrait', *Welsh Music* 8/5, p. 14.

[47]   Several commentators have noted the debt that Williams owes to Strauss's Oboe Concerto (1945–48) in her *Carillons*. See, for example, Boyd, *Grace Williams*, pp. 48–49.

Ballads for Orchestra (1968)

Other works composed in the 1960s reflected a new confidence and fluency in Williams's writing. In particular, the declamatory style and improvisatory-type textures that were such marked features of works such as *Penillion* and the Trumpet Concerto energized three works from this period. Two of these works – *Processional* for orchestra (1962) and *Castell Caernarfon* (1969) – were 'occasional' pieces, written to mark specific events. *Processional* was first performed at Llandaff Cathedral in the presence of Prince Charles on 18 June 1962 by the Royal Liverpool Philharmonic Orchestra, conducted by Charles Groves, and *Castell Caernarfon* was composed for the Prince's Investiture in 1969. The Investiture was held within the walls of Caernarfon Castle, and although not programmatic in any direct sense, the music was, according to Williams, inspired by a potent meld of imaginative sources – 'the rhythms and cadences of Welsh poetry and oratory, the Medieval legends of the *Mabinogion*', and, appropriately in this instance, 'the atmosphere of Welsh castles'.[48]

Welsh sources of 'medieval Welsh laments, proclamations, feasts [and] combats'[49] also provided the imaginative background for Williams's *Ballads* for orchestra, a four-movement suite commissioned by the 1968 National Eisteddfod of Wales which was held in Barry that year. Although *Ballads* can perhaps be described as a cycle of songs (or ballads) without words, it is interesting to note that Williams's initial conception was a work for orchestra and four solo singers (soprano, alto, tenor and bass). She was strongly attracted to ballad form and composed several vocal settings in these years, including *The Billows of the Sea* (1969) for contralto and piano. Two years earlier, she had set Vernon Watkins's *The Ballad of the Trial of Sodom* for soprano, tenor, trumpet, percussion and harp (1965), and her initial response was to search for something similar:[50]

> I want a narrative poem (tho' prose would do) that perhaps [would] be sung in Penillion style (with orchestra replacing harp – playing my music, not a traditional tune). I wish we had Welsh equivalents of the Border Ballads ... I

---

[48] Williams, programme note for *Castell Caernarfon*. The piece was written for open air performance, and is divided into a 'Prelude' for antiphonal trumpets and percussion and a 'Processional' for full orchestra. The Prelude was performed on the day from the castle towers by the trumpeters and drummers of the Kneller Hall Military School of Music, and the Processional was played by the BBC Welsh Orchestra, conducted by Wyn Morris.

[49] Williams, letter to Vivien Cutting, 28–29 November 1967, quoted in Boyd, *Grace Williams*, p. 41. *Ballads* was premiered on 10 August 1968 by the Royal Liverpool Philharmonic and Charles Groves at the Eisteddfod in Barry.

[50] The work was written for a Welsh Theatre Company presentation of Anglo-Welsh songs and poems at the 1965 Cardiff Commonwealth Arts Festival.

need something dramatic, simple, direct, easily grasped by [the] audience that has significance for the present time.[51]

Example 8.10 *Ballads* for Orchestra, IV

[Wind, brass & percussion omitted]

Source: Copyright © Oriana Publications Limited 2010. Reproduced by permission.

---

[51] Williams, letter to Enid Parry, 30 April 1967 (Williams/Parry Collection).

As had been the case with *Penillion*, however, Williams became increasingly frustrated by her inability to find the right words for her musical ideas. Searches for suitable poems through collections of Welsh verses came to nothing, as did an idea of creating her own ballad setting of the Old Testament story of Judith and Holofernes. Having failed to find a suitable narrative poem, her thoughts inevitably turned to the composition of ballads for orchestra only. Her orchestral *Ballads* share many features with the earlier *Penillion*: both are four-movement orchestral suites that employ stanzaic form, elaborate contrapuntal patterns and a declamatory style coupled with the impression of improvisation. In spite of the family resemblance, however, the two pieces are quite different in character. A powerful sense of dramatic, and often violent, lamentation pervades the later work, and its language is more terse and volatile than that of its younger cousin; indeed, in some respects, the kinship between the *Ballads* and the Second Symphony seems closer. The ornately decorated melodic lines and heraldic trumpet writing of the *Allegro* first ballad are characteristic, and their intensity is enhanced by insistent repeated notes which drive the music forward. The restlessness continues in the second ballad, *Alla Marcia solemne*, a bitingly satirical, Shostakovichian march. Towards the end of the ballad, surprising pauses disrupt the march's relentless progression. The bitter language of the march is dispelled in the more reflective third ballad (*Andante calmente*) with a gentle melody heard in violas accompanied by the sound of bells. Even here, however, the mood of serenity is briefly shattered by the intrusion of forceful and aggressive torrents in woodwind, brass and percussion to brilliant dramatic effect. The martial tone returns in the fourth and final ballad, a movement of orchestral pyrotechnics and explosive rhythmic drive (Example 8.10), which is countered by a richly lyrical and meditative central episode.

Missa Cambrensis (1968–71)

After completing the *Ballads*, Williams began writing her largest work – a setting of the Mass in Latin and Welsh for four soloists (soprano, alto, tenor and bass), mixed chorus, boys' choir, orchestra and speaker. Two years earlier, she had been approached by the chairman of the Llandaff Music Festival with an offer of a commission to write a major work. The Llandaff Festival (established 1958) was remarkable in being one of the few music festivals in Wales to be intimately connected with the Church, and its committee possessed an enlightened policy of commissioning new pieces which explored this connection. Two of the Festival's most successful large-scale commissions in the early years had been Hoddinott's *The Race of Adam* (1961) and Mathias's *St Teilo* (1962–63) – the latter largely based on the twelfth-century *Book of Llandaff* – both dramatic, liturgical masques which were specifically designed for performance in the Cathedral. Williams initially toyed with the idea of writing a cathedral opera for Llandaff (and, mischievously, of pairing it with Daniel Jones's 1967 'pagan' opera *Orestes*) but decided that a Mass would be more suitable for the magnificent setting. Furthermore, and in recognition of the special relationship between the Church of Wales and the Music Festival, this was to be a Welsh Mass. 'I am going to write a Missa Cambrensis for Llandaff for 1970', she told Maconchy. 'It may work out less than 50 mins. – & I'll have time to take on short lucrative jobs – orchestrating & scripting. (I got started on a Kyrie & Agnus Dei one day & felt it flowing …)'.[52]

That Williams, an avowed agnostic, should have chosen to write a Mass is intriguing – although one only has to look at her former teacher Vaughan Williams to find another paradoxical example of an agnostic who composed music for the church.[53] She had written only a handful of liturgical pieces in the past – *Gogonedawg Arglwydd* (1939), the *Magnificat* (1939) and, in 1965, a *Benedicite* – but her lack of blazing religious convictions did not prevent her from approaching the composition of such pieces with professionalism and a total integrity of purpose.[54] The *Missa Cambrensis* took nearly three years to write (from June 1968 to March 1971), and her creative engagement with the meaning of the Latin words and the ritual of the Mass actively informed the compositional process. Letters to friends often took the form of a heady mixture of reports of compositional progress with personal reflections on the very nature of Christian faith:

> I've begun the Credo – & incidentally worked out my own creed! The resurrection is for me simply the survival of Christ's teaching. A wonderful allegory. I don't think I believe "The good is oft interred with their bones." Goodness survives in some form or other. But faith is to me a mysterious intangible thing & I'm trying to get that sort of feeling into the orchestration – with chorus singing monotones (F♯s) & only gradually building up (a bit).[55]

The *Missa Cambrensis* is divided into the five main sections of the traditional Mass: Kyrie (I), Gloria (II), Credo (III), Sanctus and Benedictus (IV) and Agnus Dei (V). Williams departed from the conventional Mass structure, however, in the central Credo section. At the words 'et homo factus est' (and He was made man), she included her 1955 *Carol Nadolig* (A Christmas Carol), thereby giving the nativity section of the Credo a special emphasis.[56] The carol functions as a unique interlude within the Credo and is sung by a boys' choir to Welsh words. A narration of the Beatitudes follows – again, a liturgical feature not usually

---

[52] Williams, letter to Maconchy, 17 June 1968 (private collection).

[53] Note that Vaughan Williams also edited the *English Hymnal* (1906).

[54] Williams's *Benedicite* was commissioned by the 1965 National Eisteddfod (held in Newtown) and was written for the Montgomeryshire Schools' Choir and Orchestra, who gave the premiere.

[55] Williams, letter to Maconchy, 30 October 1969 (private collection).

[56] *Carol Nadolig*, Williams's first carol, was composed in 1955 in response to a request by the choir of Aberdare Hall, one of Cardiff University's student accommodation halls for girls. The Welsh words are by Saunders Lewis and Williams provided her own English translation.

included in the traditional Mass setting – where the eight Beatitudes (delivered in Welsh) are punctuated by orchestral cadences. These extra-liturgical inclusions enabled Williams to define the Mass as 'Cambrensis', but there are other, more subtle, musical features which arise naturally from her mature style – such as the extensive use of declamatory-type themes, melodic patterns derived from modal scales, and idiosyncratic rhythms – which give the work its distinctive and unmistakable signature.

Example 8.11 *Missa Cambrensis*, I 'Kyrie', opening

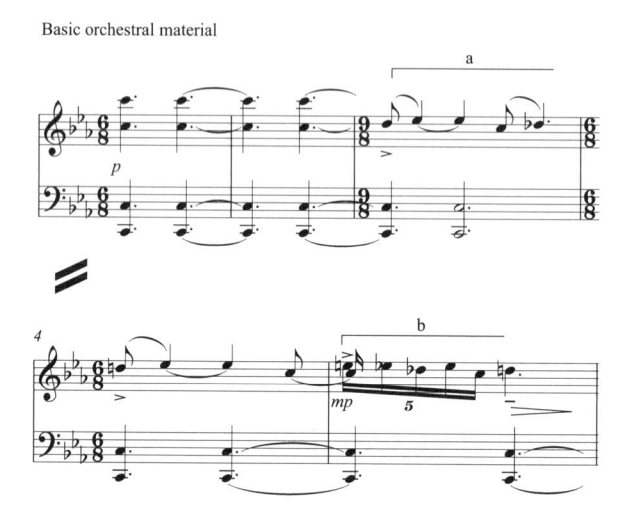

Source: Copyright © Oriana Publications Limited 2010. Reproduced by permission.

Boyd has suggested that the *Missa Cambrensis* provides 'eloquent evidence of the high regard in which Grace Williams held the music of Britten'.[57] Certainly, the Mass is in the same tradition as Britten's *War Requiem*, not least in its incorporation of extra-liturgical material into the cycle, but Williams's awareness of, for example, Vaughan Williams's *Dona nobis pacem*, Holst's choral works or Stravinsky's *Symphony of Psalms*, also may have informed the composition of the work. One feature which is fundamental to Williams's Mass is the contrast she invokes between musical material which is austere and homogenous in texture, and passages which include more fluid, quasi-improvisational gestures, a distinction which is clear from the very opening. Example 8.11 shows the opening of the brief 12-bar orchestral introduction of the Kyrie, which begins quietly with a bare octave C pedal above which the main musical ideas of the work are heard: a slow, solemn theme (a) characterized by rising semitones and tones, and a sinuous, chromatic motif (b) in quintuplet semiquavers. These ideas are expanded on in

---

[57] Boyd, *Grace Williams*, p. 60.

the five subsections of the Kyrie. In the three 'Kyrie eleisons', the impersonal, chant-like entries of the chorus, derived from (a) – see Example 8.12 – surround the more rhapsodical interwoven lines (variants of b) of the quartet of soloists in the two 'Christe eleisons'.

Example 8.12 *Missa Cambrensis*, I 'Kyrie', first chorus entry

Source: Copyright © Oriana Publications Limited 2010. Reproduced by permission.

Williams divided the ensuing Gloria (II) into six contrasting subsections, and while each division is integrated within the whole, there is a sense that she treated them as separate 'stanzas' in an unfolding musical narrative. As in the Kyrie, the soloists' lines have a melismatic, improvisatory-like quality and are heard first in alternation with the more homogenous choral entries, before combining towards the close of the section. It is not coincidental that the stark F♯ octaves heard in the orchestra at the opening of the Credo (III) directly recall the C octaves heard at the beginning of the piece. Williams described the 'Credo in unum Deum' (I believe in the one God) as being 'about the most mystical thing of all'[58] to her in the Mass cycle, and the impersonal choral chants and mellifluous solo lines of both Credo and Kyrie invoke feelings of mystery, ritual and fealty. Indeed, the link in mood and texture suggests that Williams designed her Credo to be the central pillar within the arch-like framework of the Mass, a notion strengthened by the tritonal relationship between the principal tonal centres of C (Kyrie), F♯ (Credo) and C (the final chord of the Agnus Dei). After statements of the *Carol Nadolig* and the spoken Beatitudes, the Credo's powerful sense of ritual is furthered in the ' 'Crucifixus' section by the use of bells and an oscillating ostinato bass figure itself enhanced by a high degree of chromaticism. The powerful restatement of faith which ends the Credo – 'Credo in spiritum sanctum' (I believe in the Holy Spirit) – is complemented by a return to the mysterious F♯ monotones and chant-like statements of the opening. The sound of bells is again invoked to dramatic effect in the ensuing Sanctus (IV). When the chorus sings 'pleni sunt coeli et terra' (heaven and earth are full of thy glory), for example, they are accompanied by chiming, syncopated chords in full orchestra (Example 8.13).

The mood lightens in the Benedictus which brings warmth and a less austere colour to the music, but a dramatic change of mood occurs at the end of the section. The Agnus Dei (V) begins in anguished mood, and impassioned musical themes, initially stated by all four soloists and then full chorus, dramatically invoke the sense of exalted ceremony with which the Latin rite is imbued. As if to underline this point, chorus and soloists are asked to sing '*senza misura (as in plainsong)*' to the words 'dona nobis pacem' (grant us peace), and this final section also includes recollections of both the opening Kyrie material and that of the Gloria. The work's ending is a moment of striking musical and dramatic writing. Repeated chanting by chorus and soloists gradually recedes in dynamic power and the work returns to source with a final reiteration of the theme heard at its opening and a barely audible (*pppp*) C chord in the orchestra (Example 8.14).

---

[58] Williams, letter to Vivien Cutting, 9 May 1969, quoted in Boyd, *Grace Williams*, p. 63.

Example 8.13 *Missa Cambrensis*, IV 'Sanctus'

Source: Copyright © Oriana Publications Limited 2010. Reproduced by permission.

Example 8.14 *Missa Cambrensis*, V 'Agnus Dei', final bars

Example 8.14 continued

[Musical notation: SATB voices with "pa-cem" text, and orchestra, marked pp to pppp]

Source: Copyright © Oriana Publications Limited 2010. Reproduced by permission.

Fairest of Stars (1973)
Ave Maris Stella (1973)

Several vocal works composed after the completion of the *Missa Cambrensis* reveal the musical preoccupations that occupied Williams in her final years. *Fairest of Stars*, a concert aria for soprano and orchestra, was composed in 1973 in response to a BBC Wales commission for a Welsh Arts Council concert tour. Prior to the concert premiere in February 1974 by Janet Price (soprano), the BBC Welsh Orchestra and Akeo Watanabe (conductor), the work had been included on an EMI record of Williams's music. This recording had been initiated and sponsored by the Welsh Arts Council and was part of a project that aimed to bring the music of contemporary Welsh composers to a wider audience; other composers to benefit included Jones, Mathias and Hoddinott. Roy Bohana, then Head of Music at the Welsh Arts Council, recalled that Williams was initially reluctant to have a record of her own music:

> I remember that she wrote and said, "my immediate reaction – for I am nothing if not a realist – is that there will be no sales, practically none at all." But, of course, we took no notice of that, and we carried on. EMI were very interested in the recording and we engaged the LSO [London Symphony Orchestra].

Afterwards she wrote, "I still feel that I don't deserve to have a record to myself. Nevertheless it was quite an experience to hear such performances."[59]

Williams's fears about record sales proved to be unfounded, and there can be little doubt that the understanding and appreciation of her work was boosted by the inclusion of *Fairest of Stars* on the recording. The aria is a setting of words taken from the fifth book of Milton's *Paradise Lost*: as dawn breaks over the Garden of Eden, Adam and Eve praise their 'parent of Good, Almightie ... who out of Darkness call'd up Light', and they ask all his creations (sun, moon, the elements, all plants and animals) to sing his praises. Written for the soprano Janet Price, Williams's rich and powerfully sensuous music perfectly captures the poetic imagery of Milton's song of praise. The aria's main theme is first heard in the orchestral introduction and, when the soprano enters, she elaborates around it in an improvisatory-type manner. The piece is divided into ten stanzas, and the harmony, texture and mood of the music is ingeniously varied to reflect the words. In the third stanza, for example, – beginning 'Moon, that now meets the orient Sun' – the orchestral accompaniment is changed to a more chamber-like, nocturnal texture which leads to a mystical passage (with swirling harp runs) that represents the 'mystik dance not without Song' of the 'five other wandering Fires'. The music succeeds in penetrating the different images conjured up by the text, and the soprano line is replete with skilful instances of word-painting that are not clichéd or overstated. In the sixth stanza, when the soprano sings 'His praise ye Winds ... wave your tops, ye Pines, with every plant, in sign of Worship wave', her words are framed in dramatically undulating phrases. And in the eighth stanza, the words 'Ye Birds, that singing up to Heaven-gate ascend, bear on your wings and in your notes his praise', are echoed in the trills and warbles in the orchestra.

Williams had to cope with a real-life version of Paradise Lost when the original parts of *Fairest of Stars* were stolen weeks before the London Symphony Orchestra was due to record the work for EMI. The orchestra was performing in Barry as part of their South Wales tour, and Williams gave them the parts so they could take them to London. The parcel containing the parts was placed in the boot of the orchestra's tour coach, but was stolen by vandals during the concert. A horrified Williams was notified by the caretaker of Barry Memorial Hall the next day that he had found pages of her music lying around on the ground outside. After a desperate search, the majority of the damp, mud-splattered parts that had been strewn around the hall's grounds were regained, but at least one of the parts had to be written out again.

---

[59] Roy Bohana in 'Grace Williams: A Portrait', (BBC Wales TV documentary). The other works to be included on the record (EMI ASD 3006) were the *Fantasia*, the Trumpet Concerto and *Carillons* – all performed by the London Symphony Orchestra, conducted by Charles Groves. This recording of *Fairest of Stars* was later re-released by Lyrita (SRCD.327). The other pieces were re-issued on a separate Lyrita CD of Williams's music (SRCD.323).

Fairest of Stars marked a triumphant return to a genre which had held some fascination for Williams in her earlier years. In the 1930s, she had set two songs *Tuscany* and *Tarantella* for mezzo-soprano and orchestra in which the influence of Strauss had been to the fore, particularly in the freshness and adventurousness of the orchestration.[60] As Boyd has observed, the aria 'recalls the chromaticism and rich orchestral textures'[61] of Williams's early orchestral songs, despite the distance of some 40 years. Although *Fairest of Stars* is, in its rhapsodic lyricism and masterful orchestration, the fullest expression of Williams's mature style, it is not difficult to imagine that nostalgic recollections of musical Vienna were not far from her mind when she wrote the piece; revisions to her *Carillons* for oboe and orchestra, also completed at this time, reflected a similar Straussian impulse.

Williams completed the score of *Fairest of Stars* in August 1973, a month before attending the premiere of her *Ave Maris Stella* for unaccompanied chorus at the North Wales Music Festival (established 1972). She had been delighted when William Mathias, the Festival's founding director, had asked her to write a new piece for his Festival and the BBC Singers. As soon as she discovered the eighth-century Latin hymn which hailed the Virgin Mary as 'Star of the Sea', she knew her search for the right words was over. Interestingly, the setting of *Ave Maris Stella* is remarkably un-Straussian, and is very much a work which looks to the future in Williams's own terms.

The work opens with an extended meditation on the hymn's first three words, 'ave maris stella', where 'the ebb and flow of the sea' is invoked by the choir's fluid rhythms and undulating, mellifluous lines, before giving way to the more homogenous treatment of the remaining lines of the verse. These three words are ingeniously used as an 'invocation' before each of the remaining six verses, and although the musical material is varied, the contrast between quasi-improvisatory passages and more tightly knit choral textures is retained throughout. This employment of different textures and choice of ancient liturgical text draws obvious parallels with some of the settings in the *Missa Cambrensis*, although the two works are very distinct in character. Mathias held *Ave Maris Stella* in high regard, describing the work as being 'one of the major contributions to British vocal music' of the last half century. 'I well remember her delight at the fine first performance given by the BBC Singers under John Poole', he recalled, 'and her feeling that she'd like to write more vocal music in the future'.[62]

---

[60] See Chapter 2.
[61] Boyd, *Grace Williams*, p. 67.
[62] Mathias in 'Grace Williams Memorial Tribute' (BBC Radio Wales, 10 February 1977).

Example 8.15 *Ave Maris Stella*, opening

Source: *Ave Maris Stella* by Grace Williams © Oxford University Press 1975. Extract reproduced by permission. All rights reserved.

My Last Duchess (1975)
Two Choruses (1975)

Williams did indeed go on to write more vocal music in the remaining four years of her life. Two works, in particular, act as a summation of her life's work and also reveal that Williams was keen to explore new musical territory. The first to be composed was a setting of Robert Browning's dark poem *My Last Duchess*. Written in response to a request from the baritone Louis Burkman, Williams's setting takes the form of a dramatic, ten-minute *scena*, and is quite different in character from either the more extended *Fairest of Stars* or the shorter solo songs she had composed up to this point. Although written for voice and piano, the piece is operatic in conception: an orchestral version of the piece could quite easily have been cast as a scene in an opera. Williams had, in fact, planned to adapt Browning's poem into a short stage work in the early 1960s but the idea was not realized. Even so, some notion of a staged version clearly survived in the 1975 realization of *My Last Duchess* in that the singer was asked to mime certain gestures.

The poem's theme is intriguing. A tyrannical Italian Duke (thought to be modelled on Alfonso II d'Este, Duke of Ferrara in the sixteenth century) shows a wall painting of his beautiful late wife – 'My Last Duchess' – to an emissary of a Count whose daughter he is about to marry. The piano begins wistfully with a brief introduction, after which we join the Duke and the emissary as they gaze at the fresco. The piano writing becomes more agitated when the Duke draws attention to 'the depth and passion' of his former wife's gaze and speaks of his displeasure at her behaviour when alive and her apparent lack of respect for him and his exalted social position. 'She had a heart – how shall I say? – too soon made glad' he tells the emissary. 'She liked whate'er she looked on, and her looks went everywhere'. The tone of the music chills several degrees with the suggestion that the Duke, clearly overcome by his own suspicions and jealousy, may have been the cause of his wife's sudden death. Trills and dramatic runs in the piano build to his confession – 'I gave commands; then all smiles stopped together'.

A poem concerned with themes of sex, violence and the ruthless brutality of patriarchal control in Renaissance Italy was perhaps an intriguing choice for Williams, although its resonance with the story of Bluebeard seems obvious enough. Interestingly, she seems to have been drawn to the dramatic subtleties and psychological ambiguities in Browning's monologue. As she stated in a note at the front of the score:

> One can interpret [Browning's] poem in different ways. My own interpretation is that in spite of the Duke's ruthless cruelty the justification for which he never questions, he is subconsciously aware of the Duchess's goodness.

While the piano writing is skilfully nuanced throughout, it acquires a particular significance in the Duke's more introverted moments when he appears to lose himself in his own thoughts, forgetting the emissary's presence. Immediately after his confession, for example, there is a brief, passionate piano interlude which intimates that he is haunted by feelings of love and regret over his last Duchess. Here, perhaps, music expresses the profound, underlying emotions which are left unspoken.

My Last Duchess was first performed by Louis Burkman and the pianist Paul Hamburger in a recital given at the Purcell Room, London in March 1975. Two months after the premiere, Williams was approached with the offer of a new commission for the BBC Singers. She was initially reluctant to write a new work as she had taken the decision not to accept any further commissions, but decided to honour the promise of another new piece she had made to the Singers when they had premiered her *Ave Maris Stella*. Coincidentally, she had been thinking of writing a sea song for chorus at this time – a setting of Kipling's 'Harp Song of the Dane Women' for women's voices only – but the request from the BBC caused her to revise her ideas. In the final version of her Kipling setting, the words are sung by sopranos and altos only but the verses are, for the most part, linked by more fluid passages in which the gentle ebb and flow of the sea is depicted by wordless music in tenor and bass lines. Although this approach might sound rather contrived, the resulting setting is utterly compelling. Indeed, such is the clarity and sensitivity of Williams's writing that her poignant sea song has the effect of bringing Kipling's words to life. The mood changes in the second chorus, an animated setting of the 'Mariners' Song' by Thomas Beddoes. In contrast to the first chorus, the words beginning 'To Sea! To Sea!' are sung by the men, here interspersed with sirens' songs – wordless, surging passages sung by the women. In both settings, the chorus is accompanied by an unusual but very effective ensemble of two horns and harp, and the instrumental writing complements both the poetic imagery and vocal writing throughout.

Williams's Two Choruses was her final composition and the two songs were premiered in Penarth, South Wales on 28 February 1976 by the BBC Singers and John Poole, nine days after she celebrated her 70th birthday. 'Being 70 is rather like having notice to quit', she told Gerald Cockshott after receiving his birthday card, 'and when the day comes I hope I shan't feel greedy and try to hang on. We have to go to make room for those just coming into the world'.[63] February 1976 was to be a particularly joyous and eventful month for her. Radio 3 marked the actual date of her birthday (19 February) by featuring her in a 'Composer's Portrait', and BBC Wales hosted a special concert which included a performance of the Second Symphony. Five months later, however, Williams was diagnosed with cancer and spent the summer and autumn undergoing exhaustive treatment. The treatment was not successful and in January 1977, with hopes of a return to normal life abandoned, she wrote a final farewell letter to her great friend Elizabeth Maconchy:

---

[63] Williams, letter to Cockshott, quoted in 'Williams: a Symposium', *Welsh Music* 5/6, p. 28.

Well, all along I've known this could happen and now it has I'm quite calm and prepared and can only count my blessings – that I've had such a run of good health – able to go on writing – and just being me with my thoughts and ideas and sensitivity ... From now on it won't be so good but even so there are sunsets and the sea and the understanding of friends – and a marvellous broadcast of Solti's recording of Meistersingers on Sunday.[64]

Example 8.16 'To Sea! To Sea!' from Two Choruses

Source: Reproduced by kind permission of the Estate of Grace Williams.

---

[64] Williams, letter to Maconchy, 25 January 1977, quoted in Boyd, *Grace Williams*, p. 72. Williams passed away on 10 February 1977, nine days before her 71st birthday.

Conclusion

Speaking on a radio programme shortly after Grace Williams's death, William Mathias paid tribute to her absolute integrity and professionalism. As he stated,

> she grew up between the wars at a time when one had to fight especially hard … to acquire professionalism and at a time when it was hard enough for a man to aspire to be a composer let alone a woman. She faced many more difficulties than the young music student of today, and won her fight through her professional dedication to the importance of music as a language – and in doing so made things easier for those who were to come.[1]

Although his words referred to Williams, they could equally apply to Elisabeth Lutyens and Elizabeth Maconchy. These women were rightly held in high esteem in the musical world, and their example helped to redefine the whole concept of what it was to be a modern composer, living and working in a complex age.

In exploring the work of these three fascinating individuals, I have attempted to draw attention to the fact that each wrote music of rare quality that was original, substantial, sometimes challenging and surprising. At the same time, there has always been a clear agenda for this book. Why do we carelessly neglect the music of some of our finest composers? In the case of Lutyens, Maconchy and Williams, the answer is surely not just because these composers happened to be women. Certainly, all three had to endure different forms of prejudice, particularly early on in their careers. Such hostile attitudes had the potential to cause lasting damage – most creative artists are strongly influenced by the environment in which they live and work. All three refused to be distracted by dreary arguments about 'male' and 'female' composers, however, choosing instead to focus on composing music of quality which was true to their individual visions. Significantly, none of the three subjects of this book felt that their gender made any difference to the music they wrote. As Williams remarked, 'trials and tribulations and despair have come my way, and still come my way, but they have nothing to do with my being a woman: they are wholly concerned with my being a composer'.[2] And, to echo Maconchy, can any intelligent listener really tell the difference anyway?

Listeners can only respond to music if they have a chance to experience it (a point which seems too obvious to need stating). Yet at the time of writing, much of Maconchy's music still suffers from a lack of public awareness, despite a

---

[1] Mathias in 'Grace Williams Memorial Tribute' (BBC Radio Wales, February 1977).
[2] Williams in 'Women as Composers' (BBC radio broadcast, 2 August 1973).

revival of interest in her work in recent years. Nobody has heard Lutyens's opera *The Numbered* because it has never been performed. Furthermore, in spite of a successful premiere in 1966, Williams's *The Parlour*, one of the finest examples of post-war British comic opera, has yet to be revived by a professional opera company. It is clearly time for a reevaluation of the important contribution each of these composers made to British Music. A great deal of the music discussed here urgently awaits rediscovery, and it is my sincere hope that this book will stimulate a desire in the reader to hear and/or perform the music itself.

Appendix

Berkeley, Lennox (1903–89). Studied at Oxford University before studying composition with Nadia Boulanger in Paris. Berkeley made a substantial contribution to twentieth-century British music. A meticulous musical craftsman, his compositions include the remarkable *Serenade* for string orchestra (1939), four symphonies and several chamber works, in addition to four operas and many finely crafted vocal/choral works. He served as Professor of Composition at the Royal Academy of Music, London (1946–68), inspiring several new generations of composers.

Canetti, Elias (1905–94). Studied in Germany and Austria. His experiences of the violent rise of National Socialism led to his lifelong preoccupation with crowd behaviour and the dynamics of power, concepts he explored in novels such as *Die Blendung* (Auto da Fé, 1935), and in the critical study *Masse und Macht* (Crowds and Power, 1960). He was awarded the Nobel Prize for Literature in 1981.

Canu Penillion or *Cerdd Dant*. In the medieval courts of the Welsh aristocracy, the professional bard's eulogies on the qualities of the principal nobleman took the form of public declamations of strict-metre poetry to a harp accompaniment. Although originally a soloist's art, later developments led to the popularization of the style as an amateur practice, and to the rise of choral *cerdd dant*.

Composers' Concourse (1953–57). Founded by Lutyens, Alan Bush and Arnold Cooke, the Concourse was a forum enabling professional and would-be professional composers to meet and discuss their work. A series of talks by invited speakers were programmed to stimulate discussion. Notable talks included a discussion of 12-note music by Oliver Neighbour and the premiere of John Cage's performance-lecture *45' for a Speaker* given by the composer (1954).

Craigie, Jill (1911–99). A lifelong socialist and political activist, Craigie was one of the first woman film directors to gain a national profile in post-war Britain.

Dallapiccola, Luigi (1904–75). One of the first Italian composers to adopt the 12-note system. His lifelong affinity for the voice led to the composition of a series of major vocal works – including *Tre Laudi* for soprano, tenor and 13 instruments (1937), *Tre Poemi* for soprano and 14 instruments (1949) and the operas *Il prigioniero* (1944–48) and *Ulisse* (1960–68).

Gow, Dorothy (1893–1982). Studied with Vaughan Williams and R. O. Morris at the Royal College, and later with Egon Wellesz in Vienna and Saltzburg. Intensely self-critical, Gow destroyed most of her music, but the handful of works that survive testify to the fact that she possessed an unusually distinctive and potent musical voice.

Hába, Alois (1893–1973). Studied composition in Prague and Vienna and developed a progressive, microtonal system of composition. His output includes the opera *Matka* ('The Mother'), Op. 35 (1927–29) and 16 string quartets (1919–67).

Hughes, Arwel (1909–88). Studied with Vaughan Williams and later became widely known as a composer of choral and orchestral works. In 1936 he joined the BBC's Welsh Music Department, and succeeded Mansel Thomas as Head of Music in 1965 before retiring from the post in 1971. From 1946 he conducted numerous performances by the then newly founded Welsh National Opera Company, and also composed two operas which were premiered by the company.

International Society of Contemporary Music. Founded in 1922, the ISCM aimed to transcend national barriers by promoting an international view of the different tendencies in modern music in their broadest sense. From 1923 onwards annual festivals were held in different European cities featuring the most outstanding contemporary pieces from different countries. During the first years, many of the leading names in contemporary music – including Stravinsky, Bartók and Schoenberg – were represented at festivals. Several British composers also found a wider audience for their work through their associations with ISCM festivals during the 1920s – not least Bliss, Vaughan Williams, Grainger, Lambert and Walton. Edward Dent (1876–1957), the distinguished English scholar and critic, was elected as the ISCM's first President, a post which he held until 1938.

Jones, Daniel (1912–93). An important figure in Welsh twentieth-century music, his output includes two operas, vocal and choral works as well as a fine body of chamber music. He made a significant contribution to Welsh orchestral music, composing a series of 12 symphonies. He formed a lifelong friendship with Dylan Thomas: his Symphony No. 4 is dedicated to Thomas and he also composed the music for the 1954 radio version of *Under Milk Wood*.

Jones, Granville (1922–68). Studied violin at the Royal Academy of Music, and later served as Professor of Violin there. A member of several leading chamber ensembles of the day, Jones also performed with the London Symphony Orchestra, the Boyd Neel Orchestra, and was the conductor and leader of Philomusica.

Lambert, Constant (1905–51). His prodigious talents as composer, conductor, raconteur and music critic marked him out as a leader of his day. Although his jazz-influenced *The Rio Grande* (1929) remains his most popular piece, lesser known works such as the Piano Concerto (1924) and the choral work *Summer's Last Will and Testament* (1936) reveal that he possessed a broad range of skills as a composer.

Larchet, John (1884–1967). Studied at the Royal Irish Academy of Music, Dublin, later serving as Professor from 1920 to 1955. He is primarily known as a composer of songs and choral works, and his music is thought to embody a national 'Irish' element.

Lemare, Iris (1902–97). Studied at the Jacques-Dalcroze Institute of Eurhythmics in Switzerland before entering the Royal College of Music in 1925. She was the only woman in her year to take conducting as a subject, and she went on to pursue a successful career as a professional conductor. As with her friend Anne Macnaghten, she is primarily remembered for her work with the concert series she helped to establish in the 1930s and which bears her name.

Macnaghten, Anne (1908–2001). An inspirational teacher, performer and administrator. She studied violin at the Leipzig Conservatoire and with André Mangeot, Sascha Lasserson and Antonio Brosa in England. She founded her own all-female Macnaghten String Quartet in 1931, and in that same year also founded (together with Elisabeth Lutyens and Iris Lemare) the Macnaghten–Lemare Concerts.

Mullinar, Michael (1895–1973). Although better known in his day as a pianist, Mullinar was also a composer of popular songs. He studied composition with Vaughan Williams at the Royal College, and later assisted the older composer with the preparation of piano reductions and vocal scores. He is the dedicatee of Vaughan Williams's Symphony No. 6.

National Eisteddfod of Wales. A festival of literary, musical and artistic competitions, concerts and exhibitions which is held annually in the first week of August at selected towns in either North or South Wales. Although the Eisteddfod originated in its present form in the eighteenth century, its origins reach back to the middle ages and possibly earlier.

Palmer, (Samuel) Ernest, 1st Baron of Reading (1858–1948). Director of the family biscuit manufacturing firm Huntley & Palmers Ltd., and also a generous musical benefactor. In addition to founding the Patron's Fund, he also initiated the Berkshire Scholarship and the Ernest Palmer Fund for Opera Study. He served as Vice-President and a Member of the Royal College of Music's Council.

Parry, Enid (1911–98). A fine amateur composer, poet and influential member of the Welsh Folk-Song Society.

Rawsthorne, Alan (1905–71). Studied piano at the Royal Manchester College of Music and later in Poland with the pianist Egon Petri. Rawsthorne was one of the most prominent British composers to emerge in the interwar period. He composed three symphonies, a number of concertos and an impressive collection of chamber music. Although perhaps best known for his instrumental music, his output includes several significant vocal/choral works – including *Carmen vitale* (1963) for soprano, chorus and orchestra.

Sackville-West, Victoria ('Vita') (1892–1962). Gained recognition for her novels and poems which, for the most part, were inspired by English society and Kentish countryside. She won the Hawthornden Prize twice – in 1927 for *The Land*, and in 1933 with her *Collected Poems*. Sackville-West married the diplomat, journalist and MP Harold Nicolson, and she and Nicolson designed and created the gardens at Sissinghurst Castle in Kent, their home from the 1930s onwards.

The *Mabinogion*. A collection of Welsh myths and legends. Although detailed in medieval manuscripts, the myths are commonly thought to have their origins in the pagan rituals and traditions of a much earlier age. In the story 'Pwyll, Prince of Dyfed', Rhiannon is associated with horses: her suitor, Pwyll, first sees her riding on a white horse that can never be caught, and her penance is to sit near a horse-block relating her supposed crime to all passers-by. These details reveal Rhiannon's connection with an earlier prototype, the Gaulish horse goddess Epona, who was worshipped throughout Britain and Europe.

The New Opera Company. A company that grew directly out of opera performances which had been staged at Cambridge University in the 1950s. Core members of the resourceful group of undergraduates included Peter Hemmings, Brian Trowell, Kenneth Bowen and Leon Lovett. Vaughan Williams took a lively interest in the activities of this group, and attended several performances of his operas (including *Sir John in Love* and *The Pilgrim's Progress*).

Thomas, Mansel (1909–86). A prominent figure in twentieth-century Welsh music. He composed in a wide range of musical genres, and is celebrated for being one of the finest Welsh composers of solo songs. He had a long and important association with the BBC in Wales – as assistant conductor of the BBC Welsh Orchestra (from 1936), principal conductor (from 1946), and then as Head of Music (from 1950).

Walton, William (1902–83). In his youth, Walton was part of a brilliant artistic circle centred around the Sitwell family, and as the composer of *Façade* (1922, to poems by Edith Sitwell), earned a reputation as an *enfant terrible*. Major works such as the choral *Belshazzar's Feast* (1931) and the First and Second Symphonies (1932–35 and 1959–60) later consolidated his reputation as being one of the most significant British composers of the twentieth century.

Welsh College of Music and Drama. The National College of Music and Drama (as it was initially known) opened in September 1949 and was based in Cardiff Castle. In 1970, the College moved into purpose-built premises in the Castle grounds and was renamed the Welsh College of Music and Drama. It became the Royal Welsh College of Music and Drama in 2002.

Wood, Charles (1866–1926). Studied with Stanford and Parry at the Royal College, and at Cambridge University. As a composer he is probably best known for his choral works, particularly anthems written for the Anglican tradition, but his output also includes string quartets and an opera *The Pickwick Papers*. He taught at both the Royal College and at Cambridge University, where, in 1924, he succeeded Stanford as Professor of Music. His pupils included Ralph Vaughan Williams.

Selected Bibliography

Primary Sources

Bangor University Archive: Grace Williams letters to Enid Parry.
BBC Written Archive Centre (BBC WAC): Lutyens, Composer, 1940–62.
    Maconchy, Composer, 1951–58; file RCONT1.
    Maconchy, Composer, 1963–67; file RCONT12.
    Williams, Welsh Regional Composer, 1934–37; file WAI/61/1.
    Williams, Welsh Regional Composer, 1938–41; file WAI/61/2.
    Williams, Welsh Regional Composer, 1942–48; file WAI/61/3.
    Williams, Composer, 1939–49; file Registry Services Central 1.
    Williams, Composer, 1950–62; file RCONT1.
British Library, London: Elizabeth Lutyens Collection, BL Adds 64435–64795.
Elisabeth Lutyens papers (private collection).
Elizabeth Maconchy letters to Sheila Maconchy (private collection).
Grace Williams letters from Egon Wellesz (private collection).
Grace Williams letters to Elizabeth Maconchy (private collection).
Grace Williams papers (private collection).
National Library of Wales, Aberystwyth: Grace Williams Music Manuscripts and Archive.
    Daniel Jones Archive, Grace Williams letters to Daniel Jones.
Royal College of Music Archive: Register of Students 1926.
    Concert Programmes 1924–32.
    Register of Patron's Fund Concerts 1926–32.
St. Hilda's College, Oxford: Elizabeth Maconchy Archive.

Radio and Television Sources

Dowdall, V. (director and producer), 'Grace Williams: A Portrait', BBC Wales TV documentary (1978).
Lutyens, E., 'Composer's Portrait' (BBC Third Network, 23 February 1966) [NSA Cat. No. M748R C1].
—— Interview with Stephen Plaistow (BBC Radio 3, 5 July 1971) [NSA Cat. No. P654R BD1].
—— 'Talking about Music: Elisabeth Lutyens at 70' (BBC Radio 3, 1976) [NSA Cat. No. 1LP0201961 S1 BD3 BBC TRANSC].

Maconchy, E., 'Composer's Portrait' (BBC Third Programme, 15 June 1966) [NSA Cat. No. 1CDR0003352 BD3–BD6 NSA].
—— 'The Composer Speaks' (BBC Radio 3, 17 October 1971) [NSA Cat. No. M4263W C1].
—— 'Women as Composers' (BBC radio broadcast, 2 August 1973) [NSA Cat. No. BBC Archive Cprd name: 60417 (1)].
—— 'Talk on String Quartets' (BBC Radio 3, 9 October 1976) [NSA Cat. No. NP2788AW C1].
—— Introduction to a broadcast performance of 'Settings of Poems by Hopkins' (BBC Radio 3, 15 March 1977) [NSA Cat. No. M7030BW C1].
—— Introduction to a broadcast performance of *Epyllion* (BBC Radio 3, 14 March 1978) [NSA Cat. No. NP3137BW C1].
—— 'Talking About Music' (BBC Radio 3, 1977) [NSA Cat. No. 1LP0202427 S2 BD3].
—— 'Third Ear' (BBC Radio 3, 29 March 1990) [NSA Cat. No. B5698/2].
Payne, A., Introduction to broadcast premiere of Lutyens's *Music for Orchestra IV* (BBC Radio 3, 15 December 1983) [NSA Cat. No. T6360BW C3].
Saxton, R., 'Fairest Isle: Lutyens and Maconchy' (BBC Radio 3, 11 September 1995) [NSA Cat. No. H5688/1/1].
Williams, G., 'Women as Composers' (BBC radio broadcast, 2 August 1973) [NSA Cat. No. BBC Archive Cprd name: 60417 (1)]
Williams, M. (director and producer), 'Elizabeth Maconchy: A Video Portrait' for Channel 4 (Arbor International Productions and Arts Council of Great Britain, 1984).

Printed Primary Sources

Buckley, R. and Kennedy, J. (eds), *Paradise Remembered: An Autobiography by Ursula Vaughan Williams* (London: Albion Music Ltd., 2002).
Elias, B., 'E.L. (1906–1983)', *Tempo* 145 (June 1983): 33.
Evans, J. (ed.), *Journeying Boy: The Diaries of the Young Benjamin Britten 1928–1938* (London: Faber and Faber, 2009).
Foreman, L. (ed.), *From Parry to Britten: British Music in Letters 1900–1945* (London: Batsford, 1987).
Glock, W., *Notes in Advance* (Oxford and New York: Oxford University Press, 1991).
Lambert, C., *Music Ho! A Study of Music in Decline* (London: Faber and Faber, 1934).
LeFanu, N., 'Master Musician: an Impregnable Taboo?', *Contact: A Journal of Contemporary Music* 31 (August 1987): 4–8.
Lutyens, E., *A Goldfish Bowl* (London: Cassell, 1972).
—— '*Time Off?* and *The Scene Machine*', Lutyens and Anthony Gilbert interview, *The Musical Times* 113 (February 1972): 137–139.

—— Review of Robert Craft, *Stravinsky: The Chronicle of a Friendship 1948–1971* in *Tempo* 105 (June 1973): 45–46.
Lutyens, Lady E., *Candles in the Sun* (London: R. Hart-Davis, 1957).
Lutyens, M., *To Be Young: Some Chapters of Autobiography* (London: R. Hart-Davis, 1959).
Maconchy, E., 'Vaughan Williams as a Teacher', *Composer* 2 (1959): 18–20.
—— 'A Short Symposium on Women Composers', *Composer* 6 (Spring 1961): 19–21.
—— 'The Image of Greatness: Ralph Vaughan Williams', *Composer* 15 (Spring 1965): 10–12.
—— 'Who is your Favourite Composer?', *Composer* 24 (Summer 1967): 20–21.
—— 'Serenata Concertante – an analytical note', in P. Dickinson (ed.), *Twenty British Composers* (London, 1975), pp. 50–53.
—— 'In Conversation with John Skiba', *Composer* 63 (Spring 1978): 7–10.
Manning, J., *New Vocal Repertory* (Oxford: Oxford University Press, 1986).
Saxton, R., 'Lutyens at 75', *The Musical Times* 122 (1981): 368–69.
—— 'Elisabeth Lutyens' (obituary), *RCM Magazine* 78/2 (1983): 63.
Schoenberg, A., *Style and Idea: Selected Writings of Arnold Schoenberg*, ed. L. Stein, trans. L. Black (London: Faber and Faber, 1975).
Searle, H., *Quadrille with a Raven*, available at http://www.musicweb.uk.net/searle/lesley.htm.
Shaw, G.B., *Music in London 1890–94*, 3 vols. (London: Constable, 1932).
—— *London Music in 1888–89 as heard by Corno di Bassetto* (London: Constable, 1937).
Stravinsky, I., *An Autobiography (1903–1934)* (New York: Simon and Schuster, 1936; London: Boyars, 1990).
Various authors, 'Grace Williams – a Symposium' (2 parts), *Welsh Music* 5/6 (Summer 1977): 15–30 and 5/7 (Winter 1977): 41–60.
Vaughan Williams, R., *National Music and Other Essays* (Oxford: Oxford University Press, 1987).
Williams, G., 'A Letter from Vienna', *RCM Magazine* 26/2 (1930): 64–67.
—— 'Vaughan Williams: a Tribute', *RCM Magazine* 55/1 (1959): 36–37.
—— 'How Welsh is Welsh Music?', *Welsh Music* (Summer 1973): 9–12.
—— 'Views and Revisions', *Welsh Music* 5/4 (Winter 1976–77), reprinted in 10/9–10 (Summer 2006): 9–14.
—— 'Grace Williams: A Self Portrait', Welsh Music 8/5 (Spring 1987): 7–16.

Secondary Sources

Alldis, J., 'Modern Choral Music', *Composer* 33 (Autumn 1969): 8–12.
Allsorbrook, D.I., *Music for Wales: Walford Davies and the National Council of Music 1918–1941* (Cardiff: University of Wales Press, 1992).

Bennett, R.B. and Bradshaw, S., 'Elisabeth Lutyens's Stage Works', *Tempo* (March 1977): 47–48.

Boyd, M., *Grace Williams* (Cardiff: University of Wales Press, 1980).

—— 'Benjamin Britten and Grace Williams: Chronicle of a Friendship', *Welsh Music* 6/6 1980): 6–38.

Bradshaw, S., 'The Music of Elisabeth Lutyens', *The Musical Times* 112 (July 1971): 653–56.

Burton, A., 'Maconchy: Intense But Disciplined', article for The Contemporary Music Centre, Ireland, available at http://www.cmc.ie/articles/article-maconchy.html.

Carpenter, H., *The Envy of the World: Fifty Years of the BBC Third Programme and Radio 3 1946–1996* (London: Weidenfeld and Nicolson, 1996).

Colles, H.C. and Cruft, J., *The Royal College of Music: A Centenary Record 1883–1983* (London: Royal College of Music, 1982).

Davies, E., 'A Pianist's Note on Grace Williams's *Sinfonia Concertante*', *Welsh Music* 5/9 (Summer 1978): 22–29.

—— 'Grace Williams and the Piano', *Welsh Music* 6/4 (Spring 1980): 18–25.

Doctor, J., 'Intersecting Circles: The Early Careers of Elizabeth Maconchy, Elisabeth Lutyens, and Grace Williams', *Women & Music Journal* 2 (1998): 99–109.

—— '"Working for her own Salvation": Vaughan Williams as teacher of Elizabeth Maconchy, Grace Williams and Ina Boyle', in L. Foreman (ed.), *Vaughan Williams in Perspective: Studies of an English Composer* (London: Albion Music Ltd., 1998).

—— *The BBC and Ultra-Modern Music, 1922–1936: Shaping a Nation's Tastes* (Cambridge: Cambridge University Press, 1999).

Fraser, D. (ed.), *Fairest Isle: BBC Radio 3 Book of British Music* (London: BBC, 1995).

Fubini, E., *The History of Music Aesthetics*, trans. M. Hatwell (London: Macmillan, 1990).

Fuller, S., '"Putting the BBC and T. Beecham to shame …": The Macnaghten–Lemare Concerts in the Thirties', BMus dissertation (King's College, London, 1988).

—— *The Pandora Guide to Women Composers: Britain and the United States 1629–Present* (London: HarperCollins, 1994).

Gray, C., *A Survey of Contemporary Music* (London: Oxford University Press, 1924).

Grout, D.J., *A History of Western Music*, 3rd ed. (London and Toronto: W.W. Norton, 1983).

Harries, M. and Harries, S., *A Pilgrim Soul: The Life and Work of Elisabeth Lutyens* (London: Joseph, 1989).

Henderson, Robert, 'Elisabeth Lutyens', *The Musical Times* 140 (August 1963): 551–555.

Holden, A. (ed.), *The New Penguin Opera Guide* (London: Penguin Books, 2001).

Howes, F., *The English Musical Renaissance* (New York: Stein and Day, 1966).
Kenyon, N., *The BBC Symphony Orchestra 1930–1980* (London: BBC, 1981).
Lang, P.H. and Broder, N. (eds), *Contemporary Music in Europe: A Comprehensive Survey* (New York: G. Schirmer Inc., 1965).
Leighton Thomas, A.F., 'Grace Williams', *The Musical Times* 157 (1956): 240–43.
Macarthur, S., *Feminist Aesthetics in Music* (Westpoint, CT: Greenwood Press, 2002).
Macnaghten, A., 'The Story of the Macnaghten Concerts', *The Musical Times* 100 (September 1959): 460–61.
Parsons, L., 'Music and Text in Lutyens's Wittgenstein Motet', *Canadian University Music Review / Revue de musique des universités canadiennes*, 20/1 (1999): 71–100.
Roma, C., *The Choral Music of Twentieth-Century Women Composers: Elisabeth Lutyens, Elizabeth Maconchy, and Thea Musgrave* (Lanham, MD: Scarecrow Press, 2006).
Routh, F., *Contemporary British Music: The Twenty-Five Years from 1945 to 1970* (London: Macdonald, 1972).
Schafer, R.M., *British Composers in Interview* (London: Faber and Faber, 1963).
Searle, H. and Layton, R., *Britain, Scandinavia and The Netherlands* (vol. 3 of *Twentieth Century Composers*) (London: Weidenfeld and Nicolson, 1974).
Stradling, R. and Hughes, M., *The English Musical Renaissance 1860–1940: Construction and Deconstruction* (London and New York: Routledge, 1993).
Swynnoe, J.G., *The Best Years of British Film Music 1936–1958* (Woodbridge: Boydell Press, 2002).
Temperley, N., 'Xenophilia in British Music History', in Zon, B. (ed.), *Nineteenth-Century British Music Studies* 1 (Aldershot: Ashgate, 1999).
Tenant-Flowers, S., 'A Study of Style and Technique in the Music of Elisabeth Lutyens', PhD dissertation (University of Durham, 1991).
Warkov, E.R., 'Modern Composers' Use of Welsh Texts: Some Points of View', *Welsh Music* 5/10 (Winter 1978): 31–41.
—— 'Traditional Features in Grace Williams's *Penillion*', *Welsh Music* 7/1 (Summer 1982): 15–24.
White, E.W., *Stravinsky: The Composer and His World* (London: Faber and Faber, 1979).
Whittall, A., 'Grace Williams 1906–1977', *Soundings: A Musical Journal* 7 (1978): 19–37.

Index

6 Tempi for 10 Instruments, Op. 42
  (Lutyens, 1957) 161, 169, *169*,
  170, *171*
12-note music 41, 75, 79–80
  Lutyens 1, 4, 65–66, 69–70, 73, 74, 92
  Maconchy 102–103
  Williams 270–272

Akapotik Rose, Op. 64 (Lutyens, 1966)
  159, 180n57, 182–183, *184*, 188
All Seasons shall be Sweet (Williams,
  1959) 262–263
Alldis, John 92, 162n18
Allen, Hugh 13, 28
And Suddenly It's Evening, Op. 66
  (Lutyens, 1966) 5, 165, 188–191,
  190
Ariadne for Soprano and Orchestra
  (Maconchy, 1970–71) 232, 233
Ave Maris Stella (Williams, 1973) 285, 286

Ballads for Orchestra (Williams, 1968)
  274, *275*, 276
Bartók, Bela 3, 19–20, 21, 56, 68–69,
  205n7
BBC broadcasts 33–34, 60, 82–83, 106,
  109–110, 119, 157–158
  Third Programme 83, 107, 145, 157,
  203, 204
Birthday of the Infanta, The (Lutyens,
  1931) 25–26, *26*, 27
Blue Scar (Craigie, 1949) 146
Blue Scar (Williams, 1949) 126, 146
Boethius 162
Boulez, Pierre 79
  Le Marteau sans maître (1952–54)
  166, 168
Boyd, Malcolm 56, 128, 137n28, 256–257,
  262, 278, 285
British Musical Renaissance 1, 13

Britten, Benjamin 1, 13, 52, 61, 105, 140,
  216, 222n36, 272
  Albert Herring (1947) 265
  Peter Grimes (1945) 84, 209
  Williams 53–54, 56–57, 122
Brooke, Gwydion 115–116

Camargo Society, The 27
Canetti, Elias 187, 293
Carillons for Oboe and Orchestra
  (Williams, 1965/73) 273, 285
Catena, Op. 47 (Lutyens, 1961) 178–180,
  179
Chamber Concerto No. 1, Op. 8, No. 1
  (Lutyens, 1939–40) 4, 70–73, *72*,
  83, 84
Cheltenham Festival 166, 175–176, 233,
  235, 262
Chorale for Orchestra (Lutyens, 1956)
  172–173
Clarinet Quintet (Maconchy, 1963)
  219–221, *220*
Clark, Edward 68–69, 74, 75–76, 85, 157,
  161, 172, 175
Concertino for Bassoon and String
  Orchestra (Maconchy, 1950) 115,
  116, *116*
Concertino for Clarinet and String
  Orchestra (Maconchy, 1945)
  107–108
contemporary music 3–4, 19–20, 33–34,
  44, 67–69, 119, 157–159, 168,
  173n44, 204n3, 209
Copenhagen ISCM Festival (1947) 107
Counting your Steps (Lutyens, 1972) 195
Country of the Stars, The Op. 50 (Lutyens,
  1956–57) 162, *163*
Craigie, Jill 146, 293

Dancers, The (Williams, 1953) 5, 150–152, *151–152, 153*
Dark Island, The (Williams, 1948) 145
Darke, Harold 13, 15, 24, 25
De Amore, Op. 39 (Lutyens, 1957) 160, 162, 163, *163*, 164, 191
Delius 44
Departure, The (Maconchy, 1960–61) 212–215, *213–214*
Dialogo, Op. 142 (Lutyens, 1980) 188n79, 201
Dialogue (Maconchy, 1942) 101
Diurnal, Op. 146 (Lutyens, 1980) 201
Doubles, Op. 125 (Lutyens, 1978) 201
Driving Out the Death, Op. 81 (Lutyens, 1971) 165, 195–196, *196*, 233

Elegy for String Orchestra (Williams, 1936) 57–58, *58*
Elgar, Edward 12–13, 44
Epyllion for Solo Cello and Strings (Maconchy, 1975) 5, 235–239, *236–237, 238*
Essence of Our Happiness, Op. 69 (Lutyens, 1968) 191, 192–195, *193–194*

Fairest of Stars (Williams, 1973) 142, 283–285
Fantasia on Welsh Nursery Tunes (Williams, 1939–40) 5, *127*, 127–130, *129*, 145
Five Songs (Lutyens, 1931) 42–44, *43*
Fletcher, Polyxena 10, 11
Four Mediaeval Welsh Poems (Williams, 1962) 267–268, *268–269*

Garden of Cyrus, The (Browne, 1658) 165, 166
Glendower, Owen (*Henry IV*) 126n9, 133–134, 136, 137, 256
Glock, William 89, 91–92, 158–159, 173n44, 180, 215–216, 221
Gogonedawg Arglwydd (Williams, 1939) 122n5, 149–150
Gow, Dorothy 2, 3, 15, 20, 21, 24, 47, 70, 294
Great Agrippa (Maconchy, 1933) 53

Grove, George 11

Hannibal (Williams, 1947) 145
Heart of England, The (Lutyens, 1954) 160
Heloise and Abelard (Maconchy, 1976–78) 242–244
Hen Walia (Williams, 1930) 59–60, 128, 147, 209n16
Hoddinott, Alun 266
Holst, Imogen 2, 3, 20, 24, 47
Hopkins, Gerard Manley 222–223, 262n26
  Leaden Echo and the Golden Echo, The (Maconchy) 52n51, 226–227, *228*, 229, *229*
  Six Poems (Williams) 261–262
  Three Settings of Poems (Maconchy) 223–224, *224–225*, 225, *226*
Hussey, Dyneley 74–75, 108, 205, 206

ISCM (International Society of Contemporary Music) 68n10, 294
  Clark, Edward 69, 75, 85, 161n17
  Copenhagen 107
  London 68, 74–75, 108n28
  Palermo 85
  Paris 94
  Prague 28, 34–35
  Warsaw 67, 69
Isis and Osiris, Op. 74 (Lutyens, 1969–70) 186, 195, 197–198

Jirák, Karel 35
Jungle Mariners (Lutyens, 1944) 77–78, *78*, 79

King, Thea 107–108

Lambert, Constant 15, 27, 33–34, 49, 60, 160–161, 294–295
Land, The (Maconchy, 1930) 36, 36–38, *37*, 44, 203, 212
Le Marteau sans maître (Boulez, 1952–54) 166, 168
Leaden Echo and the Golden Echo, The (Maconchy, 1978) 52n51, 226–229, *228, 229*
LeFanu, Nicola 103n15, 207, 219, 233, 235n51

Lemare, Iris 29, 44, 45, 46n36, 52, 53, 295
London Contemporary Music Centre 44, 73n20, 83n44, 98, 108n30
London ISCM Festival (1938) 68, 74–75, 108n28
Lutyens, Elisabeth 3, 5, 10–12, 13–15, 24–25, 41–42, 48–50, 61, 65–68, 159–160, 168, 202
   6 Tempi for 10 Instruments (1957) 161, 169, *169*, *170*, *171*
   12-note music 1, 4, 65–66, 69–70, 73, 74, 92
   And Suddenly It's Evening (1966) 5, 165, 188–191, *190*
   Akapotik Rose (1966) 159, 180n57, 182–183, *184*, 188
   Birthday of the Infanta, The (1931) 25–26, *26*, 27
   Catena, Op. 47 (1961) 178–180, *179*
   Chamber Concerto No. 1 (1939–40) 4, 70–73, 72, 83, 84
   Chorale for Orchestra (1956) 172–173
   Clark, Edward 69, 74, 75–76, 85, 161, 172, 175
   Counting your Steps (1972) 195
   Country of the Stars, The (1956–57) 162, *163*
   De Amore (1957) 160, 162, 163, *163*, 164, 191
   Dialogo (1980) 188n79, 201
   Diurnal (1980) 201
   Doubles (1978) 201
   Driving Out the Death (1971) 165, 195–196, *196*, 233
   Essence of Our Happiness (1968) 191, 192–195, *193–194*
   Five Songs (1931) 42–44, *43*
   Heart of England, The (1954) 160
   Isis and Osiris (1969–70) 186, 195, 197–198
   Jungle Mariners (1944) 77–78, *78*, 79
   Macnaghten-Lemare Concerts 4, 44, 45, 46, 47, 48, 202
   Mare et Minutiae (1976) 200–201
   Motet (Wittgenstein) (1953) 89–92, *90*, *91*, 157, 162n18
   Music for Orchestra
      I (1953–55) 160–161
      II (1962) 160, 168–169, 174–175, *176–177*
      III (1964) 160, 175, 176, 177–178
      IV (1981) 202
   Numbered, The (1965–67) 186, 187–188, 198, 292
   O Saisons, O Châteaux! (1946) 80–83, *81–82*, 84, 92, 109
   Pit, The (1947) 83, 84, 85
   Plenum I-IV (1972–74) 199–200, *200*
   Quincunx (1957–60) 160, 161, 165–166, *167*, 169, 176
   Requiem for the Living (1948) 84–85, *85*
   Stravinsky, Igor 172–173, 191
   String Quartets
      No. 2 (1938) 67
      No. 6 (1952) 86–88, *87–88*
   Symphonies (1960–61) 173–174, 178
   Three Salutes to the United Nations (1941–43) 76
   Three Symphonic Preludes (1942) 73–74, 160, 165
   Time Off? Not a Ghost of a Chance (1967–68) 184–186, 198
   To Sleep (1929) 25
   Triolets I and II (1983) 202
   Valley of Hatsu-Se, The (1965) 5, 159, 180–181, *181–182*
   Vaughan Williams 13
   Wind Quintet (1960) 174

Macnaghten, Anne 44, 45, 46n36, 48, 50n45, 66n3, 295
Macnaghten-Lemare Concerts 4, 44, 45, 46–47, 54
   Lutyens 4, 44, 45, 46, 47, 48, 202
   Maconchy 4, 45, 46, 47, 50, 52
   Williams 4, 47, 53, 54, 56, 57
Maconchy, Elizabeth 3, 4, 5, 15–19, 28, 34–36, 51–52, 60, 93–94, 107, 203–204, 206–209, 215–216, 239, 248, 291–292
   12-note music 102–103
   Ariadne (1970–71) 232, 233
   Clarinet Quintet (1963) 219–221, *220*
   Concertino for Bassoon and String Orchestra (1950) 115, 116, *116*

Concertino for Clarinet and String
   Orchestra (1945) 107–108
Departure, The (1960–61) 212–215,
   213–214
Dialogue (1942) 101
Epyllion (1975) 5, 235–239, *236–237*,
   238
Great Agrippa (1933) 53
Heloise and Abelard (1976–78)
   242–244
Land, The (1930) 36, 36–38, 37, 44,
   203, 212
*Leaden Echo and the Golden Echo,
   The* (1978) 52n51, 226–229, *228*,
   229
Macnaghten-Lemare Concerts 4, 45,
   46, 47, 50, 52
Music for Brass and Woodwind (1965)
   221–222
Music for Strings (1982–83) 247, *247*
My Dark Heart (1981–82) 244–247,
   245–246, *247*, 248n59
Nocturnal (1965) 222
Oboe Quartet (1972) 232–233
Patron's Fund 15–16, 20–21
Piano Concertino (1928) 27–28, *28*, 35
Proud Thames (1952–53) 115
Reflections (1960) 215
Serenata Concertante (1962) 216–219,
   217, *218*
Sofa, The (1956–57) 209–211, 212n24
Sonnet Sequence (1946–47) 109, *110*
String Quartets
   No. 1 (1933) 50–51, *51*
   No. 2 (1936) 94–98, *95–96*, *97*, 233
   No. 3 (1938) 94, 98–100, *99*, 233
   No. 4 (1942–43) 101–104, *102*,
      103–104
   No. 5 (1948) 105, 111–114, *112*,
      113
   No. 6 (1950) 114, *114*
   No. 7 (1956) 204–205, *206*
   No. 8 (1967) 230
   No. 9 (1968) 230, *231*, 231–232
   No. 10 (1972) 233, *234*, 244
   No. 11 (1977) 239–241, *240*
   No. 12 (1979) 241, *241*
   No. 13 (1984) 247–48

Suite for Strings (1924) 17
Sun, Moon and Stars (1976–77) 242
Symphony (1945–48) 108–109
Symphony for Double String Orchestra
   (1952–53) 115, 116–118, *118*, *119*
Three Settings of Poems (1964–70)
   223–226, *224–225*, *226*
Three Strangers, The (1957–58)
   211–212
Two Motets (1931) 52
Variazioni Concertante (1964–65) 221
Vaughan Williams 17, 19, 21, 24, 28,
   105, 106–107, 108–109, 117
Winter's Tale, A (1949) 109, 110
Magnificat (Williams, 1939) 122n5, 149
Mare et Minutiae, Op. 107 (Lutyens, 1976)
   200–201
McNaught, William 48, 76, 131–132
Mathias, William 269–270, 285, 291
Missa Cambrensis (Williams, 1968–71) 6,
   276–280, *278*, *279*, *281*, *282–283*,
   285
Motet, *Excerpta Tractati-Logico-
   Philosophici* (Wittgenstein), Op.
   27 (Lutyens, 1953) 89–92, *90*, *91*,
   157, 162n18
Movement for Trumpet and Chamber
   Orchestra (Williams, 1932) 54, *55*,
   55–56, *56*
Music for Brass and Woodwind
   (Maconchy, 1965) 221–222
Music for Orchestra (Lutyens)
   I Op. 31 (1953–55) 160–161
   II Op. 48 (1962) 160, 168–169,
      174–175, *176–177*
   III Op. 56 (1964) 160, 175, 176,
      177–178
   IV Op. 152 (1981) 202
Music for Strings (Maconchy, 1982–83)
   247, *247*
My Dark Heart (Maconchy, 1981–82)
   244–247, *245–246*, *247*, 248n59
My Last Duchess (Williams, 1975)
   287–288

Nocturnal for Unaccompanied Choir
   (Maconchy, 1965) 222

Numbered, The, Op. 63 (Lutyens, 1965–67) 186, 187–188, 198, 292
NYOW (National Youth Orchestra of Wales) 249, 255

O Saisons, O Châteaux!, Op. 13 (Lutyens, 1946) 80–83, *81–82*, 84, 92, 109
Oboe Quartet (Maconchy, 1972) 232–233
Oboe Quintet in One Movement (Gow, 1936) 70
opera, British 83–84, 209, 211n21

Palermo ISCM Festival (1949) 85
Paris ISCM Festival (1937) 94
Parlour, The (Williams, 1960–66) 6, 198, 250, 263–267, *265*, 292
Parry, Hubert 1, 11–12
Patron's Fund, The 15–16, 20–21, 24, 25–26, 27, 28–29
Penillion for Orchestra (Williams, 1955) 5–6, 135, 250, 251–254, *252*, *253–254*, 255–256, 276
Peter Grimes (Britten, 1945) 84, 209
Piano Concertino (Maconchy, 1928) 27–28, *28*, 35
Pit, The, Op. 14 (Lutyens, 1947) 83, 84, 85
Plenum I-IV, Opp. 87, 92, 93, 100 (Lutyens, 1972–74) 199–200, *200*
Prague ISCM Festival (1925) 28, 34–35
Proud Thames (Maconchy, 1952–53) 115

Quincunx, Op. 44 (Lutyens, 1957–60) 160, 161, 165–166, *167*, 169, 176

Reflections for Oboe, Clarinet, Viola and Harp (Maconchy, 1960) 215
Requiem for the Living, Op. 16 (Lutyens, 1948) 84–85, *85*
Rhiannon, *Four Illustrations for the Legend of* (Williams, 1939) 121–122, *123*, 123–126, *124*, *125*, 133, 145, 256
Royal College of Music 1, 2, 3, 9–10, 11–12, 13, 244
    Patron's Fund 15–16, 20–21, 24, 25–26, 27, 28–29
Royal Festival Hall 115, 159n10, 172n41, 175

Schoenberg, Arnold 33, 39, 41, 74
Schulhoff, Ervin 35
Sea Sketches for String Orchestra (Williams, 1944) 5, 113, *113*, 139, 140–143, *141*, *142*, *143*, 145, 152
Searle, Humphrey 79–80, 83
Second Viennese School 39, 41, 67–68, 70, 75
Serenata Concertante for Violin and Orchestra (Maconchy, 1962) 216–219, *217*, *218*
Severn Bridge Variations (Williams, 1965) 273
Shaw, George Bernard 6, 9–10, 20, 31
Sinfonia Concertante for Piano and Orchestra (Williams, 1940–41) 130–131, *132–133*, 145
Six Poems by G.M. Hopkins (Williams, 1958) 261–262
Smyth, Ethel 2, 27, 31, 248
Sofa, The (Maconchy, 1956–57) 209–211, 212n24
Sonnet Sequence (Maconchy, 1946–47) 109, *110*
Spencer, Penelope 26–27
Stanford, Charles Villiers 1, 11–12
Stravinsky, Igor 56n59, 98, 172–173, 191
String Quartets 205–206
    Lutyens
        No. 2 (1938) 67
        No. 6, Op. 25 (1952) 86–88, *87–88*
    Maconchy
        No. 1 (1933) 50–51, 51
        No. 2 (1936) 94–98, *95–96*, *97*, 233
        No. 3 (1938) 94, 98–100, *99*, 233
        No. 4 (1942–43) 101–104, *102*, *103–104*
        No. 5 (1948) 105, 111–114, *112*, *113*
        No. 6 (1950) 114, *114*
        No. 7 (1956) 204–205, *206*
        No. 8 (1967) 230
        No. 9 (1968) 230, *231*, 231–232
        No. 10 (1972) 233, *234*, 244
        No. 11 (1977) 239–241, *240*
        No. 12 (1979) 241, *241*
        No. 13 (*Quartetto Corto*) (1984) 247–248
suffrage movement 2–3

Suite for Chamber Orchestra (Williams, 1931) 53–54
Suite for Strings in E minor (Maconchy, 1924) 17
Sun, Moon and Stars (Maconchy, 1976–77) 242
Symphonies, Op. 46 (Lutyens, 1960–61) 173–174, 178
Symphony for Double String Orchestra (Maconchy, 1952–53) 115, 116–118, *118*, *119*
Symphony (Maconchy, 1945–48) 108–109
Symphony No. 1 (Williams, 1942–43) 5, 133, 134–139, *135*, *136*, *138*, 256
Symphony No. 2 (Williams, 1956) 6, 138, 256–261, *258*, *259*, *260*

Tarantella (Williams, 1930) 39, 149, 150, 285
Temperley, Nicholas 12
Tenant-Flowers, Sarah 49–50, 67
The Merry Minstrel (Williams, 1949) 145
Theosophical Society, The 11n6, 13–14
Third Programme, BBC 83, 107, 145, 157, 203, 204
Three Salutes to the United Nations (Lutyens, 1941–43) 76
Three Settings of Poems by G.M. Hopkins (Maconchy, 1964–70) 223–226, *224–225*, *226*
Three Strangers, The (Maconchy, 1957–58) 211–212
Three Symphonic Preludes (Lutyens, 1942) 73–74, 160, 165
Thurston, Frederick 107–108
Time Off? Not a Ghost of a Chance, Op. 68 (Lutyens, 1967–68) 184–186, 198
Tippett, Michael 1, 17, 117, 205n7, 216
To Sleep (Lutyens, 1929) 25
Triolets I and II, Opp. 160a and b (Lutyens, 1983) 198
Trumpet Concerto (Williams, 1963) 269–272, *270*, *271*
Tuscany (Williams, 1930) 38, 38–39, 149, 285
Two Choruses (Williams, 1975) 288, *289*
Two Motets for Double Chorus (Maconchy, 1931) 52

Two Psalms for Voice and Small Orchestra (Williams, 1932) 28–30, *29–30*, 209n16

Valley of Hatsu-Se, The, Op. 62 (Lutyens, 1965) 5, 159, 180–181, *181–182*
Variazioni Concertante (Maconchy, 1964–65) 221
Vaughan Williams, Ralph 1, 17–18, 20, 22, 33, 37, 114, 128, 209, 212, 277
  Lutyens 13
  Maconchy 17, 19, 21, 24, 28, 105, 106–107, 108–109, 117
  Williams 21, 23–24, 28, 40
Violin Concerto (Williams, 1950) 126, 148–149, *149*
Volanakis, Minos 186, 187

Warsaw ISCM Festival (1939) 67, 69
Webern, Anton 41, 67, 70, 73, 82n42, 90n54
Wellesz, Egon 35, 39–40, 70, 75
Williams, Grace 3, 5–6, 20, 21–24, 39–41, 60, 121–122, 126–127, 143–146, 152, 249–250, 271–273, 288–289, 291
  12-note music 270–272
  All Seasons shall be Sweet (1959) 262–263
  Ave Maris Stella (1973) 285, *286*
  Ballads (1968) 274, *275*, 276
  Blue Scar (1949) 126, 146
  Britten 53–54, 56–57, 122
  Carillons (1965/73) 273, 285
  Dancers, The (1953) 5, 150–152, 151–152, 153
  Dark Island, The (1948) 145
  Elegy (1936) 57–58, *58*
  Fairest of Stars (1973) 142, 283–285
  Fantasia on Welsh Nursery Tunes (1939–40) 5, *127*, 127–130, *129*, 145
  Four Mediaeval Welsh Poems (1962) 267–268, *268–269*
  Gogonedawg Arglwydd (1939) 122n5, 149–150
  Hannibal (1947) 145

Hen Walia (1930) 59–60, 128, 147, 209n16
Macnaghten-Lemare Concerts 4, 47, 53, 54, 56, 57
Magnificat (1939) 122n5, 149
Merry Minstrel, The (1949) 145
Missa Cambrensis (1968–71) 6, 276–280, *278*, *279*, *281*, *282–283*, 285
Movement (1932) 54, *55*, 55–56, *56*
My Last Duchess (1975) 287–288
Parlour, The (1960–66) 6, 198, 250, 263–267, *265*, 292
Patron's Fund 28–29
Penillion (1955) 5–6, 135, 250, 251–254, *252*, *253–54*, 255–256, 276
Rhiannon (1939) 121–122, *123*, 123–126, *124*, *125*, 133, 145, 256
Sea Sketches (1944) 5, 113, *113*, 139–143, *141*, *142*, *143*, 145, 152
Severn Bridge Variations (1965) 273
Sinfonia Concertante (1940–41) 130–131, *132–133*, 145
Six Poems (1958) 261–262

Suite for Chamber Orchestra (1931) 53–54
Symphony No. 1 (1942–43) 5, 133, 134–139, *135*, *136*, *138*, 256
Symphony No. 2 (1956) 6, 138, 256–261, *258*, *259*, *260*
Tarantella (1930) 39, 149, 150, 285
Trumpet Concerto (1963) 269–272, *270*, *271*
Tuscany (1930) *38*, 38–39, 149, 285
Two Choruses (1975) 288, *289*
Two Psalms (1932) 28–30, *29–30*, 58, 209n16
Vaughan Williams 21, 23–24, 28, 40
Violin Concerto (1950) 126, 148–149, *149*
Wind Quintet, Op. 45 (Lutyens, 1960) 174
Winter's Tale, A (Maconchy, 1949) 109, 110
Wittgenstein Motet *see* Motet
Wittgenstein (*Tractatus*,1921) 89
women composers 1–2, 4, 30–31, 45–46, 47–48, 207–208, 291
Wood, Henry 36, 65, 101